FORENSIC PSYCHOLOGY AND LAW

FORENSIC PSYCHOLOGY AND LAW

Ronald Roesch
Patricia A. Zapf
Stephen D. Hart

WILEY

John Wiley & Sons, Inc.

Library of Congress Cataloging-in-Publication Data

Roesch, Ronald, 1947–
    Forensic psychology and law / by Ronald Roesch, Patricia A. Zapf, and Stephen D. Hart.
       p.   cm.
    Includes bibliographical references and index.
    ISBN 978-0-470-09623-9 (cloth)
       1. Forensic psychology.   2. Criminal psychology.   3. Law—Psychological aspects.   I. Zapf, Patricia A., 1971–   II. Hart, Stephen D. (Stephen David), 1962–   III. Title.
    RA1148.R635 2010
    614'.15—dc22

                                                                                   2009024945

Printed in the United States of America

10 9 8 7 6 5 4 3 2 1

Contents

Preface

ABOUT THE TEXT

Why write another undergraduate text on forensic psychology? There is no shortage of them. Some very good ones were written by people we are proud to call colleagues and, in many instances, pleased to call friends. We have used their texts in our own teaching and were very satisfied with them.

So, when Wiley first approached us with the idea of developing a new text, we wondered what would be the point of the exercise. We didn't think we could write a text that was more comprehensive than the others—indeed, the field of forensic psychology is now so broad that even the notion of a single comprehensive text of less than a thousand pages is laughable. Neither did we think that we could write a text that was better than the others. The nature and depth of our expertise in the field is in no way superior to that of other textbook authors. But what Wiley thought we could achieve was to write a textbook that reflected a particular perspective on forensic psychology: an applied and community-oriented perspective. We define forensic psychology as the application of psychological theory and research to legal questions and problems. We have a deep respect for the idea of law, believe forensic psychologists must understand the law as it relates to their areas of expertise, and judge the usefulness of research and practice according to the extent they help answer legal questions or solve legal problems.

In our view, forensic psychology should be community-oriented. It serves and operates within the legal system, itself a rather complex web of subsystems that interact within and across various levels of society (e.g., local, regional, national, international). One of our fundamental assumptions is that forensic psychology must strive not only to understand the impact of the legal system on individuals within society, but also to improve or enhance the well-being of individuals and the society in which they live.

Our primary goal in writing this text, then, was to illustrate our perspective, developed at Simon Fraser University but influenced by colleagues all over the world, on forensic psychology. To this end, we selected topics strategically. For each topic, we discuss relevant law, focusing on but not limited to U.S. law, and point out its implications for research and practice. We make frequent reference to individual cases or research studies to illustrate key points. We hope we have achieved our goal, discussing the field in a way that is different from and complementary to that done in existing texts.

ANCILLARY MATERIALS

In addition to this text, we have developed several supplementary resources for use by students and instructors.

- On the Student Website
  - Chapter summaries
  - Sample exam questions
  - Links to journal articles, news stories, and professional organizations
- On the Instructor's Website:
  - Lecture outlines, including suggested topics
  - Powerpoint presentations (which are editable)
  - Information for instructors in Canada
  - Recommended audiovisual materials
  - Test bank (multiple choice, fill-in-the-blank, short answer, and essay questions)

Acknowledgments

Writing this text was an unexpected pleasure. This statement bears some explanation. On the one hand, it was no surprise to us that working together was a positive experience; our collaborations over many years have been both fruitful and enjoyable. But we never expected to write an undergraduate text—none of us had considered doing so until approached by our editor at Wiley, Patricia Rossi. And we never expected that writing a textbook would be gratifying in so many respects. To be sure, it was difficult to venture outside our areas of primary expertise and to write in a style so different from that required for scientific journals and books. Yet it was invigorating to immerse ourselves in new topics or think about familiar topics in new ways.

For giving us the opportunity to write this text, and for making the experience as painless as possible, we thank the professionals at Wiley. Patricia Rossi was always warm and supportive, even when deadlines were missed and extended (mostly by Steve). We received excellent feedback from a terrific Wiley production staff, including Kathleen DeChants, Katherine Glynn, and Susan Moran.

On a personal note, each of us would like to thank our families for their love, support, and patience while we worked on this project. Also, Steve and Patty would like to thank Ron for his mentorship over the years. If there does exist a strong and unique Simon Fraser University (SFU) perspective, it is thanks to Ron. Ron is the person who established and developed SFU's Program in Law and Forensic Psychology—he had the vision, recruited faculty and students, and worked tirelessly to nurture the Program. He also helped us to establish careers of our own, and for this he has our thanks, as well as our love and respect.

Chapter 1 ———————————————————————————————

INTRODUCTION TO PSYCHOLOGY AND LAW
Civil and Criminal Applications

CHAPTER OBJECTIVES

In this chapter, you will become familiar with:

- The definition of forensic psychology
- The history of forensic psychology
- The varied roles that forensic psychologists play
- The professional associations and publications relevant to forensic psychologists
- The structure of the legal system
- The similarities and differences in the fields of psychology and law
- The training opportunities for students who wish to pursue a career as a forensic psychologist

One of the questions that students in undergraduate psychology and law classes ask their professors is, "How can I become a profiler?" Clearly, television shows like *CSI* and *Criminal Minds*, as well as movies such as *Silence of the Lambs*, have piqued student interest to be involved in what is perceived as exciting and engaging work. The reality is that there is little market for profilers (see Box 1.1) and a career in forensic psychology is not the track to pursue if one has this interest. Indeed, one survey of forensic psychiatrists and psychologists found that only about 10% had ever engaged in criminal profiling and only a small percentage believe it is a scientifically reliable practice (Torres, Boccaccini, & Miller, 2006). Forensic psychology is a fascinating field that has far more to offer students who want to work at the intersection of psychology and law.

Box 1.1 On Criminal Profiling

Due to depictions in popular media (e.g., *Silence of the Lambs, Profiler, CSI*), many students express an interest in and ask questions about criminal profiling, which may be described as a criminal investigative technique based, in part, on psychological expertise and knowledge. In reality, few law enforcement agencies employ such techniques and there is little call for such professionals. Those interested in such work should consider a career in law enforcement instead of clinical-forensic psychology.

The Behavioral Sciences Unit of the FBI does employ a few FBI agents who engage in this activity. The FBI makes a distinction between mental health and law enforcement: FBI agents are law enforcement professionals, not mental health professionals. In order to work as a profiler, or with the FBI in any other role, it is necessary to become an FBI agent. Experience in criminal investigation is needed before an agent can even be considered for a profiling position, but only a small number of agents ever become profilers. Since this would be a difficult goal to achieve, the FBI encourages prospective applicants who are interested in being special agents to do so because they are interested in the range of opportunities available with the FBI, not because they want to be a profiler.

Source: Excerpt from American Psychology-Law Society website: http://www.ap-ls.org/students/careersIndex.html.

DEFINING FORENSIC PSYCHOLOGY

Forensic psychology can be conceptualized as encompassing both sides of the justice system (civil and criminal) as well as two broad aspects of psychology (clinical and experimental). It would seem that defining forensic psychology should be a straightforward task. Alas, this is not the case, and the difficulty stems from the fact that the professionals who work in forensic psychology come from a wide range of graduate and professional backgrounds. Some have degrees in clinical or counseling psychology; others have graduate training in other areas of psychology such as social, developmental, cognitive, or neuropsychology. Others have backgrounds in law, some with degrees in both psychology and law. The nature of their contributions to forensic psychology also varies. One central issue in defining forensic psychology is that forensic psychologists can work both within and outside the legal system. Some psychologists provide direct services to the court through assessments of issues such as competency to stand trial, criminal responsibility, or child custody. Others are researchers, typically based in universities, who conduct basic or applied research on such topics as eyewitness behavior or jury decision making. Still others combine both research and clinical practice. This potential for working both within and outside the legal system has led Haney (1980) to comment, "Psychologists have been slow to decide whether they want to stand outside the system to study, critique, and change it, or to embrace and be employed by it. And the law has been tentative in deciding how it will use and grant access to psychologists" (p. 152).

For these reasons, it has been difficult to arrive at a definition that encompasses all of these professional backgrounds and varied roles. Table 1.1 shows a sample of definitions that various individuals and organizations have proposed. Some, like the one used by Goldstein, use broad definitions that attempt to encompass all of the backgrounds and roles described here, and distinguish the research and practice contributions. Others, such as those used by the American Psychological Association or the Specialty Guidelines for Forensic Psychologists (Committee on Ethical Guidelines for Forensic Psychologists, 1991), focus more on the applied roles of psychologists as providers of expertise to the legal system.

The conflicts involved in arriving at a definition of forensic psychology was the subject of Professor Jack Brigham's 1999 presidential address to the American Psychology-Law Society. He posed the question, "What is forensic psychology, anyway?" His answer reflects the conflicts about clinical and nonclinical participants in forensic psychology:

> To return to my original question about what is forensic psychology, I believe that there are two levels of classification that yield two sets of definitions. At the level of ethical guidelines and professional responsibility, the broad definition fits best. Any psychologist (clinical, social, cognitive, developmental, etc.) who works within the legal system is a forensic psychologist in this sense, and the same high ethical and professional standards should apply to all. When it comes to how the legal system and the public conceptualize forensic psychology, however, there is a definite clinical flavor. The clinical/nonclinical distinction is a meaningful one, I believe. For example, educational, training, and licensing issues that are pertinent to clinical forensic psychologists may be irrelevant or inapplicable to nonclinical forensic psychologists. Further, clinicians and nonclinicians differ in their orientation to the legal process and in the role that they are likely to play in the courtroom (e.g., individual assessments vs. research-based social fact evidence). So there you have it—two varieties of forensic psychologists, clinical and nonclinical. (Brigham, 1999, p. 295)

It is of note that some graduate programs use both narrow and broad definitions to define their program. John Jay College, which has MA and PhD programs in forensic psychology, states that "In developing

Table 1.1 Definitions of Forensic Psychology

American Board of Forensic Psychology (2007)	Forensic psychology is the application of the science and profession of psychology to questions and issues relating to law and the legal system. The word *forensic* comes from the Latin word *forensis,* meaning "of the forum," where the law courts of ancient Rome were held. Today, *forensic* refers to the application of scientific principles and practices to the adversary process in which specially knowledgeable scientists play a role (http://www.abfp.com).
American Psychological Association (2001)	Forensic psychology is the professional practice by psychologists who foreseeably and regularly provide professional psychological expertise to the judicial system. Such professional practice is generally within the areas of clinical psychology, counseling psychology, neuropsychology, and school psychology, or other applied areas within psychology involving the delivery of human services, by psychologists who have additional expertise in law and the application of applied psychology to legal proceedings (http://www.apa.org/crsppp/archivforensic.html).
Goldstein (2003)	Goldstein "considers forensic psychology to be a field that involves the application of psychological research, theory, practice, and traditional specialized methodology (e.g., interviewing, psychological testing, forensic assessment, and forensically relevant instruments) to a legal question" (p. 4). Goldstein further distinguishes practice and research applications. The practice side of forensic psychology generates products for the legal system, such as reports or testimony. The research side has as its goal "to design, conduct, and interpret empirical studies, the purpose of which is to investigate groups of individuals or areas of concern or relevance to the legal system" (p. 4).
Ogloff and Finkelman (1999)	Define psychology and law quite broadly as the "scientific study of the effect the law has on people, and the effect people have on the law" (p. 3).
Committee on Ethical Guidelines for Forensic Psychologists (1991)	Defines forensic psychology to include "all forms of professional conduct when acting, with definable foreknowledge, as a psychological expert on explicitly psychological issues in direct assistance to the courts, parties to legal proceedings, correctional and forensic mental health facilities, and administrative, judicial, and legislative agencies acting in a judicial capacity" (p. 657).

Table 1.1 *(Continued)*

	Note: At the time of the writing of this book, the Guidelines were being updated. The latest draft defines forensic psychology as referring "to all professional practice by any psychologist working with any sub-discipline of psychology (e.g., clinical, developmental, social, cognitive) when the intended purpose of the service is to apply the scientific, technical, or specialized knowledge of psychology to the law and to use that knowledge to assist in solving legal, contractual, and administrative problems" (http://www.ap-ls.org/links/professionalsgfp.html).
Wrightsman and Fulero (2005)	Define forensic psychology as "any application of psychological research, methods, theory, and practice to a task faced by the legal system" (p. 2).

this program, both the broader and narrower definitions of forensic psychology are recognized. The core curriculum in the doctoral program is clinically focused. The broader definition is encompassed in non-clinical elective courses in the program and in an Interdisciplinary Concentration in Psychology and Law available to CUNY Psychology doctoral students who are interested in forensic psychology but whose interests do not require clinical training" (retrieved from http://johnjay.jjay.cuny.edu/forensicPsych/#Anchor-Q:-28528, July 18, 2007). (As this book goes to press, a second track to John Jay's doctoral program has been added. This track focuses on experimental psychology and law.)

We have adopted a broad definition for this book. **Forensic psychology** is the practice of psychology (defined to include research as well as direct and indirect service delivery and consultation) within or in conjunction with either or both sides of the legal system—criminal and civil.

HISTORY OF FORENSIC PSYCHOLOGY

There is general agreement that although medical experts testified in some criminal cases in the 1800s (see Figure 1.1), the roots of modern-day psychology and law were not established until the early part of the twentieth century. If these roots can be traced to one individual, it would perhaps be Hugo Munsterberg, who was the director of Harvard's Psychological Laboratory. Munsterberg was a strong advocate of the application of psychological research to legal issues. In his book *On the Witness Stand*, published in 1908, Munsterberg reviewed research on such topics as the reliability of eyewitness testimony, false confessions, and crime

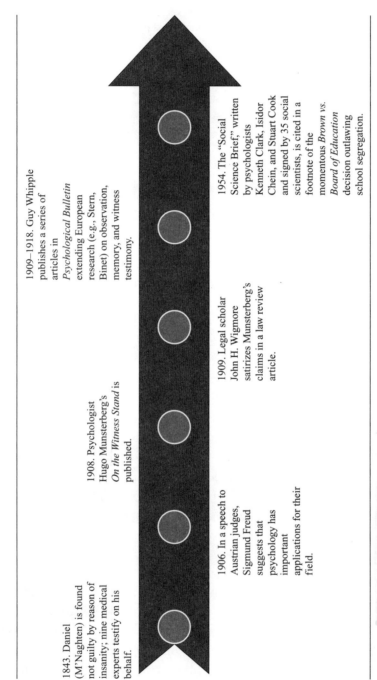

1843. Daniel (M'Naghten) is found not guilty by reason of insanity; nine medical experts testify on his behalf.

1906. In a speech to Austrian judges, Sigmund Freud suggests that psychology has important applications for their field.

1908. Psychologist Hugo Munsterberg's *On the Witness Stand* is published.

1909. Legal scholar John H. Wigmore satirizes Munsterberg's claims in a law review article.

1909–1918. Guy Whipple publishes a series of articles in *Psychological Bulletin* extending European research (e.g., Stern, Binet) on observation, memory, and witness testimony.

1954. The "Social Science Brief," written by psychologists Kenneth Clark, Isidor Chein, and Stuart Cook and signed by 35 social scientists, is cited in a footnote of the momentous *Brown vs. Board of Education* decision outlawing school segregation.

Figure 1.1   Landmark Dates in Forensic Psychology

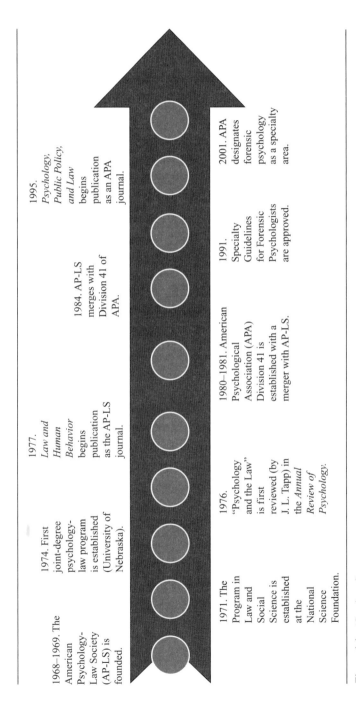

1968–1969. The American Psychology-Law Society (AP-LS) is founded.

1971. The Program in Law and Social Science is established at the National Science Foundation.

1974. First joint-degree psychology-law program is established (University of Nebraska).

1976. "Psychology and the Law" is first reviewed (by J. L. Tapp) in the *Annual Review of Psychology.*

1977. *Law and Human Behavior* begins publication as the AP-LS journal.

1980–1981. American Psychological Association (APA) Division 41 is established with a merger with AP-LS.

1984. AP-LS merges with Division 41 of APA.

1991. Specialty Guidelines for Forensic Psychologists are approved.

1995. *Psychology, Public Policy, and Law* begins publication as an APA journal.

2001. APA designates forensic psychology as a specialty area.

Figure 1.1 *(Continued)*
Source: Adapted and expanded from Brigham (1999), Table 1.

detection and prevention, and argued that the legal system should make greater use of this research. He wrote that "The courts will have to learn, sooner or later, that the individual differences of men can be tested today by the methods of experimental psychology far beyond anything which common sense and social experience suggest" (p. 63). Munsterberg was a controversial figure whose claims for the contributions of psychology to law were not supported by empirical research.

Criticisms of Munsterberg were rampant. As Doyle (2005) commented, "What Munsterberg had failed to grasp was that his knowledge about the reliability of *witnesses* was not sufficient to answer the legal system's concern for the reliability of the *verdicts*" (p. 30). Notable among the critiques by both the legal and psychological communities was one by the legal scholar, John Wigmore. In a satirical article published in a law review in 1909, Wigmore staged a mock lawsuit in which he accused Munsterberg of libeling the legal profession and exaggerating his claim of what psychology had to offer the law. He subjected Munsterberg's claims to a rigorous cross-examination in which he argued that psychological testimony about such issues such as eyewitness credibility should not be admissible in the courts. Of course, Munsterberg was found guilty. It is of interest to note that, despite his scathing critique of Munsterberg, Wigmore (1940) was positive about the potential of psychology to offer assistance to the courts on a range of legal issues, noting that the courts will be ready for psychologists when psychologists are ready for the courts. It was not until the past few decades that psychology has begun to answer Wigmore's call.

At the same time that Munsterberg published his book, Louis Brandeis, a lawyer who would later become a U.S. Supreme Court Justice, submitted, in the case of *Muller v. Oregon* (1908), a brief that summarized the social science research showing the impact that longer working hours had on the health and well-being of women. The Oregon court's decision was consistent with the conclusions Brandeis reached in the brief. This marked the first time that social science research was presented in court in the form of a brief, and subsequent briefs of this nature became known as *Brandeis briefs*. As we will see in Chapter 11, however, these briefs were not commonly presented in the courts until decades later.

Another early historical event was the publication, in the prestigious journal *Psychological Bulletin*, of a series of articles by Guy Whipple that in part related memory and the accounts of witnesses. In an article published in 1909, Whipple set the stage for later laboratory research on witness behavior. He wrote,

> If, then, the work of reporting is difficult even for the trained expert working under laboratory conditions and using a carefully refined terminology, how much more difficult must it be for the untrained individual to report with

accuracy and completeness the experiences of his daily life, when to the inadequacy of his language there must be added the falsifying influences of misdirected attention, mal-observation, and errors of memory, not to mention the falsifying influences that may spring from lack of caution, of zeal for accurate statement, or even from deliberate intent to mislead. (p. 153)

Perhaps the most cited social science brief was the one submitted in the famous desegregation case, *Brown v. Board of Education* (1954). Led by psychologists Kenneth Clark, Isidor Chein, and Stuart Cook, a brief was prepared that summarized research demonstrating that segregation has negative effects on the self-esteem and other personality characteristics of African American children. The brief was cited as a footnote in the Supreme Court's decision that segregation violated the Equal Protection and Due Process clauses of the Fourteenth Amendment. While it has since been debated whether or how much this research influenced the Court's decision (see Cook, 1985), there is no question that it marked the potential of using psychological research to inform courts about the negative consequences of social policies and practices.

The modern era of forensic psychology can perhaps be traced to the late 1960s when two psychologists, Jay Ziskin and Eric Dreikurs, began discussions that led to the creation of forensic psychology's first professional association (Grisso, 1991). These early meetings, which initially took place at the American Psychological Association Conference in San Francisco in 1968, led to the development of the American Psychology-Law Society (AP-LS). Ziskin in particular was the driving influence, and he had lofty aspirations for the impact of psychology and law. He wrote in AP-LS's first newsletter:

> While only the future can reveal the significance of a present event, I feel that [the meeting] in San Francisco will prove to be an event of historic significance . . . It may not prove grandiose to compare the potential impact of the creation of this society in its area with that of the Royal Academy of Science in Britain and the Academie des Sciences in France . . . We can perceive that we have taken on a precious responsibility, for there are few interdisciplinary areas with so much potential [as psychology and law] for improving the human condition and for acquiring and utilizing greater understanding of man. (p. 1)

Whether AP-LS will realize Ziskin's vision, it is noteworthy that AP-LS has thrived since its inception. AP-LS has now grown to over 2,000 members, has sponsored a major journal, *Law and Human Behavior*, a scholarly book series, and has developed guidelines for the professional practice of forensic psychology, among other accomplishments.

THE ROLES OF FORENSIC PSYCHOLOGISTS

There are many roles for forensic psychologists. At a broad level, one can divide these roles into research and practice, although this is an arbitrary and sometimes incorrect classification. Some forensic psychologists do focus entirely on research while others entirely focus on some form of practice. However, many of those who would identify themselves as researchers also engage in clinical forensic practice, while some clinicians are also active researchers. For example, the authors of this text are trained in clinical psychology, work in university settings but also conduct psychological evaluations for the courts. While some forensic psychologists work in universities as we do, or in other research settings, the majority of forensic psychologists are primarily practitioners who work in a wide range of settings.

The roles of forensic psychologists will be discussed in more detail in chapters throughout this book. The American Board of Forensic Psychology (ABFP) provides the following list of the types of activities of psychologists engaged in the practice of forensic psychology:

- Psychological evaluation and expert testimony regarding criminal forensic issues such as trial competency, waiver of Miranda rights, criminal responsibility, death penalty mitigation, battered woman syndrome, domestic violence, drug dependence, and sexual disorders
- Testimony and evaluation regarding civil issues such as personal injury, child custody, employment discrimination, mental disability, product liability, professional malpractice, civil commitment, and guardianship
- Assessment, treatment, and consultation regarding individuals with a high risk for aggressive behavior in the community, in the workplace, in treatment settings, and in correctional facilities
- Research, testimony, and consultation on psychological issues impacting on the legal process such as eyewitness testimony, jury selection, children's testimony, repressed memories, and pretrial publicity
- Specialized treatment service to individuals involved with the legal system
- Consultation to lawmakers about public policy issues with psychological implications
- Consultation and training to law enforcement, criminal justice, and correctional systems
- Consultation and training to mental health systems and practitioners on forensic issues
- Analysis of issues related to human performance, product liability, and safety

- Court-appointed monitoring of compliance with settlements in class-action suits affecting mental health or criminal justice settings
- Mediation and conflict resolution
- Policy and program development in the psychology-law arena
- Teaching, training, and supervision of graduate students, psychology, and psychiatry interns/residents, and law students
  (retrieved from http://www.abfp.com/brochure.asp, July 18, 2007)

Professional Associations and Publications

There are a number of professional groups that represent psychology and law. In North America, the primary group is the American Psychology-Law Society (AP-LS), which is an interdisciplinary organization devoted to scholarship, practice, and public service in psychology and law (see Grisso, 1991 for a history of AP-LS). AP-LS is both a free-standing organization as well as part of the American Psychological Association (Division 41). AP-LS has an active undergraduate and graduate student membership (see the AP-LS website for student information: http://www.ap-ls.org). The American Board of Forensic Psychology (ABFP) awards a Diploma in Forensic Psychology to those psychologists who satisfactorily complete the requirements for achieving Specialty Board Certification in forensic psychology. In Europe, the European Association of Psychology and Law (EAPL) is the representative association, and in Australia and New Zealand, it is the Australian & New Zealand Association for Psychiatry, Psychology & the Law (ANZAPPL). The three associations each have annual conferences and have held several joint conferences in order to promote international collaborations and presentation of the latest research findings.

   AP-LS member statistics. An analysis of membership data from the 2006 AP-LS member database provides an instructive profile of forensic psychologists. Nearly two-thirds of the over 2,100 members and fellows of AP-LS are male, but there are indications that this imbalance will shift in the next decade as 78% of the over 600 student members of AP-LS are female. The vast majority of members work in applied settings, with less than 20% indicating they work in academic institutions. Minorities are underrepresented. Haney's comment in 1993 that "put bluntly, psychology and law is an almost universally white and still largely male discipline" (pp. 388–389) remains true today. AP-LS member statistics show that less than 5% of members are from minority groups. This is in stark contrast to the representation of minorities in the criminal justice system, in which minorities account for the majority of defendants and prison inmates in many states.

Journals. There are also many journals that are entirely devoted to forensic psychology topics. *Law and Human Behavior* was the first journal, and it is the official publication of AP-LS. It began publication in 1977 as a quarterly journal, and expanded to six issues per year in 1990. In addition to *Law and Human Behavior*, the field has added many new journals, reflecting the substantial increases in research and practice that psychology and law has enjoyed over the past 40 years. The list is extensive but includes *Criminal Behavior and Mental Health; Behavioral Sciences & the Law; Psychology, Public Policy, and the Law;* and *Legal and Criminological Psychology.*

OVERVIEW OF LAW

This section provides an overview of the legal system, the origins of law, values, and law. This includes the organization of the courts (trial, appellate, federal, Supreme Court).

Sources of Law

Law can be thought of as the total of all the rules governing behavior that is enforceable in courts. There are four sources of law in the United States including the U.S. Constitution, state and federal statutes, administrative law, and court made law or *common law.*

U.S. Constitution

In order to understand the complexity of the American legal system, it is helpful to recall that the United States was founded as the union of 13 colonies, each one claiming independence from the British Crown. In 1787, the U.S. Constitution was put in place to govern the relationship among the 13 colonies and the national Congress. It defined the powers and authority of the federal and state governments and delineated the kinds of laws that the federal Congress and the state legislatures could pass.

The U.S. Constitution is often referred to as the "Law of the Land" because it supersedes all other laws or rules. The power of Congress and of the state legislatures to pass laws is always subject to the U.S. Constitution. Laws or rules that are inconsistent with the Constitution, either because they violate rights guaranteed by the Constitution or because the Constitution does not authorize that legislature to pass that kind of law, are *unconstitutional.* A court that finds a law to be unconstitutional will strike it down giving it no force or effect.

Statutes

As we have just seen, the Constitution gives Congress and state legislatures the power to pass legislation or laws in certain domains. Federal and state laws are known as **statutes**. The powers of Congress, or the federal legislature, to pass laws are set out in Article I of the Constitution. Examples of domains for which Congress has jurisdiction and can pass statutes include laws related to providing and maintaining a Navy, establishing post offices, and regulating commerce with foreign nations.

All powers not expressly granted to the federal legislature by the Constitution are reserved for the states. State legislatures have the power to pass laws concerning many domains of interest to forensic psychologists. For example, state legislatures have the power to enact legislation regarding criminal law, civil commitment, and family law. With respect to domains within their jurisdiction, each state will have its own statute or statutes. For example, California has enacted *The Penal Code of California* while Michigan has enacted *The Michigan Penal Code*—both statutes dealing with criminal law within their jurisdiction.

Administrative Rules and Regulations

In some cases, the federal or state government may delegate some of its powers to specialized administrative agencies through authorizing statutes. As a part of this delegation, many of these agencies will have the authority to make rules and regulations relevant to their responsibilities and within their area of expertise. These laws are referred to as *rules* or *regulations* rather than statutes, but they generally have the same force as statutes. The power of the administrative agency to enact rules and regulations is set out in the authorizing statute. One area of administrative law relevant to forensic psychologists is the laws surrounding the determination of disability and disability benefits.

Common Law

The U.S. legal system has its roots in the English common law system. Historically, English grand juries, kings, and magistrates catalogued their decisions according to the type and subject matter of the case. When subsequent cases came before them, they reviewed earlier decisions to determine whether a previous case was sufficiently similar to the current one. If so, they applied the principles set out in the earlier decision to the new decision. This body of principles came to be known as the *common law.* The common law is therefore often referred to as court- or judge-made law. Many of the principles established in English common law continue to be applied by U.S. courts today. In addition, the doctrine of *stare decisis*, Latin for "let the decision stand," remains.

That is, when a judge interprets a law, subsequent judges will often be bound by that interpretation through the process of precedence. Whether a judge is bound by a previous decision will largely depend on the jurisdiction of the court.

COURT SYSTEMS

The U.S. court system is one of the most complex in the world. It is composed of both federal and state court systems, each applying the laws of their jurisdiction. Taken together, there are thousands and thousands of individual courts in the United States! Courts are the final interpreters of law (they apply statutes, regulation and, common law) and are therefore central to the legal system.

Federal System

The Federal Court system is created like a three-level pyramid (see Figure 1.2). U.S. District Courts, the majority of courts in the federal system, make up the bottom of the pyramid. These trial courts are the entry point for most cases in the federal system. There are 94 U.S. federal judicial districts each with at least one court. Each state is composed of at least one district but many of the more populated states are made up of multiple districts. New York, for example, is composed of four federal judicial districts (i.e., Eastern, Northern, Southern,

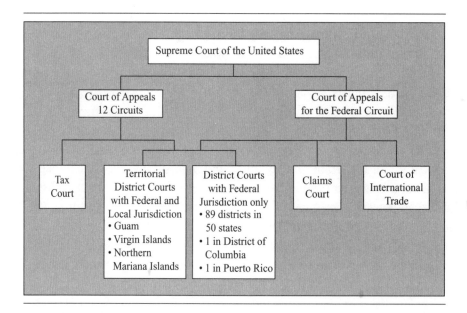

Figure 1.2   Supreme Court of the United States
Source: Encarta, http://encarta.msn.com/media_461518049_1741500781_-1_1/united_states_court_system.html.

and Western). U.S. District Courts are courts of general jurisdiction. That is, they have the authority to hear a very wide range of cases including both criminal and civil cases. If a losing party feels that a District Court made an error in reaching a decision, in many circumstances, they can appeal the decision to courts at the midlevel of the pyramid, the U.S. Courts of Appeals. The U.S. Courts of Appeals, often referred to as the U.S. Circuit Courts, are spread over 12 circuits or geographical regions. The U.S. Courts of Appeals hear appeals from District Courts within their regions. Cases at this level are decided by the majority of a three-judge panel. Decisions made by a U.S. Circuit Court will be binding on all District Courts within their jurisdiction through the doctrine of **stare decisis** (a legal term referring to the principle that prior court decisions establish precedence for current cases). A party who is dissatisfied with a decision made by a U.S. Court of Appeals may seek review by the U.S. Supreme Court by filing a motion for a **writ of certiorari** (this is a request for a higher court to direct a lower court, tribunal, or public authority to send the record in a given case for review). If the motion is successful, a higher court will then order the lower court to turn over transcripts and documents related to a specific case for review.

The U.S. Supreme Court is the single court at the top of the pyramid. It comprises nine judges, called justices, who decide cases based on a majority. The court's jurisdiction is largely discretionary. That is, when a *writ of certiorari* is filed with the U.S. Supreme Court, requesting that a U.S. Court of Appeals decision be reviewed, the nine justices will decide whether they wish to hear the case. If at least four justices agree to hear the case, *certiorari* is granted and the case is heard. Otherwise, the case is not heard and the decision of the U.S. Court of Appeals stands. The U.S. Supreme Court grants *certiorari* in only a minority of cases. The decision not to hear a case does not reflect the U.S. Supreme Court's agreement with the lower-level courts. Rather, the Court hears cases that are the most constitutionally or legally important. For example, if many Circuit Courts have interpreted identical statutes differently, the U.S. Supreme Court may agree to hear the case in order to clarify that area of law. Decisions made by the U.S. Supreme Court are binding on all other courts in the federal system. The U.S. Supreme Court is the highest arbiter of federal law and, as a result, it is sometimes called the *court of last resort*. If a losing party is unhappy with a decision made by the U.S. Supreme Court, there is no other option or remedy.

State System

The structure of state court systems vary greatly from state to state. While some states follow a pyramid structure that shares features with the federal system, many states operate complex systems involving courts with overlapping jurisdiction. Some state systems rely on four levels of courts with (1) courts of limited jurisdiction, (2) courts of general jurisdiction, (3) intermediate appellate courts, and (4) courts of last resort. In these systems, a trial will begin either at a court of limited jurisdiction or at a court of general jurisdiction depending on the subject matter and the seriousness of the case. Cases heard in a court of limited jurisdiction can often be appealed to a court of general jurisdiction. Cases first heard in a court of general jurisdiction can usually be appealed either to the intermediate appellate court or to the court of last resort depending on the nature and seriousness of the case. While this system may seem overly complex, many state systems are much more elaborate and convoluted. Students who are interested in learning about the state court system in their jurisdiction should consult their state government website for additional information.

THE COURT PROCESS

There are two distinct types of actions or lawsuits available in the United States: civil actions and criminal actions. The rules for each, the responsibilities of the court, and the rights of defendants differ considerably in both types. In addition, the outcomes can differ greatly. Some readers will remember or have heard of the O. J. Simpson trials, in which a famous ex-NFL football star was accused of killing his ex-wife and her companion. In his first trial, a criminal trial, O. J. Simpson was acquitted of the double murder. However, in his second trial, the civil trial, he was found liable for wrongful death and ordered to pay $33.5 million in damages.

Criminal Process

In a criminal action, the federal or state government prosecutes, in the name of the people, a **defendant** charged with violating a criminal law. In most criminal cases in the United States, there exists a presumption of innocence. That is, the defendant is presumed innocent unless proven guilty. The burden of proof lies with the prosecution and the level of proof, or the standard of proof, required is "beyond a reasonable doubt." That is, the **prosecutor** must convince the court that the criminal charge in the given case is true "beyond a reasonable doubt."

   The standard of proof is high in part because of the gravity of the potential outcomes in a criminal action. The penalties available are usually set out in the relevant criminal statute and they typically include a range of fines or prison time a court can impose for a given offense. In general, more severe penalties are imposed for more serious offenses and in some jurisdictions on repeat offenders.

Defendants in criminal actions are afforded a number of rights some of which are set out and protected by the U.S. Constitution. Among these rights are: the right to be free from unreasonable searches and seizures (Fourth Amendment), the right against self-incrimination (Fifth Amendment), and the right to a speedy trial (Sixth Amendment). In addition to these rights, a criminal defendant is also afforded the right to counsel. If a criminal defendant in federal and state court cannot afford an attorney, the court will appoint one, most often the **public defender**. Finally, if a criminal defendant is acquitted, the prosecution's right to appeal is virtually nonexistent.

Civil Process

Civil actions involve two or more private parties where at least one party alleges a violation of a statute or some provision of the common law. Cases involving breaches of contracts or injuries that are the result of negligence (i.e., **tort law**, which allows an injured individual to recover damages from someone who is responsible or liable for those injuries) are both examples of civil cases. The party initiating the lawsuit is the **plaintiff** while the party answering to the lawsuit is the *defendant*.

The standard of proof in civil trials is generally on the "balance of probabilities," also known as the "preponderance of evidence." This standard of proof is much lower than "beyond a reasonable doubt" and will usually be met if there is more than a 50% chance that the allegations are true or more simply, if it is more probable than not.

The many rights afforded to criminal defendants are not necessarily provided to the defendant in a civil trial. For example, in civil cases, the defendant does not have a right to counsel and is not protected against self-incrimination. For example, while O. J. Simpson was not required to testify in his criminal trial, he was required to testify at his civil trial. Many believe that his testimony coupled with the lower standard of proof accounts for the finding of liability in the wrongful death suit as opposed to the acquittal in his criminal trial.

Judges and Juries

In many civil and criminal cases, defendants are afforded the option of having their case heard before a judge alone or a judge and jury. If the defendant elects to have the case heard before a judge alone, the judge will be the arbiter of both the law and of the facts. That is, the judge decides both matters of law (e.g., which evidence to allow, how motions should be decided) and the facts of the case (e.g., decides which parties to believe, what actually transpired). The judge, therefore, decides whether the prosecution or the plaintiff has met the burden of proof and ultimately whether the defendant should be found guilty or liable. In judge and jury trials, the judge decides matters of law while the jury hears the evidence and reaches a decision about guilt or liability. Juries are made up of lay people, often referred to as *a jury of one's peers*. The jury is selected at random through a predefined procedure. In order to be eligible for jury duty, you must be at least 18 years of age, be a U.S. citizen, and have no felony convictions. Based on the facts presented at trial including the testimony of witnesses and the presentation of documents and on expert witnesses and legal arguments, the jury decides on the liability or guilt of a defendant. In coming to their decision, the jury must apply legal principles as explained by the judge. For example, a jury in a criminal trial must in making their decision apply the "beyond a reasonable doubt" standard of proof. Jury decision making is described in more detail in Chapter 7.

DIFFERENCES BETWEEN PSYCHOLOGY AND LAW

One of the difficulties faced by those in forensic psychology centers on how the two disciplines fundamentally approach their respective fields. Psychology is grounded in theory and empirical research which is used to test those theories. New research can provide evidence to support or invalidate prior research. A substantial amount of psychological research focuses on the differences between groups of individuals. The legal system, on the other hand, is ultimately concerned with the individual case. Court decisions are based on precedence, that is, what prior courts have decided in similar fact cases. There are two basic models of justice in Western societies. One is an **inquisitorial model**, which is used in a number of European countries (e.g., France, Switzerland). In this model, a judge or magistrate takes an active role in determining the facts of a case. U.S. law is based on an **adversarial model** of justice. In this model, a judge is considered to be an impartial referee between parties. There are two opposing sides, the defense and the prosecution. Each side is given the opportunity to present its version of the case. Once both sides present the evidence, the judge or jury acts as an impartial and passive fact finder, reaching a decision based in theory on an objective and unbiased review of the evidence presented in court. As discussed in Chapter 7, the ideal of a dispassionate trier of fact may not always be realized, as values and other factors may influence the decisions of judges or juries.

The adversarial system presents unique difficulties for psychologists. Psychologists are often hired by one side or the other in a criminal case or civil dispute to conduct a psychological evaluation of an individual. These evaluations may focus on such issues as competency to stand trial, the psychological impact of an assault, or risk for future violence. The individual being evaluated may perceive a psychologist as an opponent rather than an objective evaluator, and this may influence how he or she responds to the evaluator (Bush, Connell, & Denney, 2006). The adversarial nature of the legal system may also place pressure on psychologists because attorneys are primarily focused on being an advocate for their client and may attempt to influence the evaluation report. As discussed in Chapter 12, the psychologist's ethical guidelines mandate that psychologists do not take sides, but rather perform an independent evaluation.

Haney (1980) has discussed many of the conflicts that arise between law and forensic psychology:

1. Academic psychology emphasizes creative, novel, and innovativeapproaches to research questions. As Haney notes, researchers are encouraged to go beyond standard or accepted categories, and to extend them into new areas. The profession highly values the "'creative aspect' of its science . . . in hypothesis generating, methodological design, and the interpretation of data" (p. 159). The legal system, on the other hand, is more conservative in nature, and resists innovation. It operates on the principle of *stare decisis* in which prior court decisions establish precedence for current cases. Prior decisions should not be overturned unless there are strong legal reasons to do so. Haney comments that "a truly unique idea or argument is likely to lose in court" (p. 159) and adds that "the law is explicitly backward looking in its style and method" (p. 160).

2. Psychology is primarily an empirical enterprise "whose principles and propositions depend for their confirmation upon the collection of consistent and supporting data" (p. 160). The legal system in contrast is based on a hierarchical and authoritative system in which the lower courts are bound by decisions of higher courts.

3. Psychology attempts to arrive at "truth" through the application of an experimental model, in which empirical research is designed to test hypotheses. Research methodologies are designed to minimize error or bias. New research can provide evidence to support or disconfirm prior research. The law uses an adversarial system to arrive at "truth." Each side presents its version of the case and the ultimate goal is to win a case. As Haney comments, "bias and self-interest are not only permitted, they are assumed at the outset and thought to be the very strength and motive force of the procedure" (p. 162).

4. Psychology is descriptive in nature, with a goal of describing behavior as it naturally occurs. The law is prescriptive, in that laws are designed

to tell people how they should behave, and what punishment will be given if they do not.

5. Psychology is nomothetic (in which data are obtained through the investigation of groups) in nature, "concentrating upon general principles, relationships, and patterns that transcend the single instance. For the most part, it eschews case studies and principles generated from single cases" (Haney, 1980, p. 164). The law is ideographic (in which data are obtained through the investigation of one individual, usually the individual under consideration), in that it focuses on decisions in an individual case, with the facts of each case forming the basis for the decision. This difference often creates a conflict for experts who testify because the empirical basis for the testimony may lie in group data. For example, laboratory research on the reliability of eyewitnesses report high error rates in certain conditions, but there is considerable individual variation. Some individuals are accurate even if the majority may not be. This presents a problem for court testimony because the court wants to know whether a single individual is accurate. Psychology's group data cannot be used to reach an opinion that a specific individual is not reliable.

6. Psychology research is based on methods relying on probabilistic models. Psychologists characterize the relationship between cause and effect using statistics and the tools of probability theory. Hypotheses are tested with the express acknowledgment that there is always a chance of reaching the wrong conclusions. For example, choosing a probability level of 95% for a particular analysis means that there is a 5% chance that the null hypothesis will be rejected when it was actually correct. Thus, psychological research is based on the principle of probability rather than certainty. The law, in contrast, operates on a principle of certainty, in large part because the legal system demands a final definitive outcome. Criminal defendants are either guilty or not guilty. Plaintiffs in civil cases are either negligent or not. Of course, these "certain" decisions can be wrong, as shown in the many cases of convicted defendants who were later exonerated by DNA evidence.

7. Psychology is a proactive discipline. Researchers decide what hypotheses to address, and then design studies to test those hypotheses. The law is reactive, in that it waits until issues (or people) are brought to it.

8. Psychology is an academic enterprise, at least in terms of its research. As Haney comments, "Its 'issues' are commonly determined by the intellectual curiosities of psychologists and the practical reality of having to publish in order to prosper. For this reason, its concerns can and often do get far out of contact with the 'real world'" (p. 167). The law is operational and applied in nature, "its concerns are those of the real world and its problem solving is geared to application" (p. 168).

Haney's Taxonomy

Haney (1980) conceptualized the complexity and diversity of roles for psychologists in the legal system. He has suggested a threefold taxonomy to understand the multiple relationships of psychology and law: psychology *in* the law, psychology *and* law, and psychology *of* law.

Psychology in the law refers to the "explicit and conventional use of psychology by lawyers in the legal process" (p. 153). This relationship accounts for the most common role of psychologists involved in legal issues, since it encompasses the activities of psychologists who conduct court-ordered evaluations or who consult with lawyers on legal issues. Examples include psychological testimony on legal issues such as the insanity defense or competency to stand trial. It might also address questions such as whether a particular offender is at risk for reoffending. For this type of involvement, psychologists must adapt their knowledge and expertise to the legal questions that the courts or law define. To be admissible in court, psychologists must demonstrate that their evidence is relevant to the legal question. *Psychology in the law* also refers to the roles that psychologists can provide as expert consultants in various aspects of legal proceedings. Lawyers employ psychologists to consult about the selection of jurors or how jurors might react to certain defense strategies. Psychologists have also been employed to conduct studies of the effect that pretrial publicity may have on a particular case. Such research can be used by lawyers in motions arguing for a change of venue to another community. Haney notes that *psychology in the law* accounts for the most frequent roles of psychologists in the legal system, and cautions psychologists to "realize that when they are used *by* the legal system in this way they have little control over the ends to which their expertise is ultimately applied" (p. 154).

Psychology and law involves the use of "psychological principles to analyze and examine the legal system" (p. 154). Unlike *psychology in the law*, the relationship of the two disciplines of law and psychology is one that involves "coequal and conjoint use of psychological principles to analyze and examine the legal system" (p. 154). Research that follows from this relationship examines the assumptions that the law makes about behavior. Examples include research on eyewitness accuracy, coerced and/or false confessions, and judicial decision making. This type of involvement can result in changes in the way in which the legal system operates. The extensive research on police lineups in the past two decades, which demonstrated biases in how suspects were identified by witnesses, formed the basis for recommendations by an AP-LS subcommittee for changes in lineup and photospread procedures, many of which have been adopted by police throughout the United States (Wells et al., 1998). Other examples of *psychology in the law* include the study of whether adolescents have the capacity to waive their arrest rights, whether personality characteristics affect the decisions of judges or jurors, and whether the death penalty acts as a deterrent.

Psychology of law, in which psychologists study issues such as why people need the law and why people obey the law, is the third relationship Haney suggested. Two major categories fall under this approach to examining psychology's role. One, psychologists can study the origins and existence of law, in terms of the psychological functions that law serves. Two, psychologists can study how laws operate as a determinant of behavior. Haney recognizes that this approach to law is difficult for psychologists to apply to research, in part because "the unit of analysis—law qua law—is too global and pervasive, and therefore not easily manipulated or systematically varied in ways familiar to psychologists" (p. 156).

Haney notes that the roles and expectations of psychologists are different for each of these three relationships. In the first relationship, psychologists have a more passive role, since the law defines the legal concepts that psychologists are asked to address. The second and third relationships provide more autonomous roles for psychologists in that they can define the legal issues they address. Haney comments that while the majority of psychologists are involved *in* the law, it is the other two relationships in which psychologists might have the most impact on legal change through research that examines how the law actually works or studies leading to changes that might improve legal procedures.

Training in Forensic Psychology

When the field of psychology and law began to expand in the 1970s, the majority of psychologists who conducted research or engaged in practice were not specifically trained in psychology and law. This began to change with the creation of the first psychology and law graduate program in the United States at the University of Nebraska in 1973 (Krauss & Sales, 2006). Since then, programs have been established in many other universities in the United States, Canada, Europe, Australia, and elsewhere in the world.

In most states, a PhD or PsyD is required for forensic psychology practice. A doctoral degree in clinical psychology is typically based on a combination of training in research and practice, whereas in other areas of psychology (e.g., social, cognitive) it is primarily a research-based degree. A PsyD (or Doctor of Psychology) program places greater emphasis on the practice of psychology and less emphasis on independent research.

While there are now many graduate programs in which specialized training in forensic psychology is available, a doctoral degree in forensic psychology is not necessary to engage in work in the field. Many, even a majority, of psychologists have training in the traditional areas of psychology and no formal graduate training in forensic psychology. These psychologists have typically participated in workshops and other continuing education programs to keep up-to-date with the latest advances in psychology and law. The number of forensic psychologists with formal graduate training in forensic psychology has gradually increased in the past 20 years as more programs have been initiated.

Graduate programs. Graduate programs offer a number of options for training in forensic psychology (see Table 1.2 for a list of programs). Some programs adopt the scientist-practitioner model of clinical training, offering basic research and practical training in clinical psychology but with an emphasis on forensic applications. Other programs are nonclinical in nature, focusing training on more traditional fields of psychology such as social, developmental, or other experimental areas of psychology. A few programs offer joint-degree programs, with students obtaining a PhD and a law degree (see Bersoff et al., 1997, for a discussion of models of graduate training in forensic psychology).

Heilbrun (2001) has presented a table summarizing the approaches to training in forensic psychology (see Table 1.3). He conceptualizes the training in a 2 × 3 model, in which research scholarship and applied activities can be taught within three major interest areas: clinical, experimental, and legal. The model shows that each interest area includes training and experiences in research and scholarship but also in the application of psychology to the legal system. Thus, students in clinical programs learn the basic research on assessment and intervention but also how to conduct forensic assessments and provide treatment in the legal context. Experimental students study basic research in memory, perception, and other areas of experimental psychology, but also how to apply that research to consultation activities in the legal system such as jury selection and expert testimony. Students in law schools who also receive some training in behavioral science learn about mental health law and legal movements, but also how to apply that to developing new law or to consult about policy and legislative change.

An illustrative graduate program is one developed at Simon Fraser University, which uses an approach that provides graduate training in all three of these options. The Law and Forensic Psychology program offers two distinct tracks. Graduate students in the Clinical Forensic track meet all the requirements of the clinical psychology doctoral program and take additional courses to specialize in forensic psychology. Graduate students in the Experimental Psychology and Law stream or track meet all the requirements for the experimental doctoral program, and take additional courses to develop research and applied policy skills in law and forensic psychology. Due to the overlap of the two areas, students in both streams will take many of the same courses and will develop similar research

Table 1.2   Graduate Training in Forensic Psychology

Clinical PhD/PsyD Programs	University of Alabama (Clinical PhD with a psychology-law concentration) University of Arizona (PhD and/or JD) Alliant International University (PhD in Forensic Psychology or PsyD in Forensic Psychology) Arizona State University (Law and Psychology JD/PhD Program) Carlos Albizu University in Miami (PsyD in Clinical Psychology with a concentration in forensic psychology) Drexel University (JD/PhD) Drexel University (PhD with a concentration in forensic psychology) University of Florida (Counseling PhD with psychology-law concentration or JD) Fordham University (Clinical PhD with concentration in forensic psychology) Illinois School of Professional Psychology (Clinical PsyD with concentration in forensic psychology) John Jay College of Criminal Justice–CUNY (MA or PhD) University of Nebraska (joint JD and PhD or joint JD and MA in Psychology) Nova Southeastern University (PsyD with a concentration in clinical forensic psychology) Pacific Graduate School of Psychology (joint PhD/JD) Sam Houston State University (PhD in Clinical Psychology with an emphasis in forensic psychology) Simon Fraser University (PhD in Clinical-Forensic Psychology) West Virginia University (PhD in clinical with emphasis in forensics) Widener University (JD/PsyD joint degree)
Nonclinical PhD/ PsyD Programs	University of Arizona (PhD and/or JD) Alliant International University (PhD in Forensic Psychology or PsyD in Forensic Psychology) Arizona State University (Law and Psychology JD/PhD Program) Florida International University (PhD in Psychology with an emphasis in legal psychology) Georgetown University (PhD in Psychology with concentration in human development and public policy and a PhD in a joint program with an MA in public policy) John Jay College of Criminal Justice–CUNY (MA or PhD) University of Nevada–Reno (PhD in social psychology with a concentration in psychology and law) Simon Fraser University (PhD in psychology in the law and forensic psychology program) University of California–Irvine (PhD in Criminology, Law & Society) University of Florida (Developmental PhD with psychology-law concentration or JD) University of Illinois at Chicago (PhD with concentration in psychology and law) University of Minnesota (PhD in social psychology with a research concentration in social psychology and law) University of Nebraska (joint JD and PhD or joint JD and MA in Psychology) University of Texas at El Paso (PhD in Applied Psychology with the Legal Psychology Group) University of Wyoming (PhD with concentration in psychology and law)

Source: http//www.ap-ls.org/students/graduateIndex.html.

Table 1.3   Heilbrun's Conceptualization of Training in Forensic Psychology

	Law and Psychology Interest Areas (with associated training)		
	Clinical	Experimental	Legal
	(clinical, counseling, school psychology)	(social, developmental, cognitive, human experimental psychology	(law, some training in behavioral science)
Research/Scholarship	1. Assessment tools 2. Intervention effectiveness 3. Epidemiology of relevant behaviors (e.g., violence, sexual offending) and disorders	1. Memory 2. Perception 3. Child development 4. Group decision making	1. Mental health law 2. Other law relevant to health and science 3. Legal movements (law and social science, therapeutic jurisprudence, psychological jurisprudence)
Applied	1. Forensic assessment 2. Treatment in legal context 3. Integration of science (idiographic, nomethetic, reasoning) into practice	1. Consultation on jury selection 2. Consultation on litigation strategy 3. Consultation on "state of science" 4. Expert testimony on "state of science"	1. Policy and legislative consultation 2. Model law development

Source: Heilbrun (2001).

skills; however, students in the Clinical-Forensic Stream further develop their clinical training to include forensic training and practice experience. In cooperation with the University of British Columbia, the SFU Program in Law and Forensic Psychology also offers students in law and forensic psychology an opportunity to complete both a PhD and a law degree.

Undergraduate students who wish to pursue a career in forensic psychology should be aware that admission to graduate programs in forensic psychology (or psychology more generally) is highly competitive, with most programs admitting fewer than 10% of applicants. Students will usually need to major in psychology, have outstanding grades and scores on the Graduate Record Exam (GRE), and have excellent references. Students are advised to obtain as much research experience as possible, working in labs of professors as well as conducting their own research. Volunteer work or jobs in forensic psychology settings, such as juvenile detention centers or forensic hospitals, can also be helpful.

Many students inquire about whether a PhD in psychology and a law degree are necessary for engaging in either research or practice in forensic psychology. The short answer is no, but Professor Don Bersoff, one of the founders of joint degree programs, has written eloquently about the potential value of both degrees (see Box 1.2).

Box 1.2 On the Value of Joint
Degree Programs

The following excerpt, on the potential contribution that JD/PhD graduates can make to forensic psychology, was written by Professor Don Bersoff, a past president of the American Psychology-Law Society who founded one joint degree program and later directed another one.

> One of the great values of joint training is that it produces people who are comfortable and conversant in two divergent languages—that of science and that of law. Thus, graduates have the potential of serving as translators for the respective members of these two jargon-filled and technical fields. Graduates of JD/doctoral programs can translate legal principles for psychologists, helping them to understand the meaning and implications of such relevant concepts as due process, equal protection, informed consent, and insanity and the impact of the legal system on the practice of psychology. Conversely, these graduates can help inform law students, law professors, lawyers, and judges about the meaning of such legally relevant terms as falsifiability, Type I and Type II errors, multivariate analysis, test validity, psychosis, or the applicability of research on memory, perception, and group dynamics to such legal problems as eyewitness identification, the constitutionality of nonunanimous juries, or the validity of certain exculpatory "syndromes." (Bersoff, 1999, p. 392)

SUMMARY

The involvement of psychologists in the legal system dates back to the early part of the last century, but it has only been in the last 40 or 50 years that psychologists have made substantive and consistent contributions. Forensic psychology has grown dramatically during this period, as witnessed by the creation of professional associations and the publication of journals in psychology and law. We defined *forensic psychology* as encompassing both sides of the justice system (civil and criminal) as well as two broad aspects of psychology (clinical and experimental). Psychologists have made a range of contributions in both research and practice. This chapter provided numerous examples of the type of activities in which forensic psychologists contribute to the legal system. It was noted that the interaction of psychology and law is not without its difficulties. We provided an overview of Haney's model for understanding the differences between psychology and law as a way of explaining the reasons for the conflicts that often arise between the two disciplines. Training models for students wishing to pursue a career in forensic psychology were reviewed. It is essential that forensic psychologists understand the legal system, and this chapter presented an overview of how the legal system operates in the United States.

SUGGESTED READINGS AND WEBSITES

American Board of Forensic Psychology website: http://www.abfp.com.

American Psychological Association website: http://www.apa.org/crsppp/ archivforensic.html.

American Psychology-Law Society website: http://www.ap-ls.org/.

Bersoff, D. (1999). Preparing for two cultures: Education and training in law and psychology. In R. Roesch, S. D. Hart, & J. R. P. Ogloff (Eds.), *Psychology and law: The state of the discipline* (pp. 375–401). NY: Kluwer Academic/Plenum.

Brigham, J. C. (1999). What is forensic psychology, anyway? *Law and Human Behavior, 23*, 273–298.

Grisso, T. (1991). A developmental history of the American Psychology-Law Society. *Law and Human Behavior, 15*, 213–231.

Haney, C. (1980). Psychology and legal change: On the limits of a factual jurisprudence. *Law and Human Behavior, 4*, 147–199.

Haney, C. (1993). Psychology and legal change: The impact of a decade. *Law and Human Behavior, 17*, 371–398.

KEY TERMS

- *Adversarial model*
- *Defendant*
- *Forensic psychology*
- *Inquisitorial model*
- *Plaintiff*
- *Prosecutor*
- *Public defender*
- Stare decisis
- *Statutes*
- *Tort law*
- *Writ of certiorari*

References ──────────────────

Bersoff, D. N. (1999). Preparing for two cultures: Education and training in law and psychology. In R. Roesch, S. D. Hart, & J. R. P. Ogloff (Eds.), *Psychology and law: The state of the discipline* (pp. 375–401). New York: Kluwer Academic/Plenum.

Bersoff, D. N., Goodman-Delahunty, J., Grisso, J. T., Hans, V. P., Poythress, N. G., & Roesch, R. (1997). Training in law and psychology: Models from the Villanova conference. *American Psychologist, 52*, 1301–1310.

Brigham, J. C. (1999). What is forensic psychology, anyway? *Law and Human Behavior, 23*, 273–298.

Brown v. Board of Education, 375 U.S. 483 (1954).

Bush, S. S., Connell, M. A., & Denney, R. L. (2006). *Ethical practice in forensic psychology: A systematic model for decision making.* Washington, DC: American Psychological Association.

Committee on Ethical Guidelines for Forensic Psychologists. (1991). Specialty guidelines for forensic psychologists. *Law and Human Behavior, 15*, 655–665.

Cook, S. W. (1985). Experimenting on social issues: The case of school desegregation. *American Psychologist, 40*, 452–460.

Doyle, J. (2005). *True witness: Cops, courts, science, and the battle against misidentification.* New York: Palgrave MacMillan.

Goldstein, A. M. (2003). Overview of forensic psychology. In A. M. Goldstein (Ed.), *Handbook of psychology* (Volume 11: *Forensic psychology*) (pp. 3–20). New York: Wiley.

Grisso, T. (1991). A developmental history of the American Psychology-Law Society. *Law and Human Behavior, 15*, 213–231.

Haney, C. (1980). Psychology and legal change: On the limits of a factual jurisprudence. *Law and Human Behavior, 4*, 147–199.

Haney, C. (1993). Psychology and legal change: The impact of a decade. *Law and Human Behavior, 17*, 371–398.

Heilbrun, K. (2001). *Principles of forensic mental health assessment.* New York: Kluwer Academic/Plenum.

Krauss, D. A., & Sales, B. D. (2006). Training in forensic psychology: Training for what goal? In I. B. Weiner & A. K. Hess (Eds.), *Handbook of forensic psychology* (3rd ed.; pp. 851–871). New York: Wiley.

Muller v. Oregon, 208 U.S. 412 (1908).

Munsterberg, H. (1908). *On the witness stand.* Garden City, NY: Doubleday.

Ogloff, J. R. P., & Finkelman, D. (1999). Psychology and law: An overview. In R. Roesch, S. D. Hart, & J. R. P. Ogloff (Eds.), *Psychology and law: The state of the discipline* (pp. 1–20). New York: Kluwer Academic/Plenum.

Torres, A. N., Boccaccini, M. T., & Miller, H. A. (2006). Perceptions of the validity and utility of criminal profiling among forensic psychologists and psychiatrists. *Professional Psychology Research and Practice, 37*, 51–58.

Wells, G. L., Small, M., Penrod, S. D., Malpass, R. S., Fulero, S. M., & Brimacombe, C. A. E. (1998). Eyewitness identification procedures: Recommendations for lineups and photospreads. *Law and Human Behavior, 22*, 603–647.

Whipple, G. M. (1909). The observer as reporter: A survey of the psychology of testimony. *Psychological Bulletin, 6*, 153–170.

Wigmore, J. H. (1909). Professor Munsterberg and the psychology of evidence. *Illinois Law Review, 3*, 399–445.

Wigmore, J. H. (1940). *Evidence* (3rd ed.). Boston: Little, Brown.

Wrightsman, L. S., & Fulero, S. M. (2005). *Forensic psychology* (2nd ed.). Belmont, CA: Thomson Wadsworth.

Chapter 2

FORENSIC ASSESSMENT IN CRIMINAL DOMAINS

CHAPTER OBJECTIVES

In this chapter, you will become familiar with:

- The various types of competencies that determine whether an individual is able to proceed with his or her criminal proceedings
- The legal standards and procedures relevant to the determination of competency to stand trial
- The legal standards and procedures relevant to the determination of criminal responsibility or insanity
- Public perceptions of the insanity defense and insanity acquittees
- The three approaches to risk assessment
- Important risk factors for the prediction of future violent behavior

Psychologists and other mental health professionals are often called upon by the courts to assist in the determination of various legal issues. Although the final determination of any legal issue rests with the legal decision maker (judge or jury), psychologists assist the court by providing information obtained through the assessment of the person for whom the court must make a determination. The legal issues to be decided by the courts may be either civil (e.g., involuntary hospitalization, personal injury, child custody) or criminal (e.g., adjudicative competency, insanity) in nature. This chapter focuses on the role of the psychologist in the assessment of criminal forensic issues whereas the next chapter focuses on assessment of civil forensic issues. Issues having to do with juveniles or juvenile court will be discussed in Chapter 8.

Mr. Adams, a 36-year-old white male with a lengthy history of mental illness, was charged with arson after setting the walls of his apartment on fire. At his arrest, he was disheveled and unkempt and was incoherent. The police report indicates that Mr. Adams claimed that he was ridding the apartment of an evil spirit by setting the walls on fire and that he believed there to be a dead body buried within the walls. No evidence of anything unusual was found within the walls of the apartment. Mr. Adams' public defender asked the court to order an evaluation of Mr. Adams' competency to stand trial as well as an evaluation of Mr. Adams' criminal responsibility (mental state at the time of the offense). What is the difference between competency to stand trial and insanity?

Mr. Baker, a 35-year-old African American male with a lengthy history of violent and aggressive behavior, was convicted of assault with a deadly weapon after severely beating his ex-wife's boyfriend with a baseball bat. This is Mr. Baker's third conviction for a serious assault. He has served almost two years of a three-year prison sentence and will soon be eligible for parole. A risk assessment has been requested by the parole board to assist in their determination regarding Mr. Baker's parole. What factors are considered in an assessment of risk for future violence?

Mr. Cooper, a 21-year-old Hispanic male with no prior history of mental illness or criminal behavior, was charged with aggravated assault after he brutally attacked his best friend for no apparent reason. Mr. Cooper claimed he heard voices commanding him to "eliminate" his friend for the good of the world. Mr. Cooper's family, as well as the friend who was attacked, indicated that Mr. Cooper had been acting oddly for the past 3 months and often appeared to be listening and responding to internal stimuli. Mr. Cooper was referred for evaluation to determine the feasibility of an insanity defense as well as the possibility that he might be malingering. What factors would need to be considered for each of these issues?

CRIMINAL COMPETENCIES

The issue of a person's competency may arise at any stage of criminal proceedings. That is, from the time that an individual is first considered a suspect and is questioned about his or her involvement in a crime—through being arrested and charged with a crime, making initial and subsequent appearances in court, pleading guilty or going to trial, being sentenced (if found guilty), and being executed (if sentenced to death)—an individual must be competent in order for the proceedings to go forward. If a question about a defendant's competency arises at any stage of the proceedings, an evaluation by a psychologist or other mental health professional may be ordered. The results of this evaluation will be used to assist the court in making a determination about the individual's competency.

Rationale for the Competency Doctrine

According to the competency doctrine, criminal proceedings against an individual can be postponed if the defendant is unable to participate in his or her defense on account of mental disease or defect. The rationale behind this doctrine, which dates back to at least the seventeenth century and has long been a part of legal due process, is that it is unfair to try a defendant if he or she is unable to participate meaningfully in the proceedings. That is, every defendant has the right to assist legal counsel, confront his or her accusers, and testify on his or her own behalf and, if because of a mental disorder, he or she is unable to carry out these activities then it is only fair to halt the proceedings until such time as the defendant is able to carry out these activities.

In addition to protecting the rights of the individual to participate meaningfully in his or her defense, the competency doctrine also serves to protect the dignity and integrity of the court proceedings. Allowing an incompetent individual to be tried and convicted would offend the dignity and integrity of the court proceedings and the public would see the court as unfair.

Types of Criminal Competencies

The terms **adjudicative competence** or **competency to proceed** are umbrella terms that encompass all the various types of criminal competencies that may arise as an issue from the time a suspect is first arrested and charged until he or she receives a final disposition by the court or, for those sentenced to death, is executed. By far, the most common type of competency issue that arises is **competency to stand trial**. Although somewhat of a misnomer since upward of 90% of criminal defendants resolve their cases either through a guilty plea or a plea bargain and therefore never go to trial, it has been estimated that approximately 60,000 competency to stand trial evaluations are conducted each year in the United States (Bonnie & Grisso, 2000). These evaluations of competency to stand trial encompass evaluation of the defendant's abilities to understand the nature and object of the court proceedings as well as his or her ability to participate in the proceedings and assist in his or her defense (including pleading guilty or entering into a plea bargain agreement).

Surveys of attorneys regarding their client's abilities to make decisions and assist counsel in criminal cases reveal that attorneys have doubts about their client's competency in approximately 10% of all felony cases but only formally raise the issue of competency about 50% of the time (Poythress, Bonnie, Hoge, Monahan, & Oberlander, 1994). Thus, the issue of competency is raised for about 5 of every 100 felony defendants.

In addition to competency to stand trial, which is the most common type of criminal forensic assessment conducted and includes competency to plead guilty, a defendant's **competency to waive Miranda**, **competency to waive counsel** (to proceed *pro se*, that is, to proceed without legal representation), **competency to be sentenced**, and **competency to be executed** may also be questioned.

Competency to Stand Trial

This type of competency, which we have noted is by far the most common, refers to the defendant's present mental state and whether the defendant is able to understand the proceedings and assist in his or her own defense.

Competency to Waive Miranda

This type refers to the mental state of the defendant at the time that he or she was being interrogated by the police following an arrest, and whether the defendant was able to intelligently, knowingly, and willingly waive his or her right to silence (Fifth Amendment right against self-incrimination) and understand his or her rights with respect to obtaining an attorney and having that attorney present while the defendant is questioned.

Competency to Waive Counsel (Proceed Pro Se*)*

This type refers to whether the defendant is able to intelligently, knowingly, and willfully waive his or her right to the assistance of counsel and proceed to trial *pro se* (for self) by representing oneself.

Competency to Be Sentenced

This type refers to whether the defendant is able to understand the reasons why he or she is to be sentenced as well as the sentence itself.

Competency to Be Executed

This type refers to whether the defendant (now an inmate who has been sentenced to death and is living on death row) is able to understand that he or she is to be put to death as well as the reasons why he or she is to be executed.

Legal Standards for Competency

The U.S. Supreme Court decided that the standard to be used in federal cases for competency to stand trial is *Dusky v. United States* (1960). Since 1960, in addition to this standard being used in federal court, every state has also adopted the *Dusky* standard either verbatim or with some minor modification. In *Dusky*, the Court noted that in order for a defendant to be considered competent to stand trial he or she must have "sufficient present ability to consult with his [or her] lawyer with a reasonable degree of rational understanding and . . . a rational as well as factual understanding of the proceedings against him [or her]" (p. 402). Thus, as a general statement, criminal defendants must be able to understand the nature and object of the proceedings, appreciate the personal importance of their role in the proceedings, and communicate in a rational way with their defense attorney.

In 1993, the U.S. Supreme Court, in the case of *Godinez v. Moran*, decided that there was to be one standard for various types of criminal competencies. That is, the same standard—the *Dusky* standard—would apply to competency to stand trial, competency to plead guilty, and competency to waive counsel and represent oneself. This decision has been met with some criticism by legal scholars who argue that the *Dusky* standard is a lower threshold than should be required for considering someone competent to represent him- or herself.

In 1993, Colin Ferguson went on a shooting rampage on the Long Island Rail Road killing six people and wounding 19 others. There were numerous witnesses to the massacre and there was no doubt that Mr. Ferguson had committed the offenses. Although his defense team was planning to present an insanity defense, Mr. Ferguson, insisting that he did not commit the shootings, decided to fire his defense attorneys and represent himself at trial. As a result of the *Godinez* decision, the Court found Colin Ferguson competent to stand trial and, by extension, competent to represent himself. At trial, Mr. Ferguson repeatedly made a mockery of the proceedings by acting in a bizarre way, asking pointless questions, proposing conspiracy theories, referring to himself in the third person, and attempting to call President Bill Clinton as a witness for the defense. Legal scholars have called the *Ferguson* case an embarrassment to the justice system (Perlin, 1996). It is a case like this that calls into question the Court's decision in *Godinez*.

At the time of writing this book, the Supreme Court had a chance to revisit the issue of whether the same standard of competence should apply to all situations. In *Indiana v. Edwards* (2008), the Supreme Court examined the issue of whether a state can limit a defendant's right to self-representation by requiring that the defendant be represented by counsel at trial. In essence, the Supreme Court was considering the issue of whether the same standard of competence should apply for standing trial with counsel and for representing oneself at trial. The Court, in *Edwards*, reasoned that when a defendant lacks the mental capacity to represent himself at trial the state could require that the defendant be represented by counsel. Thus, the *Edwards* decision established that competency to represent oneself (to proceed *pro se*) requires a higher level of competence than competence to stand trial.

Competency Procedures

A formal inquiry into a defendant's competency status must occur whenever a *bona fide* doubt about a defendant's competency is raised. The issue of a defendant's competency can be raised by either the defense, the prosecution, or by the court more generally. Once the issue is raised, one or more mental health professionals will evaluate the defendant and will submit their conclusions in a report to the court. Research has indicated that the court agrees with the conclusions of the mental health professional in upward of 95% of the cases. Thus, while a hearing on the issue of competency may occur, it usually is not necessary.

If the defendant is found competent to stand trial, the case proceeds. If the defendant is found incompetent to stand trial, he or she is usually sent to a psychiatric hospital or forensic facility for restoration of competency. The majority of defendants will be restored to competency within a 6-month period of time (see the following discussion for more on this issue). Once the defendant is restored to competency, he or she returns to court and the case proceeds. For the small proportion of defendants who are incompetent to stand trial and who are unable to be restored to competency, the charges will usually be dropped or dismissed without prejudice. In those cases when the defendant is considered to be a risk to public safety, he or she may be committed to a psychiatric institution under civil commitment proceedings.

Until 1972, virtually all states allowed for the indefinite confinement of defendants deemed incompetent to stand trial and not restorable. The U.S. Supreme Court, in the case of *Jackson v. Indiana* (1972), decided that incompetent defendants could not be held for more than a "reasonable" period of time to determine whether their competence can be restored in the foreseeable future. Since defendants who are deemed incompetent to stand trial have not been convicted of a crime, it is unconstitutional to detain them for lengthy periods of time if there is no possibility of restoring them to competence. Thus, as a result of the *Jackson* decision, many states amended their statutes to include guidelines for the length of time that incompetent defendants can be detained. Of course, this varies by jurisdiction with some states including specific time limits in their statutes while others use the "reasonable" language of *Jackson*.

Competency Assessment

Competency to stand trial evaluations are the most common form of criminal forensic assessments conducted and, each year 2% to 8% of all felony defendants in the United States undergo this type of evaluation. Mental health professionals, including psychologists and psychiatrists in most jurisdictions as well as social workers and nurse practitioners in other jurisdictions, are called upon by the courts to conduct this type of evaluation. In general, competency to stand trial evaluations can be conducted in a relatively short period of time on an outpatient basis, although they still occur on an inpatient basis in some states. The focus of this type of evaluation is on the defendant's current mental state (as opposed to his or her mental state at another point in time, such as at the time of the offense, which is the focus of a criminal responsibility evaluation to be discussed later in this chapter).

The evaluator conducts an interview with the defendant in an attempt to assess the defendant's current mental state and to assess whether the defendant is able to perform the specific abilities required of him or her in order to proceed with the case. Although the specific abilities required of the defendant may vary by jurisdiction, in general the defendant must be able to understand the nature and object of the proceedings, understand his or her role in those proceedings, and be able to assist counsel in his or her own defense.

Several forensic assessment instruments have been developed to assist evaluators in the assessment of a defendant's competency to stand trial. These instruments may take many forms but, in general, they all serve to highlight those psycholegal abilities that are required of all defendants in order to be able to proceed. Instruments such as the *Fitness Interview Test-Revised* (FIT-R: Roesch, Zapf, & Eaves, 2006) provide questions to be asked in 16 different domains relevant to proceeding with a criminal case whereas other instruments, such as the *MacArthur Competence Assessment Tool-Criminal Adjudication* (MacCAT-CA; Poythress, Monahan, Bonnie, & Hoge, 1999) or the *Evaluation of Competency to Stand Trial-Revised* (ECST-R; Rogers, Tillbrook, & Sewell, 2004), provide standardized administration and scoring for inquiries related to relevant psycholegal abilities (see Box 2.1 for a list of competency assessment instruments).

In addition to interviewing the defendant and administering any relevant forensic assessment instruments, the evaluator may also seek third-party information, such as records that exist about the defendant's mental health or interviews with family members or others who know the defendant well and can speak about his or her current functioning within the context of his or her previous functioning. Once the evaluator has conducted the complete evaluation, he or she will usually write a report to court detailing his or her opinions regarding the defendant's abilities. As indicated earlier in this chapter, the court will then either make a determination about the defendant's competency to stand trial on the basis of the written report or will hold a hearing on the issue of competence and make a final disposition.

**Box 2.1 Forensic Assessment Instruments
for Competency to Proceed**

Numerous forensic assessment instruments have been developed to evaluate various types of competencies. The following is a sampling of some of the more well-known instruments.

Robey's (1965) Checklist. This was the first forensic assessment instrument developed and consisted of a checklist of items to guide a clinician's evaluations of competency to stand trial.

Competency Screening Test (CST; Lipsitt, Lelos, & McGarry, 1971). This 22-item, sentence-completion task was developed to identify those defendants who are clearly competent so as to minimize the need for lengthy inpatient evaluations of competence.

Competency to Stand Trial Assessment Instrument (CAI; Laboratory of Community Psychiatry, 1973). This interview-based instrument contains 13 items related to legal issues and serves to provide structure to the evaluation of competency to stand trial.

Georgia Court Competency Test (GCCT; Wildman, White, & Brandenburg, 1990). The original version of this instrument contains 17 items whereas the revision, the Georgia Court Competency Test-Mississippi State Hospital Revision (GCCT-MSH; Johnson & Mullett, 1987) contains 21 items. This instrument asks defendants to visually identify the location of various participants within the courtroom and to answer questions about the roles of various people within the courtroom as well as questions about the alleged crime, consequences, and the defendant's relationship with his or her attorney.

Competence Assessment for Standing Trial for Defendants with Mental Retardation (CAST-MR; Everington & Luckasson, 1992). This instrument, developed for use with this specialized population of defendants, contains 50 items that cover three areas: basic legal concepts, skills to assist defense, and understanding the case event. The first two sections are in multiple-choice format whereas the last section comprises open-ended questions.

Interdisciplinary Fitness Interview (IFI; Golding, Roesch, & Schreiber, 1984). This instrument and its revision, the IFI-R (Golding, 1993) was developed to assess both the legal and psychopathological aspects of competency to stand trial. The IFI-R covers 31 relatively specific psychological abilities that are organized into 11 global domains and can also be used to assist in the assessment of competency to plead guilty, to proceed *pro se*, and to confess.

Fitness Interview Test (FIT; Roesch, Webster, & Eaves, 1984). This instrument and its revision, the FIT-R (Roesch et al., 2006) was developed to assist in the evaluation of competency to stand trial by providing 70 questions in 16 different domains divided into three main areas: the ability to understand the nature or object of the proceedings, the ability to understand the possible consequences of the proceedings, and the ability to communicate with counsel.

MacArthur Competence Assessment Tool-Criminal Adjudication (MacCAT-CA; Poythress et al., 1999). This instrument contains 22 items that tap three competence-related abilities (understanding, reasoning and appreciation). The first two sections of the instrument (understanding and reasoning) are evaluated by presenting a vignette to the defendant and asking various relevant questions. The MacCAT-CA uses structured administration and scoring and provides for normative information about a defendant's competence-related abilities.

Evaluation of Competency to Stand Trial-Revised (ECST-R; Rogers et al., 2004). This instrument contains 18 items that assess four different areas: factual understanding of courtroom proceedings, rational understanding of courtroom proceedings, ability to consult with counsel, and overall rational ability. In addition, this instrument also contains 28 items that act as a screen for feigned incompetency.

Instruments for Assessing Understanding and Appreciation of Miranda Rights (Grisso, 1998). This series of four instruments evaluates various aspects involved in waiving one's Miranda rights, including: Comprehension of Miranda Rights, Comprehension of Miranda Right-Recognition, Comprehension of Miranda Vocabulary, and Function of Rights in Interrogation.

Checklist for Evaluations of Competence for Execution (Zapf, Boccaccini, & Brodsky, 2003). This is a checklist of 32 domains to be considered in the evaluation of an offender's competence to be executed. This checklist contains questions for each of the domains, which can be broken down into four different areas: understanding of the reasons for punishment, understanding of the punishment, ability to appreciate and reason in addition to simple factual understanding, and ability to assist attorney.

Characteristics of Incompetent Defendants

Research has indicated that the most common characteristics of defendants who are evaluated with respect to their competency status include being male, single, unemployed, living alone, having a history of contact with both the criminal justice and mental health systems, and being diagnosed with a major mental disorder (see, for example, Nicholson & Kugler, 1991; Roesch & Golding, 1980; Zapf & Roesch, 1998). As a general statement, approximately 20% of defendants whose competency to stand trial has been questioned and who are evaluated with respect to their competency status will be found incompetent to stand trial. Of course, the exact percentage varies by jurisdiction but on average about 20 of every 100 defendants evaluated will be found incompetent, thus leaving 80 of every 100 found competent to stand trial.

Much of the research that has been conducted in this area has examined the differences between those defendants deemed competent and those deemed incompetent. When these two groups are compared, research indicates that incompetent defendants are significantly more likely to be single, unemployed, charged with a minor offense, and diagnosed with a psychotic disorder and significantly less likely to be charged with a violent crime or to have substance use disorders than are competent defendants (Hubbard, Zapf, & Ronan, 2003). Research examining those variables that predict incompetency indicates that certain diagnoses, such as psychosis, mental retardation, schizophrenia, mood disorders, and organic brain disorders, are predictive of incompetency as are certain psychiatric symptoms indicative of severe psychopathology (Nicholson & Kugler, 1991; Warren, Fitch, Dietz, & Rosenfeld, 1991).

Competency Restoration

As indicated earlier in this chapter, defendants who are deemed incompetent to stand trial by the court are usually sent to a forensic hospital for the purposes of restoring them to competency. The most common form of treatment involves the administration of psychotropic medication; however, some jurisdictions have established treatment programs designed to increase a defendant's understanding of the legal process or programs that confront the problems that hinder a defendant's ability to participate in his or her defense (Bertman et al., 2003). As a general statement, most incompetent defendants are restored to competency within six months and the vast majority achieve competence within a one-year period.

With respect to the issue of forcible medication, the U.S. Supreme Court, in the case of *Sell v. United States* (2003), held that antipsychotic drugs could be administered against the defendant's will for the purpose of restoring competency, but only in limited circumstances. Several factors were identified that must be considered in determining whether a defendant can be forced to take medication including a finding that the medication is likely to restore competence but will not result in side effects that might affect a defendant's ability to assist counsel. In addition, forcible medication can only occur when alternative and less intrusive methods that would achieve the same result are not available.

A comparison of incompetent defendants deemed not restorable with those deemed restorable indicated that those defendants considered more likely to be restorable tended to be younger and were more likely to have a diagnosis of a nonpsychotic disorder, a previous criminal history, and a better understanding of the criminal justice system (Hubbard et al., 2003).

CRIMINAL RESPONSIBILITY

The issue of **criminal responsibility**, also known as **insanity**, has to do with a defendant's mental state at the time of the alleged offense. The basic philosophy is that to convict a person charged with a crime he or she must be considered responsible for his or her behavior. For most crimes, there are two elements that must be proved by the prosecution in order for a defendant to be found guilty: the *actus reus* or physical act of the crime and the *mens rea* or mental capacity and intention to commit the crime. Most often the issue of criminal responsibility or insanity has to do with the second element that must be proved—the *mens rea*. As a general statement, defendants for whom mental disease or defect has resulted in an inability to form the intention to commit a crime or has resulted in an inability to know right from wrong may be considered not criminally responsible for their actions and thus found not guilty of the crime for which they were charged.

Legal Standards for Criminal Responsibility

In the United States, several varieties of insanity defense standards have been used across various jurisdictions and at various points in time. Currently, the two most common insanity defense standards used are the American Law Institute's (ALI) formulation and a slightly restricted version of the traditional M'Naghten test. Each of these, as well as various other standards, are described here.

M'Naghten

The oldest test of legal insanity stems from the case of Daniel M'Naghten, which took place in England in the early 1840s. In this case, the court established what has come to be known as the **M'Naghten standard**; also called the *knowledge/right-wrong test of insanity*. This standard requires that, in order to establish a defense on the grounds of insanity,

> it must be clearly proved that, at the time of the committing of the act, the party accused was labouring under such a defect of reason, from disease of the mind, as not to know the nature and quality of the act he was doing; or, if he did know it, that he did not know he was doing what was wrong. (*M'Naghten's Case*, 1843, p. 722)

Thus, the M'Naghten test requires that: (1) the defendant be suffering from a disease of the mind (interpreted as being a mental disorder), which causes impairment in terms of either; (2) not understanding the nature and quality of his or her actions; or (3) not knowing that those actions were wrong. The careful reader will note that there is a link between the mental disorder of the accused and the impairment in either knowledge of his or her actions (he or she did not know what he or she was doing) or in knowing right from wrong (he or she did not know that what he or she was doing was wrong) such that the mental disorder must be directly related to one of these impairments.

This test has often been criticized as being either too narrow or too rigid and, as a result, other tests have been proposed including the **irresistible**

impulse standard, the **Durham rule**, the **American Law Institute standard**, and the **Insanity Defense Reform Act standard**.

Irresistible Impulse Standard

In response to criticisms that the M'Naghten test was too cognitive (recall that this test focused on whether the defendant *knew* what he or she was doing or *knew* that what he or she was doing was wrong), an irresistible impulse clause was added in order to include a volitional component to the insanity test. That is, an accused might be considered insane if he or she knew what he or she was doing and knew that it was wrong but was unable to control his or her behavior and avoid performing the action.

Durham Rule

The Durham rule, which has also been called the **product rule**, was used in the federal system for a period of time in the 1950s and 1960s and is currently only used in New Hampshire. The Durham rule was adopted in response to criticism of the M'Naghten test as being too narrow and too cognitive in focus, even with the addition of an irresistible impulse clause. Thus, the Durham or product rule established that an accused could be found not criminally responsible if his or her actions were the product of a mental disease or defect. Obviously, this significantly broadened the standard for insanity, which brought with it a host of additional problems, and the Durham rule was replaced in federal court by the American Law Institute standard.

American Law Institute (ALI) Standard

The ALI standard, also called the **Brawner rule**, was developed in an attempt to resolve the issues of the Durham rule being too broad in nature and the M'Naughten test being too cognitive in nature. The ALI standard established that an accused is not criminally responsible if,

> as a result of mental disease or defect, he [or she] lacks substantial capacity either to appreciate the criminality [wrongfulness] of his [or her] conduct or to conform his or her conduct to the requirements of the law. (American Law Institute, 1962, p. 401)

Thus, the ALI standard includes both a cognitive and a volitional component and appears to be more comprehensive than either the M'Naghten test or the irresistible impulse test while being less broad than the Durham or product rule. The ALI standard is currently used in about half of the United States.

Insanity Defense Reform Act (IDRA) Standard

In 1984, the Insanity Defense Reform Act (IDRA) was passed. The insanity standard included in this act indicated that for a defendant to be found not criminally responsible he or she needed to prove that "as a result of a severe mental disease or defect, he [or she] was unable to appreciate the nature and quality or wrongfulness of his [or her] act" (p. 201). In effect, the IDRA standard represents a slightly restricted version of the original M'Naghten standard, which includes only a cognitive prong, and eliminates the volitional prong of the ALI standard. The IDRA standard is used in federal courts and slightly restricted versions of the traditional M'Naghten test, such as the IDRA standard, are used in about half of the United States.

Guilty But Mentally Ill (GBMI)

Since the much-publicized trial of John W. Hinckley, Jr., who was found Not Guilty by Reason of Insanity (NGRI) after his attempt to kill President Regan in 1981, a great deal of court reform and legislative revision with regard to the insanity defense has occurred. Five states (Montana, Idaho, Utah, Nevada, and Kansas) have abolished the insanity defense altogether, and others have instituted alternatives such as diminished responsibility and **Guilty But Mentally Ill** (GBMI) provisions. These alternatives allow for a finding of guilt but a reduction in either the seriousness of the charge or the severity of the punishment if mental disorder was determined to have influenced the criminal act. The GBMI verdict is available in approximately 13 states and has been widely criticized on many grounds including the fact that it has not served to reduce the number of NGRI acquittals nor does it ensure that offenders receiving this verdict will receive effective treatment.

Public Perceptions of the Insanity Defense

Public perceptions of the insanity defense are that it is frequently used, frequently successful, and serves as a "loophole" guilty people use to go free (Hans, 1986); however, empirical research on whether these public perceptions are accurate reveals that the public overestimates both the use and success of the insanity defense and underestimates the length of confinement of insanity acquittees (Silver, Cirincione, & Steadman, 1994).

Although the exact rates of use and success vary by jurisdiction, as a general statement, the insanity defense is rarely used and even more rarely successful. Silver and colleagues (1994) compared public perceptions of the insanity defense with empirical data on its actual use and found that the public estimates the use of the insanity defense to be 37% (or 37 per 100 felony indictments) whereas the actual use is 0.9% (less than 1 per 100 felony indictments), representing a public estimate that is 41 times greater than its actual use. Similarly, with respect to estimates regarding the success of the insanity defense, these authors report that the public estimates the success rate to be 44% (or 44 acquittals per 100 insanity pleas) whereas the actual rate of success is 26%, representing a public estimate of success that is 81 times greater than the actual success rate. That is, there are 9 insanity pleas for every 1,000 felony cases, about only 2 of which are successful.

Silver and colleagues (1994) also examined the distribution of charges for persons pleading insanity to determine whether the public's perception—that the majority of defendants pleading insanity are murderers—was accurate. These researchers reported that approximately 14% of defendants pleading insanity were charged with murder, whereas about 54% were charged with other violent offenses and 32% were charged with nonviolent offenses. Again, public perceptions of defendants pleading insanity greatly overestimate the proportion of defendants charged with murder.

With respect to public perceptions regarding what happens to "successful" insanity acquittees, the public estimates that approximately half of these defendants are hospitalized whereas Silver and colleagues (1994) report that, in reality, about 85% are hospitalized. Similarly, these authors report that the public overestimates the proportion of insanity acquittees that "go free" upon acquittal, with a public estimate of 26% going free compared to the actual rate of 15%. These authors also indicate that if conditional release and outpatient treatment are excluded from the definition of "going free," then the actual rate drops to a mere 1%.

When Silver and colleagues (1994) compared public estimates of the length of confinement of insanity acquittees to actual lengths of confinement they found, again, that public perceptions represent an underestimate of the actual length of confinement with the public estimating an average length of confinement of just under two years (21.8 months) versus an actual average length of confinement, of over two and a half years (32.5 months) for all persons (regardless of charge) and of almost six and a half years (76.4 months) for those charged with murder.

Assessment of Criminal Responsibility

As discussed previously, the determination of competency to stand trial is based on the defendant's mental state *at the present time*. Criminal responsibility, however, takes into consideration the defendant's mental state *at the time of the alleged offense*. Thus, in this type of evaluation, the psychologist or other mental health professional is attempting to assess the defendant's mental state at some earlier point in time—so this is a retrospective evaluation. Similar to evaluations of competency to stand trial and other forensic issues, the evaluation of criminal responsibility or mental state at the time of the offense usually involves an interview with the defendant, a review of relevant records (including any available mental health records) as well as the police report, and any additional records deemed to be relevant. Interviews may be conducted with individuals who know the defendant well or who were with the defendant at or around the time of the offense, and any relevant psychological tests or forensic assessment instruments can be administered. Evaluations of mental state at the time of the offense may take place on either an inpatient or an outpatient basis, depending on the rules of the jurisdiction in which the evaluation takes place.

Although several forensic assessment instruments have been developed for use in assessments of competency to stand trial, there has only been one published instrument developed for use in assessments of criminal responsibility—*Rogers Criminal Responsibility Assessment Scales* (R-CRAS; Rogers, 1984). The R-CRAS was developed as a way to standardize the collection of information for evaluations of criminal responsibility using the ALI standard (discussed earlier) but can also be adapted for use with the GBMI and the M'Naghten standards.

Defendants who wish to pursue an insanity defense at trial will present evidence of mental impairment at the time of the offense, usually in the form of a written report by a psychologist or other mental health professional who has evaluated the defendant with respect to his or her mental state at the time of the offense. If a defendant raises the issue of his or her own mental state by using an insanity defense at trial (or by declaring his or her intention to pursue an insanity defense), the prosecution then has the right to have an evaluation of that defendant's mental state at the time of the offense conducted by an expert of their choosing. If the case proceeds to trial (recall that the vast majority of all cases are resolved by a guilty plea or a plea bargain), experts for both sides (prosecution and defense) may testify about the defendant's mental state, and the decision regarding whether the defendant is to be held accountable for his or her actions rests with the legal decision maker in the case—the jury or, if there is no jury, the judge.

Researchers have examined the process by which insanity pleas make it to court and whether insanity pleas are heard by judge or jury. Janofsky and colleagues (1996) examined the outcomes for all insanity pleas raised over a one-year period in Baltimore City's district and circuit courts and found that almost 96% of the pleas did not make it to court. The vast majority of defendants withdrew their insanity plea immediately after undergoing an insanity evaluation whereas others either had their charges dropped before trial or were found incompetent to proceed to trial. Only about 4% of the initial insanity pleas made it to court. In all these cases, the insanity pleas were not contested by either the prosecution or the defense and the defendants were found not criminally responsible.

Cirincione (1996) examined the processing of insanity pleas and determined that the vast majority of insanity cases were handled through either plea bargain (42.9%) or bench trial (42.7%), with relatively few (14.4%) being handled via jury trial. Conviction rates were approximately 88% for plea bargain cases, 45% for bench trials, and 75% for jury trials. In interpreting these results, Cirincione speculated that jury trials are more commonly used in contentious cases (involving severe crimes and less mental disorder) whereas bench trials are more likely when the prosecution does not contest the insanity claim or the judge is more likely to be convinced by the defense's arguments.

Characteristics of NGRI Acquittees

Although there are always exceptions to any rule, a relatively consistent picture of the modal insanity acquittee has emerged. Research examining the demographic characteristics of insanity acquittees in the United States (Cirincione, Steadman, & McGreevy, 1995) indicates that the typical insanity acquittee is male, between the ages of 20 and 29, single, unemployed, minimally educated, diagnosed with a major mental illness, has had prior contact with the criminal justice and mental health systems, and is acquitted for a violent offense. In terms of the types of mental illness that plague insanity acquittees, research has consistently demonstrated that the majority of insanity acquittees are diagnosed with psychotic disorders, with schizophrenia being perhaps the most common.

Treatment of NGRI Acquittees

Individuals who are found **Not Guilty by Reason of Insanity (NGRI)**, although technically acquitted of the crime with which they were charged, are rarely released upon acquittal. The majority of these individuals are sent to psychiatric hospitals or forensic institutions for a period of confinement and treatment of their mental disorder. The length of the period of confinement often varies considerably by jurisdiction. In addition, there does not appear to be a consistent pattern across jurisdictions in terms of whether insanity acquittees are held for longer or shorter periods than individuals convicted of the same type of crime—in some jurisdictions insanity acquittees are held, on average, longer than convicted individuals whereas in other jurisdictions the reverse is true and yet in others there is no difference.

Silver (1995) examined data from seven states and found that the seriousness of the offense was consistently related to the likelihood of release in that more serious offenses were associated with lower rates of release. In addition, mental disorder was related to release in only three of the seven states. Offense seriousness was found to be a stronger predictor of length of confinement than was mental disorder, suggesting that punishment may be a higher priority than treatment. Thus, although NGRI acquittees are technically found not guilty of their offenses, it appears as if they are still being punished according to the seriousness of their offenses.

RISK ASSESSMENT

The issue of a defendant's risk for committing a future offense may arise at many points in the criminal justice system, although this issue most often arises either at sentencing or release. Psychologists are increasingly being called upon by the courts to conduct assessments of a defendant's level of risk to commit a violent offense, a sexual offense, or some other type of criminal behavior. While the assessment of an individual's future risk may occur at any time, these assessments usually occur in one of two contexts: just before sentencing to inform the court about level of risk, which may affect the type of sentence that is imposed, and just before release to inform the court about the level of risk and strategies for reducing an offender's level of risk, which may affect the release decision or the conditions imposed upon that release. Risk assessment occurs in both the civil (e.g., risk for violence toward oneself or others) and criminal (e.g., risk for future sexual violence) arenas; however, the focus in this chapter is on the criminal arena.

Approaches to Risk Assessment

There are three different approaches to risk assessment. The first is known as clinical decision making or **unstructured clinical judgment**. This approach is *ideographic* (focuses on the specific individual rather than on groups of individuals) and *qualitative* (relies on subjective judgments) in nature. Thus, the clinician who is conducting a violence risk assessment in this manner will use his or her best clinical judgment regarding the likelihood that the examinee will be violent in the future. The risk markers that are taken into consideration vary by clinician, as does the weighting of each of the relevant factors for each specific case.

In contrast to the clinical decision-making approach is the **actuarial decision-making** approach. The actuarial approach is *nomothetic* (based on research involving large groups of people) and *quantitative* (statistical) in nature. Thus, the clinician who is conducting a violence risk assessment in this manner will use a formal, algorithmic, objective approach to make a decision regarding the likelihood that the examinee will be violent in the future. The clinician must incorporate his or her professional experience by using a formulaic approach that takes into consideration specific risk markers, each given a specific weight. When directly compared with unstructured clinical decision making, actuarial decisions have been found to be considerably more accurate.

The third approach to risk assessment—**structured professional judgment**—involves a melding of the clinical and actuarial approaches. In this approach, a specific array of risk markers is considered, thus ensuring that all clinicians take into consideration the same set of risk factors for each examinee. In addition, the clinician is able to introduce his or her professional experience to temper or augment the actuarial prediction. Thus, the structured professional judgment approach to violence risk assessment ensures the consideration of a relatively comprehensive set of risk factors for every examinee and allows for additional, individual factors to be considered as a supplement to the structured assessment.

Violence Risk Factors

Numerous risk factors have been identified as being related to an increased risk for violence. These risk factors include: past violent behavior; young age; relationship instability; employment instability; substance use; major mental disorder; psychopathy (discussed later); early home or school maladjustment; personality disorder; violations of conditional release; escapes or attempted escapes from incarceration; lack of insight; negative attitudes and personality states; psychiatric symptomatology; behavioral and affective instability; unresponsiveness to treatment; lack of feasible release plan; access to victims, weapons, drugs, and alcohol; lack of support and supervision; noncompliance with medication or other treatment; and stress.

These risk factors have formed the basis for a number of risk assessment instruments. Although many risk factors are important to consider across many contexts, the risk assessment instruments that have been developed have, generally, been developed for a specific purpose. That is, some instruments have been developed to assist in the evaluation of risk for violence while others have focused specifically on intimate partner violence or sexual violence.

Risk assessment instruments fall into one of two categories—those that are actuarial and those that were developed to assist in structured professional judgments of risk for violence. Instruments such as the Violence Risk

---

**Box 2.2 Forensic Assessment Instruments
for Risk Assessment**

Numerous risk assessment instruments have been developed to assist in the evaluation of an offender's future risk for violent offending. The following are a few of the better-known instruments:

HCR-20 (Webster, Douglas, Eaves, & Hart, 1997). This 20-item assessment tool includes information and criteria for evaluating 10 historical factors, 5 clinical factors, and 5 risk management factors and encompasses past, present, and future risk considerations.

SVR-20 (Boer, Hart, Kropp, & Webster, 1997). This 20-item assessment tool includes information and criteria for evaluating 11 psychosocial adjustment, 7 sexual offense, and 2 future plans variables for the evaluation of violence risk in sex offenders.

Violence Risk Appraisal Guide (VRAG; Quinsey, Harris, Rice, & Cormier, 2005). This 12-item actuarial scale is used to predict the probability of violence within a particular time frame in offenders with mental disorders.

Sex Offender Risk Appraisal Guide (SORAG; Quinsey, Harris, Rice, & Cormier, 2005). This 14-item instrument is used to predict the probability of violent and sexual recidivism in previously convicted sex offenders.

Rapid Risk Assessment for Sex Offense Recidivism (RRASOR; Hanson, 1997). This brief 4-item screening instrument is used to evaluate risk for sexual violence in previously convicted sex offenders.

STATIC-99/STATIC-2002 (Hanson & Thornton, 1999). These 10-item instruments are used to determine the long-term potential for sexual recidivism in male sex offenders.

Sex Offender Needs Assessment Rating (SONAR; Hanson & Harris, 2000). This 9-item scale is used to measure change in level of risk for sex offenders.

Minnesota Sex Offender Screening Tool (MnSOST-R; Epperson, Kaul, & Hesselton, 1998). This 16-item instrument is used to determine level of risk for sexual recidivism among rapists and intrafamilial child molesters.

Appraisal Guide (VRAG; Quinsey, Harris, Rice, & Cormier, 2005) and the Violence Prediction Scheme (VPS; Webster, Harris, Rice, Cormier, & Quinsey, 1994) are actuarial whereas the HCR-20 (Webster, Douglas, Eaves, & Hart, 1997), the Spousal Assault Risk Assessment Guide (SARA; Kropp, Hart, Webster, & Eaves, 1998) and the Sexual Violence Risk-20 (SVR-20; Boer, Hart, Kropp, & Webster, 1997) were developed to assist in structured professional evaluations of risk (see Box 2.2 for a description of risk assessment instruments).

Psychopathy and Risk Assessment

Psychopathy is a personality style that encompasses both behavioral and affective (emotional) components. Individuals who epitomize psychopathy are, among other things, glib, grandiose, callous, remorseless, reckless, manipulative, impulsive, dishonest, parasitic, and unable to experience the normal range and depth of emotional experience.

Psychopathy plays an important role in risk assessment since the available research has consistently demonstrated a significant relationship between psychopathy and violence. That is, individuals with psychopathic personality styles are more likely to engage in general criminal behavior and violent behavior than their nonpsychopathic counterparts. Moderate-to large-sized associations between psychopathy and violence have been found (Hemphill, Hare, & Wong, 1998; Salekin, Rogers, & Sewell, 1996). As Douglas and Webster (1999) have concluded, "psychopaths, in comparison with nonpsychopaths, are at an increased risk for acting violently and for doing so more quickly and in more diverse ways and across various settings, whether they are mentally disordered, sex offenders, young offenders, or just 'regular' nonmentally ill offenders" (p. 204).

Given the robustness of the relation between psychopathy and violence, it is important to take this personality style into consideration in every risk assessment.

Violence Risk Assessment

Violence risk assessment attempts to take into consideration many different factors, including: (a) the *nature* of the violence or the types of violence that may occur; (b) the *severity* or seriousness of the violence; (c) the *frequency* of the violence or how often violence might occur; (d) the *imminence* or how soon violence might occur; and (e) the *likelihood* or probability that violence will occur. Evaluators are often called upon by the courts to assess an individual's risk for violence, whether for sentencing or release purposes, and therefore must attempt to delineate each of these factors.

An informative and useful risk assessment will provide the court with the probability that the examinee will commit a particular type of violence within a particular time frame and under certain conditions. Thus, risk management is a crucial component of risk assessment. **Risk management** refers to the strategy of attempting to reduce the probability that an individual will be violent by describing the conditions under which that individual's risk for violence may increase and those under which it may decrease. Thus, to manage an individual's risk, one must know the conditions that may serve to increase and/or decrease the probability of violence so that these can be monitored and/or adjusted accordingly. For instance, the use of alcohol or drugs may serve to increase an individual's risk for violence; therefore, an appropriate risk management strategy would include treatment for substance abuse and careful monitoring to ensure that the individual abstains.

Sentencing and release decisions by the courts can then be made based on the information provided in a risk assessment, and specific sentencing and/or release conditions may be implemented in an attempt to manage the individual's risk for future violence.

As in other types of criminal forensic evaluations, an interview with the offender as well as a review of all available records and interviews with other individuals who know the offender well are involved in an assessment of an offender's risk for future violence. In addition, most risk assessments also entail the use of one or more specific forensic assessment instruments developed to assist in making a determination about an offender's level of risk.

Capital Sentencing

In the case of capital offenses—those offenses wherein the death penalty may be sought—psychologists and other mental health professionals may be called upon by the courts to conduct capital sentencing evaluations. This special type of risk assessment takes into consideration various mitigating and aggravating factors in a case, in addition to the defendant's risk for future violence, in an effort to help the court determine whether a sentence of death should be imposed. Mitigating and aggravating factors are usually statutorily (that is, by law) defined by the jurisdiction and vary accordingly. The court will weigh the mitigating and aggravating factors, along with the defendant's risk for future violence, in arriving at a decision regarding sentencing.

Dangerous Offenders and Sexually Violent Predators

In the case of certain types of offenders—generally, those who have committed numerous violent or sexually violent offenses—some jurisdictions have implemented legislation that allows for the indefinite confinement of those found at the highest risk to re-offend in a violent or sexually violent manner. In these cases, psychologists and other mental health professionals may be called upon to conduct assessments of the individual's risk for future violence or for future sexual violence in assisting the courts in making a decision about whether to institute civil proceedings against the offender that would allow for his or her indefinite confinement (after completing his or her initial sentence).

PSYCHOPATHY AND MALINGERING

There are two overarching issues that must be assessed, either formally or informally, by the examiner in any forensic evaluation: psychopathy and **malingering** (faking).

Psychopathy

Psychopathy is a constellation of affective, interpersonal, and behavioral characteristics and arises as a clinical issue in the full range of criminal forensic assessments, with specific repercussions in the assessment of risk for violence (as discussed earlier). Psychopathy is an important concept in forensic evaluations as the constellation of personality traits involved in psychopathy often has a significant impact on an individual's understanding of and functioning within his or her environment. Forensic evaluators must always consider the concept of psychopathy in any evaluation context, at least informally if not formally.

The modern concept of psychopathy was introduced by Hervey Cleckley in his classic text *The Mask of Sanity* (1941). Cleckley described the person with psychopathy as lacking emotional responsiveness, having no sense of shame, being superficially charming and manipulative, showing irresponsible behavior, and being inadequately motivated. Many researchers, but especially Robert Hare and his colleagues, have continued to develop the concept of psychopathy throughout the last three decades and have been instrumental in describing how it is distinct from (and similar to) the concept of **antisocial personality disorder (APD)**. Generally speaking, psychopathy is a broader concept than APD and encompasses an interpersonal/affective component in addition to the mainly behavioral component of APD.

Several instruments have been developed to assess the characteristics associated with psychopathy; however, there is none as well known as Hare's Psychopathy Checklist–Revised (PCL-R: Hare, 1991, 2003). The PCL-R consists of 20 items that are rated on the basis of file information and an interview with the examinee. Scores on the PCL-R range from 0 to 40 with a cutoff of 30 commonly used to denote psychopathy. In addition to the PCL-R, a screening version (PCL:SV; Hart, Cox, & Hare, 1995) and a youth version (PCL:YV; Forth, Kosson, & Hare, 2003) have been developed.

Malingering

Malingering is the feigned production or exaggeration of psychological or physical symptoms to achieve some external incentive. It must be ruled out in every legal context. The American Psychiatric Association (2000) defines malingering as "the intentional production of false or grossly exaggerated physical or psychological symptoms, motivated by external incentives such as . . . evading criminal prosecution" (p. 739). Further, malingering is to be "strongly suspected" in a "medicolegal context" (p. 739), which, of course, includes all criminal forensic evaluations.

The validity of psychological assessment instruments hinges on examinees being honest and forthright in their effort and responses and the same is true for most forensic assessment instruments. In order for results to be valid, examinees must be honest and sincere in their effort and responses. The formal evaluation of malingering might include the use of a forensic assessment instrument developed specifically for the purposes of detection of malingering. In contrast, an informal evaluation of malingering might involve only a very close scrutiny of the results of various self-reported information and various collateral sources of information without any specific testing targeted toward the issue of malingering.

There are two types of things about which an individual might attempt to malinger—psychiatric symptoms or cognitive impairment. Malingering psychiatric symptoms would involve pretending to be experiencing symptoms of a mental disorder whereas malingering cognitive impairment would involve pretending to be experiencing memory or other mental impairment. Several assessment instruments have been developed to assist in evaluating the likelihood that an individual is malingering either psychiatric symptomatology or cognitive impairment. The Structured Interview of Reported Symptoms (SIRS; Rogers, Bagby, & Dickens, 1992) and the Miller Forensic Assessment of Symptoms Test (M-FAST; Miller, 1995) are two instruments that have been developed for the assessment of malingering of psychiatric impairment whereas the Test of Memory Malingering (TOMM; Tombaugh, 1996) and the Validity Indicator Profile (VIP; Frederick, 1997) are two that have been developed to evaluate malingering of cognitive impairment.

Regardless of whether the evaluation of malingering is formal or informal, the forensic examiner must make some assessment of this issue in every case. The results of this assessment will be useful to the evaluator in determining how much weight to put on the defendant's self-reports and testing results.

SUMMARY

Psychologists and other mental health professionals assist the criminal courts in understanding issues relevant to psychology and the legal system. The courts call upon psychologists to conduct a wide variety of assessments, both formal (using assessment tools) and informal. By far, the most common type of criminal forensic assessment that occurs each year is competency to stand trial. This assessment focuses on the present abilities of the defendant. Only about 20% of defendants who have had their competency questioned are actually found incompetent to proceed.

Another common type of evaluation that psychologists are called upon to conduct is a defendant's criminal responsibility or mental state at the time of the offense (insanity). Unlike competency to stand trial, this type of evaluation focuses on the defendant's mental state at an earlier point in time (the time of the offense); therefore, is retrospective. Public perceptions of the insanity defense are that it is used often and is frequently successful; however, in reality, this defense is rarely used and even more rarely successful.

Psychologists are also called upon to conduct evaluations of an offender's risk to commit future violence. In this type of assessment, risk factors for violence are identified and evaluated in order to determine the offender's level of risk and the most appropriate means of reducing or managing his or her future risk.

Each type of evaluation involves an interview with the defendant as well as the collection of additional and varied sources of information about the defendant. In addition, specialized forensic assessment instruments may also be used to assist the evaluator in coming to an opinion regarding the defendant's competency to stand trial, criminal responsibility, or future risk for violence.

SUGGESTED READINGS

Grisso, T. (2003). *Evaluating competencies: Forensic assessments and instruments* (2nd ed.). New York: Kluwer/Plenum.

Litwack, T., Zapf, P. A., Groscup, J. L., & Hart, S. D. (2006). Violence risk assessment: Research, legal, and clinical considerations. In I. B. Weiner & A. K. Hess (Eds.), *Handbook of forensic psychology* (3rd ed., pp. 487–533). New York: Wiley.

Poythress, N. G., Bonnie, R. J., Monahan, J., Otto, R., & Hoge, S. K. (2002). *Adjudicative competence: The MacArthur studies.* New York: Kluwer/Plenum.

Quinsey, V. L., Harris, G. T., Rice, M. E., & Cormier, C. A. (2005). *Violent offenders: Appraising and managing risk* (2nd ed.). Washington, DC: American Psychological Association.

Rogers, R., & Shuman, D. W. (2000). *Conducting insanity evaluations* (2nd ed.). New York: Guilford.

Zapf, P. A., Golding, S. L., & Roesch, R. (2006). Criminal responsibility and the insanity defense. In I. B. Weiner & A. K. Hess (Eds.), *Handbook of forensic psychology* (3rd ed., pp. 332–363). New York: Wiley.

Zapf, P. A., & Roesch, R. (2006). Competency to stand trial: A guide for evaluators. In I. B. Weiner & A. K. Hess (Eds.), *Handbook of forensic psychology* (3rd ed., pp. 305–331). New York: Wiley.

KEY TERMS

- *Actuarial decision making*
- *Adjudicative competence*
- *American Law Institute (ALI) standard*
- *Antisocial personality disorder (APD)*
- *Brawner rule*
- *Competency to be executed*
- *Competency to be sentenced*
- *Competency to proceed*
- *Competency to stand trial*
- *Competency to waive counsel (proceed* pro se*)*
- *Competency to waive Miranda*
- *Criminal responsibility*
- *Durham rule*
- *Guilty But Mentally Ill (GBMI)*
- *Insanity*
- *Insanity Defense Reform Act (IDRA) standard*
- *Irresistible impulse standard*
- *Malingering*
- *M'Naghten standard*
- *Not Guilty by Reason of Insanity (NGRI), product rule*
- *Product rule*
- *Psychopathy*
- *Risk management*
- *Structured professional judgment*
- *Unstructured clinical judgment*

References

American Law Institute. (1962). *Model penal code*. Washington, DC: Author.

American Psychiatric Association. (2000). *Diagnostic and statistical manual of mental disorders* (4th ed., Text Revision). Washington, DC: American Psychiatric Association.

Bertman, L. J., Thompson, J. W. Jr., Waters, W. F., Estupinan-Kane, L., Martin, J. A., & Russell, L. (2003). Effect of an individualized treatment protocol on restoration of competency in pretrial forensic inpatients. *Journal of the American Academy of Psychiatry and Law, 31*, 27–35.

Boer, D. P., Hart, S. D., Kropp, P. R., & Webster, C. D. (1997). *Manual for the Sexual Violence Risk-20*. Vancouver: British Columbia Institute Against Family Violence.

Bonnie, R. J., & Grisso, T. (2000). Adjudicative competence and youthful offenders. In T. Grisso & R. G. Schwartz (Eds.), *Youth on trial: A developmental perspective on criminal justice* (pp. 73–103). Chicago, IL: University of Chicago Press.

Cirincione, C. (1996). Revisiting the insanity defense: Contested or consensus? *Bulletin of the American Academy of Psychiatry and Law, 24*, 165–176.

Cirincione, C., Steadman, H. J., & McGreevy, M. A. (1995). Rates of insanity acquittals and the factors associated with successful insanity pleas. *Bulletin of the American Academy of Psychiatry and Law, 23*, 399–409.

Cleckley, H. M. (1941). *The mask of sanity*. Oxford, England: Mosby.

Douglas, K. S., & Webster, C. D. (1999). Predicting violence in mentally and personality disordered individuals. In R. Roesch, S. D. Hart, & J. R. P. Ogloff (Eds.), *Psychology and law: The state of the discipline* (pp. 175–239). New York: Kluwer Academic/Plenum Publishers.

Dusky v. United States, 362 U.S. 402 (1960).

Epperson, D. L., Kaul, J. D., & Hesselton, D. (1998, October). *Final report of the development of the Minnesota Sex Offender Screening Tool—Revised* (MnSOST-R). Presentation at the 17th Annual Research and Treatment Conference of the Association for the Treatment of Sexual Abusers, Vancouver, British Columbia, Canada.

Everington, C. T., & Luckasson, R. (1992). *Competence assessment for standing trial for defendants with mental retardation*. Ohio: IDS Publishing Corporation.

Forth, A. E., Kosson, D. S., & Hare, R. D. (2003). *Hare Psychopathy Checklist: Youth Version (PCL:YV) technical manual*. Toronto, Ontario, Canada: Multi-Health Systems.

Frederick, R. I. (1997). *Validity Indicator Profile (VIP) manual*. Minneapolis, MN: NCS Pearson.

Godinez v. Moran, 113 S.Ct. 2680 (1993).

Golding, S. L. (1993). *Interdisciplinary Fitness Interview-Revised: A training manual*. State of Utah Division of Mental Health.

Golding, S. L., Roesch, R., & Schreiber, J. (1984). Assessment and conceptualization of competency to stand trial: Preliminary data on the Interdisciplinary Fitness Interview. *Law and Human Behavior, 8*, 321–334.

Grisso, T. (1998). *Instruments for assessing understanding and appreciation of Miranda rights*. Sarasota, FL: Resource Press.

Hans, V. P. (1986). An analysis of public attitudes toward the insanity defense. *Criminology, 4*, 393–415.

Hanson, R. K. (1997). *The development of a brief actuarial risk scale for sexual offense recidivism*. User Report 1997–04. Ottawa: Department of the Solicitor General of Canada.

Hanson, R. K., & Harris, A. (2000). *The Sex Offender Need Assessment Rating (SONAR): A method for measuring change in risk levels.* Use Report 2000–2001. Ottawa: Department of the Solicitor General of Canada.

Hanson, R. K., & Thornton, D. (1999). *Static-99: Improving actuarial risk assessments for sex offenders.* User Report 1999–2002. Ottawa: Department of the Solicitor General of Canada.

Hare, R. D. (1991). *Hare Psychopathy Checklist-Revised* (PCL-R). Toronto, Ontario, Canada: Multi-Health Systems.

Hare, R. D. (2003). *Hare Psychopathy Checklist—Revised (PCL-R) technical manual* (2nd ed.). Toronto, Ontario, Canada: Multi-Health Systems.

Harris, G. T., Rice, M. E., & Quinsey, V. L. (1993). Violent recidivism of mentally disordered offenders: The development of a statistical prediction instrument. *Criminal Justice and Behavior, 20,* 315–335.

Hart, S. D., Cox, D. N., & Hare, R. D. (1995). *Hare Psychopathy Checklist: Screening Version (PCL:SV) technical manual.* Toronto, Ontario, Canada: Multi-Health Systems.

Hemphill, J. F., Hare, R. D., & Wong, S. (1998). Psychopathy and recidivism: A review. *Legal and Criminalogical Psychology, 3,* 139–170.

Hubbard, K. L., Zapf, P. A., & Ronan, K. A. (2003). Competency restoration: An examination of the differences between defendants predicted restorable and not restorable to competency. *Law and Human Behavior, 27,* 127–139.

Indiana v. Edwards, 554 U.S. 208 (2008).

Jackson v. Indiana, 406 U.S. 715 (1972).

Janofsky, J. S., Dunn, M. H., Roskes, E. J., Briskin, J. K., & Lunstrum, R. M. (1996). Insanity defense pleas in Baltimore City: An analysis of outcome. *American Journal of Psychiatry, 153,* 1464–1468.

Johnson, W. G., & Mullett, N. (1987). Georgia Court Competency Test-R. In M. Hersen & A. S. Bellack (Eds.), *Dictionary of behavioral assessment techniques.* New York: Pergamon Press.

Kropp, P. R., Hart, S. D., Webster, C. D., & Eaves, D. (1998). *Manual for the spousal assault risk assessment guide* (3rd ed.). Toronto, Ontario, Canada: Multi-Health Systems.

Laboratory of Community Psychiatry, Harvard Medical School (1973). *Competency to stand trial and mental illness* (DHEW Publication No. ADM77–103). Rockville, MD: Department of Health, Education and Welfare.

Lipsitt, P., Lelos, D., & McGarry, A. L. (1971). Competency for trial: A screening instrument. *American Journal of Psychiatry, 128,* 105–109.

Miller, H. A. (1995). *Miller Forensic Assessment of Symptoms Test (M-FAST) professional manual.* Odessa, FL: Psychological Assessment Resources.

M'Naghten's Case, 8 Eng. Rep. 718 (1843).

Nicholson, R. A., & Kugler, K. E. (1991). Competent and incompetent criminal defendants: A quantitative review of comparative research. *Psychological Bulletin, 109,* 355–370.

Perlin, M. L. (1996). "Dignity was the first to leave": *Godinez v. Moran*, Colin Ferguson, and the trial of mentally disabled criminal defendants. *Behavioral Sciences and the Law, 14*, 61–81.

Poythress, N. G., Bonnie, R. J., Hoge, S. K., Monahan, J., & Oberlander, L. B. (1994). Client abilities to assist counsel and make decisions in criminal cases. *Law and Human Behavior, 18*, 437–452.

Poythress, N. G., Monahan, J., Bonnie, R. J., & Hoge, S. K. (1999). *MacArthur Competency Assessment Tool–Criminal Adjudication*. Odessa, FL: Psychological Assessment Resources.

Quinsey, V. L., Harris, G. T., Rice, M. E., & Cormier, C. A. (2005). *Violent offenders: appraising and managing risk* (2nd ed.). Washington, DC: American Psychological Association.

Robey, A. (1965). Criteria for competency to stand trial: A checklist for psychiatrists. *American Journal of Psychiatry, 122*, 616–623.

Roesch, R., & Golding, S. L. (1980). *Competency to stand trial*. Urbana: University of Illinois Press.

Roesch, R., Webster, C. D., & Eaves, D. (1984). *The Fitness Interview Test: A method for examining fitness to stand trial*. Toronto, Ontario, Canada: Research Report of the Centre of Criminology, University of Toronto.

Roesch, R., Zapf, P. A., & Eaves, D. (2006). *Fitness Interview Test-Revised: A structured interview for assessing competency to stand trial*. Sarasota, FL: Professional Resource Press.

Rogers, R. (1984). *Rogers Criminal Responsibility Assessment Scales (RCRAS) and test manual*. Odessa, FL: Psychological Assessment Resources.

Rogers, R., Bagby, R. M., & Dickens, S. E. (1992). *Structured Interview of Reports Symptoms (SIRS) and professional manual*. Odessa, FL: Psychological Assessment Resources.

Rogers, R., Tillbrook, C. E., & Sewell, K. W. (2004). *Evaluation of Competency to Stand Trial–Revised* (ECST-R). Lutz, FL: Psychological Assessment Resources.

Salekin, R. T., Rogers, R., & Sewell, K. W. (1996). A review and meta-analysis of the Psychopathy Checklist and Psychopathy Checklist-Revised: Predictive validity of dangerousness. *Clinical Psychology: Science and Practice, 3*, 203–215.

Sell v. United States, 282 F. 3d 560 (2003).

Silver, E. (1995). Punishment or treatment? Comparing the lengths of conferment of successful and unsuccessful insanity defendants. *Law and Human Behavior, 19*, 375–388.

Silver, E., Cirincione, C., & Steadman, H. J. (1994). Demythologizing inaccurate perceptions of the insanity defense. *Law and Human Behavior, 18*, 63–70.

Tombaugh, T. N. (1996). *Test of Memory Malingering (TOMM) manual*. Toronto, Toronto, Ontario, Canada: Multi-Health Systems.

Warren, J., Fitch, W. L., Dietz, P., & Rosenfeld, B. (1991). Criminal offense, psychiatric diagnoses and psycho-legal opinion: An analysis of 894 referrals. *The Bulletin of the American Academy of Psychiatry and the Law, 19,* 63–69.

Webster, C. D., Douglas, K. S., Eaves, D., & Hart, S. D. (1997). *HCR-20: Assessing risk for violence* (Version 2). Vancouver, British Columbia, Canada: Mental Health, Law, and Policy Institute, Simon Fraser University.

Webster, C. D., Harris, G. T., Rice, M. E., Cormier, C. A., & Quinsey, V. L. (1994). *The violence prediction scheme: Assessing dangerousness in high risk men*. Toronto: University of Toronto: Centre of Criminology.

Wildman, R. W., II, White, P. A., & Brandenburg, C. A. (1990). The Georgia Court Competency Test: The base rate problem. *Perceptual and Motor Skills, 70*, 1055–1058.

Zapf, P. A., Boccaccini, M. T., & Brodsky, S. L. (2003). Assessment of competency for execution: Professional guidelines and an evaluation checklist. *Behavioral Sciences and the Law, 21*, 103–120.

Zapf, P. A., & Roesch, R. (1998). Fitness to stand trial: Characteristics of fitness remands since the 1992 Criminal Code amendments. *Canadian Journal of Psychiatry, 43*, 287–293.

Chapter 3

CIVIL FORENSIC ASSESSMENT

CHAPTER OBJECTIVES

In this chapter, you will become familiar with:

- The difference between civil law and criminal law
- An overview of important topics within civil forensic assessment
- Civil commitment and civil commitment evaluations
- Parenting capacity and parenting capacity evaluations
- Child maltreatment and child maltreatment risk assessments

When most people think of law, they think about criminal law—statutes that specify proscribed acts that violate explicit and cherished social norms, procedures for determining when such acts have been committed, and punishments for the acts committed. Yet the vast majority of law is **civil law**, which is focused on regulating the day-to-day conduct of human affairs and, in particular, attempting to prevent and resolve conflicts between parties. Civil law governs our lives from before we are born until we die; it even controls our actions after we die.

Civil forensic assessments are psychological evaluations intended to assist decision making with respect to matters of civil law. The scope of forensic psychological practice with respect to civil law is as broad as the domain of civil law itself. There are too many specific types of civil forensic assessment to enumerate, let alone discuss. Instead, we begin by discussing some of the most common areas of practice in broad or general terms. We then provide a more detailed discussion of forensic assessment with respect to three issues in civil law: civil commitment, parenting capacity, and child maltreatment.

CASE STUDY

Britney Jean Spears was born to be an entertainer. Even as a child, she was a star: At age 10, she began appearing on television programs such as Star Search and The New Mickey Mouse Club. At age 17, she completed her debut album, . . . Baby One More Time, and quickly became one of the world's most famous and best-selling singer-entertainers. But she is also a tragic figure whose highly publicized personal problems, which may stem at least in part from a history of mental disorder and substance use, have led to numerous appearances in civil courts.

Spears has appeared twice in court seeking to terminate marriages. Her first marriage, to long-time friend Jason Allen Alexander, took place on January 3, 2004. She was 22 years old at the time. Two days later, she filed a complaint with the Clark County (Nevada) District Court seeking annulment on the grounds that she "lacked understanding of her actions to the extent that she was incapable of agreeing to marriage because before entering into the marriage the Plaintiff [Spears] and Defendant [Alexander] did not know each other's likes and dislikes, each other's desires to have or not have children, and each other's desires as to State of residency." The annulment was granted after only 55 hours of marriage. (For further information, see http://www.thesmokinggun.com/archive/britneyannul1.html).

Spears' second marriage, to Kevin Federline, took place later that year on September 18, 2004 (although the necessary legal documents were not filed until October 6, 2004). Spears and Federline had two sons together: Sean, born September 14, 2005, and Jayden, born September 12, 2006. But Spears began to behave erratically during her marriage to Federline, including an infamous incident in which she was photographed driving her car while holding a baby in her lap, without any proper restraints. She also expressed unhappiness with her marriage in media interviews and eventually filed for divorce in November 2006, citing irreconcilable differences. This started a legal battle, with both Spears and Federline seeking custody of the children. The couple reached an agreement in March 2007 and their divorce was finalized a few months later.

Spears' problems worsened after her divorce. She attended a substance use treatment facility in February 2007, then shaved her head completely bald with electric clippers a few hours after checking out. After a few days, she attended and completed an inpatient substance use treatment program. Her ex-husband, Federline, was concerned about her parenting capacity and requested an emergency court hearing regarding custody, but later cancelled the appearance. A detailed custody evaluation was conducted by a California psychologist, Dr. Jane Shatz, the results of which were released in a 700-page report submitted by Dr. Shatz. The court reached a decision in September 2007 that Spears and Federline would continue to have joint custody of their two children, with conditions placed on Spears including random testing for drug and alcohol use and attendance at counseling.

Despite the court-ordered conditions, Spears continued to have problems, including being charged with hit-and-run and driving without a license. In October 2007, Federline was granted full custody of both children. But after Spears ignored the court order, police were called to her residence in January 2008. The children

> *were placed in Federline's custody and Spears, who reportedly had not slept for several days, was hospitalized and held two days for an emergency mental health evaluation. As a result of this evaluation, a series of legal decisions imposed new conditions on Spears: She was involuntarily hospitalized due to mental disorder; her visitation rights were suspended indefinitely; and conservatorship (that is, control of her business and financial decisions) was granted to her father and attorney. In addition, a restraining order was granted that forbade a former business associate, who was suspected of exerting a negative influence on Spears, from having contact with her. (Subsequently, additional restraining orders were placed on two former associates.)*

The case of Britney Spears is an excellent illustration of how the civil justice system can be used to help resolve many different difficult situations, ranging from family disputes to concerns over people's ability to manage their own business affairs or make decisions about health care. It also illustrates how psychologists (and other mental health professionals) can assist the justice system to resolve these disputes. Although the results of Spears' mental health assessment and treatment remain private, there has been considerable speculation that she suffered from mood and substance-related disorders that played a major role in her personal problems. The good news is that there appears to have been a slow but steady improvement in her personal problems since her hospitalization in early 2008. She has regained some visitation rights, and the charges against her in connection with the motor vehicle accident were dismissed. She has even regained some of her former glory as an entertainer: Her 2008 album, *Circus*, and the associated concert tour (see Figure 3.1) had excellent sales, garnered her widespread acclaim, and received numerous awards. Hopefully, the worst of Britney's troubles are behind her.

CIVIL FORENSIC ASSESSMENT: MAJOR DOMAINS OF PRACTICE

Think of an area of your life—any area—and you will discover that there are laws that govern it. There are also probably one or more forms of civil forensic assessment conducted by psychologists that are relevant to it. Let's take a quick look at some of the questions addressed by psychologists in three major domains of practice in civil forensic psychology: health, children and families, and employment and education.

Figure 3.1   Britney Spears performing *Circus*, Boston, March 16, 2009.
http://en.wikipedia.org/wiki/File:Circus_Tour.jpg
Author: http://www.flickr.com/people/36292117@N00/Compulsiveprep_8&#x5D
This file is licensed under Creative Commons Attribution 2.0 License

Health

Civil forensic assessments in this realm focus on evaluating the nature and severity of psychological impairment, such as mental disorder, to determine what caused it or whether it has caused people to be unable to make sound decisions or control their own behavior. Specific legal issues include:

- *Civil commitment.* Do people pose a risk for harm on account of mental disorder to the extent that they require involuntary hospitalization or treatment? For example, should a 32-year-old man found by police walking on a bridge late at night be placed in a locked hospital ward against his wishes because he might attempt suicide?
- *Competence to consent to treatment.* Are people capable of expressing informed, rational, and voluntary preferences concerning their

health care? For example, should a 15-year-old girl who has just learned she is pregnant be allowed to make a decision about whether she will have an abortion?

- *Personal injury.* To what extent have people suffered emotional, cognitive, or physical harm due to others' actions? For example, how severe is the neuropsychological impairment demonstrated by an 8-year-old boy, to what extent can it be attributed to a recent motor vehicle accident, and what are the likely costs of rehabilitating and caring for the boy for the rest of his natural life?

Children and Families

The law governs how marriages and other civil unions are formed and dissolved, as well as what happens to the children of unions. Psychologists conduct civil forensic assessments concerning issues such as:

- *Parenting capacity.* Are parents capable of providing for a child's current and future needs, and which childrearing arrangement is best for the child? For example, following the break-up of their marriage, should a mother and father be awarded shared custody of their children, or should custody be awarded to the mother who plans to move the children to another state where they will have better living conditions?

- *Guardianship.* Are people capable of caring for themselves and living independently? For example, is a 75-year-old woman in the early stages of dementia able to manage her own finances, or should her 50-year-old son be given the power to make financial decisions on her behalf?

- *Risk for maltreatment.* Are children at risk for abuse or neglect in the family home and, if so, what should be done to minimize the risk? For example, a 15-year-old brother has inappropriately touched his 5-year-old sister; is the sister at risk for further victimization, or will the parents be able to take reasonable steps to prevent a recurrence?

Employment and Education

People have legal rights to pursue education and employment, even when they suffer from mental disorder. Psychologists are sometimes asked to help determine if such rights have been infringed on appropriately (e.g., in cases where the person poses a risk to safety due to mental disorder) or inappropriately (e.g., if people with mental disorder have been treated in a stereotypical or discriminatory manner). Specifically, psychologists may be asked to conduct assessments regarding:

- *Fitness for duty/Reasonable accommodation.* Are people incapable of performing critical job duties on account of mental disorder, or are there some changes employers could make to their conditions of employment to accommodate mental disorder? For example, a 47-year-old man was placed on temporary leave from his job as a commercial airline pilot when he experienced an episode of depression. Following treatment and apparent resolution of the depression, is he now fit to return to work?
- *Discrimination and harassment.* Have people suffered discrimination or harassment on the basis of age, gender, or physical or mental disability? For example, is there evidence to support a 54-year-old woman's claim that she was subjected to sexual harassment at her workplace, and that she suffered serious emotional distress as a result?
- *Workplace violence.* Are there reasonable grounds to believe that employees pose a risk to the health and safety of coworkers or members of the public? For example, a 28-year-old man got into an argument at work with another employee, during which he threw a stapler and screamed he was going to kill the other man. Does this employee actually pose a risk of harm, and, if so, what can or should the employer do to protect the other employees?
- *Disability.* Do people suffer from physical or mental disabilities to the extent that they are unable to engage in normal educational and employment activities and may require special assistance? For example, a 24-year-old woman was diagnosed with a schizophrenic disorder at the age of 17 and, despite being compliant with treatment, has not attended school or worked since. Is she capable of supporting herself, at least to a limited extent, or does she qualify for financial support from the government?

This list is by no means extensive or comprehensive; the topics that could be discussed are limitless. For example, specialized risk assessments may be conducted in the context of immigration and refugee hearings or firearms acquisition; or, specialized competency evaluations in the context of such things as entering into contracts, making wills, or testifying in civil court. But let's turn now to a more detailed discussion of three issues: civil commitment, parenting capacity, and child maltreatment.

CIVIL COMMITMENT

Civil commitment is involuntary treatment or hospitalization of individuals on the grounds that they pose a risk to themselves or others on account of mental disorder (Winick, 2008). The issue is, in essence, one of public safety: Governments have a legal responsibility to protect citizens, and this includes the responsibility to protect them from the harmful consequences of physical or mental illness (Gostin, 2005). In a very real sense, then, civil commitment is about containing dangerous *illnesses*, rather than dangerous *people*.

The responsibility of governments seems clear with respect to physical illness. Take the example of a disease such as tuberculosis, some forms of which are very contagious and carry a high risk of morbidity and mortality. Various levels of government in the United States have enacted laws and established regulatory and enforcement agencies to help prevent and control the spread of infectious diseases such as tuberculosis (Gostin, 2005). People entering the country may be screened for infectious tuberculosis; physicians may be mandated to report new cases to agencies responsible for surveillance; people diagnosed with the disease may be involuntary detained (i.e., quarantined), even against their will; and healthy people living or working in certain areas may be required to undergo immunization if they might be or have been in contact with an infected person. When the illness is mental rather than physical, the underlying logic for civil commitment—to prevent harm to citizens—is the same.

Laws that allow involuntary treatment and commitment of physical or mental illness clearly infringe on the basic rights and freedoms of citizens. This infringement may be legally justified on two grounds (Melton, Petrila, Poythress, & Slobogin, 2007; Morse, 2002, 2004; Schopp, 2001). First, governments have **parens patriae powers** to act as guardian or caretaker for individuals who are deemed unable to make decisions about their own health and welfare because they are physically or mentally ill. Second, governments have **police powers** to control people who threaten public order, whether or not they are physically or mentally ill.

Civil commitment on the grounds of mental disorder, then, is different from **criminal commitment**, which is a sentence following conviction for a criminal offense. Criminal commitment is inherently and deliberately punitive. It is intended to make people suffer for harms they have perpetrated and for which they are morally culpable. In this respect, it is focused on the past, on what has already happened. (For further discussion of criminal commitment, see Chapter 10.) But civil commitment is preventive. Civil commitment is intended to minimize potential harm and to look toward the future. Laws regarding civil commitment make no assumption people are morally culpable for the risks they pose, and may even assume that people are *not* culpable for the illnesses they suffer. For this reason, civil commitment is not punitive in nature, and, in fact, the procedures for and conditions of civil commitment must not be punitive if it is to be legally justified.

Two general forms of civil commitment exist (Melton et al., 2007; Schopp, 2001; Slobogin, 2007). The first, and most common, is traditional civil commitment under mental health law. It does not require that people have any history of harmful behavior, but instead requires they pose an imminent risk for serious harm to self or others due to acute mental disorder. *Imminent* typically means that the harm is likely to occur in the immediate future (i.e., in the coming hours, days, or weeks). Harm that is more distant (e.g., months or even years in the future) may be irrelevant. *Serious* typically means that the harm has the potential to result in serious injury or even death. Common examples of serious harm include life-threatening self-injurious or assaultive behavior; relatively minor or indirect forms of harm (e.g., abusing alcohol, making superficial cuts on one's own arm, threatening or slapping, damaging property) may be insufficient to justify civil commitment. Mental health law in some jurisdictions may permit civil commitment if individuals are at imminent risk for serious health problems because of failure to provide essential care for themselves (e.g., they cannot meet basic hygiene, nutritional, or health care needs). *Acute mental disorder* typically means a serious and often temporary disturbance of thought, affect, or behavior that impairs people's ability to make rational decisions or regulate their own actions. Laws may allow commitment only on an inpatient basis, or they may allow either inpatient or outpatient commitment. The time frame for commitment typically is short-term in nature, with a time horizon of days to weeks, although the laws in most jurisdictions allow for extension, if necessary. Involuntary treatment generally is permitted as part of civil commitment, although some jurisdictions permit intrusive or invasive treatments, such as medications or surgery, only when the person also is deemed incompetent to make decisions about health care.

The second form of civil commitment is under specialized statutes, such as **sexually violent predator laws** or similar laws targeting offenders with dangerous and severe personality disorders, which target criminal offenders nearing release from a custodial sentence for a violent offense (Buchanan & Leese, 2001; Janus, 2000). This newer form of civil commitment typically requires that people pose a long-term risk for harm to others due to mental disorder. *Long-term* typically means in the coming years, perhaps for the duration of the person's life. *Harm to others* typically means serious violence or sexual violence, depending on the law. *Mental disorder* typically means a chronic disturbance of thought, affect, or behavior due to conditions such as paraphilia or personality disorder. The civil commitment in this case is usually inpatient, at least initially, and the term of commitment is extended, with a time horizon of years; it may even be indefinite.

Traditional civil commitment laws have existed for hundreds of years, since the 1500s and 1600s. In contrast, the newer forms of civil commitment have existed for only a decade or so and are much more controversial, because their focus is on offenders and a long-term or indefinite time frame, making them appear to be punitive rather than preventive. (For further discussion, see Janus, 2000; Morse, 2002; Schopp, 2001.)

There are no good data concerning civil commitment rates for the United States or, for that matter, most other countries. There are many reasons for this (e.g., Høyer, 2008). One reason is that people's legal status as voluntarily or involuntarily committed or treated apparently is not considered in health care statistic databases. Another reason is that keeping statistics is complicated by the existence of several forms of civil commitment (i.e., traditional, with or without involuntary treatment versus commitment of violent or sexually violent offenders). Yet another reason is that people's legal status as voluntarily or involuntarily committed or treated can and does change quite frequently over time, even during the same course of care in a hospital or in the community, which means there are frequent errors in recording statistics. Estimated rates of civil commitment for a given country in a given year can differ greatly; trying to compare rates within a given country over time or across countries at a given time is fraught with difficulty.

Civil Commitment Procedures

The specific procedures by which people are civilly committed differ across jurisdictions, but the general procedures in the United States are as follows (e.g., Melton et al., 2007). First, a person is brought to the attention of a person in authority as someone who may pose a risk of harm to self or others on account of mental disorder. A *person in authority* means someone who is legally entitled to make decisions about civil commitment. Depending on the jurisdiction and the circumstances of the case, the person in authority may be a law enforcement officer; a health care provider, such as a physician or psychologist; a mental health tribunal or review board; or a civil court. Second, the person in authority gathers or reviews available information according to procedures outlined in law and determines whether there is sufficient evidence to commit the person. This commitment may be short-term (e.g., 24 to 72 hrs) for the purpose of further assessment of the person, or it may be long-term (e.g., weeks or longer) for the purpose of detention or treatment. Typically, police or health care providers have the power to order only short-term commitment, whereas tribunals, review boards, and courts may also order long-term commitment. Third, the case is reviewed by a tribunal, review board, or court at the end of the initial period of commitment. If the initial commitment was short-term, the new assessment results are presented and a decision is made whether to release the person, extend short-term commitment to allow further assessment, or order long-term commitment. If the initial commitment was long-term, information about the person's recent and current functioning is presented and a decision is made whether to release the person or extend long-term commitment for a period of time, at which point the third step is repeated.

The general procedure for civil commitment includes clear protections for the person who is subject to civil commitment, known as **due process protections**, something forced (or reinforced) by the U.S. Supreme Court's decision in the case of *O'Connor v. Donaldson* (1975). The due process protections include the following:

- The person has the right to legal representation through the process.
- The person has the right to regular review of commitment.
- The party seeking civil commitment is responsible for proving the person meet grounds for civil commitment.
- Decisions about civil commitment must respect the **least restrictive alternative principle**, which holds that the goal of protecting the person or the public must be accomplished in a way that minimizes any infringement on the person's rights and freedoms.

Despite due process protections, civil commitment is an inherently coercive process. By definition, the person has expressed a preference not to be subjected to the hospitalization or treatment sought by others. Unsurprisingly, coercion works. Involuntary hospitalization and treatment are at least temporarily or moderately effective in containing the risks of harm posed by people who are subject to civil commitment, and may even lead to improvement in symptoms of mental disorder. But, also unsurprisingly, detaining people against their wishes risks interfering with attempts to establish and maintain a supportive and effective treatment relationship. Put simply, civil commitment can save lives, but it can also destroy people's trust in and relationships with health care providers, family members, and others.

An important development in mental health law over the past 20 years has been the search for alternatives to traditional civil commitment. One alternative is outpatient commitment, in which people are not detained in a hospital for treatment but instead are allowed to reside in the community under conditions (Bonnie & Monahan, 2005). But treatment is still coerced: People who are subject to civil commitment may be threatened with eviction from housing, loss of social support payments, or involuntary hospitalization if they fail to comply with treatment by refusing to take medications or using alcohol and drugs (Bonnie & Monahan, 2005). Also, some critics have expressed concern that the existence of outpatient commitment may actually increase the rate of civil commitment, and especially civil commitment of people suffering from less serious mental disorders or pose relatively low risks, a process sometimes referred to as *net widening* (Geller, Fisher, Grudzinskas, Clayfield, & Lawlor, 2006). Finally, there is simply no evidence from systematic reviews that outpatient commitment is effective in reducing health service use or improving clinical outcome and social functioning relative to traditional forms of treatment, voluntary or involuntary (Kisely, Campbell, Scott, Preston, & Xiao, 2006).

Another alternative to traditional civil commitment is the use of psychiatric advance directives (Henderson, Swanson, Szmukler, Thornicroft, & Zinkler, 2008). Advance directives allow people to express their preferences for future treatment when they are fully competent to do so. In the event that they later suffer a mental disorder that impairs their competence to make decisions about competence, treatment can proceed according to the advance directives. One problem with this approach is that the advance directives cannot anticipate all possible future circumstances, including such things as changes in the nature or severity of symptoms (e.g., severe suicidality) or the advent of new treatments (e.g., a new drug with fewer side effects than older drugs). It may be possible to argue that people would have written different advance directives if they had foreseen such circumstances.

A third alternative is to provide better voluntary health care services, so that civil commitment is not necessary. For example, Greenfield, Stoneking, Humphreys, Sundby, and Bond (2008) investigated the effectiveness of a crisis residential program—an unlocked ward managed by mental health consumers (people who have experienced and received treatment for mental disorder). They randomly assigned 393 civilly committed people to either the crisis residential program or a traditional ward, which was locked and managed by health care providers. People were interviewed at admission and then at 30 days, 6 months, and 1 year after admission. People admitted to the crisis residential program exhibited significantly greater improvements in psychiatric symptoms, according to both self-report and observer ratings, than did those admitted to the traditional ward. In addition, satisfaction with health care services received was much higher among people admitted to the crisis residential program.

Evaluations for Civil Commitment

Psychologists in some states perform evaluations to determine whether people may be civilly committed. Psychology also has made important contributions to the development and evaluation of assessment procedures to assist evaluations for civil commitment. In this section, we take a look at civil commitment evaluations.

To reiterate, people may be civilly committed only if they pose a risk to self or others on account of mental disorder. Analyses of this issue by numerous psycholegal scholars (Melton et al., 2007; Morse, 2004; Schopp, 2001) concur that three general requirements must be met. First, the person must currently suffer from a mental disorder. Second, the person must currently pose certain risks. And third, the risks must be due at least in part to the mental disorder, or, put differently, there must exist a discernible **causal nexus** or causal connection between the mental disorder and the risks. These requirements are illustrated in Figure 3.2. Let's take a closer look at these requirements and how they are considered as part of civil commitment evaluations.

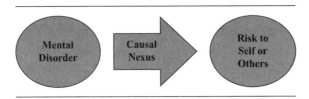

Figure 3.2   Three Requirements for Civil Commitment

Mental Disorder

Arguably, this should be the most straightforward part of civil commitment evaluations. In the United States, the law recognizes that psychologists, by virtue of their education and training they receive, have special expertise in the assessment and diagnosis of mental disorder (Melton et al., 2007). Psychologists typically evaluate the presence of mental disorder using a clinical interview and review of collateral information, but they can also utilize a wide range of tools. These tools include psychological tests, such as self-report inventories, structured interviews, and ratings scales, as well as standardized diagnostic criteria, such as those in the revised fourth edition of the *Diagnostic and Statistical Manual of Mental Disorders* (DSM-IV-TR; American Psychiatric Association, 2000), something psychologists had a hand in developing.

The task for evaluators, however, is a bit more complicated than it might appear on the surface. First, the definition of *mental disorder* used in psychology may be very different from that used in mental health law. To assist legal decision making, however, psychologists must use the definition of mental disorder that is set out in statutory or common law. A second complication is that the law is not interested in whether a person *ever* has suffered from a mental disorder, but rather whether a person *currently* suffers from a mental disorder. Lifetime diagnoses of mental disorder are generally more reliable than present state diagnoses. Third, not all forms of mental disorder are assessed and diagnosed with equivalent reliability and validity, and the general level of reliability and validity is far from ideal. Finally, not all forms of mental disorder are equally relevant to civil commitment. Evaluators need to pay careful attention to those forms of mental disorder that are established risk factors for harm to self through self-injury or self-neglect, harm to others, and incompetence to make decisions about treatment. For example, psychological research indicates that short-term risk of physical harm to others (i.e., violence) is more strongly associated with certain forms cognitive, psychotic, and mood disorders than are other forms of mental disorder such as anxiety or adjustment disorders (Friedman, 2006; Sirotich, 2008); in contrast, long-term risk for sexual violence is most strongly associated with paraphilias and personality disorders (Hanson & Morton-Bourgon, 2005). Comorbid (i.e., co-occurring) substance-related disorders further increase risk for both types of violence.

Risk of Harm

The U.S. Supreme Court emphasized in *O'Connor v. Donaldson* (1975) that civil commitment can be justified only when there is danger or risk of harm stemming from a person's mental disorder. But different jurisdictions define the nature and degree of harm that must be posed in different ways. As discussed previously, the common element across jurisdictions is risk of harm to self or others that is both imminent (i.e., in the coming hours to days) and serious (i.e., life-threatening). Other jurisdictions, however, broaden the definition to include risk that is more distal (i.e., days to weeks, months, or even years, especially for newer forms of civil commitment, such as under sexually violent predator statutes) or less serious (i.e., psychological harm, deterioration of physical or mental health).

The topic of risk assessment was raised in Chapter 2, and we will return to it frequently throughout this text, because risk assessment is central to the practice of forensic psychology. Risk assessment is always difficult because it involves speculation about what might happen in the future, whereas most psychological evaluations focus on what happened in the past or the current state of affairs. Risk assessment in the context of civil commitment is even more difficult; psychologists must keep in mind the various harms that are (and are not) legally relevant. Psychologists may have to conduct risk assessments that include risk for suicide but exclude risk for nonlethal forms of self-injury; include risk for physical assault, but exclude risk for threats or intimidating behavior; or include risk for sexual violence against strangers, but exclude risk for sexual violence against acquaintances such as family members, intimate partners, and so forth.

Psychologists have developed tools to help structure risk assessments for civil commitment. These risk assessment tools typically help to focus evaluators on a relatively small number of factors considered critical to risk. Some are highly structured tests, known as **actuarial instruments**, which tell evaluators exactly which risk factors to consider and how to combine them to estimate the probability of future harm. For example, the Classification of Violence Risk, or **COVR** (Monahan et al., 2005), is designed to estimate the likelihood that a person discharged from an emergency psychiatric unit will commit an act of physical violence—including threats made with weapons in hand—within the next 20 weeks. It comprises 40 items that are administered by computer and rated by evaluators on the basis of patient self-report and, where necessary, file information. The COVR uses adaptive testing procedures: To streamline the assessment, the items that are administered and the order in which they are administered is determined by software based on the pattern of responses. The software then gives a specific probability estimate that the person will be violent. Another example is the **STATIC-99** (Hanson & Thornton, 1999), which is designed to estimate the probability that a person who has committed a sexual offense in the past will commit another offense within 5, 10, or 15 years following release. The STATIC-99 is a 10-item rating scale completed on the basis of file information and, when necessary, interview. Items ratings are simply added to create a total score, which then can be used to estimate the probability of recidivism.

Other risk assessment tools provide a basic list of risk factors that should be considered, but they do not tell evaluators how they should be weighted or combined and cannot be used to estimate the probability of future harm. They are sometimes referred to as **structured professional judgment (SPJ)** or evidence-based guidelines. One example is the **HCR-20** (Webster, Douglas, Eaves, & Hart, 1997). The HCR-20 is designed for guide evaluations of risk for actual, attempted, or threatened physical harm of other people in institutional and community settings. It focuses evaluators on 20 primary risk factors related to a person's past functioning (*H*istorical items), current functioning (*C*linical items), and future plans (*R*isk Management items). Another example is the Sexual Violence Risk-20, or **SVR-20** (Boer, Hart, Kropp, & Webster, 1997). The SVR-20 is designed to guide evaluations of risk for sexual violence. It also focuses evaluators on 20 factors related to the person's psychosocial adjustment, history of sexual offenses, and future plans. The HCR-20 and SVR-20 manuals summarize the theoretical and empirical support for each risk factor, and also provide guidelines for assessing its presence.

The COVR and HCR-20 are potentially relevant to traditional civil commitment evaluations, whereas the STATIC-99 and SVR-20 are potentially relevant to sexually violent predator evaluations. Research supports the basic reliability and validity of all these tools: Different evaluators who evaluate the same person tend to reach similar findings, and people rated as higher risk tend to have significantly higher rates of future violence or sexual violence than do people rated as lower risk (e.g., Hanson & Morton-Bourgon, 2009). But all of them have serious limitations for use in civil commitment evaluations. First, the definition of *harm* used for each tool was not intended to match the legal definitions used in various jurisdictions. This means the findings are not necessarily legally relevant. For example, none of these instruments assesses risk for self-injury, suicide, or self-neglect. Second, none of the tools is comprehensive. Evaluators must consider whether there are circumstances or risk factors in a given case that should be considered beyond those included in any tool. This means there is always an element of subjectivity or discretion in a risk assessment, even when actuarial instruments are used. For example, the presence of many risk factors may be rendered meaningless by the fact that the person has developed a permanent and disabling medical condition; or the presence of few factors, by the fact that the person has made clear and credible statements of intent to commit harm. Third, it is impossible to estimate the specific probability that a given individual will commit harm in the future using any procedure. Actuarial instruments provide probability estimates that are based on statistical profiles of what happened in groups of other people in the past, they cannot directly calculate what a person will do in the future. SPJ guidelines do not even attempt to provide probability estimates, as they emphasize that risk of harm depends on future living circumstances.

Causal Nexus

Although civil commitment laws recognize mental disorder *may* be associated with risk to self or others, it is not *always* or even *often* associated with risk. According to psychological research, the law is correct: Most people with mental disorder do not commit serious violence, and the risk for harm to self or others associated with most forms of mental disorder is small (Choe, Teplin, & Abram, 2008). For this reason, it is not permissible under mental health law to civilly commit people solely because they have been diagnosed as suffering from mental disorder at some point in their lives. This would be stereotypical and legally discriminatory, infringing in the rights of an entire class of people (those suffering from certain mental disorders) because of problems with a few. As a consequence, civil commitment requires an individualized assessment, a demonstration that *this person* currently suffers from a mental disorder that causes *this person* to pose a risk for harm to self or others.

But how does a psychologist determine whether or to what extent any risk of harm is attributable to mental disorder? As yet, no one has developed a tool that attempts to directly evaluate or quantify the causal nexus between mental disorder and risk of harm. The problem is that a causal nexus does not exist physically, and cannot be proved or disproved through physical evidence. Rather, it is an explanation, interpretation, or account of evidence whose plausibility is judged according to the extent it coheres with the facts of the case, common sense views of the world, and (where applicable) scientific research and theory. This explanation must be based on something more than the mere co-occurrence of mental disorder and risk of harm to self or others. (In this way, the law avoids discriminating against people with mental disorder.) Evaluators must instead attempt to rule out other plausible explanations, such as chance or the presence of some other factor responsible for the risks.

PARENTING CAPACITY

Parenting capacity evaluations—also referred to as *parenting responsibility* and *child custody evaluations*—are psychological assessments of people's suitability to act as caregivers for children (Ayoub & Kinscherff, 2006; Sparta & Stahl, 2006). They are conducted when people's rights and responsibilities with respect to childrearing are in conflict. On the one hand, parents or guardians have legal rights to raise their children as they see fit but, on the other hand, they have responsibilities to provide the necessities of life to their children and provide an environment that protects the safety and well-being of children.

Conflict regarding childrearing can take many different forms. One type of conflict arises when parents' rights conflict with their responsibilities. This can happen when, for example, the religious beliefs of parents proscribe certain kinds of medical treatment that might save their child's life. In such cases, another interested party, such as a hospital or child protective services agency, may ask courts to override the rights of parents and act as a substitute decision maker concerning treatment of the child. A second type of conflict arises when the rights of one parent conflict with the rights of another parent. This can happen when parents who are not cohabiting cannot agree concerning who should have primary custody of their children. A third type of conflict is when the rights of parents conflict with the rights of their children. An example would be when children disagree with their parents about some health care decisions or about custody, access, or residence arrangements following divorce or separation. This is especially likely to happen as children age and their legal rights increase. A fourth type of conflict is when the rights and responsibilities of parents conflict with those of other interested parties such as extended family members, police, or child protection agencies. For example, in some jurisdictions grandparents may have limited rights to petition courts for access to their grandchildren, despite the wishes of one or both parents.

Most parenting capacity evaluations are conducted in the context of **custody or access disputes**, which fall into the second type of conflict already discussed. The prototypical scenario involves two parents who are in the process of dissolving their relationship (or have already done so) but disagree about where the children should reside, how much time the children should spend with each parent or other members of their extended families, or how to share responsibility for making decisions about the children's health care and education. If these disputes cannot be resolved informally, the parties may go before the courts and seek a remedy under civil law.

Scope of the Problem

There is no way to determine how often parenting capacity evaluations are conducted in the context of custody or access disputes in the United States. To give some insight into the scope of the problem, Emery, Otto, and O'Donohue (2005) noted that disputes involving family matters accounted for more than 25% of all matters filed in civil courts, and most of these disputes centered on custody and access issues. Emery and colleagues went on to summarize some relevant statistics about marriage in the United States: almost 50% of marriages end in dissolution (i.e., separation or divorce); about 60% of marriages that end in dissolution involve children; and about 50% of marriages that end in dissolution do so within 7 years. But this is only part of the picture. It is increasingly common in the United States for partners to cohabit without entering into marriage (an arrangement that may be referred to as common-law marriage in some jurisdictions). These cohabiting but unmarried couples are more likely to have children than are married couples. They are also more likely than marriages to end in dissolution, with 50% failing within 5 years. Taken together, these findings suggest that custody and access disputes may be the single biggest issue in civil law.

The picture is, however, not completely bleak. Bear in mind that perhaps 50% of all marriages and cohabiting relationships that involve children dissolve without dispute over custody or access; and even in cases that involve disputes, the majority—perhaps 60% to 85%—are settled before going to trial and without the need for parenting capacity evaluations (Bow & Quinnell, 2004; Maccoby & Mnookin, 1992). Requests for parenting capacity evaluations are typically triggered by the presence of certain factors, such as allegations that a child was abused or neglected, allegations that a parent has mental health or substance use problems, or an extreme level of conflict between parents (Bow & Quinnell, 2004).

Legal Issues

Once a custody and access dispute arises, how do courts in the United States decide the issue? Up until the mid-1800s, the decision was simple because children were viewed as the property of fathers (Emery et al., 2005), possibly a legacy of the lingering influence in British common law of the ancient Roman doctrine of *paterfamilias*. From the mid-1800s until the mid-1900s, this legal tradition was replaced by the **"tender years" doctrine**, which assumed mothers should be granted custody due to their special abilities with respect to rearing young children. But in the early to mid-1900s, the legal doctrine that emerged and eventually become dominant was the **"best interests of the child" principle**, which is now reflected in the laws of every jurisdiction in the United States (Emery et al., 2005). According to this principle, legal decisions should try to provide children with childrearing environments that are most likely to ensure optimal development in light of their unique needs and circumstances (Elrod & Spector, 2004; Melton et al., 2007), and especially their psychological needs (Emery et al., 2005). Evaluators need to determine what a child needs to grow and thrive and whether or how the parents, working jointly or individually, can provide it to the child. The specific factors considered relevant to custody and access decisions, according to the Uniform Marriage and Divorce Act (1979), include the following: the wishes of the children's parent or parents as to their custody; the wishes of the children regarding their custodian; the interaction and interrelationship of the children and their parent or parents, their siblings, and any other person who may significantly affect the children's best interests; the children's adjustment to their home, school, and community; and the mental and physical health of all individuals involved. (This list is quite representative, as many state laws are based at least in part on the Uniform Marriage and Divorce Act.) A more extensive list of specific areas addressed in parenting capacity evaluations is presented in Table 3.1.

The Practice of Parenting Capacity Evaluations

The "best interests of the child" principle may sound both simple and sensible, but custody and access evaluators have found it difficult to respect it in practice. The very things that make the principle attractive—for example,

Table 3.1 Some Specific Areas Addressed in Parenting Capacity Evaluations

Parent	Child	Parent-Child Relationship
Personality	Personality	Contact and interaction
Intellectual functioning	Intellectual functioning	Attachment
Childrearing experiences (including maltreatment)	Childrearing experiences (including maltreatment)	Nurturance and support
Relationships with intimate partners	Relationships with siblings	Supervision and discipline
Relationships with other family members	Relationships with other family members	Maltreatment
Parenting skills and attitudes	Peer relationships	
Relationships with peers and others	Educational functioning	
Educational functioning	Physical health	
Occupational functioning	Mental health	
Physical health	Substance use	
Mental health	Antisocial behavior	
Substance use	Other special problems/needs	
Antisocial behavior		

Source: Following Ayoub & Kinscherff (2006) and Sparta & Stahl (2006).

its respect for the diversity and uniqueness of children's needs—also make it difficult to conduct evaluations in a systematic, consistent manner (Emery et al., 2005). Historically, despite the frequent participation of psychologists and other mental health experts in custody and access matters, courts were often dissatisfied with their reports and testimony (Bow & Quinnell, 2004; Melton et al., 2007). A major problem identified with parenting capacity evaluations was the tendency for evaluators to work and advocate for one of the parents, rather than take a neutral and objective stance. Second, evaluators had a tendency to use traditional procedures to assess the mental health of individual parents and children, rather than using specialized procedures to assess the childrens' needs and the parents' capacity to meet those needs. Third, evaluators did not make specific comments on or recommendations that would help courts to make decisions regarding custody and access arrangements. And it wasn't only courts that were unhappy with parenting capacity evaluations—parents were unhappy too, leading to frequent complaints to professional licensing or registration bodies. To help improve parenting capacity evaluations, in February 1994 the Council of Representatives of the American Psychological Association adopted practice guidelines drafted by the American Psychological Association's Committee on Professional Practice and Standards with input from its Committee on Children, Youth, and Families. The *Guidelines for Child Custody Evaluations in Divorce Proceedings*, which were published later that same year (American Psychological Association, 1994), are summarized in Table 3.2. Similar guidelines have been published by the Association of Family and Conciliation Courts (1994, 2007) and the American Academy of Child and Adolescent Psychiatry (1997).

It appears that the efforts made by psychologists to improve parenting capacity evaluations in custody and access matters have had a substantial impact on practice. Evidence of this comes from surveys of evaluators undertaken before and after the publication of the American Psychological

Table 3.2   American Psychological Association's *Guidelines for Child Custody Evaluations in Divorce Proceedings*

I. Orienting Guidelines: Purpose of a Child Custody Evaluation	1. The primary purpose of the evaluation is to assess the best psychological interests of the child.
	2. The child's interests and well-being are paramount.
	3. The focus of the evaluation is on parenting capacity, the psychological and developmental needs of the child, and the resulting fit.
II. General Guidelines: Preparing for a Child Custody Evaluation	4. The role of the psychologist is that of a professional expert who strives to maintain an objective, impartial stance.
	5. The psychologist gains specialized competence.
	6. The psychologist is aware of personal and societal biases and engages in nondiscriminatory practice.
	7. The psychologist avoids multiple relationships.
III. Procedural Guidelines: Conducting a Child Custody Evaluation	8. The scope of the evaluation is determined by the evaluator, based on the nature of the referral question.
	9. The psychologist obtains informed consent from all adult participants and, as appropriate, informs child participants.
	10. The psychologist informs participants about the limits of confidentiality and the disclosure of information.
	11. The psychologist uses multiple methods of data gathering.
	12. The psychologist neither overinterprets nor inappropriately interprets clinical or assessment data.
	13. The psychologist does not give any opinion regarding the psychological functioning of any individual who has not been personally evaluated.
	14. Recommendations, if any, are based on what is in the best psychological interests of the child.
	15. The psychologist clarifies financial arrangements.
	16. The psychologist maintains written records.

Source: American Psychological Association (1994), Table 3.2.

Association's Guidelines in 1994. First, the before picture. Keilin and Bloom (1986) analyzed the responses of 82 custody and access evaluators, 78% of whom were psychologists, to an anonymous questionnaire that asked respondents to list the evaluation procedures they used and rank the specific factors they considered in terms of importance. Respondents indicated that they conducted evaluations as court-appointed experts only about 26% of the time. They spent an average of about 19 hours working on each evaluation. The most common assessment procedure used was interviewing: evaluators reported that they conducted interviews of parents in 100% of cases, and interviews of children in 99% of cases (remember that some children are developmentally incapable of being interviewed). Evaluators administered psychological tests to parents in 76% of cases and to children in 74% of cases; most were standard tests of intelligence or personality, and none were tests developed specifically for use in parenting capacity evaluations. Other assessment procedures included behavioral observations, interviews with collateral informants, and home and school visits. After completing the assessments, the evaluators typically spent about 2.8 hours report writing, 1.4 hours consulting with attorneys, and about 2.3 hours testifying in court.

Now, let's turn to the after picture. Since the publication of the American Psychological Association's *Guidelines*, there have been several surveys that used methods similar to those of Keilin and Bloom (1986), including: Ackerman and Ackerman (1996, 1997), Bow and Quinnell (2001; see also Quinnell & Bow, 2001), and LaFortune and Carpenter (1998). Some general conclusions can be drawn from the recent surveys about changes in the practice of parenting capacity evaluations:

- Evaluators more frequently act in the role of neutral, court-appointed evaluators.
- Evaluations are taking more time. The average number of hours spent on each case has increased by 10–20%, to about 21–24 hours.
- There have been changes in the assessment procedures used by evaluators. They still spend considerable time administering psychological tests, but now commonly use tests that were designed specifically for use in or are directly relevant to parenting capacity evaluations. (Some examples of such tests are presented in Table 3.3.) Also, evaluators spend more time reviewing documentary evidence.
- Evaluators increasingly evaluate or make specific recommendations regarding custody and access arrangements in light of a child's needs. (Not surprisingly, the time devoted to writing reports also has increased.)

Table 3.3   Examples of Specialized Psychological Tests Developed for Use in Parenting Capacity Evaluations

Test	Description
Ackerman-Schoendorf Parent Evaluation of Custody Test (ASPECT; Ackerman & Schoendorf, 1992)	A multi-item rating scale designed to index overall parenting capacity. Ratings are made by evaluators on the basis of interview, observation, and psychological testing of parents. Items were selected rationally. Item ratings are combined to yield an overall Parental Custody Index for each parent.
Bricklin Perceptual Scales (BPS; Bricklin, 1990)	A multi-item rating scale designed to tap children's perceptions of their parents. Children's responses to a series of questions related to parental competency, supportiveness, consistency, and character. Items were selected rationally. Item ratings are combined to yield three scores that compare perceptions of each parent.
Custody Quotient (CQ; Gordon & Peek, 1988)	A multi-item rating scale designed to index specific aspects of parenting capacity. Ratings are made by evaluators on the basis of interview, observation, and review of case history information. Items were selected rationally. Item ratings are combined to yield an overall Custody Quotient for each parents as well as scores on 12 subscales.
Uniform Child Custody Evaluation System (UCCES; Munsinger & Karlson, 1994)	A systematic procedure for conducting parenting capacity evaluations. Materials include 25 forms to assist gathering, transcribing, and organizing essential information and assessing response validity. Procedures developed rationally (to reflect legal and clinical considerations). Does not yield quantitative scores.

Despite some apparent improvements, there are still reasons to be concerned. One problem is that many parenting capacity evaluations do not pay sufficient attention to the legal context in which they are conducted. Evaluators too often ignore the need for their assessments to address specific legal criteria, set out clear opinions regarding issues relevant to the case at hand, and be structured in specific ways. For example, Bow and Quinnell (2004) surveyed 121 judges and attorneys in Michigan who specialized in family law issues. On the positive side, respondents rated the parenting capacity evaluation reports they reviewed as being generally quite useful, and gave high marks to those components of reports related to evaluators' discussions of psychological testing results and the psychosocial histories of parents and children. But they gave low marks to evaluators' recommendations concerning visitation and other services, comparison of parents with respect to relevant legal criteria, and identification of information that formed the basis for their findings and opinions.

A second problem is that there is little scientific support for the reliability and validity of psychological tests used so commonly in parenting capacity evaluations. As Emery and colleagues (2005) pointed out, some of these tests (e.g., projective tests) are not generally accepted as reliable and valid in any area of psychological practice; other tests (e.g., intelligence tests) are generally accepted as reliable and valid in other areas of psychological practice but their relevance to parenting capacity evaluations is often unclear; and yet other tests appear on the surface to be directly relevant to parenting capacity, but either their psychometric properties are unknown or the constructs they measure (e.g., parent alienation syndrome) are themselves unvalidated.

A third problem is that decisions about parenting capacity are value-laden. Which of a child's needs are most important? How are they best met? To what extent should the wishes of the child and parents be respected? Answering these questions requires evaluators to exercise judgment. To the extent that evaluators understand and use the values inherent in relevant legal criteria, this is acceptable; but it is unacceptable if evaluators fail to make their values explicit, reject the values reflected in law, or introduce their own personal values in the process. A major challenge facing this area of civil forensic assessment is the development of assessment procedures or decision aids to help evaluators exercise their judgment in a way that will facilitate sound, legal decision making.

CHILD MALTREATMENT

Child maltreatment is the abuse or neglect of children by parents or other people in a position of power, trust, or responsibility. **Child abuse** is the commission of acts that deliberately or recklessly threaten the safety and well-being of children. Abusive acts often are divided into three categories depending on the nature of the acts and their (potential) consequences (Krug, Dahlberg, Mercy, Zwi, & Lozano, 2002). Physical abuse involves actual, attempted, or threatened injury of a child—basically, causing bodily harm or fear of bodily harm. Sexual abuse involves actual, attempted, or threatened sexual contact that is inappropriate due to the perpetrator's age or relationship to a child. Contact includes physical contact (e.g., touching, assault) and communication, whether coercive and noncoercive. Emotional abuse involves actual, attempted, or threatened psychological or social harm of a child. It includes cruelty and exploitation. *Cruelty* is the intentional infliction of severe psychological distress (e.g., anxiety, fear, embarrassment). *Exploitation* is the use of children for commercial or sexual purposes (e.g., forced labor, military service, or prostitution) in a way that may impair their psychological or social development. In contrast, *child neglect* is the omission of acts that deliberately or recklessly threaten the safety and well-being of children (Krug et al., 2002). Neglect may involve failing to provide a child with the necessities of life, such as food, clothing, or medical care, or failing to provide a safe and secure physical environment for rearing a child.

Although the definition of child maltreatment appears to be relatively straightforward, it is influenced heavily by cultural considerations. Culture may be defined as the sum of work and thought expressed or produced by members of that population, including their social practices, beliefs, institutions, and arts (Cross & Markus, 1999; Rogler, 1999). Although culture is a reflection of people and the collective physical and social environments in which they live, it also exerts a profound influence on those same individuals, helping them to define what is normal with respect to attitudes, emotions, and behavior, including childrearing behavior. In general, acts or omissions are considered child maltreatment when they are culturally abnormal or deviant, something that may be referred to as a "violation of community standards." The impact of culture means that it is sometimes difficult to distinguish between harsh discipline and child maltreatment (Krug et al., 2002).

To illustrate the impact of culture on the definition of child maltreatment, consider the issue of physical or corporal punishment of children. Historically, it was acceptable in many European and North American cultures for caregivers—parents and other adults, including teachers—to discipline children by striking them with hands or even objects (e.g., wooden spoons, belts, rulers, or straps). But attitudes toward discipline with physical punishment have changed markedly. It is now unacceptable in some of these same cultures to strike children. For example, in Canada, the Supreme Court in *Canadian Foundation for Children, Youth and the Law v. Canada (Attorney General)* (2004) ruled that parents may use mild physical punishment, such as spanking, but its use is severely restricted: only for corrective and educational purposes; never with children under the age of 2; not with teenagers, as it may lead to aggressive or antisocial behavior; not with children who are incapable of learning from punishment due to physical or mental disability; never in a way that causes harm or fear of harm (e.g., not with objects such as rulers or belts, not slaps or blows to the head); and not in a way that is psychologically cruel or demeaning. In the same ruling, the Court also held that corporal punishment is forbidden in schools. Laws in other countries, such as the United Kingdom and the United States, are somewhat more permissive. For example, at least 1700 police departments in the United States have issued conducted electricity weapons, or Tasers®, to officers patrolling public schools. These weapons are used regularly not just to apprehend children who are breaking the law, but to control children who are simply breaking school rules by being unruly, disruptive or truant, including children as young as 6 years old. (See Box 3.1 for further discussion of cross-cultural differences in childrearing practices.)

Box 3.1 The WorldSAFE Study

Krug et al. (2002) summarized data from the World Studies of Abuse in the Family Environment (WorldSAFE), a cross-national collaborative study of disciplinary practices in Chile, Egypt, India (rural regions only), the Philippines, and the United States. The WorldSAFE survey was administered to random samples of mothers in each country. The survey comprised a core set of questions posed to mothers in all countries, as well as additional questions that were asked in only specific countries. Mothers were asked to indicate how often they had used various forms of discipline in the previous six months. The table presents some of the findings summarized by Krug et al. (2002).

A Cross-National Comparison of Disciplinary Practices

Selected Disciplinary Practices	Six-Month Incidence (%)				
	Chile	Egypt	India	Philippines	United States
Severe Physical Punishment					
Hit the child with an object (not on buttocks)	4	26	36	21	4
Kicked the child	0	2	10	6	0
Burned the child	0	2	1	0	0
Beat the child	0	25	—	3	0
Choked the child	0	1	2	1	0
Moderate Physical Punishment					
Hit the child on buttocks with hand	51	29	58	75	47
Hit the child on buttocks with an object	18	28	23	51	21
Slapped the child's face or head	13	41	58	21	4
Shook the child (older than 2 yrs)	39	59	12	20	9
Pinched the child	3	45	17	60	5
Verbal or Psychological Punishment					
Yelled or screamed at the child	84	72	70	82	85
Called the child names	15	44	29	24	17
Cursed at the child	3	51	—	0	24
Refused to speak to the child	17	48	31	15	—
Threatened to kick the child out of the household	5	0	—	26	6
Other Disciplinary Practices					
Explained why the behavior was wrong	91	80	94	90	94
Took privileges away	60	27	43	3	77
Told child to stop	88	69	—	91	—
Gave child something to do	71	43	27	66	75
Made child stay in one place	37	50	5	58	75

— = Question not asked in that country.

Scope of the Problem

Regardless of any definitional issues, child maltreatment is clearly a major public health concern due to its potentially serious consequences and high prevalence (Krug et al., 2002). The potential consequences of child maltreatment vary among individuals, depending on the severity and chronicity of maltreatment, as well as the age of the child, the child's relationship to the abuser, and response to the child's disclosure of maltreatment, the socioeconomic status of the family, and the social and community support available to the family. The effects include physical injuries ranging from minor bruises and welts to broken bones to severe neurological impairment or death, and psychological injuries range from impaired cognition and academic achievement to mental disorder and increased risk of externalizing behavior such as substance abuse, teenage pregnancy, running away, and criminality; these effects may persist into adulthood, leading to long-term need for and utilization of medical, mental health, social, and legal services (Krug et al., 2002; National Research Council, 1993).

Estimating the prevalence of child maltreatment is difficult due not only to definitional problems, as discussed previously, but also to the general problem that most incidents of child abuse and neglect, like other criminal behaviors, are not reported to police or other agencies. Looking first at official statistics, the third National Incidence Study of Child Abuse and Neglect (NIS-3) reported that more than 2.8 million children were victims of maltreatment in 1993 (Sedlak & Broadhurst, 1996). The most recent analysis of the National Child Abuse and Neglect Data System, reported by the U.S. Department of Health and Human Services (2008), estimated that there were about 3.6 million reports and about 905,000 substantiated cases of child maltreatment in the 2006 fiscal year. This represents a reporting rate of about 47.8 per 1,000 children per year, and a victimization rate of about 12.1 per 1,000 children. With respect to the type of maltreatment experienced, about 64% of victims experienced neglect, 16% experienced physical abuse, 9% experienced sexual abuse, and 7% experienced psychological abuse; in addition, 15% were recorded as having experienced "other" types of maltreatment. (These figures total more than 100% because some children were victims of more than one type of maltreatment.) In 90% of cases, the perpetrators of the abuse of neglect were the children's parents. More than 1,500 children died as a result of maltreatment. Turning next to community surveys, Straus and colleagues (1997) examined child maltreatment in a nationwide study in the United States. They estimated the victimization rate for physical abuse at 49 per 1,000 children per year—more than 10 times higher than the rate estimated from official statistics. Other social surveys have yielded similar findings with respect to the underestimate of child maltreatment based on official statistics (e.g., Gallup, 1995). Although this number seems very large, it is only the tip of the iceberg, as annual incidence rates underestimate lifetime risk of child maltreatment. Hussey, Chang, and Kotch (2006) surveyed a nationally representative probability sample of 10,828 high school students and asked them about child maltreatment victimization experiences perpetrated by parents or other adult caregivers prior to the sixth grade. With respect to child neglect, about 42% of adolescents said they had been negligently supervised on at least one occasion, and about 12% said their basic physical needs had been neglected on at least one occasion. With respect to child abuse, about 28% of adolescents said they had been physically assaulted on at least one occasion and about 5% said they had been sexually assaulted on at least one occasion.

One reason why it is so difficult to determine the rate of child maltreatment precisely is that the rate changes over time. For example, according to Jones, Finkelhor, and Halter (2006), the rate of substantiated cases increased in the 1980s and early 1990s, peaking in about 1992; since then, there has been a marked decline in the rates of physical and sexual abuse, down about 36% and 47%, respectively, between 1992 and 2003, and a small decline in the rate of neglect, down only about 7% during the same period. The reasons for the fluctuation are not entirely clear. It is likely that the rise through 1993 was more apparent than real; a reflection of more reports of maltreatment, rather than more incidents. The increased reporting may have been stimulated by changes in public attitudes toward maltreatment resulting from public education campaigns. But assuming that public attitudes have not grown more tolerant of child maltreatment since 1993, the drop in rates probably reflects a true decrease in maltreatment. A true decrease could be due to various factors, including positive changes in prevention and response at the community level (Jones et al., 2006).

The negative consequences and high prevalence of child maltreatment combine to create staggering economic consequences. At the national level, a study conducted by Prevent Child Abuse America in 2001 estimated the direct and indirect costs stemming from child maltreatment at $258 million per day, or more than $90 billion dollars per year (Fromm, 2001). At the state level, recent research in Colorado is a good example (Gould & O'Brien, 1995). They estimated the costs of child protection investigations, child welfare services, and out-of-home placements at $190 million per year; furthermore, they estimated the cost of programs and services required to deal with the long-term negative consequences of child maltreatment (special education, youth institutional and community programs, mental health programs, substance abuse programs, etc.) at an additional

$212 million per year. Other countries have reported similar findings. For example, in Canada, Bowlus, McKenna, Day, and Wright (2003) estimated the total direct and indirect costs associated with the 135,500 child maltreatment cases investigated in 1998 to be more than $15 billion.

The Role of Psychology in Child Protection

Governments have a mandate to protect children from harm not only to respond decisively to child maltreatment, but also to prevent it. This mandate is enshrined in legislation throughout the United States.

Perhaps the strongest support for governments' mandate with respect to child maltreatment comes from the **United Nations Convention on the Rights of the Child** (UNCRC; United Nations, 1989). The UNCRC is a statement of the civil, political, economic, social, and cultural rights of children. It follows in the footsteps of previous international agreements, including the World Child Welfare Charter, endorsed by the General Assembly of the League of Nations (the forerunner to the United Nations) in 1924, and the Declaration of the Rights of the Child, adopted by the General Assembly of the United Nations in 1959. According to Article 19 of the UNCRC:

1. Parties shall take all appropriate legislative, administrative, social and educational measures to protect the child from all forms of physical or mental violence, injury or abuse, neglect or negligent treatment, maltreatment or exploitation, including sexual abuse, while in the care of parent(s), legal guardian(s) or any other person who has the care of the child.
2. Such protective measures should, as appropriate, include effective procedures for the establishment of social programmes to provide necessary support for the child and for those who have the care of the child, as well as for other forms of prevention and for identification, reporting, referral, investigation, treatment and follow-up of instances of child maltreatment described heretofore, and, as appropriate, for judicial involvement.

Articles 32 to 36 prohibit other forms of maltreatment, including exploitation, and Article 39 sets out the responsibility for governments to provide appropriate services to promote physical and psychological recovery and social reintegration of victims of child maltreatment.

The UNCRC was adopted by the General Assembly of the United Nations in 1989. It is a legally binding instrument: Member nations that ratify the UNCRC are bound to it by international law, and compliance is monitored by the United Nations Committee on the Rights of the Child.

As of 2009, 193 countries have ratified the UNCRC. The United States was a signatory to the UNCRC in 1995 but did not ratify it; this makes the United States one of only two member nations (the other being Somalia), and the only member nation with an operating government, that has not ratified the convention.

Despite the federal government's hesitation, the American Psychological Association has endorsed the UNCRC. In 2001, the American Psychological Association's Council of Representatives approved a strongly worded resolution that declared the development of a national strategy for the protection of children to be "a matter of the highest urgency," affirmed its intent to adopt both the spirit and the principles of the convention in the American Psychological Association's own activities, and urged all levels of government in the United States to do the same (American Psychological Association, 2001). Based on the American Psychological Association resolution, one can identify several ways in which practice of psychology is relevant to the issue of child protection. First, psychologists have a general ethical duty to promote the adjustment of children (and other people) and protect them from harm, as well as a legal mandate to report suspected child maltreatment to the proper authorities. Second, psychological theory and research can further our understanding of children's well-being and sense of dignity, both their nature and the conditions necessary for their development, a central focus of the UNCRC. Third, psychology can assist the development and evaluation of such services designed to prevent and respond to child maltreatment. Fourth, psychological research can assist in the development and evaluation of more general public policy concerning child maltreatment.

Assessing Risk for Child Maltreatment

One area in which psychologists contribute to child protection is with respect to the assessment of risk for child maltreatment. Once a report of maltreatment is made to police or child protective services, it must be investigated to determine whether it can be substantiated and if there is any risk for future maltreatment. Prevention of maltreatment requires courts, tribunals, or other decision makers to reach an opinion—based on the findings of a risk assessment—regarding what has happened in the past, which types of harm the child faces and in which kinds of situations, and what interventions should be implemented to ensure the health and safety of the child. The plans for intervention need to specify which services should be delivered, and at what level of intensity or intrusiveness. A child who is at lower risk for maltreatment (i.e., a case in which the risk of serious abuse or neglect seems remote or unlikely) may be protected with interventions such as childrearing skills and anger management training for parents, financial aid or employment counseling for parents, assistance with housing needs for the family, regular home visits by child protective service workers to support the parents and monitor the child's adjustment, or counseling health care for the child. This is what happens in the vast majority of cases. But, in a relatively small proportion of cases, the findings of the risk assessment may suggest that the child is at high risk for abuse or neglect, and the evaluator may recommend extreme protective measures, up to and including apprehension of the child. Apprehension may result in temporary or even permanent suspension of parental rights and placement of the child in alternative residential care (e.g., under the supervision of other family members or guardians, in a foster home).

A child maltreatment risk assessment is similar to a parenting capacity evaluation in some important respects. One critical aspect of a risk assessment is to determine the unique needs of the child and whether the parents are able, either on their own or with assistance, to meet those needs. But a risk assessment also needs to consider factors that are associated, according to theory and research, with perpetration of child abuse and neglect. There is general consensus in the field that the risk assessment process should be structured to ensure critical risk factors and potential targets for intervention are considered systematically across cases (English & Pecora, 1994). The American Psychological Association's Committee on Professional Practice and Standards (1998) developed guidelines for conducting evaluations concerning child maltreatment, similar to those it developed for conducting custody and access evaluations; these are summarized in Table 3.4.

Despite consensus about the need for structure, there is considerable controversy concerning the adequacy of risk assessment instruments. There has been a proliferation of instruments used by agencies in various jurisdictions, yet none of the instruments is generally accepted or well validated. Some instruments were developed and implemented without adequate research; others are simply modifications of existing instruments, made without solid theoretical or research basis; and still others are used for purposes or with groups for which they were not intended and have not been validated (e.g., Stowman & Donohue, 2004).

An example of a structured approach to child maltreatment risk assessment is Child Abuse Potential or **CAP Inventory** (Milner, 2006). The CAP Inventory is a 160-item self-report questionnaire designed to screen parents for risk of child abuse. It is used commonly in parenting capacity evaluations, in both custody and access and child protection contexts. The items in the CAP Inventory were selected on rational or empirical grounds: rational, if they reflected potential causal risk factors for child abuse according to theory and research; and empirical, if they were shown to

Table 3.4   American Psychological Association's *Guidelines for Psychological Evaluations*
in Child Protection Matters

I. Orienting Guidelines	1. The primary purpose of the evaluation is to provide relevant, professionally sound results or opinions, in matters where a child's health and welfare may have been and/or may in the future be harmed.
	2. In child protection cases, the child's interest and well-being are paramount.
	3. The evaluation addresses the particular psychological and developmental needs of the child and/or parent(s) that are relevant to child protection issues such as physical abuse, sexual abuse, neglect, and/or serious emotional harm.
II. General Guidelines: Preparing for a Child Protection Evaluation	4. The role of psychologists conducting evaluations is that of professional expert who strives to maintain an unbiased, objective stance.
	5. The serious consequences of psychological assessment in child protection matters place a heavy burden on psychologists.
	6. Psychologists gain specialized competence.
	7. Psychologists are aware of personal and societal biases and engage in nondiscriminatory practice.
	8. Psychologists avoid multiple relationships.
III. Procedural Guidelines: Conducting a Psychological Evaluation in Child Protection Matters	9. Based on the nature of the referral questions, the scope of the evaluation is determined by the evaluator.
	10. Psychologists performing psychological evaluations in child protection matters obtain appropriate informed consent from all adult participants, and as appropriate, inform the child participant; psychologists need to be particularly sensitive to informed consent issues.
	11. Psychologists inform participants about the disclosure of information and the limits of confidentiality.
	12. Psychologists use multiple methods of data gathering.
	13. Psychologists neither overinterpret nor inappropriately interpret clinical or assessment data.
	14. Psychologists conducting a psychological evaluation in child protection matters provide an opinion regarding the psychological functioning of an individual only after conducting an evaluation of the individual adequate to support their statements or conclusions.
	15. Recommendations, if offered, are based on whether the child's health and welfare have been and/or may be seriously harmed.
	16. Psychologists clarify financial arrangements.
	17. Psychologists maintain appropriate records.

Source: American Psychological Association Committee on Professional Practice and Standards (1998).

discriminate between known groups of abusive and nonabusive parents in construction research. Parents complete the CAP Inventory by responding agree or disagree to a series of statements. Item ratings are combined to yield scores on 12 scales. One scale reflects risk for physical abuse. Eight scales reflect parent and family characteristics (distress, rigidity, unhappiness, problems with child and self, problems with family, problems with others, ego strength, and loneliness). Three scales reflect response distortion (lying, inconsistent responding, and random responding).

Research on the CAP Inventory has focused primarily on the physical abuse scale (Milner, 2008). In general, this scale appears to have adequate internal consistency and short-term test-retest reliabilities. Predictive validity research is difficult to conduct, because intervention is expected to attenuate the association between risk and subsequent maltreatment. (Hopefully, our interventions reduce risk.) There have been a few prospective studies in which the CAP Inventory physical abuse scale (or an abbreviated version of it) was administered to parents and correlated with subsequent physical health and psychological adjustment problems, some of which may have been due to child maltreatment. Other forms of validity research are much easier to conduct. Numerous studies have found that parents' scores on the physical abuse scale of the CAP Inventory are associated with a wide range of child and family problems.

But the CAP Inventory also has some important limitations. First, it focuses on general physical abuse. It is questionable whether it is relevant to sexual abuse, emotional abuse, and neglect, let alone more specific forms of maltreatment (e.g., exposing a child to dangerous chemicals by operating a drug lab in the family home). Second, there has been no research examining potential bias (i.e., lack of structural or metric equivalence) in the CAP Inventory scores across group factors such as gender, age, and ethnicity. It is uncertain, for example, if the CAP Inventory is equally useful for mothers versus fathers, younger versus older parents, or cultural majority versus minority families. Third, even focusing on the primary use of the CAP Inventory, there is no research that clearly demonstrates its ability to predict future physical abuse of children. For these reasons, psychologists (as well as others working in the field of child maltreatment) continue to develop and evaluate risk assessment instruments.

SUMMARY

Civil forensic assessment is actually a much broader and more diverse area of psychological practice than is criminal forensic assessment, because civil law regulates virtually every aspect of daily life. Psychologists conduct evaluations with respect to matters such as families, work, and health care. We focused in this chapter on three specific issues: civil commitment, parenting capacity, and child maltreatment. Although the legal questions that psychologists must try to answer in these areas are very different, a common theme is evident: A variety of assessment procedures have been developed in an effort to make sure psychological evaluations gather information that is scientifically reliable and legally relevant. As our modern societies become increasingly complex and litigious, no doubt the call for civil forensic assessment will continue to grow.

SUGGESTED READINGS

American Psychological Association. (1994). Guidelines for child custody evaluations in divorce proceedings. *American Psychologist, 49*, 677–682.

American Psychological Association Committee on Professional Practice and Standards. (1998). *Guidelines for psychological evaluations in child protection matters*. Washington, DC: American Psychological Association.

Jackson, R. L., & Richards, H. J. (2008). Civil commitment evaluations. In R. L. Jackson (Ed.), *Learning forensic assessment* (pp. 183–209). New York: Routledge.

Strachan, E. (2008). Evaluations for the civil commitment of sex offenders. In R. L. Jackson (Ed.), *Learning forensic assessment* (pp. 509–537). New York: Routledge.

U.S. Department of Health and Human Services, Administration on Children, Youth and Families. (2008). *Child Maltreatment 2006*. Washington, DC: Author. Available at: http://www.acf.hhs.gov/programs/cb/pubs/cm06.

KEY TERMS

- *Actuarial instruments*
- *"Best interests of the child" principle*
- *CAP Inventory*
- *Causal nexus*
- *Child abuse*
- *Child maltreatment*
- *Child neglect*
- *Civil commitment*
- *Civil forensic assessment*
- *Civil law*

- *COVR*
- *Criminal commitment*
- *Custody or access disputes*
- *Due process protections*
- *Guidelines for Child Custody Evaluations in Divorce Proceedings*
- *HCR-20*
- *Least restrictive alternative principle*
- *Parens patriae powers*
- *Parenting capacity evaluations*
- *Police powers*
- *Sexually violent predator laws*
- *STATIC-99*
- *Structured professional judgment (SPJ)*
- *SVR-20*
- *"Tender years" doctrine*
- *United Nations Convention on the Rights of the Child*

References

Ackerman, M. J., & Ackerman, M. (1996). Child custody evaluation practices: A 1996 survey of psychologists. *Family Law Quarterly, 30*, 565–586.

Ackerman, M. J., & Ackerman, M. (1997). Custody evaluation practices: A survey of experienced professionals (revisited). *Professional Psychology: Research and Practice, 28*, 137–145.

Ackerman, M. J., & Schoendorf, K. (1992). *Ackerman-Schoendorf Scales for Parent Evaluation of Custody (ASPECT)*. Los Angeles: Western Psychological Services.

American Academy of Child and Adolescent Psychiatry. (1997). Practice parameters for child custody evaluation. *Journal of the American Academy of Child and Adolescent Psychiatry, 36*, 57S–62S.

Association of Family and Conciliation Courts. (1994). Model standards of practice for child custody evaluation. *Family and Conciliation Courts Review, 32*, 504–513.

Association of Family and Conciliation Courts. (2007). Model standards of practice for child custody evaluation. *Family and Conciliation Courts Review, 45*, 70–91.

American Psychiatric Association. (2000). *Diagnostic and statistical manual of mental disorders* (4th ed., Text Revision). Washington, DC: Author.

American Psychological Association. (1994). Guidelines for child custody evaluations in divorce proceedings. *American Psychologist, 49*, 677–682.

American Psychological Association. (2001). *Resolution on UN Convention on the Rights of the Child and the Convention's Optional Protocols*. Approved by the APA Council of Representatives February 2001.

American Psychological Association Committee on Professional Practice and Standards. (1998). *Guidelines for psychological evaluations in child protection matters*. Washington, DC: Author.

Ayoub, C., & Kinscherff, R. (2006). Forensic assessment of parenting in child abuse and neglect cases. In S. N. Sparta & G. P. Koocher (Eds.), *Forensic mental health assessment of children and adolescents* (pp. 330–341). New York: Oxford University Press.

Beaber, R. J. (1982). Custody quagmire: Some psychological dilemmas. *Journal of Psychiatry & Law, 10*, 309–326.

Boer, D. P., Hart, S. D., Kropp, P. R., & Webster, C. D. (1997). *Manual for the Sexual Violence Risk-20: Professional guidelines for assessing risk of sexual violence*. Burnaby, British Columbia: Mental Health, Law, and Policy Institute, Simon Fraser University.

Bonnie, R. J., & Monahan, J. (2005). From coercion to contract: Reframing the debate on mandated community treatment for people with mental disorders. *Law and Human Behavior, 29*, 487–505.

Bow, J. N., & Quinnell, F. A. (2001). Psychologists' current practices and procedures in child custody evaluations: Five years after American Psychological Association guidelines. *Professional Psychology: Research and Practice, 32*, 261–268.

Bow, J. N., & Quinnell, F. A. (2004). Critique of child custody evaluations by the legal profession. *Family Court Review, 42*, 115–127.

Bowlus, A., McKenna, K., Day, T., & Wright, D. (2003). *The economic costs and consequences of child abuse in Canada*. Ottawa: Law Commission of Canada.

Bricklin, B. (1984). *Bricklin Perceptual Scales*. Furlong, PA: Village.

Buchanan, A., & Leese, M. (2001). Detention of people with dangerous severe personality disorders: A systematic review. *Lancet*, 358, 1955–1959.

Canadian Foundation for Children, Youth and the Law v. Canada (Attorney General), SCC 4 [2004], 1 S.C.R. 76 (2004).

Choe, J. Y., Teplin, L. A., & Abram, K. M. (2008). Perpetration of violence, violent victimization, and severe mental illness: Balancing public health concerns. *Psychiatric Services, 59*, 153–164.

Cross, S. E., & Markus, H. R. (1999). The cultural constitution of personality. In L. A. Pervin & O. P. John (Eds.), *Handbook of personality* (pp. 378–396). New York: Guilford.

Elrod, L. D., & Spector, R. G. (2004). A review of the year in family law: Children's issues remain the focus. *Family Law Quarterly, 37*, 527–575.

Emery, R. E., Otto, R. K., & O'Donohue, W. T. (2005). A critical assessment of child custody evaluations: Limited science and a flawed system. *Psychological Science in the Public Interest, 6*, 1–29.

English, D. J., & Pecora, P. J. (1994). Risk assessment as a practice in child protective services. *Child Welfare, 73*, 451–473.

Friedman, R. A. (2006). Violence and mental illness—How strong is the link? *New England Journal of Medicine, 355*, 2064–2066.

Fromm, S. (2001). *Total estimated cost of child abuse and neglect in the United States: Statistical evidence*. Chicago: Prevent Child Abuse America.

Gallup. (1995). *Gallup poll finds far more of America's children are victims of physical & sexual abuse than officially reported*. Princeton, NJ: Author.

Geller, J. L., Fisher, W. H., Grudzinskas, A. J., Clayfield, J. C., & Lawlor, T. (2006). Involuntary outpatient treatment as "deinstitutionalized coercion": The net-widening concerns. *International Journal of Law and Psychiatry, 29*, 551–562.

Gordon, R., & Peek, L. A. (1988). *The custody quotient*. Dallas, TX: Wilmington Institute.

Gostin, L. (2005). The future of communicable disease control: Toward a new concept in public health law. *Milbank Quarterly, 83*(4), 1–17.

Gould, M., & O'Brien, T. (1995). *Child maltreatment in Colorado: The value of prevention and the cost of failure to prevent*. Denver: Center for Human Investment Policy, University of Colorado at Denver.

Greenfield, T. K., Stoneking, B. C., Humphreys, K., Sundby, E., & Bond, J. (2008). A randomized trial of a mental health consumer-managed alternative to civil commitment for acute psychiatric crisis. *American Journal of Community Psychology, 42*, 135–144.

Hanson, R. K., & Morton-Bourgon, K. E. (2005). The characteristics of persistent sexual offenders: A meta-analysis of recidivism studies. *Journal of Consulting and Clinical Psychology, 73*, 1154–1163.

Hanson, R. K., & Morton-Bourgon, K. E. (2009). The accuracy of recidivism risk assessments for sexual offenders: A meta-analysis. *Psychological Assessment, 21*, 1–21.

Hanson, R. K., & Thornton, D. (1999). *STATIC-99: Improving actuarial risk assessments for sex offenders*. Ottawa: Ministry of the Solicitor General of Canada.

Henderson, C. R., Swanson, J. W., Szmukler, G., Thornicroft, G., & Zinkler, M. (2008). A typology of advance statements in mental health care. *Psychiatric Services, 59*, 63–71.

Høyer, G. (2008). Involuntary hospitalization in contemporary mental health care: Some (still) unanswered questions. *Journal of Mental Health, 17*, 281–292.

Hussey, J. M., Chang, J. J., & Kotch, J. B. (2006). Child maltreatment in the United States: Prevalence, risk factors, and adolescent health consequences. *Pediatrics, 118*, 933–942.

Janus, E. S. (2000). Sexual predator commitment laws: Lessons for law and the behavioral sciences. *Behavioral Sciences and the Law, 18*, 5–21.

Jones, L. M., Finkelhor, D., & Halter, S. (2006). Child maltreatment trends in the 1990s: Why does neglect differ from sexual and physical abuse? *Child Maltreatment, 11*, 107–120.

Keilin, W. G., & Bloom, L. J. (1986). Child custody evaluation practices: A survey of experienced professionals. *Professional Psychology: Research and Practice, 17*, 338–346.

Kisely, S., Campbell, L. A., Scott, A., Preston, N., & Xiao, J. (2006). Randomized and nonrandomized evidence for the effect of compulsory community and involuntary outpatient treatment on health service use: Systematic review and meta-analysis. *Psychological Medicine, 37*, 3–14.

Krug, E. G., Dahlberg, L. L., Mercy, J. A., Zwi, A. B., & Lozano, R. (Eds.). (2002). *World report on violence and health*. Geneva: World Health Organization.

LaFortune, K. A., & Carpenter, B. N. (1998). Custody evaluations: A survey of mental health professionals. *Behavioral Sciences and the Law, 16*, 201–224.

Maccoby, E. E., & Mnookin, R. H. (1992). *Dividing the child: Social and legal dilemmas of custody*. Cambridge, MA: Harvard University Press.

Melton, G. B., Petrila, J., Poythress, N., & Slobogin, C. (2007). *Psychological evaluations for the courts: A handbook for attorneys and mental health professionals* (3rd ed.). New York: Guilford.

Milner, J. S. (2006). *The Child Abuse Potential Inventory manual* (2nd ed.). Lutz, FL: Psychological Assessment Resources.

Milner, J. S. (2008). Child Abuse Potential (CAP) Inventory. *Encyclopedia of psychology and law* (pp. 69–70). Thousand Oaks, CA: Sage.

Monahan, J. A., Steadman, H. J., Appelbaum, P. S., Grisso, T., Mulvey, E. P., Roth, L. H., Robbins, P. C., Banks, S., & Silver, E. (2005). *Classification of Violence Risk (COVR)*. Lutz, FL: Psychological Assessment Resources.

Morse, S. J. (2002). Uncontrollable urges and irrational people. *Virginia Law Review, 88*, 1025–1078.

Morse, S. J. (2004). Preventive confinement of dangerous offenders. *Journal of Law, Medicine, and Ethics, 32*, 56–72.

Munsinger, H. L., & Karlson, K. W. (1994). Uniform child custody evaluation system. Lutz, FL: Psychological Assessment Resources.

National Clearinghouse on Child Abuse and Neglect Information. (2004). *Child abuse and neglect fatalities: Statistics and interventions*. Retrieved June 2005, from http://nccanch.acf.hhs.gov/pubs/factsheets/fatality.cfm.

National Research Council. (1993). *Understanding child abuse and neglect*. Washington, DC: National Academy of Science Press.

O'Connor v. Donaldson, 422 U.S. 563 (1975).

Quinnell, F. A., & Bow, J. N. (2001). Psychological tests used in child custody evaluations. *Behavioral Science and the Law, 19*, 491–501.

Rogler, L. H. (1999). Methodological sources of cultural insensitivity in mental health research. *American Psychologist, 54*, 424–433.

Schopp, R. F. (2001). *Competence, condemnation, and commitment: An integrated theory of mental health law*. Washington, DC: American Psychological Association.

Sedlak, A. J., & Broadhurst, D. D. (1996). *Third national incidence study of child abuse and neglect*. Washington, DC: U.S. Department of Health and Human Services.

Sirotich, F. (2008). Correlates of crime and violence among persons with mental disorder: An evidence-based review. *Brief Treatment and Crisis Intervention, 8*, 171–194.

Slobogin, C. (2007). *Proving the unprovable: The role of law, science, and speculation in adjudicating culpability and dangerousness.* New York: Oxford University Press.

Sparta, S. N., & Stahl, P. N. (2006). Psychological evaluation for child custody. In S. N. Sparta & G. P. Koocher (Eds.), *Forensic mental health assessment of children and adolescents* (pp. 203–229). New York: Oxford University Press.

Stowman, S. A., & Donohue, B. (2004). Assessing child neglect: A review of standardized measures. *Aggression and Violent Behavior, 10,* 491–512.

Straus, M. A., Sugarman, D., & Giles-Sims, J. (1997). Spanking by parents and subsequent antisocial behavior of children. *Archives of Pediatric and Adolescent Medicine, 151,* 761–767.

Uniform Marriage and Divorce Act, 9A Uniform Laws Annotated, Sec. 316 (1979).

United Nations. (1989). *Convention on the rights of the child.* Adopted and opened for signature, ratification, and accession by General Assembly resolution 44/25 of November 20, 1989.

U.S. Department of Health and Human Services, Administration on Children, Youth and Families. (2008). *Child Maltreatment 2006.* Washington, DC: Author.

Webster, C. D., Douglas, K. S., Eaves, D., & Hart, S. D. (1997). *HCR-20: Assessing risk for violence* (Version 2). Burnaby, British Columbia: Simon Fraser University.

Winick, B. J. (2008). Civil commitment. In B. Cutler (Ed.), *Encyclopedia of psychology and law* (pp. 89–92). Thousand Oaks, CA: Sage.

Chapter 4

FORENSIC TREATMENT

CHAPTER OBJECTIVES

In this chapter, you will become familiar with:

- Competency restoration procedures for individuals deemed incompetent to stand trial
- Treatment and release procedures for defendants found not guilty by reason of insanity
- The treatment of mentally disordered offenders
- The treatment of sexual offenders and offenders considered at high risk for violence
- The treatment of offenders to reduce the risk of general recidivism
- The importance of continuing care into the community after release

This chapter describes the different types of treatments or interventions that are typically used with the forensic population. Since forensic treatment may encompass many different elements, and since there are many different groups included in the forensic population, we begin by categorizing the forensic population into three general groups based on the extent to which mental disorder is involved in their contact with the legal system. While it has been noted in earlier chapters that the term *forensic* applies to both the criminal and civil sides of the legal system, this chapter only discusses psychological treatments for individuals who come into contact with the criminal justice system since the psychological treatments that individuals involved with civil litigation or civil commitment receive are no different than those offered to the general public.

With respect to treatment, the criminal forensic population can be broken down into three broadly defined groups. These groups are determined by the extent to which mental disorder is the target of treatment (intervention). The first group encompasses those individuals for whom mental disorder is the most significant factor in their involvement with the criminal justice system and for whom treatment to target their mental disorder is primary. This group includes those individuals who have been found incompetent to stand trial (recall the discussion of competency from Chapter 2) or not guilty on the basis of mental disorder (recall the discussion of Not Guilty by Reason of Insanity [NGRI] from Chapter 2). The second group encompasses those individuals for whom mental disorder is not necessarily a primary target of treatment but is still considered to be a contributing factor to their involvement with the criminal justice system and thus should receive some focus in treatment. Individuals in this group include **mentally disordered offenders** (MDOs) and sexual offenders or those individuals who are considered to be at high risk for violence and for whom intervention strategies would target risk reduction or risk management. The third group encompasses those individuals for whom mental disorder may play only a minor role in their involvement with the criminal justice system and may or may not be a focus of intervention. This group is comprised mainly of offenders who fall under the purview of the criminal justice system (are either in jail or prison or out on probation or parole) and for whom **recidivism** (re-offending) and rehabilitation is the primary focus of intervention.

MENTAL DISORDER AS A PRIMARY FOCUS OF INTERVENTION

For some individuals who come into contact with the criminal justice system, mental disorder becomes a primary issue in their involvement with this system and, as such, becomes the primary focus of intervention or treatment. There are two types of cases in which this occurs: when defendants are found incompetent to stand trial (or to proceed with some aspect of their case) and when defendants are found not guilty (or not criminally responsible) on account of mental disorder. In these two instances, mental disorder becomes a primary issue in the individual's involvement with the criminal justice system; thus, the focus of intervention is on that mental disorder.

Incompetent Defendants

Recall from the discussion of the assessment of competence from Chapter 2 that individuals who are found incompetent to proceed are then committed for treatment in order to restore their competence. In most instances, this occurs on an inpatient basis whereby the defendant is sent to a forensic facility to undergo treatment for some period of time. Note that although an increasing number of jurisdictions permit outpatient commitment for

> *Mr. Smith, a 37-year-old white male, was charged with unlawful confinement of his 65-year-old mother after he locked her in the bathroom of her apartment and barricaded the door. Mr. Smith was acting "weird" at the time and was agitated and yelling something about needing to keep his mother locked up so she would not bite him and infect him with rabies. Mr. Smith's mother was extremely fearful and suffered a nonfatal heart attack while she was locked in the bathroom. Mr. Smith has a lengthy history of mental illness (schizophrenia, paranoid type) and was found incompetent to stand trial. He was sent for treatment to restore his competency. What type of treatment is most commonly used to restore a defendant to competency? How long does restoration usually take?*

the purposes of restoring competence, this tends to occur less frequently than inpatient commitment.

How Many Incompetent Defendants Are There?

Approximately 60,000 competency evaluations are conducted annually in the United States (Bonnie & Grisso, 2000). Although the proportion of those evaluees who are found incompetent varies by jurisdiction, an average estimated rate of incompetence of about 20% translates into about 12,000 individuals found incompetent to stand trial each year in the United States. The vast majority of these 12,000 defendants will be committed for the purposes of restoring their competence. Pendleton (1980) noted that defendants who are found incompetent to stand trial make up the largest group of psychiatric patients admitted to mental hospitals by way of the criminal justice system.

Treatment of Incompetent Defendants

The most common form of treatment for the restoration of competence involves the administration of psychotropic medication; however, some jurisdictions have established educational treatment programs designed to increase a defendant's understanding of the legal process or individualized treatment programs that confront the problems that hinder a defendant's ability to participate in his or her defense (Bertman et al., 2003). In addition, some jurisdictions have implemented treatment programs specifically targeted toward those defendants with mental retardation who are found incompetent to proceed.

The success of treatment programs for the restoration of competence is variable and dependent upon the type of treatment program and the type of defendant targeted. Anderson and Hewitt (2002) examined treatment programs designed to restore competency in defendants with mental retardation (MR) and found that only 18% of their sample was restored.

These researchers concluded, "for the most part, competency training for defendants with MR might not be that effective" (p. 349). Other researchers and commentators have found similar results and have noted the difficulty in treating a chronic condition such as MR (Daniel & Menninger, 1983; Ellis & Luckasson, 1985).

Treatment programs that target defendants with various other types of mental disorders have met with more success in that larger proportions of the defendants are restored to competency. However, it is not clear that individualized treatment programs that target specific underlying deficits (such as the particular defendant's understanding and appreciation of his or her charges and their consequences) for each defendant are any more effective than educational programs that teach defendants about their legal rights (Bertman et al., 2003). The research findings suggest that successful restoration is related to how well the defendant responds to psychotropic medications administered to alleviate the symptoms of the mental disorder.

As a general statement, most incompetent defendants are restored to competency within six months and the vast majority achieve competence within a one-year period. An examination of those conditions associated with a greater inability to be restored to competence show that there are two groups for whom restoration is difficult. The first group is comprised of defendants whose incompetence stems from irremediable cognitive disorders, such as mental retardation, whereas the second group is comprised of defendants who are chronically psychotic and who have a history of lengthy inpatient hospitalizations (Mossman, 2007).

One final note on competence restoration: In comparison to the literature and research on other aspects of competency, such as the assessment of competence, there is a serious lack of literature and research on the treatment or restoration of competence.

Defendants Found Not Guilty by Reason of Insanity

Recall from the discussion of insanity in Chapter 2 that this defense is rarely used and even more rarely successful (although public perception is that it is used often and mostly successfully). Research examining the characteristics of **insanity acquittees** (people who have successfully used an insanity defense) shows that this group is mainly "male, between the ages of 20 and 29, unmarried, unemployed, minimally educated, has been acquitted for a violent offense and diagnosed with a major mental illness, and has had prior contact with both the criminal and mental health systems" (Lymburner & Roesch, 1999, p. 215).

> *Mr. Cook, a 29-year-old white male with a lengthy history of schizophrenia, was charged with trespassing and assault on a police officer after he punched a police officer who was attempting to have Mr. Cook leave the premises of a local grocery store after the grocery store owner had complained about Mr. Cook's loitering. The arresting police officer describes Mr. Cook as "agitated and confused." Mr. Cook was initially found incompetent to stand trial, sent for treatment, and was restored to competency within four months. Mr. Cook was subsequently found Not Guilty by Reason of Insanity at trial. What will happen to Mr. Cook after being found NGRI? Will he be locked up? How long will he be detained? What criteria will be used to determine when he will be released?*

After Acquittal

What happens to an insanity acquittee after he (or she) is acquitted varies according to jurisdiction. In general, there are three things that may happen:

1. The individual may be unconditionally released whereby he or she is allowed to leave the court and go home.
2. The individual may be conditionally released whereby he or she is permitted to live in the community but under certain conditions.
3. The individual may be committed to a mental health facility for treatment.

The majority of insanity acquittees are committed to public state mental health or forensic facilities for extensive evaluation and treatment for their mental illness. It is rare that an individual is simply let go (unconditionally released) upon acquittal.

Criteria for Detention and Release

In general, two criteria are used to determine the detention and/or release of an insanity acquittee: mental illness and dangerousness. That is, individuals who have a mental illness and who are considered to be dangerous to themselves or others are detained and treated until they are no longer mentally ill and dangerous. These two criteria are evaluated periodically for each insanity acquittee throughout detention. Once an insanity acquittee is no longer considered to be mentally ill or dangerous, he or she is usually conditionally discharged and is permitted to live in the community under certain conditions. Common conditions usually include taking prescribed medications regularly, being evaluated by a mental health professional periodically, and not carrying a weapon.

Length of Confinement

Research examining the length of confinement of insanity acquittees appears to indicate that there is a relation between the length of confinement and the severity of the crime for which the individual was acquitted. Silver (1995) examined data from a large, multistate study of the insanity defense and found that offense seriousness was a stronger predictor of length of confinement than was mental disorder in persons found NGRI. In addition, Silver (1995) found that persons who raised an insanity defense but who were found guilty (unsuccessful insanity defendants) were more likely to be released without ever being confined than were persons who were found NGRI. Silver concluded that length of confinement and release decisions for insanity acquittees appears to reflect a punishment model wherein punishment seems to be a higher priority than treatment for these individuals.

Research comparing the lengths of confinement for insanity acquittees with their matched civilly committed counterparts (individuals committed to mental hospitals who were matched to the insanity acquittees in terms of their mental illness) shows that insanity acquittees spend longer in confinement even though they appear to show better functioning in terms of their personal care skills and social acceptability and lower rates of aggressiveness (Shah, Greenberg, & Convit, 1994). The actual amount of time that insanity acquittees spend in confinement varies widely according to jurisdiction. In some jurisdictions, insanity acquittees spend more time in confinement than they would have had they been found guilty of the same offense whereas in other jurisdictions they spend less time (Lymburner & Roesch, 1999).

Conditional Release

Research examining the rates of conditional release of insanity acquittees shows wide variation across jurisdictions in terms of the proportions of insanity acquittees who are released as well as the types of variables or characteristics related to conditional release (Callahan & Silver, 1998a). An investigation of the factors associated with revocation of conditional release revealed that minority status, substance abuse diagnosis, and a prior criminal history were predictive of having a conditional release revoked (Monson, Gunnin, Fogel, & Kyle, 2001). Those factors that have been found to be associated with the successful maintenance of conditional release include being white, married, and employed (Callahan & Silver, 1998b).

Recidivism and Rehospitalization

Research examining recidivism and rehospitalization of insanity acquittees shows, not surprisingly, wide variation depending upon jurisdiction.

Lymburner and Roesch (1999) concluded that "rearrest rates during conditional release ranged from 2% to 16%, with these numbers increasing substantially for longer-term follow-up periods (i.e., 42–56%) (p. 230). Heilbrun and Griffin (1993) determined that rehospitalization rates for insanity acquittees on conditional release also varied widely, ranging from 11% to 78% (but the majority fell between 11% and 40%).

Treatment Issues for Insanity Acquittees

Salekin and Rogers (2001) provided a review of treatment issues for insanity acquittees and, as might be expected, inpatient treatment of insanity acquittees varies by treatment facility. Salekin and Rogers noted that the most predominant diagnostic category for insanity acquittees is psychotic disorders, with personality disorders being the second most frequent diagnostic category. Substance abuse disorders are also a common co-occurrence for these individuals. Thus, a primary focus of inpatient treatment programs is the reduction or management of psychotic symptomatology (such as delusions or hallucinations), most commonly through the use of psychotropic medications. In addition to the administration of medication and specialized treatment programs, such as **dialectical behavior therapy**, targeting personality disorders in this group of individuals have been found to be effective in the management of the symptoms associated with personality disorders (Vitacco & Van Rybroek, 2006).

Of some concern is the apparent focus on primary disorders to the neglect of secondary or co-occurring disorders such as substance abuse. Salekin and Rogers (2001) argue that NGRI patients with substance abuse disorders would benefit maximally from treatment programs that address both their primary disorders as well as their substance abuse disorders. Programs such as **relapse prevention training** or **cognitive-behavioral therapy** have been effective in treating substance abuse.

Rogers (1986) noted that, while mood disorders such as depression are not commonly the primary diagnosis for an NGRI acquittee, a substantial proportion of these individuals experience symptoms of mood disorders at the time of the offense. In addition, Rogers also noted that a substantial proportion of insane defendants experienced severe or pervasive anxiety. Thus, treatment programs that target symptoms such as anxiety and depression in insanity acquittees appear appropriate. In addition to treatments that target symptoms of mental disorder, **life skills training**, **social skills training**, and the management of anger, aggression, and violence appear to have a place in the treatment of insanity acquittees (Salekin & Rogers, 2001).

MENTAL DISORDER AS A SECONDARY FOCUS OF INTERVENTION

The second group of offenders that we discuss includes those individuals for whom mental illness is not necessarily a primary factor in their involvement with the criminal justice system, but rather, is a factor nonetheless and thus should receive some focus in treatment. This group includes offenders who have mental illnesses, sometimes referred to as *mentally disordered offenders* (MDOs), as well as offenders for whom mental disorder is relevant to their offense behavior, such as sexual offenders or offenders who are at high risk for violence. Although the term *MDO* can also encompass those individuals who are found incompetent to stand trial and those who have been acquitted on account of insanity, we have discussed these groups already and so eliminate them from our discussion here.

Mentally Disordered Offenders

In this section, we work from the premise that the primary emphasis of treatment is the offender's criminal behavior; the offender's mental disorder is a secondary focus of treatment. However, in many cases treatment programs focus on both mental disorder and criminal behavior and so attempts to tease these two foci apart are unnecessary.

Prevalence of Mental Illness in Jails and Prisons

There is considerable variation in estimates of the proportion of inmates in jails and prisons for whom mental disorder is an issue. Depending upon the type of institution (jail or prison; see distinction in the next section), the definitions of mental disorder used (whether estimates include personality disorders and substance use disorders), whether the institution draws inmates from rural, urban, or suburban areas, and the sampling procedures used (how estimates of mental illness are calculated), rates of mental illness in the offender population can range from less than 5% to over 60% (Mobley, 2006).

A number of conclusions can be drawn from a review of studies investigating the prevalence of mental illness in jails and prisons. First, there are a large number of persons in jails and prisons with significant mental disorders. Substantial numbers of inmates (perhaps as many as 10%) suffer from psychotic disorders and an even greater proportion (estimates indicate between 15% and 40%) suffers from depression, anxiety, or other moderate mental illnesses. Larger yet is the proportion that suffers from substance use disorders or personality disorders (estimated at up to 90%

of inmates) (Ogloff, Roesch, & Hart, 1994). Second, these disorders cause significant impairment in inmates' social functioning, both within and outside of the institution. Finally, the rates of mental illness in correctional populations are significantly higher than the rates in the general population from comparable socioeconomic backgrounds (Ogloff et al., 1994; Roesch, Ogloff, Zapf, Hart, & Otto, 1998). Thus, what is clear is that mental illness is a significant issue for some proportion of offenders housed in jails and prisons.

The Distinction Between Jails and Prisons

An important distinction exists between jails and prisons in terms of the populations that they serve as well as the types of treatments that they are able to offer inmates. Jails are short-term facilities that house offenders who have been charged, but not yet convicted, of a crime, and thus are at the pretrial stage of proceedings. In addition to pretrial inmates, jails may also house offenders who have been convicted but sentenced to relatively short periods of incarceration (typically one year or less). Prisons house inmates who have been convicted of a crime and for whom a sentence of greater than one year has been received. Thus, it is generally the case that a greater proportion of mentally ill offenders will be found in jails as compared to prisons and that fewer treatment options are available in jails since offenders typically have shorter stays and are less able to engage in longer-term treatments even if they were to be offered.

Mental Health Services in Jails and Prisons

Jails have typically provided little in the way of mental health services. A national survey of jail mental health services found that the areas of emphasis in jails were the identification of problems (screening and evaluating offenders for mental illness, suicide risk, or institutional adjustment problems) and the dispensing of medication; drug or alcohol services were available in the majority of jails but psychological counseling was available in less than one-half of the jails surveyed (Steadman, McCarty, & Morrissey, 1989). The type of mental health services available in prisons varies considerably. Similar to jails, the most common form of treatment offered in prisons is the administration of psychotropic medication; however, other forms of therapy, such as behavioral or cognitive-behavioral treatments, are also popular (Gudjonson, 1990).

Many states have either special prisons, which function essentially as maximum-security hospitals, or special sections of regular prisons specifically targeted to the needs of MDOs. These facilities generally house offenders who have the most serious and chronic mental disorders and employ staff who have been specifically trained to deal with the special

needs of these offenders (in some states, the state mental hospital or forensic facility may be used to house these types of offenders). Thus, offenders
who have the most serious types of mental disorders are housed in these
special facilities whereas offenders who have less severe mental illnesses
are housed with the rest of the general prison population. Offenders who
experience an intensification of their mental illness (e.g., offenders
who become psychotic) may be transferred to one of these special facilities for treatment until their symptoms are controlled, at which time they
may be transferred back.

Goals of Treatment

Although the specific goals of treatment may vary by facility or by
offender, in general the two most common treatment goals include the
reduction of the symptoms of mental illness and the reduction of criminal recidivism. Various programs and interventions have been developed
in an attempt to accomplish these goals. The programs and interventions
offered vary by facility (prison hospital, special MDO prison ward, regular prison ward) and are dependent upon the availability of treatment staff
(psychologists, psychiatrists, social workers, counselors), which also varies
by facility. Rice and Harris (1997) identified seven areas that are generally
targeted in the treatment of MDOs, including: active psychotic symptoms,
aggression and problems of institutional adjustment, criminal propensity,
depression, life skills deficits, social withdrawal, and substance abuse.

Treatment Programs for MDOs

A review of treatment programs and interventions for MDOs has identified
interventions that appear to be most promising in each of the seven aforementioned areas (Rice & Harris, 1997). In general, behaviorally oriented
treatments (to change an offender's behavior), skills training (to improve
an offender's social skills and life skills), and pharmacological treatment
(to reduce an offender's mental illness symptoms through the use of psychotropic medications) have been shown to be effective for reducing active
psychotic symptoms, for reducing aggression and increasing institutional
adjustment, and for reducing depression (Rice & Harris, 1997). In addition, behaviorally oriented treatments (including cognitive-behavioral therapy) and skills training (life skills and social skills) have been shown to
be effective for reducing criminal propensity, substance abuse, social withdrawal, and life skills deficits (Rice & Harris, 1997).

As is the case with competency to stand trial and insanity, there are few
empirical studies of the effectiveness of various types of treatments for
MDOs. This is an area that is ripe for development in terms of determining
the effectiveness of those treatment programs that currently exist as well as

developing alternative treatment programs. What seems clear is that effective treatment programs for MDOs must target both the symptoms of mental disorder as well as the criminal behavior of the offender.

Sexual Offenders

Sexual offenders constitute only a small proportion of the total number of MDOs; however, various treatment programs have targeted the special needs of this group of offenders. In general, treatment programs for sexual offenders fall into three different categories: nonbehavioral psychotherapy, pharmacological, and behavioral or cognitive-behavioral therapy (Rice & Harris, 1997).

Treatment Programs for Sexual Offenders

A review of the research and literature on these three types of programs indicates that there is little empirical support for the effectiveness of nonbehavioral psychotherapeutic interventions (Rice & Harris, 1997). Pharmacotherapy, the use of drugs as therapy, has proven effective for reducing sex drive in sexual offenders. However, the link between reduced sex drive and reduced sexual recidivism is less clear. Some authors have speculated that offenders who voluntarily accept drugs to reduce their sex drive are also those who are highly motivated for treatment and thus reduced recidivism in this group may be accounted for by either drug therapy, or motivation, or perhaps both (Rice & Harris, 1997).

By far, the most promising treatments for sexual offenders are behavioral or cognitive-behavioral in nature and have as their goal the normalization of deviant sexual preferences. In addition, it appears that training in social competence is a key component of effective treatment programs (Rice & Harris, 1997).

One of the most important aspects in the treatment of sexual offenders is the monitoring and case management of these offenders once they leave the institution and become integrated back into the community. (Case management and community re-integration are discussed in more detail in the next section.) For many offenders, but especially for sexual offenders, case management and community follow-up is an important component of their continued treatment and success.

Offenders at High Risk for Violence

Examination of the factors that are related to high risk for violence indicates that certain clinical characteristics are important and should be a focus in the treatment and risk management of these offenders. Risk for violence has been studied in both offender groups as well as in nonoffender community samples and some differences between these two groups have been found.

Mental Disorder and Violence

In nonoffender community samples, research suggests that there is a positive relation between some symptoms of mental illness and violent behavior. For example, 10,000 American adults were surveyed as part of the National Institute of Mental Health's Epidemiological Catchment Area study and results indicated that persons who met criteria for certain serious mental disorders (schizophrenia, major depression, mania, or bipolar disorder) were six times more likely to self-report violent behavior within the past year than non-MDOs (Swanson, Holzer, Ganju, & Jono, 1990). In addition, persons who met criteria for substance abuse or dependence were even more likely to self-report being violent. Similarly, researchers in the MacArthur study of mental disorder and violence found that the presence of a co-occurring diagnosis of substance abuse or dependence to be a significant factor for violence (Monahan et al., 2001). Link, Andrews, and Cullen (1992) found a positive relationship between psychotic symptoms and violence in a nonoffender sample such that the greater the number of psychotic symptoms a person endorsed experiencing, the greater the number of self-reported recent violent acts. Thus, in nonoffender samples, it appears that psychotic symptoms and substance abuse or dependence are important risk factors for violence.

In research that examines samples of criminal offenders, however, it appears that this link between psychotic symptoms and violence becomes less clear (Rice & Harris, 1997). Instead, diagnoses of personality disorders (especially **antisocial personality disorder** and **psychopathy**) and substance abuse have been linked to violent behavior (Harris, Rice, & Cormier, 1991). It is important to note, however, that in the studies of MDOs, it is likely that the psychotic offenders were on medication and thus had their psychoses under control (as it would be unlikely that a psychotic offender would be released without medication). Therefore, this may explain the lack of a relation between psychotic symptoms and violence in these groups (Rice & Harris, 1997). Thus, it appears that antisocial personality disorder, psychopathy, and substance abuse are important risk factors for violence in offender samples. It is therefore reasonable to assume that treatment programs and programs for managing risk in offenders should focus on these features.

Treatment of Violent Offenders

The most effective treatment programs are those that target the specific needs of the particular offender. Promising treatment programs for targeting personality disorders and substance abuse include dialectical behavior therapy and relapse prevention training, respectively. Harris and Rice (1994) examined the treatment literature and offered the following three guidelines for the treatment of violent offenders:

1. *Risk.* More intensive services should be provided to higher-risk cases.
2. *Needs.* Service should target criminogenic needs; that is, personal characteristics that contribute to the commission of crime. Known criminogenic targets include changing antisocial attitudes, promoting familial affection and supervision, increasing self-control, replacing lying and aggression with prosocial skills, reducing substance abuse, and improving interpersonal and vocational skills. Inappropriate targets include self-esteem, increasing the cohesiveness of antisocial peer groups, and focusing on intrapsychic forces not empirically linked with criminality.
3. *Style of treatment.* Behavioral or cognitive-behavioral treatments consistently produce larger treatment effects than other styles of treatment (nondirective, punitive, insight-oriented, psychodynamic, evocative and relationship-dependent therapies). There is no guarantee that these same principles apply to treatment for violent (as opposed to general criminal) behavior. However, in the absence of evidence to the contrary, we propose that these principles be applied in selecting treatments for violent clients (p. 472).

As has been mentioned in each of the earlier sections of this chapter, there is limited research on the effectiveness of treatment programs and interventions for offenders at high risk for violence. More research on the assessment of violence risk and treatment or management is needed.

Difficulties in Implementing Effective Treatment Programs

In general, it appears that we have come to a point in each of the aforementioned areas (competency, insanity, MDOs, sexual offenders, and offenders at high risk for violence) where the focus in the future needs to be on designing, implementing, and evaluating treatment programs. Of course, this is a statement that is easier to make than to fulfill. Numerous obstacles exist to successfully implementing effective treatment programs, including the fact that the political climate in the United States has become more focused on the punishment of offenders than on their rehabilitation. Another important obstacle is the difficulty of attempting to implement behaviorally oriented treatment programs in institutions that are not run in a behaviorally oriented way. That is, the treatment literature to date has indicated that the most effective treatments are those that are behavioral in nature but "the idea that prisons should provide treatment is quite foreign to most staff in correctional institutions. It is difficult to retrain frontline medical or security staff to take an approach that emphasizes a behavioral model of patients' problems, gives patients an active role in their own recovery, and promotes skills training and contingency management as the primary treatment options" (Rice & Harris, 1994, p. 162).

RECIDIVISM AND REHABILITATION AS THE FOCUS OF INTERVENTION

The third group of offenders that we discuss includes those for whom mental illness is not necessarily a significant factor in their involvement with the criminal justice system but for whom symptoms of mental illness may be present and may become a focus of treatment. As reported, many offenders housed in jails and prisons meet criteria for mental disorders and an even greater proportion experience some symptoms of mental disorder (especially anxiety or depression) although they may not necessarily meet diagnostic criteria for a particular disorder. In general, treatment programs for those offenders who are not designated as MDOs focus on general recidivism rather than on mental disorder or the symptoms of mental disorder with the exception of substance abuse treatment programs which, technically, focus on issues related to mental disorder, since substance abuse and dependence are relevant diagnostic categories. Thus, our discussion in this section focuses on treatment for general criminal recidivism and substance abuse.

General Recidivism and Rehabilitation

Until the 1970s, the preeminent philosophy in corrections was the rehabilitation, rather than punishment, of offenders. Beginning in the mid-1970s, however, this began to change. More and more the main philosophy in the United States regarding offenders began to focus on punishment rather than their rehabilitation. Martinson (1974) analyzed the outcomes of 231 treatment studies of offenders and arrived at the conclusion that "nothing works." This "nothing works" conclusion served, over time, to focus treatment providers and researchers, once again, on the issue of offender treatment and rehabilitation. Since that time, much research has focused on the factors that make for successful rehabilitation of offenders.

Treatment Programs for Recidivism

In general, successful rehabilitation refers to a decrease in recidivism (the likelihood that an offender will commit crime in the future). Gendreau, Coggin, French, and Smith (2006) examined the vast literature on offender rehabilitation and concluded that a number of variables are associated with successful offender treatment programs. These researchers concluded that treatment programs that are behavioral in nature, that target the crimino-genic needs of the offender, and that target the most high-risk offenders are the most successful.

Behavioral treatment programs focus on the specific behaviors of the offender in an attempt to help offenders recognize the sequence of events or patterns that lead up to their criminal behavior. The pattern or sequence of events might include becoming stressed out, not talking about this stress but, rather, drinking alcohol, then becoming intoxicated and thus disinhib-ited, which in turn leads to fighting with his or her spouse, which in turn leads to an assault charge. Awareness of this pattern may assist the offender in making changes to his or her typical behaviors thus leading to a reduced probability that this pattern of behaviors will lead to violence in the future. In addition to recognizing patterns of behavior, treatment programs that are behavioral in nature encourage the offender to determine more appropriate actions that can be substituted for their typical pattern of responding. For instance, teaching the aforementioned spousal assaulter that he or she could call a friend who is a good source of social support when he or she becomes stressed out, rather than turning to alcohol, may serve to prevent the typical pattern of behavior that results in an assault charge.

Treatment programs that target the criminogenic needs of the offender focus on changeable variables such as antisocial attitudes and thought pat-terns, procriminal associates, and personality factors such as poor impulse control and poor self-control (Gendreau et al., 2006). Treatment programs that help offenders learn to become more self-controlled, to change their atti-tudes and thought patterns to become more prosocial, and to associate with noncriminal individuals are more effective in reducing the probability that the individual will commit crime in the future.

Finally, programs that target those offenders who are at the highest risk to re-offend are more effective. In addition to targeting those at the highest levels of risk, treatment programs that match treatment providers to offend-ers on the basis of such characteristics as ability to relate and communicate are most effective. For example, matching offenders with lower IQs to treat-ment providers who are able to relate to the more concrete style of thinking of these offenders will be more effective than having treatment providers who are more abstract and conduct insight-oriented work with low IQ individuals.

Substance Abuse

Substance use is a problem for a large proportion of criminal offenders and is often a contributing factor to criminal behavior. The vast majority of jails and prisons offer substance abuse treatment programs of some sort; however, the success of these programs is variable.

Treatment Programs for Substance Abuse

A large-scale examination by Miller and colleagues (1995) of the available treatment approaches for alcohol abuse indicated that the treatment approaches with the most empirical support primarily include behavioral and cognitive-behavioral approaches, including behavioral contracting, social skills training, behaviorally oriented therapy, and relapse prevention. Those treatments that had the least empirical support included Alcoholics Anonymous (AA), education, lectures, and nonbehavioral therapies (Miller et al., 1995). Unfortunately, as Miller and colleagues have pointed out, those treatments that have the least empirical support (such as AA) are those that are the most frequently used in North America.

Relapse prevention is a treatment approach that was originally developed as a means of dealing with substance abuse and other addictive disorders and includes both behavioral skills training procedures and cognitive techniques. This treatment approach has shown success when individuals can maintain behavior change and control addictive behaviors. More recently, relapse prevention has been used in the treatment of sex offenders and other impulsive behaviors, such as domestic violence, and might also be successful in the treatment of both the psychiatric symptoms and criminogenic needs of MDOs (Rice & Harris, 1997). What appears to set relapse prevention approaches apart from other treatment programs is its strong emphasis on continued monitoring, social support, and general lifestyle change for the successful maintenance of the desired behavioral changes. Follow-up and monitoring are crucial components of any successful treatment program.

COMMUNITY-BASED TREATMENT

Up to this point, the discussion of forensic treatment has focused on what occurs in some type of inpatient or institutional setting; however, forensic treatment extends into the community and such settings as outpatient clinics, halfway houses, and crisis stabilization units. With the exception of those offenders who have been sentenced to serve life sentences without the possibility of parole, eventually every offender gets released back into the community. For some, the criminal justice system maintains some aspect of control over their lives for some period of time through **parole** or **probation**. Successful reintegration into the community depends heavily on community-based treatment and monitoring.

Three key features for the successful monitoring and treatment of individuals on parole or probation include:

1. Centralized responsibility wherein one decision maker or body has primary authority over and responsibility for these individuals.
2. A uniform system of treatment and supervision.
3. A network of community services.
   (Heilbrun & Griffin, 1999)

Heilbrun and Griffin (1999) underscore the "importance of integrating decision making, treatment, and treatment compliance-enhancing strategies, such as careful monitoring" (p. 261).

Perhaps the most important component of any treatment program is the follow-up or monitoring of program completers. Intensive follow-up and monitoring appear to be crucial for the maintenance of behavior change. Thus, supporting MDOs and non-MDOs in making the transition from institution to community becomes an important key to success. Effective monitoring is important for improving treatment compliance and treatment outcomes. In addition, case management and communication between the various parties involved in the mental health and criminal justice systems is important to the treatment and success of offenders and MDOs. Generally, it will be the case manager or probation officer who is responsible for coordinating communication among the courts, the offender, and the various other parties involved in the mental health and criminal justice systems. Monitoring of treatment compliance and compliance with the conditions of release is another important role that falls to the case manager or probation officer.

The existing treatment literature is clear that the most effective treatment is that which occurs in the least restrictive environment, preferably in the community (Andrews et al., 1990). Treating individuals in the least restrictive environment—the community—often calls into play a delicate balance among the rights of the individual, the need for treatment, and the safety of the community (Heilbrun & Griffin, 1999). Heilbrun and Griffin (1999) highlight the importance of promoting health care adherence with clients/offenders who are to be treated in the community. Better adherence to treatment can often be accomplished by developing a contract with the client/offender that contains very clear conditions to which the client/offender must adhere as well as the consequences for violating these conditions.

Frequent components of such a contract include medication compliance, attendance at scheduled sessions with therapists and case managers, abstinence from alcohol and drug use (and blood or urine screening, if indicated, to monitor adherence), disallowance of weapons possession, housing (including where the person will live, applicable rent and how it will be paid, adherence to housing rules), and the consequences for violating conditions. More specific conditions—no contact with the victim, employment, specialized forms of treatment and monitoring, and transportation—can be included as needed. (p. 267)

In addition, it is often useful to include family members in these agreements if they are able and willing because their involvement serves to increase client/offender compliance.

SUMMARY

Perhaps the most common theme throughout this chapter is that there is far less research and commentary on the treatment of various types of offenders and on what makes an effective treatment program than there is on other related areas such as the assessment of offenders. Research on the development and implementation of effective treatment programs is certain to be an important area of focus for the future.

Forensic treatment, as discussed in this chapter, can encompass the treatment of both MDOs and non-MDOs; however, the focus of treatment for these various groups of offenders varies somewhat. The primary focus of treatment for offenders who have been found incompetent to stand trial or not guilty on account of mental disorder (by reason of insanity) is the reduction of the symptoms of mental disorder. To accomplish this goal, the administration of psychotropic medication appears to be a common and relatively effective treatment option.

For incarcerated MDOs, including sexual offenders and offenders at high risk for violence, treatment goals include the reduction of the symptoms of mental illness as well as the reduction of future criminal behavior. It appears that behaviorally oriented treatment programs show the highest levels of promise and effectiveness. This is also true for the treatment of general recidivism in non-MDOs and for the treatment of substance abuse, which is a common problem in all offender populations.

Finally, perhaps one of the most important keys to successful treatment programs lies in the continuity of care in the transition from the institution to the community. It is important that treatment services be provided in the community and crucial that released offenders are able to access these services.

SUGGESTED READINGS

Ashford, J. B., Sales, B. D., & Reid, W. H. (2001). *Treating adult and juvenile offenders with special needs*. Washington, DC: American Psychological Association.

Marlatt, G. A., & Gordon, J. R. (1985). *Relapse prevention: Maintenance strategies in the treatment of addictive behaviors*. New York: Guilford.

National Institute on Drug Abuse Website on the Treatment of Offenders. Accessed at: http://www.nida.nih.gov/drugpages/CJfactsheet.html.

Rice, M. E., & Harris, G. T. (1997). The treatment of mentally disordered offenders. *Psychology, Public Policy, and Law, 1*, 126–183.

Salekin, R. T., & Rogers, R. (2001). Treating patients found not guilty by reason of insanity. In J. B. Ashford, B. D. Sales, & W. H. Reid (Eds.), *Treating adult and juvenile offenders with special needs* (pp. 171–195). Washington, DC: American Psychological Association.

Steadman, H. J., McCarty, D. W., & Morrissey, J. P. (1989). *The mentally ill in jail: Planning for essential services*. New York: Guilford.

KEY TERMS

- *Antisocial personality disorder*
- *Cognitive-behavioral therapy*
- *Dialectical behavior therapy*
- *Insanity acquittee*
- *Life skills training*
- *Mentally disordered offender (MDO)*
- *Parole*
- *Probation*
- *Psychopathy*
- *Relapse prevention training*
- *Recidivism*
- *Social skills training*

References ───────────────────────────

Anderson, S. D., & Hewitt, J. (2002). The effect of competency restoration training on defendants with mental retardation found not competent to proceed. *Law and Human Behavior, 26*, 343–351.

Andrews, D. D., Zinger, I., Hoge, R. D., Bonta, J., Gendreau, P., & Cullen, F. T. (1990). Does correctional treatment work? A clinically relevant and psychologically informed meta-analysis. *Criminology, 28*, 369–404.

Bertman, L. J., Thompson, J. W., Jr., Waters, W. F., Estupinan-Kane, L., Martin, J. A., & Russell, L. (2003). Effect of an individualized treatment protocol on restoration of competency in pretrial forensic inpatients. *Journal of the American Academy of Psychiatry and Law, 31*, 27–35.

Bonnie, R. J., & Grisso, T. (2000). Adjudicative competence and youthful offenders. In T. Grisso & R. G. Schwartz (Eds.), *Youth on trial: A developmental perspective on criminal justice* (pp. 73–103). Chicago, IL: University of Chicago Press.

Callahan, L., A., & Silver, E. (1998a). Factors associated with the conditional release of persons acquitted by reason of insanity: A decision tree approach. *Law and Human Behavior, 22*, 147–163.

Callahan, L. A., & Silver, E. (1998b). Revocation of conditional release: A comparison of individual and program characteristics across four U.S. states. *International Journal of Law and Psychiatry, 21*, 177–186.

Daniel, A. E., & Menninger, K. (1983). Mentally retarded defendants: Competency and criminal responsibility. *American Journal of Forensic Psychiatry, 4*, 145–156.

Ellis, J. W., & Luckasson, R. A. (1985). Mentally retarded criminal defendants. *George Washington Law Review, 53*, 414–493.

Gendreau, P., Coggin, C., French, S., & Smith, P. (2006). Practicing psychology in correctional settings. In I. B. Weiner & A. K. Hess (Eds.), *The handbook of forensic psychology* (3rd ed., pp. 722–750). Hoboken, NJ: Wiley.

Gudjonson, G. H. (1990). Psychological treatment for the mentally ill offender. *Issues in Criminal Legal Psychology, 16*, 15–21.

Harris, G. T., & Rice, M. E. (1994). The violent patient. In M. Hersen & R. T. Ammerman (Eds.), *Handbook of prescriptive treatments for adults* (pp. 463–486). New York: Plenum.

Harris, G. T., Rice, M. E., & Cormier, C. A. (1991). Psychopathy and violent recidivism. *Law and Human Behavior, 15*, 625–637.

Heilbrun, K., & Griffin, P. A. (1993). Community-based forensic treatment of insanity acquittees. *International Journal of Law and Psychiatry, 16*, 133–150.

Heilbrun, K., & Griffin, P. A. (1999). Forensic treatment: A review of programs and research. In R. Roesch, S. D. Hart, & J. R. P. Ogloff (Eds.), *Psychology and law: The state of the discipline* (pp. 241–274). New York: Kluwer/Plenum.

Link, B. G., Andrews, H., & Cullen, F. T. (1992). The violent and illegal behavior of mental patients reconsidered. *American Sociological Review, 57*, 275–292.

Lymburner, J. A., & Roesch, R. (1999). The insanity defense: Five years of research (1993–1997). *International Journal of Law and Psychiatry, 22*, 213–240.

Martinson, R. (1974). What works? Questions and answers about prison reform. *The Public Interest, 35*, 22–54.

Miller, W. R., Brown, J. M., Simpson, T. L., Handmaker, N. S., Bien, T. H., Luckie, L. F., Montgomery, H. A., Hester, R. K., & Tonigan, J. S. (1995). What works: A methodological analysis of the alcohol treatment outcome literature. In R. K. Hester & W. R. Miller (Eds.), *Handbook of alcoholism treatment approaches* (2nd ed., pp. 12–44). Toronto, ON: Allyn & Bacon.

Mobley, M. J. (2006). Psychotherapy with criminal offenders. In I. B Weiner & A. K. Hess (Eds.), *The handbook of forensic psychology* (3rd ed., pp. 751–789). Hoboken, NJ: Wiley.

Monahan, J., Steadman, H. J., Silver, E., Appelbaum, P. S., Robbins, P. C., Mulvey, E. P., Roth, L. H., Grisso, T., & Banks, S. (2001). *Rethinking risk assessment: The MacArthur study of mental disorder and violence.* New York: Oxford.

Monson, C. M., Gunnin, D. D., Fogel, M. H., & Kyle, L. L. (2001). Stopping (or slowing) the revolving door: Factors related to NGRI acquittees' maintenance of a conditional release. *Law and Human Behavior, 25*, 257–267.

Mossman, D. (2007). Predicting restorability of incompetent criminal defendants. *Journal of the American Academy of Psychiatry and Law, 35*, 34–43.

Ogloff, J. R. P., Roesch, R., & Hart, S. D. (1994). Mental health services in jails and prisons: Legal, clinical, and policy issues. *Law and Psychology Review, 18*, 109–136.

Pendleton L. (1980). Treatment of persons found incompetent to stand trial. *American Journal of Psychiatry, 137*, 1098–1100.

Rice, M. E., & Harris, G. T. (1997). The treatment of mentally disordered offenders. *Psychology, Public Policy, and Law, 1*, 126–183.

Roesch, R., Ogloff, J. R. P., Zapf, P. A., Hart, S. D., & Otto, R. K. (1998). Jail and prison inmates. In A. S. Bellack & M. Hersen (Series Eds.) and N. N. Singh (Vol. Ed.), *Comprehensive clinical psychology: Vol. 9. Application in diverse populations.* New York: Elsevier.

Rogers, R. (1986). *Conducting insanity evaluations.* New York: Van Nostrand Reinhold.

Salekin, R. T., & Rogers, R. (2001). Treating patients found not guilty by reason of insanity. In J. B. Ashford, B. D. Sales, & W. H. Reid (Eds.), *Treating adult and juvenile offenders with special needs* (pp. 171–195). Washington, DC: American Psychological Association.

Shah, P. J., Greenberg, W. M., & Convit, A. (1994). Hospitalized insanity acquittees' level of functioning. *Bulletin of the American Academy of Psychiatry and Law, 22*, 85–93.

Silver, E. (1995). Punishment or treatment? Comparing the lengths of confinement of successful and unsuccessful insanity defendants. *Law and Human Behavior, 19*, 375–388.

Steadman, H. J., McCarty, D. W., & Morrissey, J. P. (1989). *The mentally ill in jail: Planning for essential services.* New York: Guilford.

Swanson, J. W., Holzer, C. E., Ganju, V. K., & Jono, R. T. (1990). Violence and psychiatric disorder in the community: Evidence from the epidemiological catchment area surveys. *Hospital and Community Psychiatry, 41*, 761–770.

Vitacco, M. J., & Van Rybroek, G. J. (2006). Treating insanity acquittees with personality disorders: Implementing dialectical behavior therapy in a forensic hospital. *Journal of Forensic Psychology Practice, 6*, 1–16.

Chapter 5

EYEWITNESS IDENTIFICATION

<table>
<tr><td colspan="2" align="center">**CHAPTER OBJECTIVES**</td></tr>
<tr><td colspan="2">

In this chapter, you will become familiar with:

- Witness characteristics that may impact accurate eyewitness identification
- Situational characteristics that may impact accurate eyewitness identification
- Postevent factors that may limit the accuracy of eyewitness identifications
- The limitations of children as eyewitnesses
- The special accommodations given to child victims asked to testify as witnesses
- Investigation procedures that serve to reduce the likelihood of mistaken eyewitness identifications
- Courtroom procedures that serve to safeguard against convicting an innocent person on the basis of mistaken eyewitness identification

</td></tr>
</table>

Eyewitness identification and subsequent eyewitness testimony are important and integral components of our criminal justice system. The difference between an acquittal and a conviction can rest on the testimony of an eyewitness. Eyewitness testimony is often some of the most compelling evidence offered in a trial. Loftus (1984) examined 347 cases for which the only evidence presented was eyewitness testimony and found that the defendant was convicted in three-quarters of the cases. In half of those cases of conviction, there was only one eyewitness. Cutler and Penrod (1995) found that mock jurors would convict a defendant twice as often when the defendant was identified by a credible eyewitness than when there was no eyewitness identification. It has been estimated that eyewitness evidence plays a significant role in over 75,000 criminal cases annually in the United States (Goldstein, Chance, & Schneller, 1989).

Of course, *mistaken* eyewitness identifications are of great concern, especially in light of the significant weight placed on the testimony of an eyewitness. Penrod and Cutler (1999) estimated that mistaken eyewitness identifications account for approximately 4,500 wrongful convictions each year and Costanzo (1997) estimated that about a dozen people are executed each year for crimes they did not commit, many involving faulty eyewitness identification. In fact, mistaken eyewitness identifications have led to more wrongful convictions than all other causes together (Wells et al., 1998). We start this chapter by examining the various factors that may account for faulty eyewitness identification (See Box 5.1).

Box 5.1 The Case of the Mistaken Identity of Tony Ford

On December 18, 1991, two men broke into the home of Myra Murillo in El Paso, Texas, demanding to see "the man of the house" and demanding to know where "the money" was. When their demands were met with confusion, one of the men shot and killed Ms. Murillo's 18-year-old son, Armando, and then shot Ms. Murillo and her two daughters. Ms. Murillo and her daughters survived.

The prosecution's case at trial centered around the daughters' identification of Tony Ford from a photospread as one of the two men who broke into their house and as the man who did the shooting. In his defense, Tony Ford testified that he was not involved in the home break-in, but that he had driven the two men to the Murillos' house. He testified that he was outside waiting in the car for the two men when the break-in and murder occurred and that he did not know that the men were planning to break into the home and kill people.

A man named Van Belton was charged along with Tony Ford with breaking into the Murillos' home. Both daughters said that Van was the second man involved in the break-in but that he was not the shooter. After Van was arrested, he told police that Tony Ford was the other person. In Tony's statement to the police and in his testimony at trial, he confirmed that Van was one of the two men who broke into the Murillos' home, but testified that the second man was Van's brother, Victor Belton.

At trial, the critical factual question for the jury was whether the Murillo girls' subsequent identification of Tony Ford from a photospread was reliable. Based on all the other evidence, the Murillo sisters' identification of Tony appeared to be a mistake as there was no other evidence that connected him directly to the crime.

To show how the Murillos could have mistakenly identified Tony, defense counsel introduced a booking photograph of Victor Belton (Victor was arrested for assaulting the police officers who were attempting to arrest his brother, Van, for this crime). The defense also introduced the booking sheets for both Tony and Victor since the physical characteristics of Victor and Tony were so strikingly similar (both men were 5'8" tall; Victor weighed 156 lbs while Tony weighed 150 lbs; Victor was 17 years, 8 months old and Tony was 18 years, 6 months old). As the photographs of Victor and Tony showed, they also look quite similar. An eyewitness could have easily misidentified Victor Belton as Tony Ford. (To view the photos, go to http://www.justicedenied.org/issue_30/tony_ford.html.)

The defense counsel's request to hire and use an expert on eyewitness identification was denied. Tony Ford was convicted on July 9, 1993, and sentenced to death.

In response to one of Tony's appeals, he was granted the funds to hire an expert on eyewitness identification. This expert, Dr. Roy Malpass, one of the leading researchers on eyewitness identification, conducted two studies to determine the possibility of a mistaken identification. The first study showed that Tony and Victor were, by far, more similar looking than Tony and any of the people in the photospread. Thus, someone who had seen Victor actually commit the crime and who was shown the photospread with Tony's photo (but not with Victor's photo) would have been drawn to Tony's photo. The second study examined whether the photospread from which the Murillo sisters selected Tony was "suggestive" (composed of people different enough in appearance from Tony that he stood out and was more likely to be picked by persons who were only given a verbal description of Tony's features). The results of this second study showed that Tony's photo was selected four times more often than the other photos (a fair and nonsuggestive photospread would have lead research participants to pick out each photo with approximately the same frequency). The importance of these two studies was that they established that Victor looked remarkably like Tony and that the photospread was biased. Thus, if the person that the Murillo sisters saw shoot their brother was Victor they would have been highly likely to pick Tony out of the photospread (remember that Victor was not included in the photospread).

In addition, a number of other relevant issues (which will be discussed in more detail in this chapter) were important: (1) the Murillos were Latino and the suspects were black and research shows that there is a high likelihood of mistakes in cross-racial identifications; (2) the presence of a weapon decreases the chances of an accurate identification; (3) one of the Murillo sisters saw a photo of Tony in the newspaper identifying him as a suspect in the case before she viewed the photospread (exposure of an eyewitness to a photo of the suspect before viewing the photo as part of a photospread increases the likelihood of selecting the same suspect in the photospread); and (4) the Murillo sisters' unwavering certainty of their identification of Tony is not a good indicator of the accuracy of this identification (there is no relationship between confidence and accuracy).

Eight days before Tony Ford's scheduled December 7, 2005, execution, he was granted a temporary stay so that DNA testing could be performed on the clothing Victor was wearing at the time of his arrest. As this book goes to print, further DNA testing is being conducted.

This case was reprinted with the permission of Mr. Richard Burr, defense counsel for Tony Ford.

FACTORS THAT MAY ACCOUNT FOR MISTAKEN EYEWITNESS IDENTIFICATION

There are many factors that may account for mistaken eyewitness identification. Wells (1978) distinguished between **system variables** and **estimator variables**. *System variables* affect the accuracy of eyewitness testimony that the criminal justice system has some control over. For example, the way a question is worded or the way a lineup is constructed may impact the accuracy of eyewitness identification. In these instances, the justice system has some control over these variables. *Estimator variables*, on the other hand, are those that may affect the accuracy of eyewitness testimony but that the criminal justice system does not have any control over. These variables have to do with the characteristics of the eyewitness or the circumstances surrounding the event witnessed. For example, the amount of attention that an eyewitness paid to a perpetrator, how long an eyewitness viewed a perpetrator, or the lighting conditions under which a perpetrator was viewed would be examples of estimator variables since they have to do with the eyewitness or the circumstances surrounding the event. The criminal justice system does not have any control over these variables. The vast majority of the research on eyewitness identifications deals with system variables since they are under the control of the justice system and thus can be modified accordingly to improve the accuracy of eyewitness identifications and testimony.

We now turn to a discussion of the various factors that affect the accuracy of eyewitness identifications.

The Issue of Memory

Wells, Wright, and Bradfield (1999) advocate maintaining a clear distinction between what witnesses report and memory, as it is traditionally construed. These authors define memory as "the mental trace of a previously experienced event" (p. 56) and do not believe that memory processes *per se* completely encompass what governs a witness' report of some previously observed event. Various theories of memory exist and so what governs a witness' report of a prior event will depend, in part, upon which theory of memory one endorses. For example, much research has shown that asking an eyewitness misleading questions will influence his or her subsequent reports of a prior observed event (Loftus, 1975, 1979, 2000). Some theorists contend that the misleading questions serve to alter the original memory trace. Thus, a stop sign, for example, is replaced in memory with a yield sign or an empty field is replaced in memory with a field containing a red barn (see Loftus, 1975; Loftus & Palmer, 1974). Other theorists, on the other hand, contend that the original memory trace is not altered by the misleading questions, but rather, one of several other processes (e.g., creation of a second memory, demand characteristics) serves to bias the witness' report toward the misleading information (see McCloskey & Zaragoza, 1985). However, regardless of which theory of memory one believes, the outcome (that the eyewitness account is influenced by the misleading information) is the same. Thus, for the purposes of this chapter, it is irrelevant whether the original memory trace is or is not altered by intervening events. What is relevant is that memory is but one element that places constraint on a witness' testimony; thus, testimony and memory are not necessarily the same thing. Our discussion turns to the specific factors that have been shown to impact eyewitness accuracy.

Witness Characteristics

Race, gender, and age are three characteristics that have been examined to determine the extent to which they impact eyewitness accuracy. Each is an estimator variable and, therefore, out of the control of the justice system. With respect to age, the majority of the research has examined the differences between adults and children in terms of eyewitness testimony. These differences are discussed later in the chapter when we take a look at children as witnesses.

Research on gender differences in eyewitness identification indicates that there is no evidence that females are any better or worse than males. Similarly, there is no evidence that members of one race are better or worse at eyewitness identification than members of another race. However, there is evidence to suggest that people are better at recognizing the faces of members of their own race than they are at recognizing the faces of members of other races.

Meissner and Brigham (2001) conducted a meta-analysis of 39 studies and found that within-race identifications were significantly more likely to be accurate than cross-race identifications (also known as **own-race bias**). Various reasons have been proposed for why people are better at identifying others from their own race more accurately. Some researchers have suggested that we classify the facial features of someone from our own race in more detail, and less superficially, than the facial features of someone from another race (Fiske & Taylor, 1991; Malpass & Kravitz, 1969). This may be a result of a greater familiarity with those from our own race. Meissner and Brigham (2001) found that as our contact with members of different racial groups increases, we improve in our ability to recognize faces from those racial groups.

Situational Factors

Aside from witness characteristics, situation factors may play a role in mistaken eyewitness identifications. The following sections review the research on various situational factors.

Stress/Arousal

The relationship between stress/arousal and performance is characterized by an inverted U; thus looking something like ∩.

If we think of this as a graph, with level of stress/arousal falling along the x-axis and level of performance falling along the y-axis, the optimal level of performance falls at a point of moderate stress/arousal. Performance is lowest at very high and very low levels of stress/arousal. This is known as the **Yerkes-Dodson law**. When we apply this law to eyewitness identification, we find this same relationship between stress/arousal and eyewitness performance (Deffenbacher, 1983). Thus, eyewitnesses who experience high levels of stress/arousal, as the case may be when one witnesses a serious or violent criminal event, often are less accurate in their identifications and less reliable in their testimony. One study showed that witnesses to a nonviolent act were able to provide more detailed and accurate recall than were witnesses to a violent act (Clifford & Scott, 1978).

Weapon Focus

Research has indicated that eyewitnesses are significantly influenced by the visual presence of a weapon. When a weapon, such as a knife or gun, is present, witnesses' memory for other details is impaired (Kramer, Buckhout, & Eugenio, 1990). While emotional stress/arousal may certainly be increased in situations when a weapon is present, it appears that eyewitnesses narrow their attention so that they spend more time focusing on the weapon and thus pay less attention to other aspects of the situation, including the physical characteristics of the perpetrator. This **weapon focus effect** has been demonstrated to occur even in simulated situations when people watch a film of a crime being committed (Tooley, Brigham, Maass, & Bothwell, 1987).

Environmental Factors

Several environmental factors can affect the accuracy of eyewitness recall. The amount and type of light available at the crime scene is related to how well an eyewitness is able to see, and therefore, how well he or she is able to perceive the events as they unfold. Research has indicated that it is difficult to accurately detect colors in monochromic lighting, such as that given off by a streetlight. Fog as well as the presence of rain, snow, or other precipitation also affect visibility and thus serve to lower the potential for accurate eyewitness information. The distance between the witness and the observed event is a factor as is whether there was additional simultaneous activity or other distracters.

Duration of Event

The research on facial recognition suggests a positive relationship between time and accuracy such that the longer a witness is exposed to a perpetrator, the more accurate his or her eyewitness testimony (Memon, Hope, & Bull, 2003). There is, however, a tendency for people to overestimate the duration of brief events and to underestimate the duration of lengthy events. Thus, since the majority of crimes occur during a brief period of time, witnesses tend to overestimate the amount of time that they were exposed to the perpetrator. Penrod and Cutler (1999) have indicated that these overestimates tend to be about three or four times the actual length of the event. Therefore, a witness who sees a perpetrator for only 30 seconds may estimate that he or she was exposed to the perpetrator for 2 minutes. An exposure time of 30 seconds does not allow the witness much time to pay attention to and note facial and other physical features of the perpetrator. Of course, as discussed previously, if the perpetrator has a weapon, the witness will spend even less time observing his or her facial and physical features.

Postevent Factors

Aside from witness characteristics and situational factors that occur at the time of the event, postevent factors may also play a role in mistaken eyewitness identifications. Let's consider some of the more common postevent factors that may account for mistaken identification.

Passage of Time

As with any memory, recall drops off as time passes. Ebbinghaus (1964) determined that the rate of forgetting is steepest immediately after the event and then levels off. The amount of time that passes between the event witnessed and the opportunity to make eyewitness identification will serve to decrease the accuracy of an eyewitness account. It may be that the eyewitness was unaware that he or she was observing an event that would later come under the scrutiny of the criminal justice system or it may be that the police did not make an immediate arrest. Regardless, eyewitnesses forget things over time and, therefore, accuracy diminishes as more time passes (Flin, Boone, Knox, & Bull, 1992).

Shepard (1983) exposed witnesses to an irate stranger for 45 seconds and then asked the witnesses to pick the stranger out of a video lineup at varying delays. After a 1-week delay, 65% of the witnesses were able to make an accurate identification whereas after an 11-month delay, only 10% of the witnesses made an accurate identification. Thus, the rate of accurate identifications decreased over time. Cutler, Penrod, and Martens (1987) also found the opposite to be true: that false identifications increase over time.

There is also an interaction between time and suggestion. The more time that passes between a witnessed event and a misleading question or other attempt to implant a suggestion, the more effective the suggestion will be in distorting the accuracy of the eyewitness' report (Hoffman, Loftus, Greenmun, & Dashiell, 1992).

Misleading Information

Misleading information, often in the form of leading questions or suggestive comments, can affect the accuracy of an eyewitness' recall. The research of Loftus and colleagues has demonstrated that the recall of eyewitnesses can be influenced by information introduced after the event, in the form of misleading questions or statements as well as in the way that questions are asked (the wording used).

In one series of studies, Loftus and Palmer (1974) showed participants a film of a car crash. Half of the participants were asked about the speed of the car when it "turned right" and half were asked to estimate the speed when the car "ran the stop sign." Later, participants were asked whether they saw a stop sign: 35% of the group who were asked about the speed of the car when it turned right indicated that they saw a stop sign whereas 53% of the group who had been asked about the speed of the car when it ran the stop sign reported seeing a stop sign. When a suggestion about the presence of a barn was included in the questioning, 17% of participants reported seeing a barn when, in fact, none existed. In addition to showing that suggestions implanted within questions can influence the recall of eyewitnesses, Loftus and her colleagues also showed that the way in which questions are worded could also influence eyewitness recall. Participants were asked to estimate the speed of two cars when they "contacted," "hit," or "smashed" each other. The estimated speeds varied significantly as a function of the wording used. Participants estimated the cars to be traveling at a slower speed when the word *contacted* was used than when the word *smashed* was used in the question. In addition, participants were much more likely to recall seeing a broken headlight when they were asked whether they saw "the" broken headlight than when they were asked whether they saw "a" broken headlight. Thus, subtle variations in wording or subtle suggestions implanted within the context of a question or a statement about the event can result in substantial variation in the eyewitness' recall of the event.

Wells, Wright, and Bradfield (1999) delineated three conditions under which misleading information tends to affect the accuracy of eyewitness accounts: (1) when the strength of the original memory trace is weaker rather than stronger (such as when an eyewitness does not get to observe the event for very long, or when a great deal of time has passed since the event), (2) when the misinformation is not recognized as being incorrect at the time (such as when the misinformation is about a peripheral detail rather the central gist of the event), and (3) when the misinformation is being delivered by a credible source (such as a police officer).

Unconscious Transference

When a witness remembers a face but inaccurately attributes the face to a different context it is referred to as **unconscious transference**. Unconscious transference occurs when you see a barista from your favorite coffeeshop on the street and place her as someone you've seen at your healthclub. Similarly, unconscious transference occurs when an eyewitness mistakenly identifies an innocent bystander who was present at the crime scene as the perpetrator. Robert Buckhout (1974), a psychologist who studied eyewitnesses, staged a mock assault in front of 141 students in his psychology class. When he asked the students in his class to pick the perpetrator out of a photo lineup seven weeks later, only about 40% were able to make an accurate identification. What is interesting is that two-thirds of those who were unable to make an accurate identification selected someone from the lineup who was present in the classroom on the day of the "crime" as an innocent bystander. Thus, the phenomenon of unconscious transference is one means by which innocent people may be considered suspects within the criminal justice system.

Lineups and Photospreads

Given that a suspect almost immediately becomes a culprit once he or she has been selected from a photospread (sometimes called a photo array) or a lineup, much research has focused on the sources of potential errors in eyewitness identification pertaining to photospreads and lineups. Wells and colleagues (1999) identified three broad domains as sources of eyewitness identification errors in photospreads and lineups: instructions, structure, and procedure.

If police instruct the witness prior to viewing the lineup or photospread that the perpetrator might or might not be present, inaccurate or false identifications can be reduced. In addition, the witness should be warned not to guess. If these instructions are not provided, most witnesses will assume that the perpetrator is present (otherwise, why conduct the lineup?) and will usually select the individual that most closely approximates the perpetrator.

Asking a witness to select a perpetrator from a photospread or a lineup places a high degree of demand on the witness. Most witnesses feel a desire to assist the police and, therefore, experience psychological pressure to identify someone from the lineup or photospread as the perpetrator. It appears difficult for witnesses to indicate that the perpetrator is not present in a lineup or photospread. Malpass and Devine (1981) found that 78% of eyewitnesses identified someone from a perpetrator-absent lineup when they were led to believe that the perpetrator was in the lineup. However, this false identification rate fell to 33% when the eyewitnesses were warned that the perpetrator might not be in the lineup. Steblay (1997) found that this warning resulted in reduced identifications when the perpetrator was not in the lineup but had no effect when the perpetrator was in the lineup.

To reduce false identifications, a lineup or photospread must be structured so that all members of the lineup or photospread match the witness' description of the perpetrator. In addition, only one member of the lineup or photospread should be the suspect while the others should be foils or distractors (individuals who are known to be innocent) who match the witness' description of the perpetrator. Obviously, if the witness has described the perpetrator as a short, white male with blond hair and blue eyes, it biases the lineup to include men who are from other racial groups, are very tall, or have dark hair. Research shows that the rate of selecting an innocent person who fits the description of the perpetrator increases substantially when the others in the lineup or photospread do not fit the description (Lindsay & Wells, 1980; Wells, Rydell, & Seelau, 1993).

Finally, presenting the lineup or photospread in a sequential manner rather than simultaneously can reduce the rate of false identifications. In addition, the use of dual lineup procedures can also reduce false identifications. The dual lineup procedure involves the use of a **blank lineup** (i.e., a lineup where *all* the members are known to be innocent by the police; thus a blank lineup does not contain any suspects). With the blank lineup, the witness is not told that there are no suspects in the lineup, but rather, is given instructions with the warning that the perpetrator might not be present. Blank lineups can be used as a "lure" to determine whether the witness is able to resist the temptation of selecting someone when the actual perpetrator is not present (Wells et al., 1998). Wells (1984) found that eyewitnesses who did not make an identification when shown a blank lineup were significantly less likely to make a false identification on the actual lineup than were those who either were not given the blank lineup test or who failed the blank lineup test (i.e., they selected someone from the blank lineup as the perpetrator). It seems that the use of a blank lineup can help to weed out those eyewitnesses who are prone to make mistakes.

   Presenting members of a lineup or photospread sequentially, rather than simultaneously, can also help reduce the chance of a false identification (Lindsay & Wells, 1985). In a traditional lineup or photospread, the members are all shown to the witness all at once. In this situation, the eyewitness tends to use relative judgments and selects the person from the lineup or photospread who most closely resembles the perpetrator. In a sequential lineup or photospread, the members are shown to the witness one at a time. Thus, the witness must decide whether the member being viewed is the perpetrator without seeing the other possibilities. This serves to prevent the use of relative judgments and, therefore, to reduce the rate of false identifications.

Demand Characteristics

The psychological pressure on a witness to give a description of a perpetrator or to make a positive identification from a photospread or lineup is great. This pressure, which can be either implicit or explicit, can heighten the witness' anxiety and/or desire to assist the police in the investigation and prosecution of the crime. This increased anxiety or desire may lead to errors in identification and testimony. Conducting a lineup or photospread sets up an implicit expectation that the perpetrator is present and increases the chance that an identification will be made, unless, as discussed earlier, the witness is explicitly warned that the perpetrator might not be present. Asking the witness to point out the perpetrator in the courtroom is another situation that sets up a high demand for the witness to select the individual whom he or she has previously identified in a lineup or photospread.

Witness Confidence

Research indicates that highly confident witnesses are persuasive with jurors. The problem, however, is that confidence is not related to accuracy. Highly confident witnesses may be inaccurate while less confident witnesses may be accurate. In addition, research indicates that confidence is highly malleable. That is, it is relatively easy to manipulate the confidence of eyewitnesses. Finally, confidence tends to increase over time and successive identifications such that a witness who was only slightly confident when identifying the perpetrator in a photospread, becomes somewhat more confident when identifying the perpetrator during a live lineup, and ends up being very confident when identifying the perpetrator when on the witness stand during the trial. Of course, this is regardless of whether the identified perpetrator is the actual perpetrator. Successive identifications increases a witness' confidence which, in turn, increases his or her persuasiveness but not his or her accuracy.

Wells and Bradfield (1998) demonstrated the malleability of eyewitness' confidence when they had hundreds of witnesses view a security video of a man entering a store and then told the witnesses that the man had killed a security guard. They then asked the witnesses to identify the man from a photospread. The 352 witnesses who made a false identification (selected the wrong man from the photospread) were then randomly assigned to one of three groups. One group was told that they identified the correct perpetrator, one group was told that they identified the wrong man and were then told who the actual perpetrator was in the photospread, and the third group was not given any feedback. At the time of the initial identification, the three groups were equally confident about their selections. Later on, the eyewitnesses were asked to indicate how certain they were at the time they made the initial identification. Those who had been given the confirming feedback that they had selected the correct perpetrator recalled being very certain at the time of the initial identification whereas those who were told that they had identified the wrong man recalled being uncertain. In addition, those who were told that they made the correct identification indicated that they made the identification more easily, recalled having a better view of the perpetrator, and indicated that they paid more attention to the event than those in the group who were told that they made an incorrect identification. This research indicates how easily witness confidence can be manipulated.

There are many factors that may contribute to a mistaken identification. The multitude of factors ensures that mistaken identifications can occur at any of a number of points from the time of the crime (poor lighting conditions, brief encounter, presence of a weapon) through the investigation procedures used by the police (witness questioning, photospreads, lineups) and up to identifying the perpetrator in the courtroom (witness confidence, demand characteristics). For many of these factors (estimator variables), there is not much that can be done to limit their impact on inaccurate identifications. However, for other factors (system variables), there are some procedures that can be used to reduce the number of mistaken or inaccurate identifications and we will discuss these safeguards later in the chapter.

CHILDREN AS EYEWITNESSES

As a general statement, children differ from adults in terms of the accuracy and completeness of their eyewitness accounts (Wells et al., 1999). When asked to provide free recall of a previously witnessed event, children tend to provide less information overall as well as less accurate information than that provided by adults. These tendencies become even more pronounced when children are asked to respond to specific questions

(Luus & Wells, 1992; Poole & White, 1991, 1993). In addition, it appears that children's narrative accounts are more accurate when they actually participated in an incident as opposed to merely observing it (Tobey & Goodman, 1992).

As discussed earlier, errors in adult eyewitness identification can occur as a result of the way in which photospreads and lineups are constructed and used. Children generally experience the same types of difficulties as adults (Wells et al., 1999). There is, however, one area in particular that children appear to have more difficulty than adults: when the actual perpetrator is not present in the photospread or lineup. Recall that, in general, eyewitnesses find it difficult to indicate that none of the people in the lineup or photospread are the perpetrator and, instead, tend to select the person in the lineup or photospread who most closely resembles the actual perpetrator (see Wells 1984, 1993; Wells et al., 1998). When a child eyewitness is shown a lineup or a photospread that does not include the perpetrator, the tendency to make an identification is even more pronounced than with adults (Dekle, Beal, Elliott, & Huneycutt, 1996). Thus, children find it very difficult to indicate that the perpetrator is not present. This may reflect a greater weakness in children's memory compared to an adult's memory, since perpetrator-absent lineups are a tougher test of the eyewitness' memory (Wells et al., 1999). Alternatively, it may reflect the greater suggestibility of children since the inherent suggestion in a lineup is that the perpetrator is present (Wells et al., 1999).

It appears that children, especially children of preschool age, are far more suggestible than adults (Ceci & Bruck, 1993, 1995). In fact, very young children—under 6 years of age—often have difficulty distinguishing between real events that actually occurred from those that were only imagined (Ceci & Bruck, 1995; Johnson & Foley, 1984). Thus, careful interviewing of child witnesses is necessary to minimize the possibility that the child will be influenced by the interviewer or by any possible suggestions implanted during the interrogation.

The Wee Care Nursery School case that occurred in Maplewood, New Jersey, in 1985 illustrates some of the potential problems that can occur when children are interrogated as if they were adults. (See Box 5.2.) The children in this case were interrogated and interviewed repeatedly and in a suggestive and coercive manner. Peterson and Bell (1996) demonstrated that children under 5 years of age are sensitive to repeated and coercive questioning and that erroneous answers increased dramatically when leading, as opposed to open-ended, questions were used. Ceci and Bruck (1995) also demonstrated that almost 60% of children who initially said an event never occurred would give detailed descriptions of the supposed event after repeated questioning by adults.

**Box 5.2 Case Study: The Wee Care
Nursery School**

On April 26, 1985, 26-year-old Margaret Kelly Michaels left her job at the Wee Care Nursery School in Maplewood, New Jersey, for a better-paying position. Four days later, a 4-year-old boy, who was a former student of Michaels, was having his temperature taken rectally at the doctor's office and told the nurse, "That's what my teacher does to me at school." The boy's mother notified child protective services that afternoon. Two days later, a prosecutor interviewed the boy. As part of the interview, the boy inserted his finger into the rectum of an anatomical doll and told the prosecutor that two other boys also had their temperatures taken in this manner. Neither of these two other boys confirmed this claim but one of the boys said that Michaels had touched his penis. The first boy's mother told another parent, who was a member of the school board, and when he questioned his own son, his son told him that Michaels had touched his penis with a spoon.

The Wee Care Nursery School was made aware of these claims and sent a letter home to all parents indicating that a former employee was being investigated "regarding serious allegations made by a child." The parents were invited to a presentation by a social worker who encouraged the parents to look for signs that their children had been abused, such as genital soreness, bed-wetting, masturbation, nightmares, or other changes in behavior. Over the next several months several therapists and investigators interviewed the children and their families to determine the extent of the abuse. Many children were repeatedly interviewed and questioned persistently. Some bizarre allegations came out, including that Michaels had played the piano naked, had licked peanut butter off the children's genitals, had forced the children to drink her urine and eat her feces, and had raped the children with forks, knives, spoons, and Lego blocks. These events had all allegedly happened during regular school hours and over the course of many months, although none of them had been reported to any of the parents or noticed by any of the staff members and none of the parents noticed any unusual behavior in their children over this period of time.

On August 2, 1988, Michaels was convicted of 115 counts of sexual abuse, based on the testimony of 19 three- to five-year-old children and sentenced to 47 years in prison. After serving five years of her sentence, her conviction was overturned on the grounds that the interviews and interrogations of the children were highly coercive and suggestive. In 1994, all charges against Michaels were dropped.

A large proportion of the testimony given by children in court have to do with child sexual abuse cases since the child victim is often the only witness. As a general statement, children are generally viewed as less credible witnesses than are adults. Interestingly, however, it appears that younger children who testify in sexual abuse cases are perceived as more credible and are more likely to be believed by jurors than are adolescents or adults. The explanation for this appears to be that jurors believe that younger children lack the sexual sophistication to fabricate such allegations (Bottoms & Goodman, 1994).

The Sixth Amendment of the Constitution allows defendants the right to confront their accusers and to cross-examine them in court. This right, however, can pose a special problem when a child is the accuser since defense lawyers and the courtroom experience often intimidate children and the thought of testifying in front of the person they are accusing can be frightening. The courts have considered this right against the possible psychological harm or trauma that might occur for the child and, in at least 41 states, will allow an exception to the hearsay rule for a child victim. The hearsay rule specifies that a witness cannot repeat someone else's out-of-court statements and have these admitted as evidence. In the special case of the child victim, however, this rule can be waived and, instead of having the child testify, evidence of abuse can be admitted as hearsay testimony by a parent, teacher, psychologist, physician, police officer, or social worker. One of these adults would take the stand and repeat the out-of-court statements made by the child. This way, the child is spared having to take the witness stand.

An interesting and informational study on hearsay testimony was conducted by Myers, Redlich, Goodman, Prizmich, & Imwinkelried (1999) who administered a questionnaire to 248 individuals who had just served as jurors in child molestation or a child exploitation trials. In each trial, at least one child testified about the abuse that he or she suffered and at least one adult provided hearsay testimony about the child's out-of-court statements regarding the abuse. The results of the questionnaire suggested that the adult hearsay testimony was perceived by jurors as more credible, consistent, complete, and accurate than the direct testimony of the child. The researchers speculated that this might have been because the adult witnesses' professional status as police officers or teachers gave them more credibility with the jurors. In addition, the researchers found that the jurors were very attentive to the demeanor of the child witnesses and speculated that the jurors' verdicts may have been influenced by the children's facial expressions, eye contact, nervousness, hesitations, gestures, and speech errors whereas the adult witnesses' mannerisms did not appear to impact the jurors' verdicts.

Another protection sometimes offered to child witnesses is the option to testify by closed circuit television rather than in front of the defendant in the courtroom. Children who would likely experience significant emotional trauma by testifying in front of the defendant can testify in a different room while their testimony is displayed on a large television in the actual courtroom. Goodman and her colleagues (1998) conducted a study to compare live testimony with testimony via closed circuit television. These researchers had 5- to 6-year-olds and 8- to 9-year-olds play individually with a male confederate who helped the child place stickers on either their bare skin (arms, toes, bellybutton; "defendant guilty" condition) or on their clothing ("defendant not guilty" condition). Later on, each child then testified about the play session in a mock trial held in a courtroom. The testimony was either presented live in open court or via closed circuit television. Community mock jurors viewed the trials and the testimony and deliberated until reaching a verdict. The researchers found that closed circuit television reduced the amount of pretrial emotional distress experienced by the children and increased the accuracy of their testimony while having no effect on juror perceptions of fairness to the defendant or likelihood of conviction. However, the children who testified in open court were seen as more believable than those who testified via closed circuit television (even though they were less accurate). The results of this research are generally favorable toward the use of closed circuit television and at least 33 states currently allow the use of closed circuit television for child testimony.

SAFEGUARDS AND PROTECTIONS

To this point, we have discussed many of the factors that contribute to mistaken identifications. We now turn to some of the safeguards or protections that can be used to decrease the chances that an innocent person who was mistakenly identified will be convicted of a crime. These safeguards or protections fall into two main categories: those that can be implemented during police investigation procedures, especially lineups and photospreads, and those that can be implemented within the courtroom setting.

Investigation Procedures

In 1996, the American Psychology-Law Society (AP-LS; Division 41 of the American Psychological Association) assembled a subcommittee to review the research on eyewitness identifications and to put forth a number of recommendations regarding the best procedures for conducting lineups and photospreads. Gary Wells, one of the preeminent research psychologists in the area of eyewitness identification, led this subcommittee, which put forth four recommended rules (Wells et al., 1998). In addition to the recommendations made by Gary Wells and the AP-LS subcommittee, other researchers have also offered recommendations that would serve to reduce the number of mistaken identifications.

Rule 1: Who Conducts the Lineup

Wells and his colleagues (1998) recommended that the first rule be that "the person who conducts the lineup or photospread should not be aware of which member of the lineup or photospread is the suspect" (p. 627). This rule comes from studies that demonstrate the powerful effects of experimenter expectancy (Rosenthal, 1976). Participants in research studies are able to pick up on the experimenter's expectations when the experimenter is not blind to the condition and, many times, the participants will act accordingly.

For example, recall the story of Clever Hans from your introductory psychology course. Clever Hans was a horse who could supposedly perform arithmetic and who would answer math questions by counting out the correct answer by tapping his hoof on the ground. It was discovered, however, that in fact Clever Hans was just very good at reading his trainer and would tap until he received a clue from his trainer that he had arrived at the correct answer at which point he would stop tapping. The trainer was unaware that he was providing any clues to Clever Hans (the trainer would lean forward slightly until Clever Hans approached the correct number of taps, at which point the trainer would lean back). Likewise, human research participants can pick up on the nonverbal cues of an experimenter and can alter their behavior accordingly. This has been demonstrated in lineup situations in which the detective administering a photospread mistakenly obtained a photograph of someone he believed to be the suspect but who was not. The eyewitness selected the photo of the person who the detective believed to be the suspect. When the error was discovered and the photospread reconstructed with the correct photo, the eyewitness chose the correct suspect. In addition, when 50 people were shown the actual photo of the suspect and asked to select the person from the original photospread that most closely resembled the suspect, none of these people chose the person selected by the eyewitness (Wells et al., 1998). It seems that, as in the case of Clever Hans, the eyewitness was picking up on some nonverbal cues from the detective, which influenced the initial identification. Because experimenter expectancy is so influential, it is now common practice for the experimenters to be blind to the participants' conditions.

The lead detective or investigator on a case is most often the person who assembles and conducts the lineup or photospread. Thus, like in the experimenter situation, it is quite possible that the lead investigator can convey verbal and nonverbal cues to the eyewitness regarding which member of the lineup is the suspect. For these reasons, it has been recommended that the person who conducts the lineup or photospread should be blind as to which member is the suspect.

Rule 2: Instructions on Viewing

The second rule proposed by Wells and colleagues (1998) is that "eyewitnesses should be told explicitly that the person in question might not be in the lineup or photospread and therefore should not feel that they must make an identification. They should also be told that the person administering the lineup does not know which person is the suspect in the case" (p. 629). As discussed earlier in this chapter, eyewitnesses find it difficult not to select someone from a lineup or photospread and, instead of indicating that the perpetrator is not present, will most often select the person from the lineup or photospread that most closely resembles the perpetrator. Administering the lineup or photospread in such a way reduces the chances that he or she will make a false identification.

The second part of this rule is related to the first rule; the eyewitness must be told that the person conducting the lineup does not know who the suspect is, thereby reducing the possibility that the eyewitness will look to the person conducting the lineup for cues as to which person to select or whether the person selected is the "correct" choice.

Rule 3: Structure of Lineup or Photospread

The third rule that Wells and colleagues (1998) recommended was that "the suspect should not stand out of the lineup or photospread as being different from the distractors based on the eyewitness' previous description of the culprit or based on other factors that would draw extra attention to the suspect" (p. 630). The critical issue here is to ensure that the suspect in the lineup or photospread does not stand out in any significant way from the distractors that would cause this person to be selected more than would be expected on the basis of chance. One way to test whether this rule has been met with any particular lineup is through the use of a mock witness procedure. Mock witnesses (people who have never seen the perpetrator) are given the eyewitness' description of the perpetrator and then shown the lineup and asked to select the person who they think matches the description. If the mock witnesses are able to figure out who the suspect is, this suggests a problem with the lineup. In theory, if there are six members of a lineup or photospread who all match the description given by the eyewitness, the mock witnesses should select each member about one-sixth of the time.

Rule 4: Obtaining Confidence Statements

The fourth rule recommended by Wells and colleagues (1998) is that "a clear statement should be taken from the eyewitness at the time of the identification and prior to any feedback as to his or her confidence that the identified person is the actual culprit" (p. 635). As discussed earlier in this chapter, an eyewitness' confidence tends to increase over time, with successive identifications and with postidentification information provided to the eyewitness. In addition, we know that jurors can be strongly persuaded by a witness' level of confidence, even though confidence is not related to accuracy. If an eye-witness is provided feedback that he or she identified the person that the police suspected, this raises his or her confidence in the identification. In addition, asking an eyewitness to recall the level of confidence that he or she had at the time of the identification is not reliable, especially when he or she has been given feedback about the identification. Thus, the only way to accurately assess the eyewitness' confidence in the identification is to ask for their confidence level at the time of the identification. This way, any significant discrepancy between the level of confidence indicated by the eyewitness at the time of the identification and during testimony at trial can be noted by the jury and considered accordingly.

Rule 5: Videotaping the Lineup and Witness Identification

Kassin (1998) argued that a fifth rule should be added to the recommenda-tions: that the lineup and identification procedures should be routinely videotaped. Kassin argued that videotaping would allow for an objective record of the structure of the lineup (rule 3), the person conducting the lineup and the instructions used (rules 1 and 2), the length of time that an eyewitness took to make the identification, as well as his or her confidence in the identification (rule 4). Although Wells and colleagues (1998) were reluctant to include videotaping as one of their rules because they made a concerted effort to include only those rules that would serve to reduce the likelihood of a mistaken identification and that would not cause unneces-sary burden to police departments, it seems that Kassin's proposed fifth rule would allow an opportunity for police departments to document adher-ence to the four rules proposed by Wells and colleagues (see Box 5.3).

Box 5.3 Research Being Put into Practice

Gary Wells and his subcommittee of eyewitness identification researchers were called upon by Attorney General Janet Reno and the U.S. Department of Justice to form part of a larger working group whose goal it was to develop a series of guidelines that would serve as recommended procedures for law enforcement when conducting lineups and photospreads and obtaining eyewitness evidence. The product of this working group was a manual entitled *Eyewitness Evidence: A Guide for Law Enforcement*, which was distributed to police departments across the country in 1999. Each of the recommendations in this manual followed directly from the results of psychological research on eyewitness identification. This is one example of how research can be implemented into practice. A consequence of this manual's recommendations is that the results of psychological research are being directly implemented into police practices across the United States regarding the collection of eyewitness evidence.

Courtroom Procedures

In the first part of this chapter we noted that eyewitness evidence plays a significant role in over 75,000 cases each year in the United States but mistaken identifications account for approximately 4,500 wrongful convictions each year. These numbers are staggering and underscore the importance eyewitness evidence plays in our criminal justice system. We know from research that the likelihood of a conviction is far greater when there is an eyewitness than when there is not. In addition, it appears that jurors are so swayed by eyewitness evidence that even information indicating that an eyewitness did not view the perpetrator under adequate conditions does not change the chances of conviction significantly.

In a classic study, Loftus (1979) presented three groups of mock jurors with evidence from a criminal case. The first group heard circumstantial evidence only; the second group heard the circumstantial evidence plus eyewitness identification evidence; and the third group heard the circumstantial evidence, the eyewitness identification evidence, as well as evidence regarding the fact that the eyewitness had very poor eyesight and was not wearing glasses on the day of the crime. Of the first group, 18% voted to convict the defendant; of the second group, 72% voted to convict the defendant; and of the third group, 68% voted to convict the defendant. Thus, the mock jurors appear to have been strongly influenced by the eyewitness evidence, regardless of whether the evidence appeared to be credible.

Research on eyewitness identification has also demonstrated that eyewitness confidence is one of the most important variables used to determine whether the eyewitness is being truthful (Cutler, Penrod, & Stuve, 1988). However, it has also been demonstrated that level of confidence is not indicative of accuracy (Penrod & Cutler, 1995). In addition, there are many factors (previously discussed) that account for mistaken eyewitness identifications, including stress, the presence of a weapon, the amount of time an eyewitness has to observe the event, the viewing environment, the amount of time that passes between the event and the identification, as well as the way in which questions are worded, information provided to the eyewitness after the event, and how lineups and photospreads are conducted. Thus, one of the challenges for the defense in any trial is to attempt to educate the jury about the factors that may impact an eyewitness' accurate identification. Aside from cross-examining the eyewitness in an attempt to bring to light possible weaknesses in his or her identification of the defendant, educating the jury about some of these factors can be done in two other ways: expert testimony about eyewitness identification and judicial instructions.

Expert Testimony

Psychologists may be called as experts to testify about eyewitness identifications. In general, this type of testimony focuses on the factors that may impact accurate eyewitness identification in an attempt to educate the jury about the possibility of false or mistaken identifications. The psychologist would explain the research on eyewitness identifications to the jury but would not comment on whether the characteristics of the particular eyewitness in the case or whether the eyewitness was mistaken in his or her identification of the perpetrator.

In many cases, judges are reluctant to allow expert testimony on eyewitness identification fearing that the trial may turn into a battle of the experts, or believing that much of the information that the expert would provide is common knowledge to laypersons (who serve as jurors) or that the research in this field has not been sufficiently established. However, research suggests that mock jurors (laypersons) are insensitive to those factors that can cause mistaken eyewitness identifications (Cutler, Penrod, & Dexter, 1990a). In addition, it appears that many of the findings from research in this area have been sufficiently established (see Box 5.4). In recent years, the courts have become more open to allowing expert testimony on eyewitness identification when the evidence relies heavily on the testimony of a single eyewitness.

Box 5.4 Consensus among Eyewitness Experts

Kassin, Ellsworth, and Smith (1989) conducted a survey of the leading researchers on eyewitness identification to determine the degree of consensus among these experts regarding whether various research findings were reliable enough to serve as the basis for expert testimony on eyewitness identification.

The highest rate of agreement among the experts (96.8%) related to the finding that an eyewitness' recall of events can be affected by the wording of questions. This was followed closely by the finding that police instructions during a lineup can affect the willingness of a witness to make an identification or the likelihood that a witness will make an identification (95.1%).

Over 80% of the experts agreed that the following findings were reliable enough to be included as expert testimony on eyewitnesses in court:

- Postevent information is reflected in the eyewitness' recall of events (87.1%).
- Eyewitness confidence is not predictive of eyewitness accuracy (87.1%).
- An eyewitness' attitudes and expectations can affect recall of an event (86.9%).
- An eyewitness' recall is affected by exposure time; the less time the eyewitness has to observe an event, the less accurate he or she will recall the event (84.7%).
- Unconscious transference can interfere with an eyewitness' recall such that the eyewitness may identify someone from another situation or context as the perpetrator (84.5%).

- Show ups (i.e., when one person is shown to the eyewitness rather than a full lineup) increase the chances of false identifications (83.1%).
- Forgetting follows a curve; the greatest rate of forgetting occurs immediately following an event and levels off over time (82.5%).

Over 70% of the experts agreed that the following findings were reliable enough to be included as expert testimony on eyewitnesses in court:

- White eyewitnesses are better at identifying white perpetrators than they are at identifying black perpetrators (79.4%).
- The likelihood that an eyewitness' identification is accurate increases when the members of the lineup resemble the perpetrator (77.2%).
- Eyewitnesses tend to overestimate the duration of short events (74.5%).
- Eyewitness accuracy is reduced when the eyewitness experiences high levels of stress during the event (70.5%).

Cutler and his colleagues (1990b) conducted a series of studies to examine the impact of expert testimony. In one of the conditions, as part of the trial evidence presented, some participants heard expert testimony regarding the limitations of eyewitness identifications while other participants were not presented with expert testimony. The results indicated that the presentation of expert testimony at trial caused participants to place less emphasis on eyewitness confidence as an indicator of accuracy and sensitized participants to the importance of considering factors that may reduce or enhance eyewitness accuracy. Those participants who were not presented with expert testimony on eyewitness identifications at trial were more likely to use confidence as an indicator of accuracy and did not consider those factors that are known to reduce accuracy (Cutler, Penrod, & Dexter, 1990b). Thus, it seems that the presentation of expert testimony at trial can serve to educate jurors about the relevant factors for evaluating eyewitness testimony.

Judicial Instructions

An alternative to expert testimony is for the judge to provide instructions to the jury to alert them to some of the limitations of eyewitness identification. While this alternative may avoid the concern that the trial will turn into a battle of the experts, research on judicial instructions has demonstrated that juries often have a difficult time understanding and implementing the instructions. Often, the instructions, which can be quite lengthy, are read aloud to the jury and jurors are not given copy of the instructions to read for themselves. In addition, although the defense will usually request that the judge provide instruction to the jury on the limitations of eyewitness identification, it is not always the case that the judge will oblige.

In 1972, the court in *Neil v. Biggers* set out five criteria to be considered when considering the accuracy of an eyewitness' identification; these five criteria were affirmed five years later in *Manson v. Braithwaite*. The criteria are as follows:

1. The witness' opportunity to observe the perpetrator.
2. The witness' level of attention.
3. The accuracy of the witness' previous description of the perpetrator.
4. The degree of certainty displayed by the witness.
5. The amount of time between witnessing the event and making the identification.

These five criteria have been the subject of much criticism by researchers in the field. Wells and colleagues (1998) indicated that these criteria are problematic because research has demonstrated that at least three of them (eyewitness' reports of their certainty, attention, and opportunity to view) are influenced by suggestive procedures. Eyewitness confidence or certainty can be influenced by the instructions used in a lineup or photospread procedure, the structure of the lineup, or suggestions or information regarding which person in a lineup or photospread is the suspect. Thus, Wells and colleagues (1998) argue, "it is ironic, therefore, that the elevated certainty of a witness resulting from a suggestive procedure should then be used to dismiss the suggestive procedure on grounds that the witness displays high certainty" (p. 631).

SUMMARY

Eyewitness identification and testimony are important components of our criminal justice system. Unfortunately, errors in eyewitness identification frequently occur and are the cause of many cases of wrongful conviction each year in the United States. Many types of factors may account for errors in eyewitness identification, including witness characteristics (such as age, race, or gender) or situational factors (such as stress, the presence of a weapon, environmental conditions, or the duration of the event). Postevent factors account for many mistaken identifications as well. These factors include the simple passage of time, misleading information, unconscious transference, demand characteristics, witness confidence, and many aspects of lineups and photospreads.

Estimator variables, those having to do with the characteristics of the eyewitness or the situation, are not under the control of the criminal justice system and, therefore, their effects cannot be minimized. System variables, those factors that are under the control of the criminal justice system and have to do with interrogation tactics or the collection of evidence, can be minimized by careful consideration of the research in this area. Some of the most important procedural considerations are rules 1 through 4 proposed by Wells and colleagues (1998).

The differences between and weight placed on child and adult eyewitnesses are important to note. As a result, special protections are often provided for child victims who are called to testify in court. Finally, various safeguards and protections, both with respect to investigation procedures as well as courtroom procedures, have been used to minimize the chances that an innocent person will be the victim of a false or mistaken eyewitness identification.

SUGGESTED READINGS

Kassin, S. M., Ellsworth, P. C., & Smith, V. L. (1989). The "general acceptance" of psychological research on eyewitness testimony: A survey of the experts. *American Psychologist, 44*, 1089–1098.

Penrod, S. D., & Cutler, B. L. (1999). Preventing mistaken convictions in eyewitness identification trials. In R. Roesch, S. D. Hart, & J. R. P. Ogloff (Eds.), *Psychology and law: The state of the discipline* (pp. 89–118). New York: Kluwer Academic/Plenum.

Wells, G. L. (1993). What do we know about eyewitness identification? *American Psychologist, 48*, 553–571.

Wells, G. L., Small, M., Penrod, S., Malpass, R. S., Fulero, S. M., & Brimacombe, C. A. E. (1998). Eyewitness identification procedures: Recommendations for lineups and photospreads. *Law and Human Behavior, 22*, 603–647.

Wells, G. L., Wright, E. F., & Bradfield, A. L. (1999). Witnesses to crime: Social and cognitive factors governing the validity of people's reports. In R. Roesch, S. D. Hart, & J. R. P. Ogloff (Eds.), *Psychology and law: The state of the discipline* (pp. 53–87). New York: Kluwer Academic/Plenum.

KEY TERMS

- *Blank lineup*
- *Estimator variables*
- *Own-race bias*
- *System variables*
- *Unconscious transference*
- *Weapon focus effect*
- *Yerkes-Dodson law*

References

Bottoms, B., & Goodman, G. S. (1994). Perceptions of children's credibility in sexual assault cases. *Journal of Applied Social Psychology, 24*, 702–732.

Buckhout, R. (1974). Eyewitness testimony. *Scientific American, 231*, 23–31.

Ceci, S. J., & Bruck, M. (1993). The suggestibility of the child eyewitness: A historical review and synthesis. *Psychological Bulletin, 113*, 403–439.

Ceci, S. J., & Bruck, M. (1995). *Jeopardy in the courtroom: A scientific analysis of children's testimony*. Washington, DC: American Psychological Association.

Clifford, B. R., & Scott, J. (1978). Individual and situational factors in eyewitness testimony. *Journal of Applied Psychology, 63*, 352–359.

Costanzo, M. (1997). *Just revenge: Costs and consequences of the death penalty*. New York: St. Martin's Press.

Cutler, B. L., & Penrod, S. D. (1995). *Mistaken identification: The eyewitness, psychology and the law*. Cambridge, UK: Cambridge University Press.

Cutler, B. L., Penrod, S. D., & Dexter, H. R. (1990a). Juror sensitivity to eyewitness identification evidence. *Law and Human Behavior, 14*, 185–191.

Cutler, B. L., Penrod, S. D., & Dexter, H. R. (1990b). Nonadversarial methods for sensitizing jurors to eyewitness evidence. *Journal of Applied Social Psychology, 20*, 1197–1207.

Cutler, B. L., Penrod, S. D., & Martens, T. K. (1987). Improving the reliability of eyewitness identification: Putting context into context. *Journal of Applied Psychology, 72*, 629–637.

Cutler, B. L., Penrod, S. D., & Stuve, T. E. (1988). Juror decision making in eyewitness identification cases. *Law and Human Behavior, 12*, 41–55.

Deffenbacher, K. (1983). The influence of arousal on reliability of testimony. In S. M. A. Lloyd-Bostock & B. R. Clifford (Eds.), *Evaluating eyewitness evidence: Recent psychological research and new perspectives* (pp. 235–251). Chichester, England: Wiley.

Dekle, D. J., Beal, C. R., Elliott, R., & Huneycutt, D. (1996). Children as witnesses: A comparison of lineup versus showup identification methods. *Applied Cognitive Psychology, 10*, 1–12.

Ebbinghaus, H. E. (1964). *Memory: A contribution to experimental psychology*. New York: Dover.

Fiske, S. T., & Taylor, S. E. (1991). *Social cognition*. New York: McGraw-Hill.

Flin, R., Boone, J., Knox, A., & Bull, R. (1992). The effect of a five-month delay on children's and adult's eyewitness memory. *British Journal of Psychology, 83*, 323–336.

Goldstein, A. G., Chance, J. E., & Schneller, G. R. (1989). Frequency of eyewitness identification in criminal cases: A survey of prosecutors. *Bulletin of the Psychonomic Society, 27*, 71–74.

Goodman, G. S., Tobey, A. E., Batterman-Faunce, J. M., Orcutt, H., Thomas, S., Shapiro, C., & Sachsenmaier, T. (1998). Face-to-face confrontation: Effects of closed-circuit technology on children's eyewitness testimony and jurors' decisions. *Law and Human Behavior, 22,* 165–203.

Hoffman, H. G., Loftus, E. F., Greenmun, N., & Dashiell, R. L. (1992). The generation of misinformation. In F. Losel, D. Bender, & T. Bliesener (Eds.), *Psychology and law: International perspectives* (pp. 292–301). Berlin: Walter de Gruyter.

Johnson, M. K., & Foley, M. A. (1984). Differentiating fact from fantasy: The reliability of children's memory. *Journal of Social Issues, 40,* 33–50.

Kassin, S. M. (1998). Eyewitness identification procedures: The fifth rule. *Law and Human Behavior, 22,* 649–653.

Kassin, S. M., Ellsworth, P. C., & Smith, V. L. (1989). The "general acceptance" of psychological research on eyewitness testimony: A survey of the experts. *American Psychologist, 44,* 1089–1098.

Kramer, T. H., Buckhout, R., & Eugenio, P. (1990). Weapon focus, arousal, and eyewitness memory: Attention must be paid. *Law and Human Behavior, 14,* 167–184.

Lindsay, R. C. L., & Wells, G. L. (1980). What price justice? Exploring the relationship between lineup fairness and identification accuracy. *Law and Human Behavior, 4,* 303–314.

Lindsay, R. C. L., & Wells, G. L. (1985). Improving eyewitness identification from lineups: Simultaneous versus sequential lineup presentations. *Journal of Applied Psychology, 70,* 556–564.

Loftus, E. F. (1975). Leading questions and the eyewitness report. *Cognitive Psychology, 7,* 560–572.

Loftus, E. F. (1979). *Eyewitness testimony.* Cambridge, MA: Harvard University Press.

Loftus, E. F. (1984). Expert testimony on the eyewitness. In G. L. Wells & E. F. Loftus (Eds.), *Eyewitness testimony: Psychological perspectives* (pp. 273–283). New York: Cambridge University Press.

Loftus, E. F. (2000). Suggestions, imagination, and transformation of reality. In A. A. Stone, J. S. Turkkan, C. A. Bachrach, J. B. Jobe, H. S. Kurtzman, & V. S. Cain (Eds.), *The science of self-report: Implications for research and practice* (pp. 201–210). Mahwah, NJ: Erlbaum.

Loftus, E. F., & Palmer, J. C. (1974). Reconstruction of an automobile destruction: An example of the interaction between language and memory. *Journal of Verbal Learning and Verbal Behavior, 13,* 585–589.

Luus, C. A. E., & Wells, G. L. (1992). The perceived credibility of child eyewitnesses. In H. Dent & R. Flin (Eds.), *Children as witnesses* (pp. 73–92). New York: Wiley.

Malpass, R. S., & Kravitz, J. (1969). Recognition of faces of own and other race. *Journal of Personality and Social Psychology, 13,* 330–334.

Malpass, R. S., & Devine, P. G. (1981). Eyewitness identification: Lineup instructions and the absence of the offender. *Journal of Applied Psychology, 66,* 482–489.

Manson v. Braithwaite, 432 U.S. 98 (1977).

McCloskey, M., & Zaragoza, M. (1985). Misleading postevent information and memory for events: Arguments and evidence against memory impairment hypotheses. *Journal of Experimental Psychology: General, 114*, 1–16.

Meissner, C. A., & Brigham, J. C. (2001). Thirty years of investigating the own-race bias in memory for faces: A meta-analytic review. *Psychology, Public Policy, and Law, 7*, 3–35.

Memon, A., Hope, L., & Bull, R. (2003). Exposure duration: Effects on eyewitness accuracy and confidence. *British Journal of Psychology, 94*, 339–354.

Myers, J. E. B., Redlich, A. D., Goodman, G. S., Prizmich, L. P., & Imwinkelried, E. (1999). Jurors' perceptions of hearsay in child sexual abuse cases. *Psychology, Public Policy, and Law, 5*, 388–419.

Neil v. Biggers, 409 U.S. 188 (1972).

Penrod, S. D., & Cutler, B. L. (1995). Witness confidence and witness accuracy:Assessing their forensic relation. *Psychology, Public Policy, and Law, 1*, 817–845.

Penrod, S. D., & Cutler, B. L. (1999). Preventing mistaken convictions in eyewitness identification trials. In R. Roesch, S. D. Hart, & J. R. P. Ogloff (Eds.), *Psychology and law: The state of the discipline* (pp. 89–118). New York: Kluwer Academic/Plenum.

Peterson, C., & Bell, M. (1996). Children's memory for traumatic injury. *Child Development, 567*, 3045–3070.

Poole, D. A., & White, L. T. (1991). Effects of question repetition on the eyewitness testimony of children and adults. *Developmental Psychology, 27*, 975–986.

Poole, D. A., & White, L. T. (1993). Two years later: Effect of question repetition and retention interval on the eyewitness testimony of children and adults. *Developmental Psychology, 29*, 844–853.

Rosenthal, R. (1976). *Experimenter effects in behavioral research.* New York: Irvington.

Shepard, J. W. (1983). Identification after long delays. In S. Lloyd-Bostock & B. R. Clifford (Eds.), *Evaluating witness evidence* (pp. 173–187). Chichester, England: Wiley.

Steblay, N. M. (1997). Social influence in eyewitness recall: A meta-analytic review of lineup instruction effects. *Law and Human Behavior, 21*, 283–298.

Tobey, A. E., & Goodman, G. S. (1992). Children's eyewitness memory: Effects of participation and forensic context. *Child Abuse and Neglect, 16*, 779–796.

Tooley, V., Brigham, J. C., Maass, A., & Bothwell, R. K. (1987). Facial recognition: Weapon effect and attention focus. *Journal of Applied Social Psychology, 17*, 845–859.

Wells, G. L. (1978). Applied eyewitness testimony research: System variables and estimator variables. *Journal of Personality and Social Psychology, 36*, 1546–1557.

Wells, G. L. (1984). The psychology of lineup identifications. *Journal of Applied Social Psychology, 14*, 89–103.

Wells, G. L. (1993). What do we know about eyewitness identification? *American Psychologist, 48*, 553–571.

Wells, G. L., & Bradfield, A. L. (1998). "Good, you identified the suspect": Feedback to eyewitnesses distorts their reports of the witnessing experience. *Journal of Applied Psychology, 83*, 360–376.

Wells, G. L., Rydell, S. M., & Seelau, E. P. (1993). On the selection of distractors for eyewitness lineups. *Journal of Applied Psychology, 78*, 835–844.

Wells, G. L., Small, M., Penrod, S. D., Malpass, R. S., Fulero, S. M., & Brimacombe, C. A. E. (1998). Eyewitness identification procedures: Recommendations for lineups and photospreads. *Law and Human Behavior, 22*, 603–647.

Wells, G. L., Wright, E. F., & Bradfield, A. L. (1999). Witnesses to crime: Social and cognitive factors governing the validity of people's reports. In R. Roesch, S. D. Hart, & J. R. P. Ogloff (Eds.), *Psychology and law: The state of the discipline* (pp. 53–87). New York: Kluwer Academic/Plenum.

Chapter 6

POLICE INVESTIGATIONS, INTERROGATIONS, AND CONFESSIONS

CHAPTER OBJECTIVES

In this chapter, you will become familiar with:

- The rights of individuals when arrested and subjected to interrogation
- Strategies police use to elicit confessions
- The reasons people confess to crimes
- The frequency of false confessions

POLICE INTERROGATIONS AND CONFESSIONS

A confession is perhaps the most compelling evidence that can be presented in a criminal trial. A confession, even when subsequently retracted, can influence jury verdicts (Kassin & Sukel, 1997). Most jurors view confessions as accurate accounts of a defendant's culpability. Indeed, it is likely that the majority of confessions are valid, in that the suspect actually committed a criminal act. However, it is sometimes the case that confessions are false. In these cases, a suspect confesses to a crime he or she did not actually commit. In this chapter, we consider the factors that can lead to a false confession.

In order to understand the factors that can contribute to a false confession, one must distinguish between *personal* and *situational risk factors* (Kassin & Gudjonsson, 2004). Some individuals are more susceptible to respond to interrogative coercion by being more compliant or more suggestible. Younger suspects, particularly adolescents, or individuals with mental health problems may be more vulnerable to interrogation tactics. Intelligence, drug or alcohol use, and stress are other personal risk factors that may increase the likelihood of a false confession. In contrast, situational risk factors involve the particular techniques used to extract the confession, the time of day the interrogation was conducted, or the length of the interrogation. We review both personal and situational risk factors later in this chapter.

Most people believe that they would never falsely confess to a crime, so they cannot imagine that others would do so. People also tend to believe that confessions stem from individual rather than situational factors. This is known as a **fundamental attribution error**, which is the tendency to overemphasize dispositional or personality-based explanations for an individual's behavior while minimizing situational or external causes (Ross, 1977). When applied to confession evidence, this suggests that jurors would interpret a confession as reflecting the actual guilt of a defendant and discount the possibility of external causes, such as coercion.

Hugo Munsterberg, whose seminal book, *On the Witness Stand*, is discussed in Chapter 1 of this text, was perhaps the first psychologist to write about the false confession phenomenon. Munsterberg was convinced that a man who had been hanged for murder had falsely confessed to the crime. The press at the time heard of Munsterberg's comments on this case and he became the target of news stories and editorials attacking his view. It is unknown whether this man had actually falsely confessed, but the notion that it is possible that people do falsely confess remained difficult to accept until a number of cases surfaced beginning in the 1960s showing that false confessions can and do occur.

Review of Legal Cases

Given the implications of a confession, it is not surprising that there is a considerable amount of case law and research that has addressed the issue of ensuring that a suspect's rights are protected and that a confession is made voluntarily and without coercion. The landmark case of *Miranda v. Arizona* (1966) held that prior to interrogating a suspect, police must inform individuals of their legal rights. Ernesto Miranda was an indigent defendant who was arrested in Arizona on charges of kidnapping and rape. He was interrogated and signed a confession, and was ultimately found guilty of the charges. He did not have a lawyer present during interrogation nor was he asked if he wanted to have an attorney present. In a prior case, the U.S. Supreme Court in *Escobedo v. Illinois* (1964) recognized a suspect's right to an attorney during police interrogation. In *Miranda*, the Supreme Court extended this ruling by requiring police to warn suspects prior to interrogation or questioning of several rights, including the right to remain silent, that anything they say can be used against them in a court of law, the right to the presence of an attorney, and the right to free counsel if they cannot afford the cost of an attorney. These warnings are viewed as strengthening an individual's protection against self-incrimination during police interrogation. *Miranda* requires that an interrogation must cease if at any time prior to or during questioning a suspect states a wish to remain silent or to have an attorney present. Once an attorney is requested, the suspect must be given an opportunity to confer with the attorney and to have the attorney present during any subsequent questioning. Miranda's conviction was overturned, but he was subsequently tried without the confession evidence. He was convicted and served 11 years in prison.

A suspect may waive his or her rights under *Miranda*, but this requires that the rights be waived "voluntarily, knowingly and intelligently before interrogation can commence, otherwise the resulting confession will be inadmissible" (*Miranda*, p. 479), and further that "any evidence that the accused was threatened, tricked or cajoled into a waiver will, of course, show that the defendant did not voluntarily waive the privilege" (*Miranda*, p. 475). *Miranda* thus requires first that a suspect understand the nature of the rights that are being waived, and second, that any waiver of those rights is made voluntarily. The *Miranda* decision has survived a number of challenges, including an attempt by Congress to overturn it, but it has been affirmed in subsequent cases (see *Dickerson v. United States*, 2000).

It is perhaps surprising that only about one in five suspects exercise their *Miranda* rights (Leo, 1996). Police estimate that 81% of suspects waive their rights. Given that interrogation is inherently a stressful and risky situation, the exercise of the right to silence would make a good deal of sense as an avoidance response. So why do so many suspects waive their rights? Costanzo (2004) suggests several reasons, including the fact that detectives deemphasize Miranda warnings, innocent suspects want to show they have nothing to hide, and guilty suspects don't want to appear uncooperative. Costanzo adds that many suspects may not fully appreciate they are waiving their rights. White (2003) writes that police may use a variety of coercive techniques that are questionably legal, but adds that these techniques are difficult to prove that they resulted in a nonvoluntary waiver of Miranda rights.

Kassin and Norwick (2004) conducted a laboratory experiment to understand why most people waive their rights. The study involved 72 participants who were guilty or innocent of a mock theft. Prior to their interrogation, they were given instructions to avoid going to trial or be acquitted at trial. The participants were confronted by either a neutral, sympathetic, or hostile male "detective" who sought a waiver of their Miranda rights. Overall, about 58% of all suspects waived their rights, but over 80% of the innocent suspects waived their rights. Kassin and Norwick noted that these participants had a "naïve faith in the power of their own innocence to set them free" (p. 218), and they conclude that "Miranda warnings may not adequately protect from police authority the people who may need it most, those falsely accused of crimes they did not commit" (p. 218).

The issue of appreciation of rights is central to a valid waiver. Grisso (1981) conceptualizes appreciation of the significance of rights to comprise three main parts:

- One: Suspects must recognize the interrogative nature of police questioning.
- Two: Suspects must perceive the defense attorney as an advocate for them, and be willing to disclose confidential information to him or her (appreciation of the right to counsel).
- Three: Suspects must perceive the right to silence as a right that cannot be revoked, and that statements made by suspects can be used in court (appreciation of the right to silence).

An intelligent waiver of rights suggests that a suspect understands the language used in Miranda warnings. A number of studies suggest that the vocabulary used in some Miranda warnings may exceed the comprehension and reading level of some suspects. For example, Rogers, Hazelwood, Sewell, Harrison, and Shuman (2007) studied 356 different (written) English language versions of Miranda warnings (that there are so many variations of the Miranda warning is somewhat troubling in itself). They tested each version for reading level and found that they varied from elementary school to college. They found that the majority of the warnings required at least a seventh-grade reading level, with less than 1% of the warnings readable at a fifth-grade level (about 1% required college level reading ability!). Thus, the reading level of most Miranda warnings may exceed the capability of a substantial number of suspects.

Factors such as mental illness or mental retardation may also affect the accused's ability to make a knowing and voluntary waiver. Suspects with anxiety disorders, for example, may make a false confession as a way of escaping from the anxiety of an interrogation (Leo & Ofshe, 1998). Individuals with intellectual deficits may become confused, have a desire to please authority figures such as detectives, be more suggestible, or not fully appreciate the implications of a confession. Gudjonsson (2003) cites the case of Earl Washington, a mentally retarded man who confessed to murder and rape and was convicted and sentenced to death, despite the fact that he recanted his confession. His case was appealed on the basis that he had not voluntarily confessed and that he did not knowingly and intelligently waive his Miranda rights. He spent 18 years in prison before DNA evidence showed that he could not have committed the crime.

Rogers, Harrison, Hazelwood, and Sewell (2007) estimated that nearly 700,000 individuals with mental disorders are arrested annually in the United States. These authors administered Miranda comprehension measures to a sample of 107 mentally disordered defendants (MDOs), and found that most defendants lacked good comprehension on all but the simplest Miranda warnings (those requiring less than a sixth-grade reading level). About one-fourth of the sample had substantial deficits on measures of intellectual ability and general personality adjustment. This study raises serious questions about the ability of many mentally disordered suspects to waive their arrest rights.

Youth Capacity to Understand Arrest Rights

The *Kent* and *Gault* decisions (see Chapter 8 for a review of these two cases) establish the rights of youth in a variety of legal contexts. The age at which youth can be charged varies by state, but generally is between 8 and 18. Prior to *Gault*, youth were rarely represented by an attorney. Case law has now established that youth do have the right to an attorney. In *Fare v. Michael C.* (1979), the Supreme Court adopted the adult standard in a case involving a youth, and noted that the test allowed judicial review of factors such as a juvenile's age, experience, education, background, and intelligence in evaluating whether the youth had the capacity to understand the warnings, the nature of his or her rights, and the consequences of waiving those rights. Thus, the rights established in *Miranda* apply to youth, and police now routinely read youth their rights prior to interrogation. As we will see, the age of young suspects may require special protections to ensure their rights are protected. The likelihood of false confessions is higher for youth compared to adults. Drizin and Leo (2004), in a study discussed in more detail later in this chapter, reported that 35% of their sample of 125 proven false confessions were under the age of 17.

An example of a Miranda waiver form used by police for juvenile suspects in Washington State is shown in Box 6.1. It includes the four traditional Miranda warnings as well as two additional prongs utilized in some U.S. jurisdictions. Roesch, McLachlan, and Viljoen (2007) reported that a Flesch-Kincaid reading level analysis conducted on the Washington State warning form yielded a reading grade level of 9.2. This suggests that in order for youth to be able to read this warning, they would have to be able to read at about a ninth-grade level. This difficulty level is concerning, given the fact that youth much younger than 14 years old (a typical age for ninth-grade students) may be presented with the same form, and also that even those who are 14 years or older may have reading levels below the ninth-grade level. Indeed, research by Viljoen and Roesch (2005) indicated that the average IQ of a sample of youth in detention was 83, with reading levels well below ninth-grade. This study suggests that many youth would have difficulty understanding the vocabulary used in Miranda warnings.

Box 6.1 Washington State's Miranda Warning for Youth

- I have the right to remain silent and not make any statement at all.
- Any statement that I do make can and will be used against me in a court of law.
- I have the right to consult with and have an attorney present before and during questioning or the making of any statement.
- If I desire an attorney but cannot afford one, an attorney will be appointed for me at public expense prior to any questioning.
- I may exercise these rights at any time before or during questioning.
- If I am under 18 years of age I am considered a juvenile, but I do realize that this matter may be remanded to adult court for criminal prosecution, where I would be treated as an adult in all respects.

After initialing each of the above statements, the youth is asked to sign the form after reading the following:

- I understand each of these rights that I have read or had read to me. I understand that I may exercise these rights at any time before or during questioning. I do wish to waive my right to remain silent, and I do wish to waive my right to an attorney at this time.

From R. Roesch, K. McLachlan, & J. L. Viljoen (2007), p. 268.

Assessing Understanding and Appreciation of Rights

Grisso (1998) developed a forensic assessment instrument called the *Instruments for Assessing Understanding and Appreciation of Miranda Rights* to assist mental health professionals in evaluating whether an individual made a knowing and intelligent waiver of rights at the time of interrogation. Four subtests measure various aspects of comprehension and understanding of rights. Each of the subtests are scored separately and judged relative to one another to determine the level of understanding and appreciation of interrogation rights, and no total comprehension score is derived. The four subtests are:

Comprehension of Miranda Rights (CMR) assesses examinees' understanding of the four elements of a standard rights warning by asking them to paraphrase the meaning of each right in four items (e.g., "You do not have to make a statement and have the right to remain silent.").

Comprehension of Miranda Rights-Recognition (CMR-R) requires little verbal skill and requires examinees to compare the four elements of a typical rights warning with a pool of statements including accurate and inaccurate rewordings of each of the sentences. This subtest comprises 12 items, with three semantic comparison items for each of the standard rights prongs.

Comprehension of Miranda Vocabulary (CMV) requires examinees to provide definitions of six words contained in the interrogation warnings (e.g., *attorney* and *interrogation*).

Function of Rights in Interrogation (FRI) assesses the examinee's appreciation of the importance of rights in an interrogation and legal situations generally. This subtest comprises three subsections, each assessing appreciation of the significance of the warning in different areas including: recognition of the nature of interrogation (NI), significance of the right to counsel (RC), and significance of the right to silence (RS). Examinees are presented with a series of four pictures in which youth are shown interacting with various criminal justice figures, including police officers, a lawyer, and a court scenario. They are read a short description of what is happening in a given picture, and then asked questions about the scenario (e.g., "What is it that the police want Joe to do?").

Research has shown that younger children are more likely to have reduced capacity to understand their rights. In one study, Viljoen and Roesch (2005) administered Grisso's measure to 152 male and female defendants aged 11 to 17 in a detention center in Washington State. They found that age significantly predicted overall comprehension of rights, with younger adolescents demonstrating more impaired comprehension than older adolescents. Roesch and colleagues (2007) commented that coupled with anxiety that may be present under questioning by police, it is possible that many youth, especially younger ones, do not adequately understand their rights.

Given these findings, what can be done to protect the rights of youth? One suggestion is to require the presence of an adult before a youth could waive rights. This could be an attorney, but some states also allow a parent or other interested adult as a substitute. However, the expectation that parents would help ensure understanding and protect the rights of their child may sometimes not be realized in practice. Parents may place coercive pressures on youth to talk to the police because they are upset or angry with their child. They also may advise their children to waive their right to an attorney, encourage them to cooperate, and even adopt an adversarial attitude toward their own children. In their study of youth in pretrial detention, Viljoen, Klaver, and Roesch (2005) found 89% of youth indicated their parents wanted them to confess or tell the truth, 11% indicated that their parents wanted them to deny the offense, and none reported that their parents advised them to remain silent.

INTERROGATION TECHNIQUES

In 1930, police detectives interrogated Tony Colletti, an 18-year-old man whose wife had been murdered. Although he denied any involvement, police suspected he had killed his wife. Leo (2004) describes his interrogation:

At the station house during the next 26 hours, Colletti was questioned continuously in relays, lied to, threatened, yelled at, cursed, deprived of food and water, made to stand for hours, forced to stay awake, slapped, slugged with bare fists, stripped naked, and beaten with a rubber hose until he no longer denied killing his wife and finally agreed to sign a confession acknowledging guilt. (pp. 37–38)

Colletti later recanted the confession, claiming it was made under duress. It is not known whether he did kill his wife, because he hanged himself in jail prior to his trial. Leo (2004) notes that the techniques used to extract his confession, known in the popular culture as the **third degree**, were widely used by police in the 1920s and 1930s. The practice declined in the 1940s and by the 1950s, a new approach began to emerge. Modern interrogation techniques no longer use such strong-arm tactics, but rely instead on a more psychological approach that may involve deceptive techniques, including the presentation of false evidence.

Police officers and detectives receive extensive training on interviewing suspects. The most popular training approach is the **Reid Technique**. This approach was first introduced by Inbau and Reid in 1962, and it has since been revised and developed in several editions, with the most recent one authored by Inbau, Reid, Buckley, and Jayne in 2001.

Inbau and colleagues provide a detailed procedure for interrogating suspects, including advice about how to set up an interrogation room. The room should have minimal furniture (straightback chairs and a table), with nothing on the walls. One-way mirrors are common, to allow for observation from another room. Once the suspect is seated, interrogation begins, with the interrogator following the nine sequential steps that comprise the Reid Technique (Gudjonsson, 2003; Inbau et al., 2001; Leo, 2004):

1. Begin by confronting the suspect with his or her guilt. The interrogator states this confidently, even in the absence of clear evidence. The accusation of guilt may be repeated several times. The interrogator observes the reactions of the suspect, looking for signs of deception.
2. Develop psychological "themes" that justify or excuse the crime. The interrogator displays understanding and sympathy as a means of obtaining the suspect's trust. The themes suggested by the interrogator are designed to minimize guilt or provide possible excuses for committing the crime. "In this way the suspect can accept physical responsibility for the crime while at the same time either minimizing the seriousness of it or the internal blame for it" (Gudjonsson, 2003, p. 13).
3. Interrupt all statements of denial. "Repeated denials by the suspect are seen as being very undesirable because they give the suspect a psychological advantage" (Gudjonsson, p. 17). Inbau and colleagues (2001) argue that there are differences in denials by guilty and innocent suspects. "Innocent suspects' denials are said to be more spontaneous,

forceful, and direct, whereas denials of guilty suspects are more defensive, qualified, and hesitant" (Gudjonsson, p. 17).

4. Overcome the suspect's factual, moral, and emotional objections to the charges.

5. Ensure that the increasingly passive suspect does not tune out. The interrogator may do this by moving closer to the suspect, maintaining eye contact, and touching the suspect.

6. Show sympathy and understanding and urge the suspect to tell the truth.

7. Offer the suspect a face-saving alternative explanation for his or her guilty action. The interrogator presents two possible alternatives to explain the crime, with one alternative serving a face-saving function while the other represents a more callous or repulsive motivation. Both implicate the suspect, but one is seen as a more positive explanation for the crime. Gudjonsson comments, "It is a highly coercive procedure where suspects are pressured to choose between two incriminating alternatives when neither may be applicable" (p. 19).

8. Get the suspect to recount the details of the crime. This step follows from step 7 in which the suspect has accepted one of the alternative explanations. Once this occurs, the suspect is then asked to orally provide details.

9. Convert that statement into a full written confession. The suspect signs the confession.

Kassin and McNall (1991) observed that the strategies used by interrogators following the Reid Technique fell into two general categories. In **maximization**, the interrogator uses "scare tactics" designed to intimidate a suspect into a confession. This intimidation is achieved by emphasizing or even overstating the seriousness of the offense and the magnitude of the charges. Detectives might also make false or exaggerated claims about the evidence (e.g., by staging an eyewitness identification or a rigged lie-detector test, by claiming to have fingerprints or other types of forensic evidence, or by citing admissions that were supposedly made by an accomplice). In **minimization**, interrogators provide a false sense of security by offering face-saving excuses, moral justification, blaming a victim or accomplice, or playing down the seriousness of the charges. In the Central Park Jogger case (see Box 6.2), each of the five boys who confessed minimized their own involvement while placing more blame on the other boys (Kassin & Gudjonsson, 2003). Contrasting the two types of interrogation categories, Costanzo (2004) comments that "maximization *implies* a threat of severe punishment and minimization *implies* a promise of leniency" (p. 39).

Box 6.2 The Central Park Jogger

In 1989, a female jogger was beaten senseless raped, and left for dead in New York City's Central Park. Her skull had multiple fractures, her eye socket was crushed, and she lost three quarters of her blood. She managed to survive, but she was and still is completely amnesic for the incident (Meili, 2003). Within 48 hours, solely on the basis of police-induced confessions, five African American and Hispanic American boys, 14 to 16 years old, were arrested for the attack. All were ultimately tried, convicted, and sentenced to prison. The crime scene betrayed a bloody, horrific act, but no physical traces at all of the defendants. Yet it was easy to understand why detectives, under the glare of a national media spotlight, aggressively interrogated the boys, at least some of whom were "wilding" in the park that night. It was also easy to understand why the boys were then prosecuted and convicted. Four of their confessions were videotaped and presented at trial. The tapes were compelling, with each and every one of the defendants describing in vivid—though, in many ways, erroneous—detail how the jogger was attacked, when, where, and by whom, and the role that he played. One boy stood up and reenacted the way he allegedly pulled off the jogger's running pants. A second said he felt pressured by the others to participate in his "first rape." He expressed remorse and assured the assistant district attorney that he would not commit such a crime again. Collectively, the taped confessions persuaded police, prosecutors, two trial juries, a city, and a nation.

Thirteen years later, Matias Reyes, in prison for three rapes and a murder committed subsequent to the jogger attack, stepped forward at his own initiative and confessed. He said that he had raped the Central Park jogger and that he had acted alone. Investigating this new claim, the Manhattan district attorney's office questioned Reyes and discovered that he had accurate, privileged, and independently corroborated knowledge of the crime and crime scene. DNA testing further revealed that the semen samples originally recovered from the victim—which had conclusively excluded the boys as donors (prosecutors had argued at trial that the police may not have captured all the perpetrators in the alleged gang rape, but this did not mean they did not get some of them)—belonged to Reyes. In December 2002, the defendants' convictions were vacated. The case of the Central Park jogger revealed five false confessions resulting from a single investigation.

Excerpt from Kassin & Gudjonsson (2004, p. 34).

Kassin and McNall (1991) conducted several laboratory studies to examine how potential jurors perceived these interrogation approaches. They used transcripts from an actual interrogation in which these techniques were used and asked participants about their expectations for the sentence that might be received. Kassin (1997) concluded that these studies indicated that "(a) the use of maximization raised sentencing expectations, leading participants to expect a harsher sentence . . . and (b) minimization lowered sentencing expectations, which led participants to anticipate leniency" (p. 224). Gudjonsson (2003) comments that the Kassin and McNall studies "are important because they show that the techniques advocated by Inbau and his colleagues are inherently coercive in that they communicate implicit threats and promises to suspects" (p. 21).

DETECTING DECEPTION

One of the assumptions made in the Reid Technique is that detectives can distinguish between truthful and untruthful suspects. Psychological research suggests there is little support for the assumption that investigators can rely on verbal and nonverbal cues to make accurate judgments about whether a suspect is lying or telling the truth (Meissner & Kassin, 2004).

Kassin and colleagues (2007) surveyed 574 investigators from 16 police departments in five U.S. states and 57 customs officials from two Canadian provinces. They asked a series of questions about the inter-rogation process. In response to a question about their ability to detect lies, 77% said they could detect truthful and dishonest suspects. Kassin and colleagues comment that this figure far exceeds research findings on accuracy, as other research by Kassin (Kassin, Meissner, & Norwick, 2005) has shown that although police are more confident about their judg-ments of accuracy, they are actually no more accurate than lay people in detecting lies. Indeed, even with training, accuracy is only slightly better than chance.

Kassin's research is consistent with one of the first studies done on the ability to detect lying in interview situations. Ekman and O'Sullivan (1991) asked seven groups of participants to view videotaped inter-views of 10 university-aged women. They were told that half of the women were lying when they responded to questions about a film they had seen. The seven groups were (1) Secret Service agents, (2) federal polygraphers, (3) robbery investigators, (4) judges, (5) psychiatrists, (6) a group of students who had taken a university extension course on deceit, and (7) undergraduate psychology students. Participants were asked to decide if each woman was lying or telling the truth. Were any of the groups accurate in detecting deception? Only one group, Secret Service agents, performed better than chance. Ekman and O'Sullivan comment that many Secret Service agents had been assigned to protection work, guarding important government officials from potential attack. They speculate that this type of work may increase reliance on nonverbal cues (e.g., through scanning crowds), so that Secret Service agents paid greater attention to nonverbal behavior in their study. However, a study by Mann, Vrij, and Bull (2004), which used videotapes of actual sus-pects, found that police officers in England were able to detect truth or lies at a rate better than chance (65%), with more experienced officers performing better than less experienced ones. Even this more positive finding indicates that detectives are frequently wrong in their judgments of suspects.

The finding that investigators may not be accurate in judgments of guilt is particularly troubling because research has shown that a presumption of guilt can affect how the interrogation proceeds. Kassin, Goldstein, and Savitsky (2003) found that student interrogators in a controlled laboratory study who presumed guilt asked more guilt-presumptive questions, used a greater number of interrogation techniques, exerted more pressure on suspects to confess, and made innocent suspects sound more defensive and guilty to observers.

The presumption of guilt can lead to what has been referred to as **investigative bias**. Investigators will develop a theory about a crime, presume a suspect is guilty, and conduct the interrogation with the goal of obtaining a confession that fits that theory of the crime (Meissner & Kassin, 2004). The presumption of guilt is also related to the advocacy of more aggressive interrogation tactics. This approach may, as Saul Kassin (2005) has commented, put innocent individuals at a greater risk for making a false confession.

FALSE CONFESSIONS

A **false confession** occurs when individuals confess to a crime they did not commit or exaggerate involvement in a crime they did commit. As discussed in this chapter, there are many documented cases of false confessions that have resulted in a conviction. Box 6.3 summarizes one of these cases.

Box 6.3 A Case of a False Confession

Eddie Joe Lloyd was convicted of the 1984 murder of a 16-year-old girl in Detroit after he wrote to police with suggestions on how to solve various recent crimes. During several interviews, police fed details of the crime to Lloyd, who was mentally ill, and convinced him that by confessing he was helping them "smoke out" the real killer. Lloyd eventually signed a confession and gave a tape-recorded statement. The jury deliberated less than an hour before convicting him and the judge said at sentencing that execution, which had been outlawed in Michigan, would have been the "only justifiable sentence" if it were available. In 2002, DNA testing proved that Lloyd was innocent and he was exonerated. As mandated in a settlement with Lloyd's family, Detroit police officials said in 2006 that they would start videotaping all interrogations in crimes that could carry a sentence of life.

Source: http://www.innocenceproject.org/understand/False-Confessions.php.

Why would an innocent person confess to a crime that he or she didn't commit? In Lloyd's case (see Box 6.3), investigators fed him information that he could not otherwise have known, including details about the victim's clothing and location of her body. Lloyd spent 17 years in prison before being exonerated in 2002, becoming the 110th person to be released through the introduction of DNA evidence.

Kassin and McNall (1991) estimated a relatively small rate of less than 60 alleged false confessions occur annually in the United States, while others have set the rate much higher, perhaps over 600 (Huff, Rattner, & Sagarin, 1986). The rate is difficult to assess accurately because, for example, it is unknown what percent of recanted confessions are valid. Obviously, some guilty suspects may come to regret their confession and subsequently claim it was coerced. The only hard evidence for a false confession is the conviction of another person who actually committed the crime or through DNA testing exonerating the individual who had falsely confessed. Of course, this will underestimate the number of false confessions given that some innocent individuals who confessed are convicted and their false confessions are never proven.

DNA technology allowed researchers to provide estimates of the contribution of false confessions to wrongful convictions. For example, Connors, Lundregan, Miller, and McEwen (1996) found that 5 of 28 convictions in which DNA evidence established innocence were attributable to false confessions. The Innocence Project tracks cases in which convicted individuals have been exonerated. The Project has found that in more than 25% of over 200 DNA exoneration cases, innocent defendants made incriminating statements, delivered outright confessions, or pled guilty. As shown in Box 6.4, there are many reasons that may explain why this occurs, including mental impairment, as in the case of Eddie Joe Lloyd.

Box 6.4 The Innocence Project

The Innocence Project (www.innocenceproject.org) tracks cases in which individuals have been exonerated, most commonly due to DNA evidence proving that the convicted person was innocent.

- Why do innocent people confess? A variety of factors can contribute to a false confession during a police interrogation. Many cases have included a combination of several of these causes:
  - duress
  - coercion
  - intoxication
  - diminished capacity
  - mental impairment

- ignorance of the law
- fear of violence
- the actual infliction of harm
- the threat of a harsh sentence
- misunderstanding the situation

Some false confessions can be explained by the mental state of the confessor:

- Confessions obtained from juveniles are often unreliable. Children can be easily manipulated and are not always fully aware of their situation. Children and adults both are often convinced that they can "go home" as soon as they admit guilt.
- People with mental disabilities have often falsely confessed because they are tempted to accommodate and agree with authority figures. Further, many law enforcement interrogators are not given any special training on questioning suspects with mental disabilities. An impaired mental state due to mental illness, drugs, or alcohol may also elicit false admissions of guilt.
- Mentally capable adults also give false confessions due to a variety of factors like the length of interrogation, exhaustion, or a belief that they can be released after confessing and prove their innocence later.

One of the most shocking examples of false confessions is the Central Park Jogger case (refer back to Box 6.2). For many years, the victim was unknown and referred to only as the "Central Park Jogger" in media reports. Trisha Meili later identified herself, telling her story in a book entitled *I Am the Central Park Jogger*. Police apparently used a variety of tactics to get five young boys (all between the ages of 14 to 16) to confess, including fairly constant interrogation over a period ranging from 14 to 30 hours. Each of the boys subsequently retracted their confessions, stating that they did so because they expected they could go home (Kassin & Gudjonsson, 2004).

Research on False Confessions

Edwin Borchard (1932) was one of the first to identify cases in which innocent individuals were convicted. His work, although largely descriptive in nature, established that individuals can be falsely convicted, and led researchers to begin focusing on the reasons for false convictions as well as what can be done to prevent these outcomes.

It wasn't until the 1980s that researchers began to conduct empirical studies of wrongful convictions. Bedau and Radelet (1987) found that 49 of 350 cases (14%) of wrongful conviction in potentially capital cases in the United States from 1900–1987 were attributed to false confessions. False confessions resulting in convictions represent a high cost, both in terms of loss of liberty for individuals wrongly convicted as well as the cost of imprisonment. Drizin and Leo (2004) analyzed 125 cases of proven interrogation-induced false confessions. First, they found that 81% of the cases involved charges of murder, with convictions resulting in lengthy sentences or even the death penalty. One shocking finding was that the average length of interrogation was 16.3 hours, a figure many times higher than the less than two-hour average interrogation in over 90% of all cases in which suspects are interrogated. Their study also shows the high financial cost associated with false confessions. Only 44 of the 125 cases resulted in a conviction, because many cases were either never charged or did not result in successful prosecution. Of the 44 cases, 18 (41%) individuals were sentenced to more than 20 years or life in prison, and 9 (20%) were sentenced to death. Many of the individuals who were never convicted nevertheless spent considerable time in jail while awaiting trial; 24% of those never convicted spent more than a year in jail.

In addition to understanding false confessions through actual cases, it is possible to study this issue in the laboratory setting. Kassin and Kiechel (1996) used a creative approach to determine whether experimenters could use police interrogation techniques to get participants in an experiment to confess to a crime they did not commit. They were also interested in examining whether participants would make up details about the crime and whether they could come to believe that they actually committed the crime. Their experimental paradigm involved bringing participants into a lab ostensibly for a reaction time study. The 75 participants were seated at a keyboard across a table from a confederate who read a list of letters. The participants were instructed to type the letters but to avoid hitting the ALT key, as they were told that hitting this key would crash the computer and all the data would be lost. Although no one actually hit the ALT key, the computer crashed after 60 seconds. The participants had been randomly assigned to one of four groups in a 2 (high versus low vulnerability) × 2 (presence versus absence of a false incriminating witness) factorial design. Vulnerability was simulated by reading the letters at a slow or a fast pace (43 versus 67 letters per minute), and the confederate for half of the participants said she saw the participant hit the ALT key. Once the computer crashed, the experimenter appeared upset and accused the participant of crashing the computer. All participants initially denied the accusation. Upon further questioning, and the introduction of the false incriminating witness, the participants were asked to sign a confession.

The results of this study support the notion that participants will confess to a crime they did not commit. The researchers reported that 69% of the participants signed the confession, 28% evidenced internalized guilt (they believed they had pressed the ALT key), and 9% confabulated details to support their false beliefs. The results also showed different effects by condition. In the low vulnerability/no witness group, only 35% signed the confession, no one exhibited internalization or confabulated details. However, in the high vulnerability/witness group, all participants signed the confession, 65% came to believe they were guilty, and 35% made up details. The researchers noted that these results support the hypothesis that people can be induced to confess, to internalize guilt even when innocent, and that the risk for a false confession is increased when false evidence is produced.

Another laboratory study provides some evidence that age is a factor in explaining false confessions. Goldstein, Condie, Kalbeitzer, Osman, and Geier (2003) studied a sample of 57 adolescent boys, ranging in age from 13 to 18, drawn from a residential, postadjudication, juvenile justice facility. They administered the *Perceptions of Coercion during Holding and Interrogation Procedures (P-CHIP)*, a measure that assessed the participants self-reported likelihood of offering false confessions while various police interrogation techniques were applied to a hypothetical situation. The participants read a vignette describing a police interrogation of an adolescent falsely accused of stealing a watch and kicking a boy. Twenty-six police behaviors were systematically added to the interrogation that were based on the Reid Technique (e.g., police told the child if he confessed, they would allow him to leave; police told the child if he did not confess at that moment, he would spend the rest of his life in prison; police told the child if he did not confess, his parents would be very disappointed in him). Following the description of each of the 26 police behaviors, participants were asked their likelihood (on a 6-point scale) of offering a false confession. As shown in Figure 6.1, this study found that age was the most important risk factor for self-reported likelihood of offering a false confession, as most participants 15 years or younger had substantially higher rates of false confessions. Overall, 25% said they would definitely give a false confession in at least one scenario. Goldstein and colleagues conclude that police should be particularly cautious about ensuring for youth, especially those younger than 16 years.

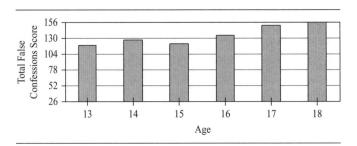

Figure 6.1   Total self-reported likelihood of false confession score by age

While laboratory studies provide valuable information, it is not clear whether the results reported by Kassin and Keichel or Goldstein and colleagues can be generalized to actual interrogation situations. The consequences of confessing in a laboratory setting are trivial compared to the real-life consequences of confessing to police in a criminal investigation. Nevertheless, studies such as these generate intriguing questions about the manner in which confessions are elicited.

Types of False Confessions

There are three types of false confessions.

A **voluntary false confession** occurs when an innocent person confesses without being prompted by the police. Cases in which there is considerable media attention often draw voluntary false confessions. For example, John Mark Karr was detained in Thailand and returned to the United States after he had voluntarily confessed to the still unsolved murder of JonBenet Ramsay. Evidence later showed that he could not have been her killer. The motivation for this type of false confession may be to gain fame or notoriety. A desire to protect friends or relatives is another motivation for a voluntary false confession.

A **coerced-compliant false confession** occurs when a suspect wishes to escape from the stress of the interrogation, to avoid a threat of harm or punishment, or to gain a promised or implied reward such as being allowed to sleep, eat, or make a phone call. The Central Park jogger case is an example of a coerced-compliant false confession, because the boys were interrogated over lengthy periods, were deprived of sleep, and thought they would be allowed to go home if they confessed.

Box 6.5 Case Study: Using Polygraph Results to Elicit a Confession

On the night of September 28, 1973, Barbara Gibbons of Canaan, Connecticut, was brutally killed in her home. Her throat was slashed almost severing her head, and her legs were broken, apparently after she was killed. There was evidence she had been sexually molested. There were multiple cuts to her body, and the bedroom was splashed with blood. Peter Reilly, her son, claimed that he returned home and found his mother on the floor of her bedroom, covered with blood and breathing with difficulty.

State police who questioned Peter immediately suspected him because he appeared to express no grief. The fact that he claimed to have found his mother alive, and that her legs were apparently broken after she died, raised police suspicions about his involvement. But when police examined him, they found no blood on his clothes or on his body. After his explanation to the police, he was held overnight, then interrogated. At some point, he requested a polygraph test, in the apparent belief that its results would clear him of any suspicion. However, he had not slept the night before, and as the questioning wore on for more than six hours, he eventually agreed with the police that he might have killed his mother but then blocked the event from his memory. His interrogation was recorded, and later transcripts revealed that although he was not intimidated or threatened physically, he became more and more confused and eager to please his questioners during the lengthy process.

He later recanted the confession, and after extensive community effort, he appealed for a new trial based on new evidence. His petition for a new trial was granted, but the state never brought him to a second trial and charges against him were dismissed.

The following is an excerpt from the interrogation transcript:

Peter: The polygraph test is giving me some doubts right now. Disregarding the test, I don't think I hurt my mother.

Det.: You're so damned ashamed of last night that you're trying to just block it out of your mind.

Peter: I'm not purposely denying it. If I did it, I wish I knew I'd done it. I'd be more than happy to admit it if I knew it. But I don't remember it. . . . Have you ever been proven totally wrong? A person, just from nervousness responds that way?

Det.: No, the polygraph can never be wrong because it is just a recording device, recording from you.

Peter: But if I did it, and I didn't realize it, there's got to be some clue in the house.

Det.: I've got this clue here, the polygraph charts. This is a recording of your mind.

Peter: Would it definitely be me? Could it be someone else?

Det.: No way, not from these reactions.

Source: http://law.jrank.org/pages/3232/Peter-Reilly-Trial-1974–1976-Son-Confesses.html.

A **coerced-internalized false confession** results from highly suggestive interrogations. As Kassin (1997) notes, a suspect who is coerced, tired, and highly suggestible actually comes to believe that he or she committed the crime. The case of Peter Reilly (see Box 6.5) is an example of this type of false confession. Kassin comments that two factors account for this type of false confession. One is a internal factor, involving a vulnerable suspect with a malleable memory due to youth, interpersonal trust, naiveté, suggestibility, lack of intelligence, stress, fatigue, alcohol, or substance use. The second is an external factor, involving the presentation of false evidence such as the false polygraph feedback provided to Peter Reilly.

Kassin and Gudjonsson (2004) summarize the case of 14-year-old Michael Crowe as an example of a coerced-internalized false confession:

> At first, Michael vehemently denied that he had stabbed his sister Stephanie. Eventually, however, he conceded that he was a killer: "I'm not sure how I did it. All I know is I did it" (see Drizin & Colgan, 2004, p. 141). This admission followed three interrogation sessions during which Michael was told that his hair was found in Stephanie's grasp, that her blood was in his bedroom, that all means of entry to the house were locked, and that he had failed a lie test—all claims that were false. Failing to recall the stabbing, Michael was persuaded that he had a split personality, that "good Michael" had blocked out the incident, and that he should try to imagine how "bad Michael" had killed Stephanie. . . . the charges against the boys were later dropped when a local vagrant seen in the area that night was found with Stephanie's blood on his clothing. (p. 50)

The Role of Compliance and Suggestibility

Two psychological constructs are important in understanding false confessions. The first is **compliance**, which is the tendency to go along with people in authority. The second is **suggestibility**, which is the tendency to internalize information communicated during questioning. Compliance is a factor in coerced-compliant false confessions, while suggestibility is related to coerced-internalized confessions.

The distinction between compliance and suggestibility is an important one. A compliant suspect would confess to a crime, even one that he or she didn't commit, in an effort to please an interrogator or avoid conflict or confrontation. A suggestible suspect might confess to a crime because he or she has come to believe or internalize information communicated during the interrogation process. Gisli Gudjonsson, a British researcher, has developed scales to measure both of these constructs.

The *Gudjonsson Compliance Scale* (GCS) contains 20 true/false items that measure two types of interview behavior (Gudjonsson, 2003). The first type of interview behavior measured assesses the tendency to comply with requests and obey instructions for instrumental gain, such as the termination of the interrogation, release from custody, avoidance of conflict, or eagerness to please the interviewer. The second type of interview behavior measured assesses susceptibility to pressure from others to commit an offense. Examples of items are "I tend to give in to people who insist that they are right," "I try hard to please others," and "I generally believe in doing as I am told." Research on the GCS suggests that this is a promising measure of compliance. Gudjonsson reports that the GCS is correlated with other measures with which it is theoretically related, such as social desirability and social conformity. In a naturalistic study, Gudjonsson found that the GCS discriminated between false confessors and those suspects who resisted police pressure to confess.

Gudjonsson's Suggestibility Scales (GSS) measure interrogative suggestibility, and tap into two distinct forms of suggestibility: the extent to which people *yield* to misleading questions, and the extent to which people *shift* their answers after receiving negative feedback (Gudjonsson, 2003). The scales are designed to measure "individual differences in the degree to which they may yield to suggestions by police officers" (Grisso, 2003, p. 164), and whether a person's confession may have been distorted or false (Gudjonsson, 2003). The measure is presented as a memory test, and it employs one of two narrative paragraphs describing a fictitious story that is played on audiotape. After listening to the story, individuals are asked to recall as many details from the story as they can, both immediately and again after a 50-minute delay. The second portion of the GSS asks participants 20 specific questions about the content of the story, 15 of which are misleading. Regardless of actual performance on these questions, participants are provided with negative feedback from the examiner who informs them that they have made a number of errors. They are then sternly asked to respond to the same set of questions again and to try and provide more accurate answers. The extent to which individuals give in to the misleading questions is scored as a yield, and any change in the person's answers from the previous trial is noted as shift. The yield and shift scores are then added together for a Total Suggestibility score.

Research shows that children are more suggestible than adolescents and adults, as measured by the GSS (Gudjonsson, 2003), and that suggestibility decreases steadily as age increases (Warren, Hulse-Trotter, & Tubbs, 1991). Gudjonsson (2003) has suggested that interrogative suggestibility is possibly related to the likelihood of false confession. Most of the research on this possibility has been conducted in labs. In one such study, Redlich and Goodman (2003) demonstrated that younger and more suggestible adolescent participants were more likely than young adults to falsely take responsibility for crashing a computer in an experimental paradigm. Interestingly, they found that while participants' GSS shift scores were unrelated to confession, those who were more likely to yield to misleading questions were also more likely to agree with an experimenter's request to (falsely) sign a confession form.

Suggestibility may also be a factor in understanding arrest rights. Redlich, Silverman, and Steiner (2003) investigated the relationship between Miranda rights comprehension and suggestibility in a sample of 18 juveniles (14 to 17 years old) and 17 young adults (18 to 25 years old) recruited from various community settings. They found that higher suggestibility in terms of yielding to misleading questions (GSS yield) significantly predicted increased comprehension and overall scores of Miranda rights understanding. Further, they found that higher suggestibility in terms of shifting answers after receiving negative feedback (GSS shift) was associated with lower comprehension. One implication of this research is that those individuals who are more susceptible to waiving arrest rights may also be at an increased risk for false confessions.

Recommendations for Reducing False Confessions

False confessions do occur. So, what can be done to reduce them? The Innocence Project has recommended specific changes in the practice of suspect interrogations in the United States, including the mandatory video recording of interrogations, which has been shown to decrease the number of false confessions and increase the reliability of confessions as evidence. The Project recommends that the entire custodial interrogation be recorded, and in fact, this is now the practice in over 500 jurisdictions nationwide, including the states of Alaska, Minnesota, and Illinois. Recording allows a later assessment of the accuracy of a confession. The Project notes that in some false confession cases, police may inadvertently communicate details of the crime. When a suspect later recounts these details, the police take the knowledge as evidence of guilt. The Project also notes that threats or promises may be made to the suspect off camera and then the camera is turned on for a false confession. Recording the entire interrogation would prevent this from happening. To avoid contaminating a confession with facts provided to the suspect, Leo and Ofshe (1998) recommended that investigators evaluate the suspect's postadmission narrative to determine the extent to which the details provided in the statement are consistent with known facts in the case. Investigators should not provide a suspect with details of the crime during the course of an interrogation (including evidentiary materials, crime scene photographs, or visits to the crime scene).

A model for police interrogation has been developed in England and Wales (Bull & Milne, 2004). Coercive interrogation techniques are explicitly forbidden. The approach includes extensive training of police officers in noncoercive interview techniques aimed at obtaining accurate information from a suspect. Interviewers are instructed to keep an open mind about the innocence or guilt of the suspect and to treat all suspects fairly. Vulnerable suspects are to be treated with special consideration.

Another safeguard is to allow expert testimony about the research on false confessions. This type of testimony would not focus on the validity of a particular confession but rather on the research on interviewing and interrogation, as well as the factors that may increase the risk of a false confession. Many, but not all, states do allow this form of testimony (Fulero, 2004).

SUMMARY

This chapter provides a review of the arrest and interrogation process. The process begins with an arrest, at which time a suspect is read their Miranda rights. The majority of suspects waive those rights, despite the risks involved in submitting to an interrogation. Particular attention was paid to issues surrounding waiver of rights by youth and mentally disordered suspects, as research shows that many individuals in these groups may not fully understand their rights and may be more susceptible to making false confessions. Police strategies for soliciting a confession were reviewed, including the commonly used Reid Technique. A confession is perhaps the most compelling evidence that can be presented in a criminal trial, and police are motivated to obtain a confession once they believe a suspect is guilty. Although the heavy-handed tactics used in the past are no longer relied upon, police are now trained in a variety of sophisticated psychological strategies designed to convince a suspect to confess. Many do, although some of these confessions turn out to be untrue. Reasons for false confessions were reviewed, and strategies for reducing the risk of false confessions were presented.

SUGGESTED READINGS

Ekman, P., & O'Sullivan, M. (1991). Who can catch a liar? *American Psychologist, 46,* 913–920.

Kassin, S. M., & Gudjonsson, G. H. (2004). The psychology of confessions: A review of the literature and issues. *Psychological Science in the Public Interest, 5,* 35–67.

Meissner, C. A., & Kassin, S. M. (2004). "You're guilty, so just confess!" Cognitive and behavioral confirmation biases in the interrogation room. In G. D. Lassiter (Ed.), *Interrogations, confessions, and entrapment* (pp. 85–106). New York: Kluwer Academic.

Rogers, R., Hazelwood, L. L., Sewell, K. W., Harrison, K. S., & Shuman, D. W. (2007). The language of Miranda warnings in American jurisdictions: A replication and vocabulary analysis. *Law and Human Behavior, 37,* 401–418.

KEY TERMS

- *Coerced-compliant false confession*
- *Coerced-internalized false confession*

- *Compliance*
- *False confessions*
- *Fundamental attribution error*
- *Investigative bias*
- *Maximization*
- *Minimization*
- *Reid Technique*
- *Suggestibility*
- *Third degree*
- *Voluntary false confession*

References

Bedau, H. A., & Radelet, M. L. (1987). Miscarriages of justice in potentially capital cases. *Stanford Law Review, 40*, 21–179.

Borchard, E. (1932). *Convicting the innocent.* New York: Garden City.

Bull, R. and Milne, R., (2004). Attempts to improve police interviewing of suspects. In G. D. Lassiter (Ed.), *Interrogation, confessions and entrapment* (pp. 181–196). New York: Kluwer/Plenum.

Connors, E., Lundregan, T., Miller, N., & McEwen, T. (1996). *Convicted by juries, exonerated by science: Case studies in the use of DNA evidence to establish innocence after trial.* Washington, DC: National Institute of Justice.

Costanzo, M. (2004). *Psychology applied to law.* Belmont, CA: Wadsworth/ Thomson Learning.

Dickerson v. United States, 120 S. Ct. 2326 (2000).

Drizin, S. A., & Colgan, B. A. (2004). Tales from the juvenile confessions front. In G. D. Lassiter (Ed.), *Interrogations, confessions, and entrapment* (pp. 127–162). New York: Kluwer Academic.

Drizin, S. A., & Leo, R. A. (2004). The problem of false confessions in the post-DNA world. *North Carolina Law Review, 82*, 891–1007.

Ekman, P., & O'Sullivan, M. (1991). Who can catch a liar? *American Psychologist, 46*, 913–920.

Escobedo v. Illinois, 378 U.S. 478 (1964).

Fare v. Michael *C.*, 442 U.S. 707 (1979).

Fulero, S. M. (2004). Expert psychological testimony on the psychology of interrogations and confessions. In G. D. Lassiter (Ed.), *Interrogations, confessions, and entrapment* (pp. 247–263). New York: Kluwer Academic.

Goldstein, N. E. S., Condie, L. O., Kalbeitzer, R., Osman, D., & Geier, J. L. (2003). Juvenile offenders' Miranda rights comprehension and self-reported likelihood of offering false confessions. *Assessment, 10*, 359–369.

Grisso, T. (1981). *Juveniles' waiver of rights: Legal and psychological competence.* New York: Plenum.

Grisso, T. (1998). *Instruments for assessing understanding and appreciation of Miranda rights.* Sarasota, FL: Professional Resources.

Grisso, T. (2003). *Evaluating competencies: Forensic assessments and instruments* (2nd ed.). New York: Kluwer Academic/Plenum.

Gudjonsson, G. H. (2003). *The psychology of interrogations and confessions.* London: Wiley.

Huff, C. R., Rattner, A., & Sagarin, E. (1986). Guilty until proved innocent: Wrongful conviction and public policy. *Crime & Delinquency, 35,* 518–544.

Inbau, F. E., & Reid, J. E. (1962). *Criminal interrogation and confessions.* Baltimore: Williams & Wilkins.

Inbau, F. E., Reid, J. E., Buckley, J. P., & Jayne, B. C. (2001). *Criminal interrogation and confessions* (4th ed.). Gaithersburg, MD: Aspen.

Kassin, S. M. (1997). The psychology of confession evidence. *American Psychologist, 52,* 221–233.

Kassin, S. M. (2005). On the psychology of confessions: Does *innocence* put *innocents* at risk? *American Psychologist, 60,* 215–228.

Kassin, S. M., Goldstein, C. J., & Savitsky, K. (2003). Behavioral confirmation in the interrogation room: On the dangers of presuming guilt. *Law and Human Behavior, 27,* 187–203.

Kassin, S. M., & Gudjonsson, G. H. (2004). The psychology of confessions: A review of the literature and issues. *Psychological Science in the Public Interest, 5,* 35–67.

Kassin, S. M., & Kiechel, K. L. (1996). The social psychology of false confessions: Compliance, internalization, and confabulation. *Psychological Science, 7,* 125–128.

Kassin, S. M., Leo, R. A., Meissner, C. A., Richman, K. D., Colwell, L. H., Leach, A., & La Fon, D. (2007). Police interviewing and interrogation: A self-report survey of police practices and beliefs. *Law and Human Behavior, 31,* 381–400.

Kassin, S. M., & McNall, K. (1991). Police interrogations and confessions: Communicating promises and threats by pragmatic implication. *Law and Human Behavior, 15,* 233–251.

Kassin, S. M., Meissner, C. A., & Norwick, R. J. (2005). "I'd know a false confession if I saw one": A comparative study of college students and police investigators. *Law and Human Behavior, 29,* 211–227.

Kassin, S. M., & Norwick, R. J. (2004). Why suspects waive their *Miranda* rights: The power of innocence. *Law and Human Behavior, 28,* 211–221.

Kassin, S. M., & Sukel, H. (1997). Coerced confessions and the jury: An experimental test of the "harmless error" rule. *Law and Human Behavior, 21,* 27–46.

Leo, R. A. (1996). *Miranda*'s revenge: Police interrogation as a confidence game. *Law and Society Review, 30,* 259–288.

Leo, R. A. (2004). The third degree and the origins of psychological police interrogation in the United States. In G. D. Lassiter (Ed.), *Interrogations, confessions, and entrapment* (pp. 37–84). New York: Kluwer Academic.

Leo, R. A., & Ofshe, R. J. (1998). The consequences of false confessions: Deprivations of liberty and miscarriages of justice in the age of psychological interrogation. *Journal of Criminal Law and Criminology, 88,* 429–496.

Mann, S., Vrij, A., & Bull, R. (2004). Detecting true lies: Police officers' ability to detect suspects' lies. *Journal of Applied Psychology, 89,* 137–149.

Meili, T. (2003). *I am the Central Park jogger: A story of hope and possibility.* New York: Scribner.

Meissner, C. A., & Kassin, S. M. (2004). "You're guilty, so just confess!" Cognitive and behavioral confirmation biases in the interrogation room. In G. D. Lassiter (Ed.), *Interrogations, confessions, and entrapment* (pp. 85–106). New York: Kluwer Academic.

Miranda v. Arizona, 384 U.S. 336 (1966).

Redlich, A. D., & Goodman, S. (2003). Taking responsibility for an act not committed: The influence of age and suggestibility. *Law and Human Behavior, 27,* 141–156.

Redlich, A. D., Silverman, M., & Steiner, H. (2003). Pre-adjudicative and adjudicative competence in juveniles and young adults. *Behavioral Sciences and the Law, 21,* 393–410.

Roesch, R., McLachlan, K., & Viljoen, J. L. (2007). The capacity of juveniles to understand and waive arrest rights. In R. Jackson (Ed.), *Learning forensic assessment* (pp. 265–289). New York: Routledge.

Rogers, R., Harrison, K. S., Hazelwood, H. L., & Sewell, K. W. (2007). Knowing and intelligent: A study of Miranda warnings in mentally disordered defendants. *Law and Human Behavior, 31,* 401–418.

Rogers, R., Harrison, K. S., Shuman, D. W., Sewell, K. W., & Hazelwood, L. L. (2007). An analysis of Miranda warnings and waivers: Comprehension and coverage. *Law and Human Behavior, 31,* 177–192.

Rogers, R., Hazelwood, L. L., Sewell, K. W., Harrison, K. S., & Shuman, D. W. (2007). The language of Miranda warnings in American jurisdictions: A replication and vocabulary analysis. *Law and Human Behavior, 37,* 401–418.

Ross, L. (1977). The intuitive psychologist and his shortcomings: Distortions in the attribution process. In L. Berkowitz (Ed.), *Advances in experimental social psychology* (Vol. 10, pp. 173–220). New York: Academic Press.

Viljoen, J. L., Klaver, J., & Roesch, R. (2005). Legal decisions of preadolescent and adolescent defendants: Predictors of confessions, pleas, communication with attorneys, and appeals. *Law and Human Behavior, 29,* 253–257.

Viljoen, J. L., & Roesch, R. (2005). Competence to waive interrogation rights and adjudicative competence in adolescent defendants: Cognitive development, attorney contact, and psychological symptoms. *Law and Human Behavior, 29*, 723–742.

Warren, A., Hulse-Trotter, K., & Tubbs, E. C. (1991). Inducing resistance to suggestibility in children. *Law and Human Behavior, 15*, 273–285.

White, W. (2003). *Miranda's waning protections: Police interrogation practices after Dickerson*. Ann Arbor, MI: The University of Michigan Press.

Chapter 7

JURIES AND LEGAL DECISION MAKING

CHAPTER OBJECTIVES

In this chapter, you will become familiar with:

- The definition of **legal decision making**
- The various contexts in which legal decision making takes place
- The unique characteristics of juries as legal decision makers
- The difference between grand and petit (trial) juries
- The basic structure and functions of petit juries
- The different models of jury decision making
- The process of juror selection

In this chapter, we examine the psychology of juries. Juries represent one form of legal decision making, which is the process of using procedural and substantive law to settle disputes heard in public forums. We begin by discussing the nature of legal decision making, identifying its unique features, differentiating it from other types of decision making, and considering various contexts in which it is used. We then focus in detail on juries, discussing the law and reviewing the research to gain a better understanding of how they are formed and how they function.

CASE STUDY

In a story that quickly garnered national media attention in the United States, 27-year-old Laci Peterson was reported missing from her Modesto, California home by her husband, Scott Peterson, on December 24, 2002. What made the case so compelling was not that Laci went missing on Christmas Eve, but that she was eight months pregnant at the time. Police searched in vain for Laci for several months. Scott, supported by Laci's family and friends, spoke about the case at several press conferences.

Investigators eventually focused on Scott as a potential suspect based on several reasons. First, his statements contained inconsistencies about what was he was doing when his wife disappeared. Initially, he had reported that he was golfing but later maintained that he had been fishing. A second reason was the revelation that he had been having extramarital affairs. The third reason was that one of the women with whom Scott had an affair came forward and gave damning information to police. She said Scott told her about two weeks before Laci disappeared that he had recently lost his wife and would be spending Christmas alone. During the Christmas holidays, Scott phoned her, claiming to be on vacation in Paris when he was actually attending a candlelight vigil for Laci, who was still missing at the time.

In April 2002, the body of the Peterson's unborn child, already named Conner, was found only a few miles from the place where Scott said he had gone fishing the day Laci went missing. Laci's body was recovered close by the next day. Autopsy could not determine a specific cause of death for Laci, but did reveal she had suffered broken ribs prior to her death that could not be explained by accidental drowning. The only other piece of forensic evidence was the discovery of one of Laci's hairs on a pair of pliers in Scott's toolbox. Despite the lack of evidence tying Scott directly to Laci's disappearance, police arrested him on April 18, 2002, and charged him with her murder and the murder of his unborn son. At the time of his arrest, Scott's physical appearance had changed—he had dyed his hair and goatee—and he also had in his possession various articles (e.g., camping equipment, various credit cards and driver's licenses) that gave rise to suspicion he was intending to flee or go into hiding.

Media coverage of the Peterson case became even more intense, and public sentiment toward Scott grew increasingly negative. As the time for trial approached, a change of venue was ordered from Modesto to Redwood City. This was an attempt to increase the chances of selecting an unbiased jury. But after a jury was selected and the trial of People of the State of California vs. Scott Peterson started in June 2004, problems with the jury became apparent. During the trial itself, one juror was dismissed and replaced by an alternate after being seen exchanging words with Laci Peterson's older brother. Later, only four days after the start of deliberation, the jury foreman approached the judge and asked to be dismissed, citing problems getting along with other jurors who felt he was too controlling. The request was denied by the judge who admonished the jury and instructed it to resume deliberations. Then, a second juror was dismissed for misconduct and replaced by an alternate, after the juror admitted she had gathered her own evidence outside the court. When the jury learned they would need to start deliberations all over again, they also voted for a new foreman; this led to the dismissal of the previous foreman (at his request) and the appointment of yet another alternate. After only seven hours of deliberation, the reconstituted jury—satisfied with the circumstantial evidence presented by the prosecution and unconvinced by the defense theory that someone else was responsible for the murders—voted unanimously to convict Scott Peterson of first-degree murder with special circumstances in the death of Laci and second-degree murder in the death of his unborn son.

But the jury's work wasn't done. They reconvened a month later for the penalty phase of the trial. They heard evidence and then began deliberations; and once again, the deliberations were difficult. For a time the jury was deadlocked, with 10 jurors favoring the death penalty and two favoring life in prison. In an effort to avoid a hung jury, the foreman took several steps, including asking jurors to look once again at photos of the victims and to state their reasons behind their votes. When they took another vote a short time later the result was unanimous, and the jury recommended the death sentence for Peterson.

After the jury was discharged, jurors finally were able to discuss their experiences and they eventually published them in the book, We, the Jury: Deciding the Scott Peterson Case (Berattis et al., 2007). Their stories are compelling: learning to cope with the stresses of trial; struggling to decide how the process of deliberations should be organized; and dealing with emotions after reaching their verdicts. The story of the Peterson case reveals both the strengths and flaws of the jury system, and the book provides a fascinating glimpse inside the private world of the jury itself.

LEGAL DECISION MAKING: A SEARCH FOR JUSTICE

Justice is, in essence, the moral correctness, fairness, peace, or harmony of people's collective conduct—how we interact, share resources, respond to disputes and wrong-doing, and repair harm. It is central to our conception of society and civilization. Commonsense notions of justice incorporate three basic elements: fair rules, fair play, and fair outcome. *Fair rules* means the laws that govern people are explicit, and the same laws apply to everyone. *Fair play* means that laws are administered and enforced routinely and consistently. *Fair outcome* means that the net result of the laws and their administration and enforcement is the expected and proper one. This commonsense notion of justice is reflected in the many representations of Justitia, also known as Lady Justice, which can be found outside courts and other public buildings throughout Europe and the Americas. According to Roman mythology, Justitia (*Iustitia* in Latin) was one of the four Virtues, along with Prudence, Fortitude, and Temperance. Justitia embodied the attributes of mythological figures from more ancient civilizations, including the Greek goddesses Themis and Dike, and the Egyptian goddess Ma'at. For the Romans, Justitia personified the natural and divine rightness of law; her image has come to personify the moral basis of the legal system throughout the Western world (Capers, 2006). She is often depicted as a bare-breasted or lightly cloaked woman, carrying scales, a sword, and a scroll of laws, and is often blindfolded (see Figure 7.1). The

Figure 7.1   Justitia (Lady Justice)
Statue of Justitia by John Massey Rhind From Image:JMR-Memphis1.jpg on en.wikipedia photo by Einar Einarsson Kvaran aka Carptrash 19:52, 12 October 2006 (UTC). *Permission is granted to copy, distribute and/ or modify this document under the terms of the **GNU Free Documentation License**, Version 1.2 or any later version published by the Free Software Foundation; with no Invariant Sections, no Front-Cover Texts, and no Back-Cover Texts. A copy of the license is included in the section entitled "GNU Free Documentation License."*

symbolism is clear (Capers, 2006; Luban, 2001). On the one hand, Justitia is a young woman, full of passion and emotion, with the power to nurture others out of compassion or strike them down, seeking vengeance. On the other hand, Justitia's powers are limited by the scales, blindfold, and scroll of laws, which force her to carefully listen to and weigh information and follow tradition in reaching an impartial decision.

Legal decision making seeks justice. Legal decision making is quite different from what can be termed **operational decision making** by justice professionals, which is the process of using personal knowledge, skills, and abilities to determine the most appropriate course of action in a given situation. First, with respect to the nature of the decision, legal decision making is used to resolve disputes about the interpretation or application of specific laws in light of particular circumstances. Disputes about the interpretation and application of law are referred to as *matters of law*, and legal decision makers dealing with such matters are called **triers of law**. Disputes about the circumstances of a dispute are referred to as *matters of fact*, and legal decision makers dealing with matters of this sort are called **triers of fact**. In contrast, operational decisions involve matters of practice or procedure in which laws and circumstances are not in dispute (e.g., "What should I do in this situation?"). A legal decision may be considered an end in itself, whereas an operational decision is a means to some other end. Second, with respect to the way in which decisions are made, legal decision making is formal (fixed or structured) and time consuming, whereas operational decision making is often rapid and informal or intuitive. The process of legal decision making always involves gathering or receiving information, reviewing it, and rendering a decision according to established rules and conventions. The law provides structure concerning the issues to be decided (substantive law) and how they should be decided (substantive and procedural law). The process of operational decisions is highly variable, and decision makers have considerable discretion concerning what information they use and how they use it. Third, with respect to who makes the decision, legal decision making involves people who are appointed and given special powers to make certain decisions, and quite possibly only to make a decision in the case at hand, whereas operational decision making involves people who are expected to make a wide range of practical decisions. Finally, with respect to the situational context of the decision, legal decision making takes place at a predetermined time and in a special setting, usually a public building that is decorated with official or traditional trappings to underscore its legitimacy, whereas operational decision making occurs whenever and wherever the need arises. Even people who are involved in legal decision making need to make operational decisions on a day-to-day basis throughout the process.

To make these differences clear, the following are some concrete examples of legal decision making:

- An academic tribunal at a university—comprising representatives of the administration, faculty, and student body—sits to hear the case of a student accused of cheating on a final exam. The tribunal will hear the evidence, determine whether the student violated the university's code of conduct and if so, decide how the student should be punished.
- An employee believes she has been improperly passed over for promotion at work and files a grievance against her employer according to her

union's collective bargaining agreement. The grievance will be heard by a board comprising an independent arbitrator and representatives of the employer and the union. They will determine if the grievance is legitimate and, if so, how the situation should be remedied.

- Two men wearing turbans and *kirpans* (the ceremonial knives worn by baptized members of the Sikh religion) are refused service in a coffee shop. They make a complaint to a human rights commission that they were the victims of religious discrimination. A commissioner will hear the case, decide whether a human rights violation occurred and, if so, determine what remedies are appropriate.

- A parole board, comprising three members, meets to review the case of an offender who has served 10 years of a 15-year sentence for killing another man during a bar fight. The parole board will hear evidence from the offender and the corrections service, then decide whether the offender is suitable for release and whether special conditions should be put in place.

- A coroner and five jury members have been convened in coroner's court to review the death of three children who died in a school bus crash. Together, they will decide which witnesses to call, review the evidence presented by the witnesses, determine the cause of death, and then decide whether to make recommendations designed to prevent such incidents in the future.

- A judge presiding over a civil court hears a case involving two large banks. One bank claims the other bank breached a contract, resulting in a financial loss totaling tens of millions of dollars. The judge will listen to months of evidence from bank officials and expert testimony from dozens of forensic accountants, then determine whether there was a breach of contract and, if so, how much one bank should pay to the other.

- A judge and jury sitting in criminal court are hearing the case of a man charged with aggravated assault. The defendant claims he was provoked into a fight by the alleged victim and, therefore, is not guilty of any wrongdoing. The judge will make sure the prosecutor and defense counsel make arguments and present evidence according to the law and then give instructions to the jury; the jury then will be sequestered to discuss the evidence and reach a verdict concerning the defendant's guilt or innocence.

The description of legal decision making offered here may give the impression that the process is fixed, neutral, and objective. If so, the impression is mistaken. Although legal decision making differs from operational decision making in many ways, both are intrinsically human. They require people to function as part of a social group to analyze information and develop action plans. To this end, people will use their cognitive, affective, interpersonal, and behavioral functions; and everything they do will be colored by their own attitudes, beliefs, biases, feelings, preferences, relationships, stereotypes, and values. Its dual, conflicting nature—cold and impersonal on the one hand, yet inescapably emotional and personal on the other—is exactly what is captured so beautifully in images of Justitia, and the very thing that makes legal decision making such a fascinating topic.

JURIES

A **jury** is a group of people convened to make a legal decision by functioning as a trier of fact. Juries play a role in many legal systems; indeed, the word *jury* derives from the Latin *juris*, meaning "law." A person who sits on a jury is called a **juror**.

Juries are used in a small minority of legal disputes. The vast majority of disputes are decided prior to a trial, either through a plea bargain in criminal matters or a settlement in civil matters. Even legal disputes that proceed to trial are decided primarily by judges or administrative bodies such as tribunals and review boards. Yet juries remain a topic of considerable interest to psycholegal scholars and researchers.

Juries are diverse in terms of membership, function, structure, and operation. With respect to membership, jurors can be legal professionals (judges or lawyers); people with special status, knowledge, or ability; or ordinary citizens. With respect to function, juries may be charged with answering questions of law (i.e., to interpret the law), questions of fact (i.e., to interpret and draw inference from evidence), or both. These questions may be simple or narrow in scope, or they may be broad and far-reaching. With respect to structure, juries vary greatly in terms of size, ranging from small (e.g., six or fewer) to large (e.g., 23 or more), and manner of selection (e.g., appointment by an administrative authority or with input from the parties to a legal proceeding). With respect to operation, juries vary in terms of how they deliberate, reach, and communicate decisions.

The definition and description offered here may come as a surprise to some people. This is because contemporary use of the term *jury* is much more restricted, typically referring to a group of ordinary citizens who are selected more or less at random to represent the general population and serve as impartial triers of fact in a criminal or civil court, hearing evidence, deliberating in secrecy, reaching a decision by a vote, and communicating the decision, often without giving reasons (e.g., Diamond, 2004). Juries of this sort play a relatively minor role in some nations where the legal system is based in part on continental European civil law (e.g., Belgium, Brazil, France, and Spain), and a larger role in nations where the legal system is based on English common law, including the United Kingdom and many territories that were at one time part of or administered by the British Empire (e.g., Australia, Belize, Canada, Ireland, New Zealand, and the United States; Roberts, 2004). (Some of these nations have regions or areas of law based on other legal traditions; examples include Québec in Canada, Scotland in the United Kingdom, and Louisiana in the United States, which rely in part on a continental European civil law tradition. Also, many other nations and territories have legal systems that reflect a blending between English common law and another legal tradition; examples include continental European civil law in Hong Kong, Nicaragua, Sri Lanka, and South Africa; Islamic law in Bangladesh and Pakistan; and multiple traditions in India, Israel, and Nigeria.) For reasons that will be made clear later, juries are a particularly important part of the administration of justice in the United States. Indeed, the majority of all trials by jury take place in the United States (Diamond, 2004).

The History of Juries

The origin of juries, as they are used today in the United States, can be traced back to Viking Age Britain (Diamond, 2004; Roberts, 2004). The first Viking raid in the British Isles at Lindisfarne in 793 CE was followed by permanent settlements, including what became the *Danelaw.* (The Vikings who settled England were mostly Danes.) The Danelaw was a large region that encompassed much of what is now the north and east of England. Its political, legal, and military administration followed Norse traditions. These traditions were reinforced by the conquest of Britain in 1066 by the Normans, who were descended from Danish Vikings (also known as "Norsemen") who had raided, conquered, and settled the region of what is now northern France.

One important feature of traditional Norse government was that the king or chieftain had limited power, ruling as a leader among peers and advised by an assembly of elders (as opposed to a king with unlimited power, ruling by divine right or by right of inheritance). In the British Isles, the Norse traditions of the Danelaw and, ultimately, the Norman conquerors merged with those of the Anglo-Saxons and native Britons. One level of governmental administration in Norman Britain was that of the *shire* or *borough*, governed by a *reeve*, who functioned as the king's representative. A shire or borough was divided into smaller regions, called *wapentakes* (sometimes spelled *vapontakes*) or *hundreds*, that comprised a hundred or so families and the land necessary to sustain them. In legal matters, the shire reeve, or sheriff, appointed a *gemot* or assembly of a dozen or so *thegns* (also spelled *thanes*)—senior men—from the local hundred who swore an oath to make a decision according to the law. The gemot played a role in every aspect of legal decision making, from giving evidence to hearing evidence, and advising the sheriff on matters of both fact and law. The involvement of thegns not only ensured the sheriff had the benefit of the community's knowledge and values, but also helped to balance power, both legitimizing and limiting the authority of the king (Diamond, 2004).

As British society evolved, becoming increasingly centralized and urban, the common law system also evolved (Roberts, 2004). Responsibility for legal decision making was handed over from sheriffs and assemblies of elders to courts, presided over by judges. The move toward reliance on judges—independent, expert, and professional decision makers appointed by the government—had potential advantages and disadvantages. On the one hand, it could help to ensure consistency and fairness in legal proceedings. But on the other hand, it could lead to feelings of disempowerment and alienation among the populace, weakening the perceived legitimacy of the government. To avoid these potential problems, legal proceedings included several specific roles for local citizens—not just elders, but virtually any man of standing (i.e., a property owner)—who sat together as a panel of jurors.

In most countries where the legal system follows the common law tradition, the use of juries has declined over time. There are many possible explanations for this trend. One is that trials have become increasingly long and complex. This means serving on a jury can be a heavy responsibility for many people. A second is that modern democratic societies have many mechanisms that limit the power of their central governments, including a constitution, judicial independence, and high levels of openness. Arguably, juries are no longer necessary to help protect against the unreasonable exercise of power by governments. Third, many people who work in the justice system, including judges and lawyers, have expressed serious doubt that a group of laypeople had the knowledge or training necessary to make good legal decisions. Whatever the reasons, most common law jurisdictions now use juries only in trials for serious crimes.

But the trend away from juries was resisted in the United States, where juries are considered a crucial means of protecting citizens from the unreasonable exercise of power, as well as an important way of educating citizens about and involving them in the administration of justice. The right to trial by jury is established in the Sixth Amendment to the Constitution, and the U.S. Supreme Court has ruled the right may be exercised whenever defendants face the possibility of punishment that exceeds six months of imprisonment (*Chaff v. Schnackenberg*, 1966; *Duncan v. Louisiana*, 1968). Trial by jury is also widely available for civil matters in state and federal courts. In most other common law jurisdictions, defendants may have the right to trial by jury only when charged with serious crimes (e.g., in Canada, when facing a sentence of five years or longer, or in some other criminal and civil matters).

It is important to keep in mind that although parties to a proceeding may have the right to trial by jury, they may also have the right to waive trial by jury if they so desire. Jury trials are more likely to be waived in civil than criminal matters.

Types of Juries

Today, two major types of juries exist in common law jurisdictions. A **grand jury** comprises a large panel of jurors who consider allegations of crimes (or, less commonly, provide financial oversight of public institutions) to determine if there has been any wrongdoing and whether further investigation or prosecution is warranted. A grand jury typically comprises a large group of jurors—depending on the jurisdiction, ranging from a minimum of 11 or 12 to 23 or more—who sit in closed court, or privately, and hear evidence presented by a complainant or prosecutor (although they have the authority to compel additional testimony). The grand jury then deliberates and decides whether to issue an indictment. Virtually the only place grand juries are used today is the United States, and even then only in a small number of jurisdictions and in restricted circumstances. Most other common law jurisdictions, including Canada, have not used grand juries for many years.

A **petit jury**, also known as a trial jury, comprises a small group of jurors who serve as the trier of fact in a criminal or civil trial, under the guidance of a judge who interprets and instructs them with respect to matters of law. A petit jury typically comprises a relatively small group of people—depending on the jurisdiction and the nature of the matter, ranging from a minimum of 5 or 6 up to 12 or even 15—who sit in open court to hear evidence presented by all parties, with little or no influence over what or how evidence is presented. It then deliberates privately and issues a decision with respect to the issues at hand (e.g., verdict, liability). It is estimated that each year more than 250,000 criminal or civil trials by jury are held in the United States (Diamond, 2004).

Other types of juries exist, but are rarely used. For example, some jurisdictions can impanel a jury to review fatalities in coroner's court. As discussed previously, a coroner's jury may play a much more active role in eliciting and questioning evidence and render complex decisions that include recommendations for preventing deaths.

Researching Juries

Research on juries is complicated because jurors are often required by law not to discuss their deliberations, and they typically do not have to explain the reasoning behind their decisions. In Canada, for example, the law strictly prohibits jurors in criminal trials from ever discussing their deliberations or decisions. In the United States, jurors are often free to discuss deliberations or discussions *after* they have been discharged, but in most cases not while serving on a jury. This means researchers are generally unable to directly observe juries in action, and must use other strategies to gather information.

One alternative to direct observation is *archival research*. This type of research involves studying court records of jury trials and recording information about jurors, the cases they hear, and their verdicts. But official records typically contain only limited information. A second alternative is to *survey jurors or officers of the court* (e.g., lawyers and judges) after trial. This relies on the willingness of people to participate in research, and also may be prone to bias with respect to what they know, remember, or are willing to report. A third alternative is to conduct *field experiments*. These experiments involve systematic manipulation of various aspects of court proceedings, such as whether jurors are permitted to take notes during presentation of evidence, followed by a survey of jurors or officers of the court or by an examination of verdicts. But this type of research is difficult—judges tend to be uncomfortable with the idea of random assignment of juries or trials to various experimental conditions—and also does not provide insight into underlying processes. Finally, **mock jury research** involves simulation. People recruited to acts as jurors are presented with summaries or excerpts of trial evidence and legal instructions, and afterward they may complete questionnaires individually or deliberate as a group. Although this approach allows tight controls and true experimental designs, it is not clear whether the findings generalize to actual juries.

Characteristics and Processes of Petit Juries

Because petit juries are the type most commonly used, and most commonly studied, let's take a closer look at them.

The size of a petit jury varies not only across jurisdictions, but also across different types of trials within jurisdictions. The ancient rule was that a gemot should comprise the 12 leading thegns of the shire or borough, assembled by the reeve. This is still the standard or most common size for a jury, although some jurisdictions permit smaller juries, comprising only five or six jurors, for some or all trials. Smaller juries are easier to impanel, especially in jurisdictions with small populations.

In the United States, the Sixth Amendment—which establishes the right to trial by jury—is silent on the issue of jury size. In the second half of the twentieth century, several states began using smaller juries, most commonly comprising six jurors. The U.S. Supreme Court eventually weighed in on this practice, ruling that smaller juries were constitutionally permissible in both criminal and civil trials (*Colgrove v. Battin*, 1973; *Williams v. Florida*, 1970). But how small a jury is permissible? This question was addressed in *Ballew v. Georgia* (1978), in which the Supreme Court held that a jury of six was the constitutional minimum.

It is sometimes difficult to keep a jury intact after jurors have been selected. Jurors may be excused before a verdict is reached due to personal circumstances (e.g., illness, family or work problems) or, in rare circumstances, misconduct (e.g., ignoring instructions from a judge not to discuss evidence with others prior to deliberation). Typically, the law governing a trial specifies a target size for the jury, as well as a minimum size, and may also allow for the selection of one or more "extra" jurors, called ***alternates***. Alternates function as regular jurors, listening to the presentation of evidence, and can replace regular jurors in the event they are excused prior to deliberation; once deliberations begin, alternates are excused and do not participate further. In rare cases, jurors may be excused during the course of deliberation or there may be no alternates available to replace those excused, and the jury may be smaller than the target size. This is usually not a problem, unless the jury size exceeds any minimum specified by law (e.g., six in the United States), as the law recognizes there is nothing magical about a particular number of jurors.

Selection

When a matter proceeds to trial by jury, a jury is empanelled before any evidence is presented in court. The process of selecting jurors comprises two major steps. The first step is to identify a large pool of potential jurors, sometimes referred to as **venirepersons**, using a few general criteria. Typically, the law requires that potential jurors are adults (usually at least 18 or 19 years old), citizens of the nation in which the trial will be held, and residents of that jurisdiction. Potential jurors are often identified through official records (e.g., people registered as voters or possessing driver's licenses). This step is designed to ensure the pool of potential voters is representative of the community at large, although reliance on official records may introduce some systematic bias (e.g., excluding people who cannot afford telephones or automobiles, or who change address frequently).

The second step is to select a short list of actual jurors. A large group of venirepersons is subpoenaed to attend court and undergoes examination designed to identify people who may be inappropriate to serve as jurors. Potential jurors may be deemed inappropriate if they have personal experience with the administration of justice, general knowledge of the law, or specific knowledge of the case at hand. It is common to exclude from jury duty people who are employed (or have family members who are employed) in the justice system or who have been convicted of serious criminal offenses. To illustrate, according to the *Jury Selection and Service Act* (1968), a person is automatically excluded from jury duty in the United States if he or she:

1. Is not a citizen of the United States is not at least 18 years old, or has not resided for a period of one year within the judicial district;
2. Is unable to read, write, and understand the English language with a degree of proficiency sufficient to fill out satisfactorily the juror qualification form;
3. Is unable to speak the English language;
4. Is incapable, by reason of mental or physical infirmity, to render satisfactory jury service; or
5. Has a charge pending against him for the commission of, or has been convicted in a State or Federal court of record of, a crime punishable by imprisonment for more than one year and his civil rights have not been restored.

Potential jurors may also be deemed inappropriate if they have personal experiences, attitudes, or beliefs relevant to the case at hand that may bias their judgment. For example, people who have been victims of sexual assault or who believe all sex offenders deserve the death penalty may be excluded from jury duty if the trial is for someone charged with sexual assault. The goal of this second step is to ensure the jury is impartial.

Voir Dire

The most common method of examining jurors is the **voir dire**, a French term that means "to speak truthfully." The *voir dire* is a special minitrial in which venirepersons are sworn as witnesses and answer questions posed by the judge or the trial parties intended to reveal possible bias. Other methods of examination may be used. An example is a written questionnaire developed by the judge and parties specifically for that trial; the questionnaires are completed individually by jurors and then reviewed by the judge and parties in private. Based on the information available to them, parties may object to a venireperson serving on the jury through either a **peremptory challenge** or a **challenge for cause**. A peremptory challenge can be used to remove a prospective juror without having to specify a reason. The parties have a specified number of peremptory challenges depending on legal issues at hand. In contrast, a challenge for cause must be based on an argument that the prospective juror cannot serve impartially. When a challenge for cause is raised, the opposing party is allowed to respond and the judge then decides whether to exclude the juror. There are no limits to a challenge for cause. Possible reasons for a challenge for cause include being a relative of the defendant, having prior experience with a similar case, expressing a bias against the defendant's race or religion, or stating they are unable to follow the law in a given case (e.g., jurors in capital sentencing cases who state they are unable to vote for the death penalty; see Box 7.1).

Box 7.1 Death-Qualified Juries

Capital murder cases represent a unique basis for challenging a prospective jury. In a capital case, the proceedings are divided into two stages. In the first stage, juries are asked to reach a verdict of guilt or innocence. If the defendant is found guilty, the case moves to the second phase, the sentencing phase. Here, the jury determines whether the death sentence should be imposed. Jurors may be excluded for cause if they are categorically opposed to the imposition of a death sentence, or if they believe that the death penalty must be imposed in all instances of capital punishment.

The use of a death-qualified jury has been affirmed by the Supreme Court (*Witherspoon v. Illinois*, 1968; *Lockhart v. McCree*, 1986). The screening of jurors in death penalty cases is controversial because it may result in jurors more likely to convict as well as impose the death penalty. Craig Haney (2005), in a highly influential book on the death penalty, concluded, "Death qualification facilitates death sentencing by insuring that the only jurors allowed to decide whether a capital defendant lives or dies have been selected on the basis of their willingness to impose the death penalty. Of course, a group selected on this basis is more likely to actually impose the death penalty than one selected through non-death qualifying voir dire" (p. 111). Psychological research supports this conclusion. A well-designed laboratory study by Cowan, Thompson, and Ellsworth (1984) divided participants into two groups of juries. Nine juries were composed entirely of death-qualified participants (death-qualified juries) while 10 juries included from 2 to 4 excludable participants (mixed juries). The juries viewed a two-and-a-half hour trial videotape and then deliberated to reach a verdict. They found that death-qualified jurors were less likely to vote not guilty (22.1% vs. 46.7%) on predeliberation ballots, and less likely to vote for acquittal following deliberation (13.7% vs. 34.5%). Also, compared to excludable jurors, death-qualified jurors trust prosecution witnesses more and defense witnesses less. A meta-analysis of

14 studies showed that this finding has been consistently supported. Allen, Mabry, and McKelton (1991) estimated that the bias resulting from holding favorable attitudes toward the death sentence was associated with a 44% increase in the probability of a juror favoring conviction. They concluded that research had shown that "the more a person favors the death penalty, the more likely that person is to vote to convict a defendant" (p. 724).

Research has also shown that death-qualified jurors are different from those who were not qualified in a number of ways. Butler (2007), in a study of individuals called for jury duty, found that more positive attitudes toward the death penalty were correlated with more negative attitudes toward women and higher levels of homophobia, modern racism, and modern sexism. Personality differences were reported in a study by Butler and Moran (2007), who found that death-qualified participants were also more likely to have a high belief in a just world, espouse legal authoritarian beliefs, and exhibit an internal locus of control (i.e., internal rather than external events control one's life).

This research, however, has not influenced court decisions. In *Witherspoon*, the Court rejected the research as "too tentative and fragmentary to establish that jurors not opposed to the death penalty tend to favor the prosecution in the determination of guilt" (p. 520). At the time, this decision spurred a considerable amount of research, so that by the time *Lockhart v. McCree* was decided in 1986, the Court had more evidence about the effects of death-qualified juries. The American Psychological Association submitted an *amicus curiae* brief (Bersoff & Ogden, 1987). The Court reviewed this research, but noted serious methodological flaws. The Court wrote that "We will assume for purposes of this opinion that the studies are both methodologically valid and adequate to establish that 'death qualification' in fact produces juries somewhat more 'conviction-prone' than 'non-death-qualified' juries. We hold, nonetheless, that the Constitution does not prohibit the States from 'death qualifying' juries in capital cases" (p. 1764).

The nature and scope of the questions that can be asked in *voir dire*, as well as the frequency with and reasons for which potential jurors can be excluded, are limited by the laws of the jurisdiction. The purpose of the limitations is to maintain the representativeness of juries. In some countries, the ability to examine and exclude potential jurors is more restricted. For example, Canada limits the scope of questions that can be asked of potential jurors, allows fewer peremptory challenges, and has a complex system for challenging by cause in criminal matters. In contrast, there is considerable latitude to examine and exclude jurors in the United States. Venirepersons cannot be challenged on the basis of race, gender, sexual orientation, or religion (e.g., *Batson v. Kentucky*, 1968), but beyond that, almost anything goes. This has led to the development of the practice known as **scientific jury selection** (SJS), which is the application of social science to assist attorneys in the selection of jurors. (See Box 7.2 for more information on SJS.)

Box 7.2 Scientific Jury Selection: A Closer Look

Perhaps the first use of scientific jury selection (SJS) was in the trial of the Harrisburg Seven in the 1970s. This trial involved a group of defendants charged with a number of crimes related to their activity in the Vietnam antiwar movement. Concerned that the government set the trial in a politically conservative community that would be more likely to convict, a group of social scientists surveyed residents about their values and attitudes in an attempt to develop a profile of the ideal juror (Schulman, Shaver, Coleman, Emrich, & Christie, 1973). Their objective was to assist the attorneys in selecting an impartial jury. The trial ended in a hung jury, with the majority voting for acquittal. The defendants were not retried.

Schulman and his colleagues continued to be involved in other political trials (Lieberman & Sales, 2006), but since then, the business of trial consultants focusing on jury selection and other trial consulting has developed into a vast industry employing large numbers of psychologists and other social scientists who are now involved in a range of criminal and civil trials. SJS typically employs a community survey of jury-eligible citizens, but sometimes uses other activities such as trial simulations and the use of focus groups to obtain reactions to evidence that may be presented at trial. The results of these activities are intended to be used by attorneys in *voir dire*. Trial consultants present attorneys with individual characteristics that are thought to predict verdicts. Trial consultants are more commonly used in civil trials involving potentially high damage awards, but they are also used in criminal cases, notably high profile cases such as the murder trial of O. J. Simpson.

There are two basic approaches to jury selection. One focuses on broad attitudes and traits, by measuring such characteristics as juror bias (whether a juror has a pro-prosecution or pro-defense bias), or personality characteristics such as liberalism, authoritarianism, or need for social approval. Psychologists have developed measures of these constructs, such as the *Legal Attitudes Questionnaire* (Boehm, 1968), the *Juror Bias Scale* (Kassin & Wrightsman, 1983), and the *Belief in a Just World Scale* (Rubin & Peplau, 1975). The second approach is case-specific. As the name implies, this approach attempts to identify juror biases that are relevant to a particular case. The Harrisburg Seven trial is an example of this case-specific approach the social science team focused on attitudes specific to the trial, such as attitudes toward government property, the police, and patriotism, as well as pro-prosecution attitudes (see Posey & Wrightsman, 2005, for a discussion of this case).

Is SJS effective? In other words, would the trial outcome be different if SJS were not used? This is a difficult question to answer. One major difficulty is that SJS is typically used in cases in which the defendant or plaintiff has the funds to afford the cost of trial consultants. In these cases, they would be likely to have the best legal representation, and other trial tactics may simultaneously be employed (e.g., shadow juries, focus groups). Thus, even if the outcome were favorable, one would not be able to discern how much SJS contributed to the outcome. In an extensive review of the literature, Lieberman and Sales (2006) note that research shows that attitudinal, personality, and demographic variables are poor predictors of verdicts, typically accounting for only about 10% to 15% of verdict variance. They conclude, however, that even if SJS doesn't affect the outcome in a specific case, it is unlikely that it would harm the case, and the client may be reassured that every effort is being made to mount the defense.

The Special Problem of Pretrial Publicity

Pretrial publicity can greatly complicate the process of jury selection, because a large number of people can be exposed to information that may make it impossible for them to serve as impartial jurors. (Recall the trial of Scott Peterson, discussed at the start of the chapter.) This is especially true in the United States; in contrast, many other countries have strict limits concerning what can be reported before or during the trial. The media may report details about the crime, the fact that a defendant confessed to the crime, or other details that may prejudice prospective jurors. On occasion, the media may have reported evidence, such as a confession or evidence seized at the time of arrest, that later is ruled inadmissible in the trial itself. In these cases, jurors have information they are instructed to ignore. Is it possible to do so? That is the issue that is raised when considering the effects of pretrial publicity on juries.

One of the first cases that addressed the issue of pretrial publicity was the murder trial and conviction of Dr. Sam Sheppard. Sheppard was charged with the murder of his wife. He claimed that he had fallen asleep while watching television and was awakened by his wife calling his name. He ran to their bedroom and was struck on the head from behind. When he woke up, he found his wife covered in blood. He checked her pulse and found none. He then heard a noise from downstairs and chased after a man he saw running in his backyard. He reported that he caught up to the man, they struggled, and he lost consciousness again. When he came to, the man was gone, and he returned to his house to find his wife had been murdered.

The facts of this case may be familiar to many readers, as it was the basis of a television series and later a movie called *The Fugitive*. Dr. Sheppard's trial was covered extensively by the media, and the coverage was largely negative. Jurors were exposed to this information both before and during the trial. He was convicted and sentenced to life in prison. He appealed, arguing that the negative publicity had prejudiced the jury. The appeals took many years, but ultimately the U.S. Supreme Court ruled that Sheppard's trial had indeed been prejudiced by pretrial publicity (*Sheppard v. Maxwell*, 1964). By then, he had already spent over 10 years in prison. The Court vacated his conviction and ordered a new trial, and Dr. Sheppard was acquitted at the second trial. Sadly, he died just four years later of liver failure (Cooper & Sheppard, 1995).

A key issue regarding pretrial publicity is balancing the First Amendment right to free speech and a free press with the Sixth Amendment right to a fair and impartial jury. The American Bar Association (ABA) has developed standards in an attempt to address concerns about the prejudicial effects of pretrial publicity. As shown in Box 7.3, the ABA suggests extensive

---

Box 7.3 American Bar Association Standard 8–3.5:
Selecting the Jury

The following standards govern the selection of a jury in those criminal cases in which questions of possible prejudice are raised:

a. If there is a substantial possibility that individual jurors will be ineligible to serve because of exposure to potentially prejudicial material, the examination of each juror with respect to exposure should take place outside the presence of other chosen and prospective jurors. . . . The questioning should be conducted for the purpose of determining what the prospective juror has read and heard about the case and how any exposure has affected that person's attitude toward the trial, not to convince the prospective juror that an inability to cast aside any preconceptions would be a dereliction of duty.

b. Whenever prospective jurors have been exposed to potentially prejudicial material, the court should consider not only the jurors' subjective self-evaluation of their ability to remain impartial but also the objective nature of the material and the degree of exposure. The court should exercise extreme caution in qualifying a prospective juror who has either been exposed to highly prejudicial material or retained a recollection of any prejudicial material.

c. Whenever there is a substantial likelihood that, due to pretrial publicity, the regularly allotted number of peremptory challenges is inadequate, the court should permit additional challenges to the extent necessary for the impaneling of an impartial jury.

d. Whenever it is determined that potentially prejudicial news coverage of a criminal matter has been intense and has been concentrated in a given locality in a state (or federal district), the court should, in jurisdictions where permissible, consider drawing jurors from other localities in that state (or district).

Source: http://www.abanet.org/crimjust/standards/fairtrial_blk.html.

---

questioning of prospective jurors to determine the possible impact of any prior knowledge. Other possible remedies include a **change of venue** (i.e., moving the trial to another jurisdiction that has not been exposed to publicity), **judicial instruction** (i.e., instructing the jury to disregard information they obtained outside of the trial), or a **continuance** (i.e., delaying the start of a trial).

Research on pretrial publicity reinforces the perspective that such publicity can have prejudicial effects in both criminal and civil cases (Bornstein, Whisenhunt, Nemeth, & Dunaway, 2002; Greene, 1990). A number of studies have shown that knowledge of pretrial publicity is associated with an increased presumption of guilt of a defendant and that a juror's statement that he or she would be impartial despite this knowledge should not be taken at face value (Kovera, 2002; Moran & Cutler, 2006; Steblay, Besirevic, Fulero, & Jimenez-Lorente, 1999). Research also suggests that a judge's instruction to a jury to ignore extra-trial information, or even information they heard in a trial but is ruled inadmissible, is not effective, and in fact, may result in jurors paying more attention to inadmissible evidence (Lieberman & Arndt, 2000). Moving the trial to another jurisdiction may be the most effective method for minimizing the impact of pretrial publicity, although even this option may be impossible in high-profile cases that have received national attention.

Instructions

As jurors are not knowledgeable about matters of law, they receive general and special instructions from the trial judge. General instructions may be given at any time, and typically are intended to help jurors understand and follow the procedures set out in law. A set of special instructions, also known as the **charge to the jury**, concerns the decisions to be made by the jury in the case at hand. In criminal trials, the jury typically is charged with reaching a verdict concerning guilt (e.g., "guilty" versus "not guilty"), although it may also be asked to pass or recommend a sentence (e.g., in some capital murder cases). In civil trials, the jury is most often charged with finding liability (e.g., "for the plaintiff" versus "for the respondent [defendant]"), and may also be asked to award or recommend monetary damages. The trial judge is responsible for instructing the jury. The instructions may be guided by some combination of precedent, standard, or pattern instructions provided to judges in a given jurisdiction and legal arguments made by the parties.

Hearing Evidence

Many trials are brief, lasting only a day or two, but some trials are considerably longer. The murder trial of O. J. Simpson took nearly a year, during which a large amount of evidence, some of it highly complex such as the DNA evidence, was presented. Should jurors be allowed to take notes during the trial so that they can recall the evidence presented and understand the complex evidence? The American Bar Association (ABA, 2005) recommended in its *Principles for Juries and Jury Trials* that juries should be allowed to take notes during the trial, and the courts have become increasingly favorable to this practice, particularly for trials lasting for more than two days. The ABA notes that juries should be permitted, but not required, to take notes, and that they should receive appropriate cautionary instructions on note taking and note use. The practice of note taking, however, has been a controversial issue, as some have argued that jurors who take notes may, during deliberation, exert greater influence on those who choose not to take notes, or that note taking would be distracting during trial.

Research has addressed this issue. Horowitz and Bordens (2002) conducted a mock jury study in which jury-eligible participants were divided into 6- or 12-person juries who watched a videotaped civil trial. Half of the juries were allowed to take notes. They found differences for size of jury as well as note taking versus no note taking. The six-person juries that did not take notes awarded multiple plaintiffs the highest amounts of compensation, and awarded the highest punitive damages. Compared to the smaller juries, 12-person juries deliberated longer, recalled more probative information, and relied less on evaluative statements and nonprobative evidence.

Penrod and Heuer (1997) summarized the results from two studies they conducted. One study was a Wisconsin State study of 67 trials, and the second was a national sample of 75 civil and 85 criminal trials. They found that about two-thirds of the jurors in Wisconsin and 87% of the national sample elected to take notes. The note taking was often not extensive, as national sample jurors took on average about a half page of notes per trial. With respect to the controversies about note taking, Penrod and Heuer found that note taking did not serve as a useful memory aid, but jurors who took notes reported feeling more involved and satisfied with the trial procedure and verdict. They also found that note taking did not serve as a distraction and that jurors who took notes did not have an undue influence on those who did not. Although Penrod and Heuer did not find positive effects of note taking, they also noted that their findings also showed no negative effects, concluding that note taking is relatively innocuous. Given that the disadvantages are minimal and that jurors are more satisfied when allowed to take notes, they suggested that this practice continue to be allowed.

Deliberations

After receiving instructions, jury members deliberate. Deliberation is the *raison d'être* of the jury. The collective knowledge and wisdom of a jury is, in principle, superior to that of individual jurors and less likely to result in decisions that are idiosyncratic or unreflective of community values. Deliberations follow many steps.

- First, the jury appoints or elects a foreperson from among the jurors, if this has not already been done. The foreperson usually has primary responsibility for chairing the jury's deliberations (i.e., ensuring they are orderly), for communications between judge and jury during deliberations (e.g., if the jury poses questions for the judge), and for communicating the jury's final decisions (although individual jurors may also be polled, that is, asked to state their own decisions).

- Second, the jury reviews and discusses the evidence heard. To this end, jurors may be allowed to consult any written notes they have taken, evidence presented in the form of exhibits, and in some cases, trial transcripts or even public documents not entered into evidence. They also have the opportunity to discuss the meaning and interpretation of evidence. Exactly how the deliberations proceed is a matter for the jury to decide, guided by three general principles: first, the jury must base its decision solely on the evidence deemed admissible by the judge; second, jurors must reach decisions independently, free from coercion or other undue influence by other jurors; and third, the jury must make the decision on its own, not communicating with and free from the influence of outsiders. To help them deliberate properly, juries receive general instructions not to discuss the case with outsiders and not to have contact with parties during the trial, and they may be sequestered (isolated) during deliberations.

- Third, the jury reaches (or attempts to reach) a consensual decision through voting. Again, exactly how the voting proceeds is a matter for the jury to decide. It is common for the foreperson to solicit votes at the outset of the deliberations (a "straw poll"), before any in-depth discussion commences, so the jurors have some idea of each other's leanings or preliminary opinions. If there is unanimity of views at the outset, the review and discussion of evidence that follows may be brief; if there is a divergence of opinion, it may be much longer. The discussion may continue, with periodic votes (formal or informal), until each juror has reached a firm decision as an individual. It is expected that each juror will participate to some degree in the review and discussion, and that each will vote to express an individual decision.

How and to what extent does the process of deliberation sway jurors' verdicts? The answer to this question is not clear (Diamond, 2004). The role of deliberation is probably relatively small when the charge to the jury is simple and a clear majority view exists (and is expressed) from the outset. In such circumstances, the process appears to focus on pressuring the minority to change its vote and the final verdict is quite predictable. But when the charge is complex, or when no clear majority exists or is expressed, the process appears to focus on reviewing the evidence and the final verdict is less predictable. Research also suggests that time spent deliberating is a good indicator of dissent among jurors: the greater the dissent, the longer the deliberations, and the greater the likelihood of a hung jury.

Jury Decision Rules

The deliberations reach a natural end once there is unanimity or once further discussion fails to change the opinions of individual jurors. At this point, the jury must determine whether it has reached a decision according to the judge's charge. The charge includes a **decision rule**, the voting pattern required for a jury to reach a consensual decision. Decision rules vary across jurisdictions and across legal issues within jurisdictions. Historically, the decision rule required unanimous voting, with no specified time limit; failure to achieve the required unanimity meant that no decision was reached and thus no action was taken. Modern decision rules require either unanimity or a voting pattern that could be characterized as somewhere between a "clear majority" and a "virtual unanimity." In the United States, for example, a few states allow up to two or even three dissenters in a 12-person jury (*Apodaca v. Oregon*, 1972; *Johnson v. Louisiana*, 1972), but most require unanimity. The U.S. Supreme Court has held that six-person juries must be unanimous (*Burch v. Louisiana*, 1979).

At the natural end of the deliberations, the foreperson communicates to the trial judge whether the jury has been able to reach a decision and, if so, the decision itself. When a jury is unable to reach a decision, the judge may question jurors to determine why. If it appears there is some chance of reaching a decision within a reasonable time frame, the judge may order the jury to resume deliberations. But if there is a **hung jury**—a jury whose deliberations are deadlocked and is therefore unable to reach a proper decision within a reasonable time frame—the judge may declare a mistrial, dismiss the jury, and order a new trial.

Jury Nullification

When a criminal jury reaches a legal decision that flies in the face of the evidence presented at trial, either by acquitting a defendant who is obviously guilty or by convicting a defendant who is obviously not guilty, *jury nullification* occurs. Decisions of this sort are a communication that the jurors reject the validity of the law as it applies to the facts of the case. Consider the murder trials of Dr. Jack Kevorkian, a physician who helped a number of his terminally ill patients to commit suicide. On three different occasions, Dr. Kevorkian was acquitted of murder despite incontrovertible evidence of his involvement in the deaths of his patients, a rather clear message that the juries did not believe physician-assisted suicide of terminally ill patients should be considered a crime.

Since juries deliberate in secret and are not obliged to explain or justify their verdicts, it is difficult to ascertain whether jury nullification has occurred unless jurors acknowledge disagreement with the law was the basis for their verdicts. For example, the verdict of the jury in the O. J. Simpson murder trial is considered by many to be an example of jury nullification, but it may also be the case that jurors accepted defense arguments that Simpson had been framed by the investigating detectives.

The possibility of jury nullification is a concern to the judicial system. Some studies have shown that giving instructions about jury nullification makes guilty verdicts less likely (Meissner, Brigham, & Pfeifer, 2003; Niedermeier, Horowitz, & Kerr, 1999). Trial judges, however, do not instruct juries about the possibility of nullification, even when the defense requests such instructions. For example, in *United States v. Dougherty* (1973), a defense request to provide a nullification instruction to the jury in a trial of antiwar activists was rejected.

MODELS OF JURY DECISION MAKING

The study of how legal decision makers understand and use evidence to reach verdicts can be traced to the legal scholar, John Henry Wigmore (Wigmore, 1909, 1913). Wigmore developed a sophisticated method for analyzing and synthesizing trial evidence. "Wigmore charts" or "evidence charts" summarized chains of inferential reasoning from evidence to the propositions underlying legal arguments. Since that time, the study of legal decision making has followed two very different routes. One route elaborates on Wigmore's original methods, leading to "modified Wigmorean analysis" (e.g., Twining, 2007) or develops even more sophisticated models (e.g., Kadane & Schum, 1996; Thagard, 2004). The goal of this approach is to explicate the specific cognitive processes used by triers of fact to infer causality and evaluate arguments within the context of a legal trial. The other route views legal decision making as a process in which triers of fact develop stories that help them understand the decision-making context, explain the evidence presented to them, and reach a decision (e.g., Bennett, 1978). Following Jerome S. Bruner (1985, 1991, 2003)—a distinguished cognitive-developmental psychologist who now holds positions in the Department of Psychology and School of Law at New York University—we will refer to these two models as *paradigmatic models* and *narrative models.*

Paradigmatic Models

Paradigmatic models assume that people's thought processes are mechanical or rule-governed in nature and can be conceptualized in terms of the application of basic logical operators to information (Bruner, 1985, 1991; Pennington & Hastie, 1981). Although the logical operators may appear simple when considered in isolation, in combination they are capable of generating incredibly sophisticated answers to complex problems. They allow human beings, born with a *tabula rasa* (a cognitive "blank slate"), to perceive associations between objects or events in their environments and perform inductive tasks such as categorization and causal reasoning that permit them to develop and evaluate theories about how the world works. The two major types of paradigmatic models differ from each other in terms of the emphasis given to roles for innate or learned knowledge structures, such as beliefs, schemas, and conditional interventions (Gopnik & Tenenbaum, 2007; Shultz, 2007). The first type, simple association models, require only classical or operant conditioning and have no need to include concepts related to abstract learning or knowledge structures. Learning is viewed as the process of directly linking inputs in the form of information about the environment to outputs in the form of behavior. The second type, connectionist models, posit that abstract learning or knowledge structures may emerge out of simple associations, but they are implicit or hidden. Learning is viewed as a process of linking inputs to outputs that is mediated by learned mental activity, although people may not be conscious or aware of this activity.

In a now-classic article, Pennington and Hastie (1981) discussed paradigmatic models that have been used to study legal decision making. The models differ in some important respects. Some assume that triers of fact begin the trial process with no preference for one verdict or the other; others assume they enter the trial with a naïve (i.e., uninformed) assumption in favor of one verdict before they hear any evidence. Some assume that each piece of evidence is given a rating of probity (i.e., the extent to which it factors one verdict versus the other) as soon as it is heard, whereas others assume ratings are not assigned until all the evidence has been heard. Some assume that the probity ratings take the form of scalar variables (like a rating on a 7-point scale), whereas others assume they are estimates of the odds in favor of one verdict. Some assume the probity ratings are combined using simple arithmetic algorithms (e.g., sum, average) after all the evidence is received, whereas others assume they are combined using more complex algorithms (e.g., Bayes' theorem) or sequentially throughout the trial process. Finally, some focus on the decision-making processes of individual triers of fact, whereas others focus on a general process discernible only across triers of fact (i.e., the "on average" process).

As an example, Louden and Skeem (2007) investigated the impact of attitudes toward the insanity defense on decision making by jurors, relative to jurors' prototypes of insanity. They conducted an experiment using as participants 113 prospective jurors, people who had reported for jury duty at a county courthouse and voluntarily completed the study after being excused from jury duty. Participants individually completed a questionnaire that evaluated their prototypes of insanity and their attitudes toward the insanity defense, then made decisions (case judgments and verdicts) for each of four brief case vignettes. The data were aggregated and analyzed using bivariate and multivariate statistics. The findings indicated that attitudes toward the insanity defense were associated with prototypes of insanity. But attitudes were much more strongly associated with jurors' decisions than were prototypes, which had only a small independent association with juror's decisions.

Narrative Models

Narrative models, also called *explanatory models*, of decision making assume that people think about the world in terms of stories, particularly when they think about interactions among human beings (Bruner, 1985, 1991, 2003; Schank & Abelson, 1995). A *story* is a communicative device in which multiple events or incidents are sequenced and unified into a single entity by means of a plot, or "a narrative of particular events arranged in time and forming a meaningful totality" (Twining, 2006, p. 223). Human beings are social, communicative creatures, and narratives are quintessentially human—perhaps the most intricate form of communication or expression known to us. According to Polkinghorne (1995), narrative is "uniquely suited for displaying human existence as situated action. . . . [It] is the linguistic form that preserves the complexity of human action with its interrelationships of temporal sequence, human motivation, chance happenings, and changing interpersonal and environmental contexts" (pp. 5–7). According to narrative models of decision making, people strive to explain what has happened, is happening, or might happen in the future, and this explanation in turn determines their reactions or actions. They view people as engaged constantly and actively in the construction of meaning.

Narrative cognition has its own characteristic rules and operations. It functions as a symbolic system (like language) that, although it may have a neuropsychological basis, is largely a product of culture (Bruner, 1985, 1991; Schank & Abelson, 1995). According to Twining (2006), stories have three basic characteristics:

1. *Particularity* is raw material in the form of critical elements of information that can be used to elucidate the emotional and motivational meaning of people's behavior.
2. *Temporality* is the chronological ordering of information in the form of events or occurrences.
3. *Coherence* or *unity* is the establishment of causal links between the information elements by means of a plot.

Bennett (1978) was among the first to outline a narrative model of legal decision making. It was elaborated by Pennington and Hastie (1981, 1992) and popularized in psychology as the story model. (Other elaborations have been developed, including the anchored narrative model of Wagenaar, van Koppen, & Crombag, 1993; but as many of the basic elements are similar, we will focus on the story model here.) According to the **story model**, legal decision making comprises three different processes: *story construction, verdict representation*, and *story classification*.

1. *Story construction* is the process by which triers of fact evaluate the evidence presented to them. Evaluating evidence requires considerable cognitive effort, as evidence typically is presented bit by bit, over an extended period of time (hours or days), and pieces of evidence are interdependent, making it is impossible to determine their relevance or importance until all the pieces have been presented. Triers of fact develop narrative accounts that help them remember, organize, and explain evidence. The narratives they develop are based not only on information about the case at hand, but also on information about similar incidents or situations and their general understanding of narrative structure. Several narratives may be developed that fit the evidence, but their adequacy may be judged according to their coverage (the extent to which a narrative accounts for all the evidence presented), coherence (the extent to which the elements of a narrative are consistent, complete, and plausible), and uniqueness (the extent to which a narrative lacks viable competing or alternative narratives).

2. *Verdict representation* is the process in which triers of fact understand the legal decision they must reach, that is, the alternatives open to them under the law. The alternatives depend on the relevant law, as well as the specific circumstances of the case at hand. For example, in a given criminal trial, the verdicts available to triers of fact might be "guilty," "not guilty by reason of insanity," or "not guilty," or they may be asked to decide whether a person convicted of murder should receive the death penalty; in a given civil trial, the available verdicts might be "for the plaintiff" or "for the respondent," or jurors may be asked to determine the amount of compensatory or punitive damages to be awarded following a verdict for the plaintiff; or in a coroner's inquest, triers of fact may be asked to decide the identity and cause of death of a victim or to make recommendation for preventing similar deaths in the future. The process of legal decision making generally includes some formal discussion of the law and decisions alternatives, but triers of fact may also be influenced by other factors, including their own personal knowledge and beliefs. Verdict representation may occur after or in parallel with story construction.

3. *Story classification* comes after story construction and verdict representation, and is the process by which triers of fact determine which decision

or verdict fits their preferred narrative best. This process is simpler to the extent that the narratives developed by triers of fact contain information that is directly relevant to their verdict representations.

An example of research using the story model is a study by Weiner, Richmond, Seib, Rausch, and Hackney (2002). They investigated whether people used a common script or prototype to construct narratives in murder trials, or whether they used multiple exemplars (i.e., specific versions) of the same general script or prototype. Participants in the study were 76 people, recruited through newspaper advertisements, who were eligible to serve on a jury and "death qualified" (i.e., willing to consider sentencing someone to the death penalty under state law). Participants were interviewed individually, asked to think about a scenario in which someone perpetrated first-degree (i.e., capital) murder, and then asked to describe the scenario in detail. Interviewers asked questions to make sure the scenarios were as detailed as possible. The interviews were recorded and researchers developed a scheme that was used to code the presence of 13 common story features (motivational theme, location, emotional state of the perpetrator, the number of victims involved, the acquaintanceship between perpetrator and victim, etc.), the level of premeditation and intent on the part of the perpetrator, and the presence of aggravating and mitigating factors in death penalty cases according to state law. Statistical analyses suggested the presence of three general exemplars.

- The first typically involved perpetrators who did not know their victims, encountered them while committing other crimes, and then killed them in an unemotional and unplanned manner.
- The second typically involved a perpetrator planning to shoot an acquaintance and following through on the plan.
- The third involved a perpetrator motivated by anger or jealousy, often killing multiple acquaintance victims at a residence.

Each of the general clusters also contained multiple exemplars. The researchers concluded that the scenarios generated by participants were strikingly diverse; there was no evidence that a single script or prototype was used to construct the murder narratives.

An important strength of paradigmatic models is that they are highly structured and explicit. Because of the specific information inputs, the operations used to manipulate information, and decision outputs, they easily lend themselves to experimental and statistical evaluation. Narrative models are inherently less structured, which makes them harder to evaluate. But the strengths of paradigmatic models comes at a cost:

- Paradigmatic models are normative, focusing on how decisions should be made by hypothetical rational beings. In contrast, narrative models are descriptive, focusing on how people actually make decisions.

• Paradigmatic models assume that the decision-making process is stable, that is, the same process is used by different triers of fact or by the same trier of fact across trials. Narrative models make no such assumption, although they acknowledge certain story elements may be stable.

• Paradigmatic models view trials as "closed systems." They assume triers of fact base their decisions solely on the evidence presented at trial and evaluate only the legal arguments put forward by parties to the proceedings. In contrast, narrative models assume triers of fact may be just as interested in evidence that was not presented; they also accept that triers of fact may construct their own story to explain evidence, rejecting all the legal arguments put forward by parties and drawing unexpected inferences from the evidence presented.

• Paradigmatic models view the legal decision as a simple binary choice, for example, a choice between accepting or rejecting a particular legal argument (e.g., "guilty" versus "not guilty") or between accepting one of the legal arguments advanced by opposing parties (e.g., "Jones suffered injury due to negligent acts by Smith" versus "Jones suffered injury due to acts by Smith, but Smith did not act negligently"). But many legal decisions are much more complicated. For example, the "decision" in a coroner's court may require the trier of fact to determine the cause of death in a given case and to make recommendation for preventing future deaths.

• Paradigmatic and narrative models both tend to focus on the trier of fact as an individual person, even when that person is part of a group (e.g., an administrative tribunal, review board, jury, or panel of judges). Both models ignore the interpersonal or social dimension of legal decision making.

EVALUATING JURIES

The jury system allows ordinary citizens to play a role in the administration of justice by cleaving the process of legal decision making in two: (1) juries function as triers of fact using the wisdom of a group and (2) judges function as triers of law using the wisdom of an individual. But does using a jury system lead to better—or even different—decisions?

Research using various methods has compared the legal decision made by jurors (mock or actual) to those of legal professionals (lawyers or judges) based on the same facts and legal instructions. According to Diamond (2004), the differences between the two groups are rather small. The rate of agreement between laypeople and experts with respect to final decisions generally is very high, ranging from 74% to 90%. Also, laypeople and experts are influenced by evidence in very similar ways. For example, both groups have trouble ignoring evidence deemed inadmissible, are susceptible to the hindsight bias, and put little weight on statistical evidence. Perhaps the only reliable difference is that when laypeople disagree with experts with respect to final decisions, laypeople more often vote in favor the defendant or respondent.

SUMMARY

Legal decision making strives for justice by considering matters of law and fact. Legal decisions are made by a range of people acting as individuals (e.g., judges) or as groups (e.g., judicial panels, tribunals, review boards, and juries). The unique characteristic of modern juries is that they are made up of ordinary citizens. In common law jurisdictions, all legal decision makers are expected to be impartial. But jurors are also expected, and indeed selected, to have no special knowledge concerning matters of fact in the case at hand or concerning matters of law, either in the case at hand or more generally. It is ironic that the jury, originally developed in part because it had specific knowledge that might assist the trier of law, has evolved into a group chosen because it is specifically ignorant. Psycholegal scholars have attempted to overcome the considerable obstacles to research, and their findings reveal jurors as neither incompetent amateurs nor the last bastions of justice, but rather human beings struggling collectively to overcome their individual limitations to reach a just decision.

SUGGESTED READINGS

Beratlis, G., Marino, T., Belmessieri, B., Lear, D., Nice, R., Guinasso, J., Zanartu, J., Swertlow, F., & Stambler, L. (2006). *We, the jury: Deciding the Scott Peterson case.* Beverly Hills, CA: Phoenix Books.

English, P. W., & Sales, B. D. (2005). *More than the law: Behavioral and social facts in legal decision making.* Washington, DC: American Psychological Association.

Kaplan, M. F., & Martín, A. M. (Eds.). (2006). *Understanding world jury systems: Through social psychological research.* New York: Psychology Press.

KEY TERMS

- *Alternates*
- *Challenge for cause*
- *Change of venue*
- *Charge to the jury*
- *Continuance*

- *Decision rule*
- *Grand jury*
- *Hung jury*
- *Judicial instruction*
- *Juror*
- *Jury*
- *Justice*
- *Legal decision making*
- *Mock jury research*
- *Narrative models*
- *Operational decision making*
- *Paradigmatic models*
- *Petit jury*
- *Peremptory challenge*
- *Scientific jury selection*
- *Story model*
- *Triers of law*
- *Triers of fact*
- *Venirepersons*
- *Voir dire*

References

Allen, M., Mabry, E., & McKelton, D. M. (1991). Impact of juror attitudes about the death penalty on juror evaluations of guilt and punishment: A meta-analysis. *Law and Human Behavior, 23*, 715–731.

American Bar Association (ABA). (2005). *Principles for juries and jury trials.* Chicago: ABA.

Apodaca v. Oregon, 406 U.S. 408 (1972).

Ballew v. Georgia, 435 U.S. 223 (1978).

Batson v. Kentucky, 476 U.S. 79 (1968).

Bennett, W. L. (1978). Storytelling in criminal trials: A model of social judgment. *Quarterly Journal of Speech, 64*, 1–22.

Berattis, G., Marino, T., Belmessieri, M., Lear, D., Nice, R., Guinasso, J. (2007). We the jury: Deciding the Scott Peterson Case. Beverly Hills, CA: Phoenix Books.

Bersoff, D. N., & Ogden, D. W. (1987). In the Supreme Court of the United States: *Lockhart v. McCree* Amicus curiae brief for the American Psychological Association. *American Psychologist, 42*, 59–68.

Boehm, V. R. (1968). Mr. Prejudice, Miss Sympathy, and the authoritarian personality: An application of psychological measuring techniques to the problem of jury bias. *Wisconsin Law Review, 1968*, 734–750.

Bornstein, B. H., Whisenhunt, B. L., Nemeth, R. J., & Dunaway, D. L. (2002). Pretrial publicity and civil cases: A two-way street? *Law and Human Behavior, 26*, 3–17.

Bruner, J. S. (1985). *Actual minds, possible worlds.* Cambridge, MA: Harvard University Press.

Bruner, J. S. (1991). The narrative construction of reality. *Critical Inquiry, 18*, 1–21.

Bruner, J. S. (2003). *Making stories: Law, literature, life.* Cambridge, MA: Harvard University Press.

Burch v. Louisiana, 441 U.S. 130 (1979).

Butler, B. (2007). Death qualification and prejudice: The effect of implicit racism, sexism, and homophobia on capital defendants' right to due process. *Behavioral Sciences & the Law, 25*, 857–867.

Butler, B., & Moran, G. (2007). The impact of death qualification, belief in a just world, legal authoritarianism, and locus of control on venirepersons' evaluations of aggravating and mitigating circumstances in capital trials. *Behavioral Sciences & the Law, 25*, 57–68.

Capers, I. B. (2006). On Justicia, race, gender, and blindness. *Michigan Journal of Race and Law, 12*, 203-233

Chaff v. Schnackenberg, 384 U.S. 373 (1966).

Colgrove v. Battin, 413 U.S. 149 (1973).

Cooper, C., & Sheppard, S. R. (1995). *Mockery of justice.* Boston: University Press.

Cowan, C. L., Thompson, W. C., & Ellsworth, P. C. (1984). The effects of death qualification on jurors' predisposition to convict and on the quality of deliberation. *Law and Human Behavior, 8*, 53–79.

Diamond, S. L. (2004). Juries. In N. J. Smelser & P. B. Baltes (Eds.), *International encyclopedia of the social and behavioral sciences* (pp. 8031–8037). New York: Elsevier.

Duncan v. Louisiana, 391 U.S. 145 (1968).

Gopnik, A., & Tenenbaum, J. B. (2007). Bayesian networks, Bayesian learning and cognitive development. *Developmental Science, 10*, 281–287.

Greene, E. (1990). Media effects on jurors. *Law and Human Behavior, 14*, 439–450.

Haney, C. (2005). *Death by design: Capital punishment as a social psychological system.* New York: Oxford University Press.

Horowitz, I. A., & Bordens, K. S. (2002). The effects of jury size, evidence complexity, and note taking on jury process and performance in a civil trial. *Journal of Applied Psychology, 87*, 121–130.

Johnson v. Louisiana, 406 U.S. 356 (1972).

Jury Selection and Service Act, 28 U.S.C. §§ 1861–1869 (1968).

Kadane, J. B., & Schum, D. A. (1996). *A probabilistic analysis of the Sacco and Vanzetti evidence.* New York: Wiley.

Kassin, S. M., & Wrightsman, L. S. (1983). The construction and validation of a juror bias scale. *Journal of Research in Personality, 17*, 432–442.

Kovera, M. B. (2002). The effects of general pretrial publicity on juror decisions: An examination of moderators and mediating mechanisms. *Law and Human Behavior, 26*, 43–72.

Lieberman, J. D., & Arndt, J. (2000). Understanding the limits of limiting instructions: Social psychological explanations for the failures of instructions to disregard pretrial publicity and other inadmissible evidence. *Psychology, Public Policy, & Law, 6*, 677–711.

Lieberman, J. D., & Sales, B. D. (2006). *Scientific jury selection.* Washington, DC: APA Books.

Lockhart v. McCree, 476 U.S. 162 (1986).

Louden, J. E., & Skeem, J. L. (2007). Constructing insanity: Jurors' prototypes, attitudes, and legal decision-making. *Behavioral Sciences & the Law, 25*, 449–470.

Luban, D. J. (2001). Law's blindfold. In M. Davis & A. Stark (Eds.), *Conflict of interest in the professions* (pp. 23–48). Oxford: Oxford University Press.

Meissner, C. A., Brigham, J. C., & Pfeifer, J. E. (2003). Jury nullification: The influence of judicial instruction on the relationship between attitudes and juridic decision-making. *Basic and Applied Social Psychology, 25*, 243–254.

Moran, G., & Cutler, B. L. (2006). The prejudicial impact of pretrial publicity. *Journal of Applied Social Psychology, 21*, 345–367.

Niedermeier, R., Horowitz, I. A., & Kerr, N. L. (1999). Informing jurors of their nullification power: A route to a just verdict or judicial chaos? *Law and Human Behavior, 23*, 331–352.

Pennington, N., & Hastie, R. (1981). Juror decision-making models: The generalization gap. *Psychological Bulletin, 89*, 246–287.

Pennington, N., & Hastie, R. (1992). Explaining the evidence: tests of the story model for juror decision making. *Journal of Personality and Social Psychology, 62*, 189–206.

Penrod, S. D., & Heuer, L. (1997). Tweaking commonsense: Assessing aids to jury decision making. *Psychology, Public Policy, and Law, 3*, 259–284.

Polkinghorne, D. E. (1995). Narrative configuration in qualitative analysis. In J. A. Hatch & R. Wisniewski (Eds.), *Life history and narrative* (pp. 5–23). London: Falmer Press.

Posey, A. J., & Wrightsman, L. S. (2005). *Trial consulting.* New York: Oxford University Press.

Roberts, S. (2004). Common law. In N. J. Smelser & P. B. Baltes (Eds.), *International encyclopedia of the social and behavioral sciences* (pp. 2279–2283). New York: Elsevier.

Rubin, Z., & Peplau, L. (1975). Who believes in a just world? *Journal of Social Issues, 31*, 65–89.

Schank, R., & Abelson, R. (1995). Storytelling and understanding: The basis for human memory. In Robert S. Wyer, Jr. (Ed.), *Knowledge and memory: The real story* (pp. 1–82). Mahwah, NJ: Lawrence Erlbaum Associates, Inc.

Schulman, J., Shaver, P., Coleman, R., Emrich, B., & Christie, R. (1973). Recipe for a jury. *Psychology Today, 37*, 37–44.

Sheppard v. Maxwell, 384 U.S. 333, 358 (1964).

Shultz, T. R. (2007). The Bayesian revolution approaches psychological development. *Developmental Science, 10*, 357–364.

Steblay, N. M., Besirevic, J., Fulero, S. M., & Jimenez-Lorente, B. (1999). The effects of pretrial publicity on juror verdicts. *Law and Human Behavior, 23*, 219–235.

Thagard, P. (2004). Causal inference in legal decision making: Explanatory coherence vs. Bayesian networks. *Applied Artificial Intelligence, 18*, 231–249.

Twining, W. (2006). *Rethinking evidence: Exploratory essays.* New York: Cambridge University Press.

Twining, W. (2007). Argumentation, stories and generalizations: A comment. *Law, Probability, and Risk, 6*, 169–186.

United States v. Dougherty, 473 F2d 1113 (1973).

Wagenaar, W. A., van Koppen, P. J., & Crombag, H. F. M. (1993). *Anchored narratives. The psychology of criminal evidence.* London: Harvester Wheatsheaf.

Weiner, R. L., Richmond, T. L., Seib, H. M., Rausch, S. M., & Hackney, A. A. (2002). The psychology of telling murder stories: Do we think in scripts, exemplars, or prototypes? *Behavioral Sciences & the Law, 20*, 119–139.

Wigmore, J. H. (1909). Professor Muensterberg and the psychology of testimony. *Illinois Law Review, 3*, 399–434.

Wigmore, J. H. (1913). *The principles of judicial proof.* Boston: Little, Brown.

Williams v. Florida, 399 U.S. 78 (1970).

Witherspoon v. Illinois, 391 U.S. 510 (1968).

Chapter 8

JUVENILES IN THE LEGAL SYSTEM

CHAPTER OBJECTIVES
In this chapter, you will become familiar with:
• The history of juvenile justice
• Different theories about delinquent behavior
• Forensic assessments of juveniles
• Interventions with children and youth

HISTORY OF JUVENILE JUSTICE

The concept of a separate juvenile court was created in Illinois in 1899. Prior to that, age was an irrelevant consideration if a crime had been committed, except that children under age 7 were considered too young to commit a criminal offense. Thus, juveniles were tried in adult courts, and if convicted, were subjected to the same sentences as adults, including imprisonment and the death penalty. The Illinois Juvenile Justice Court Act (see Fox, 1996) initially created a separate division within the adult court to deal with juveniles, and this was expanded just a few years later to become an independent juvenile court. In addition to a shift of focus from punishment to rehabilitation, the Act provided for confidentiality of records, physical separation of youth from adults if incarcerated in the same facility, and a ban on jail detention for those under 12 years old. The reform that began in Illinois quickly caught on in other jurisdictions. By 1910, 32 states adopted similar provisions and by 1925, all but two states had a separate juvenile court.

It is important to note that the Illinois Act was designed to provide a separate system for dealing with all youth in need of protection. Thus, unlike modern juvenile courts, this prototype juvenile court had jurisdiction over youth under the age of 16 who were delinquent, neglected, or dependent.

The Illinois Juvenile Justice Court Act (1899) defined dependency and neglect in the following manner:

1. Any child who for any reason is destitute or homeless or abandoned;
2. Has not proper parental care or guardianship;
3. Who habitually begs or receives alms;
4. Who is found living in any house of ill fame or with any vicious or disreputable person;
5. Whose home, by reason of neglect, cruelty, or depravity on the part of its parents, guardian or other person in whose care it may be, is an unfit place for such a child;
6. Any child under the age of 8 years who is found peddling or selling any article or singing or playing any musical instrument upon the street or giving any public entertainment.

Delinquent acts under the jurisdiction of the juvenile court included criminal acts for which adults could be charged but also status offenses. The primary focus of the juvenile court was rehabilitation and protection, and the courts quickly adopted the doctrine of **parens patriae**. Under this doctrine, the courts were seen in a paternalistic, benevolent role, and the state had the right to intervene in the lives of youth, even over the parents' objection, when it considered intervention in the child's best interest. Since the goal was rehabilitation rather than punishment, due process rights of youth were not paramount. Indeed, juveniles were not considered to have the same rights afforded adults, and lawyers were rarely present in juvenile court.

Judge Ben B. Lindsey perhaps set the standard for the *parens patriae* approach. He helped establish a juvenile court in Colorado in 1903. Fox summarized his approach:

> Under Judge Lindsey's aegis, the Denver court uniquely embodied a deeply personal judicial involvement in the lives of the juvenile court children. His juvenile court was a vigorous machine for social engineering, reaching out to reform everything that adversely affected children, from the corruption of the police to the need for playgrounds. But reaching out to foster a close relationship with each individual child was the quintessence of Lindsey's juvenile court . . . . Children who came to the Denver court were "his boys" and were seen by him as fundamentally good human beings whose going astray was largely attributable to their social and psychological environment. According to Lindsey, the role of the juvenile court judge was to strengthen the child's belief in himself and make available to him all of the support and encouragement from outside the court that the judge could harness on his behalf. (1996, pp. 34–35)

Judge Lindsey and other juvenile court judges may have had the best of intentions, but they operated at the expense of fundamental constitutional rights. This practice was challenged in two cases in the 1960s, and the Supreme Court's decisions fundamentally changed the nature of the juvenile court since that time.

Kent v. United States (1966)

Kent v. United States (1966) is a landmark case establishing the rights of young offenders in juvenile court (see Box 8.1). Morris Kent's waiver to adult court, and his subsequent conviction and sentence, were appealed. His case ultimately was heard by the U.S. Supreme Court, which held, in a 5–4 decision, that a juvenile court may not waive jurisdiction in the absence of a hearing and accompanying safeguards. Writing for the majority, Justice Abe Fortas commented,

> We do not consider whether, on the merits, Kent should have been trans-
> ferred; but there is no place in our system of law for reaching a result

---

Box 8.1 A Landmark Case Establishing the Rights of Young Offenders

Morris A. Kent Jr., was first arrested at age 14, and was given probation on charges of several housebreakings and an attempted purse snatching. Two years later, he was arrested after his fingerprints were found at the site of a housebreaking, robbery, and rape. He was taken to police headquarters and interrogated by police officers, with the interrogation lasting about seven hours. He admitted committing the offenses and was sent to an emergency temporary shelter for children. He was again interrogated by police the next day, and this also lasted about seven hours. It is not clear when his mother was notified, but she retained an attorney the day after his arrest. His attorney was notified that the case might be transferred to adult court. The attorney voiced his objection and arranged for Kent to be evaluated by two psychiatrists and a psychologist. One of the psychiatrists noted that Kent was "a victim of severe psychopathology" and recommended hospitalization in a mental health facility. Kent's lawyer submitted a motion to the court arguing that Kent could be rehabilitated if retained under the jurisdiction of the juvenile court. He also requested the court to gain access to Kent's social service record. The juvenile court judge did not rule on these motions, did not hold a hearing, but ruled that Kent should be waived to adult court. Kent was subsequently found Not Guilty by Reason of Insanity (NGRI) on the rape charge but Guilty of housebreaking and robbery. Kent was sentenced to serve 5 to 15 years on each of the convictions, or a total of 30 to 90 years in prison for the housebreaking and robbery convictions, but he was first sent to a mental hospital for treatment because he was also found not guilty by reason of insanity on the other charge. He was to remain in the mental hospital until sanity was restored, and then he would be transferred to prison.

of such tremendous consequences without ceremony—without hearing, without effective assistance of counsel, without a statement of reasons. It is inconceivable that a court of justice dealing with adults with respect to a similar issue would proceed in this manner. It would be extraordinary if society's special concern for children, as reflected in the District of Columbia's Juvenile Court Act, permitted this procedure. We hold that it does not.

The Court also held that Kent's lawyer should have had access to the social service records. Finally, the Court listed eight determining factors that must be considered by a judge in deciding whether the Juvenile Court's jurisdiction over such offenses will be waived (see Box 8.2). These criteria have since guided the courts in determining transfers, a topic that will be

---

**Box 8.2 Transfer to Adult Court Criteria
Established in *Kent v. United States* (1966)**

The determinative factors that will be considered by the Judge in deciding whether the Juvenile Court's jurisdiction over such offenses will be waived are the following:

1. The seriousness of the alleged offense to the community and whether the protection of the community requires waiver.
2. Whether the alleged offense was committed in an aggressive, violent, premeditated or willful manner.
3. Whether the alleged offense was against persons or against property, greater weight being given to offenses against persons especially if personal injury resulted.
4. The prosecutive merit of the complaint, i.e., whether there is evidence upon which a Grand Jury may be expected to return an indictment (to be determined by consultation with the United States Attorney).
5. The desirability of trial and disposition of the entire offense in one court when the juvenile's associates in the alleged offense are adults who will be charged with a crime in the U.S. District Court for the District of Columbia.
6. The sophistication and maturity of the juvenile as determined by consideration of his home, environmental situation, emotional attitude and pattern of living.
7. The record and previous history of the juvenile, including previous contacts with the Youth Aid Division, other law enforcement agencies, juvenile courts and other jurisdictions, prior periods of probation to this Court, or prior commitments to juvenile institutions.
8. The prospects for adequate protection of the public and the likelihood of reasonable rehabilitation of the juvenile (if he is found to have committed the alleged offense) by the use of procedures, services and facilities currently available to the Juvenile Court.

From *Kent v. United States*, 383 U.S. 541 (1966), pp. 566–567.

discussed in more detail later in this chapter. More importantly, the *Kent* decision provided a clear message to juvenile courts that they would need to provide due process protections for juveniles. This message was made more explicit when the Supreme Court heard *In re Gault* the following year.

In re Gault (1967)

The Supreme Court's decision in this case extended the procedural safe-guards noted in *Kent* to all juveniles in any delinquency proceeding. Gerald Francis Gault was a 15-year-old boy living with his parents in Arizona. He was accused, with a friend, of making an obscene telephone call to a neighbor and he was taken into custody at his home by the Sheriff of Gila County. Gerald's parents were not home at the time of his arrest, and received no notice that he was taken into custody. His mother came home later that day and became worried about her son's absence. She later learned from a friend of her son's that he had been arrested. She attempted to visit him in custody but she was not allowed to see him. She was informed that there would be a hearing the next day. Mrs. Gault attended the hearing but no record was made so it is not clear what transpired at this hearing or at a subsequent hearing a week later. It is known that Gerald was not represented by counsel and that the complainant neighbor did not appear to testify at either hearing.

The Court was highly critical of the legal and philosophical premises of juvenile court:

> The early reformers were appalled by adult procedures and penalties and by the fact that children could be given long prison sentences and mixed in jails with hardened criminals. . . . The idea of crime and punishment was to be abandoned. The child was to be "treated" and "rehabilitated" and the proce-dures, from apprehension through institutionalization, were to be "clinical" rather than punitive. These results were to be achieved, without coming to conceptual and constitutional grief, by insisting that the proceedings were not adversary, but that the state was proceeding as *parens patriae*. The Latin phrase proved to be a great help to those who sought to rationalize the exclu-sion of juveniles from the constitutional scheme; but its meaning is murky and its historic credentials are of dubious relevance. . . . If his parents default in effectively performing their custodial functions—that is, if the child is "delinquent"—the state may intervene. In doing so, it does not deprive the child of any rights, because he has none.

The Court concluded that "Juvenile Court history has again demonstrated that unbridled discretion, however benevolently motivated, is frequently a poor substitute for principle and procedure." It held that juveniles must be afforded certain constitutional rights, including the right to have notice of the charges against them, the right to an attorney, the right to invoke the privilege against self-incrimination, and the right to confront and cross-examine witnesses.

The next section provides an overview of how these cases have affected the operation of the juvenile court.

The Juvenile Justice System Today

Chapter 1 provided an overview of the criminal justice system and its court process. In many respects, particularly given the *Kent* and *In re Gault* decisions, the juvenile justice system (JJS) now parallels the adult system. Juveniles have the same procedural rights afforded adults, including the right to an attorney. There are, however, some important differences. For example, juveniles do not have a right to a trial by jury (unless of course they are waived to adult court), and the juvenile court retains a more rehabilitation rather than punishment philosophy.

Juveniles can be charged with the same range of offenses as adults, but there are also a number of offenses, called **status offenses**, that only apply to juveniles. These include curfew violations, incorrigibility (refusal to obey parents), running away, truancy, and underage alcohol consumption. Except for few short-term exceptions, status offenders may not be held in secure detention facilities.

Unlike the adult system, a primary goal of the JJS is rehabilitation. There is less emphasis on detention and greater use of diversion programs. In diversion programs, a youth must admit guilt, but then is allowed to participate in community programs and/or make restitution to victims.

The Juvenile Justice and Delinquency Prevention Act (JJDPA), first passed by Congress in 1974 and amended several times since, was designed to establish a comprehensive nationwide program of juvenile delinquency prevention, offender rehabilitation, and juvenile justice system improvements (see http://www1.cj.msu.edu/~outreach/jj/booklet_2002.html). The Act outlines four requirements: (1) deinstitutionalization of status offenders and nonoffenders; (2) separation of juveniles from adult offenders; (3) removal of juveniles from adult jails and lockups; and (4) address disproportionate minority confinement if the number of juveniles from minority groups who are confined in secure detention facilities exceeds the proportion such groups represent in the general population.

Another difference in the JJS is that the court hearings are closed in many jurisdictions. As of 2004, the majority of states held either closed hearings or limited open hearings for certain cases, while 14 states have delinquency hearings open to the general public.

Violent Crime Rates

As Figure 8.1 shows, there was a surge of violent crime committed by juveniles in the 1980s and early 1990s. This led to increased public fears and calls for more punitive sanctions, including transfer to adult court. However, the surge in the 1980s and early 1990s has since been followed by a decline. The arrest rates for juvenile violent crimes declined by 44% from 1994 to 2001 (Synder, 2003). Figure 8.2 shows that the juvenile arrest rates for homicide from 1993 to2003 have declined dramatically during this period. The decline may be largely accounted for by the substantial drop in the rates of minority males killing other minority males (see Box 8.3).

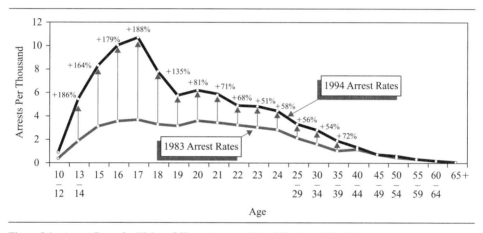

Figure 8.1   Arrest Rates for Violent Offenses by Age of the Offender, 1983–1994
Source: From "Trends in At-Risk Behaviors of Youth in Washington: A Report to the Washington State Legislature as Directed in RCW 70.190.050," by S. Aos, R. Lieb, and R. Barnoski, 1996. All calculations made by the Washington State Institute for Public Policy.

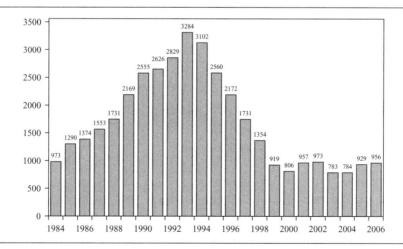

Figure 8.2   Juvenile Arrests for Homicide in the United States, 1984–2006
Source: Federal Bureau of Investigation, *Crime in the United States, 1984–2006*: Uniform Crime Reports. http://www.fbi.gov/ucr/ucr.htm.

Box 8.3 highlights statistics on juvenile offending and victims from a 2006 U.S. Department of Justice national report. This report documents increases in female delinquency, the overrepresentation of African American youth in the juvenile justice system, and the disproportionate involvement of youth gangs in violent and nonviolent offenses.

Box 8.3 Highlights from Juvenile Offenders and Victims: 2006 National Report

The female proportion of delinquency cases increased steadily from 19% in 1991 to 26% in 2002.

In 2002, African Americans comprised 16% of the juvenile population but 29% of the delinquency caseload. The African American proportion was greater for person offense cases (37%) and lower for drug cases (21%) than for property (28%) or public order (29%) cases.

Juvenile courts waived fewer cases to criminal court in 2002 (7,100) than in 1985 (7,200). In 2002, waived cases accounted for less than 1% of petitioned delinquency cases.

Reoffending data from studies of juveniles released from state incarceration found that rearrest rates were substantially higher than rates based on other measures of recidivism.

Across studies with a 12-month follow-up period, the average rate of rearrest for a delinquent or criminal offense was 55%, the average reconviction or readjudication rate was 33%, and the average reincarceration or reconfinement rate was 24%.

Juvenile courts handled 1.6 million delinquency cases in 2002—up from 1.1 million in 1985. However, the volume of delinquency cases has declined since 1997 for most offense categories (11% overall).

In 2002, 1 in 12 murders in the United States involved a juvenile offender. One-third of murders committed by a juvenile offender also involved an adult offender.

The large decline in the number of murders committed by juveniles from the mid-1990s to 2002 stemmed primarily from a decline in minority males killing minority males.

The violent crime peak in the after-school hours on school days is seen in the crimes committed by male, female, white, and African American youth.

Six percent of high school students said they carried a weapon (e.g., gun, knife, or club) on school property in the past 30 days—down from 12% in 1993. The proportion that carried a weapon to school was about one-third of those who said they had carried a weapon anywhere in the past month.

Although the number of law enforcement agencies reporting gang problems appears to have stabilized, and the prevalence of youth gangs declined in nonurban areas, gangs remain a substantial urban problem. Gang members are responsible for a disproportionate share of violent and nonviolent offenses.

Source: http://ojjdp.ncjrs.gov/ojstatbb/nr2006/downloads/NR2006_HL.pdf, accessed September 26, 2007.

Figure 8.1 also shows that the level of criminal activity peaks in the adolescent years and declines steadily from that point on. Thus, adolescents account for a larger percentage of crime than any other age group, and as people age, they become less likely to engage in criminal behavior.

Developmental Theory and Psychosocial Development

Dr. Terrie Moffitt, a researcher who pioneered longitudinal studies of the development of criminal behavior over the course of life, has contributed substantially to our understanding of developmental pathways to delinquent and criminal behavior (Moffitt, 1993, 2003). Based initially on research conducted in New Zealand, Moffitt identified two groups of delinquents. The first group, called **life-course-persistent offenders**, have conduct problems that begin in early childhood. The childhood predictors Moffitt identified in her research showed that the life-course-persistent path is characterized by undercontrolled temperament and delayed motor development by age 3, low verbal ability, attention deficit and hyperactivity problems, and neuropsychological impairments (Moffitt & Caspi, 2001). These children may engage in bullying behavior in elementary school and have difficulties in interpersonal peer relations. These individuals are at higher risk for later delinquent and adult criminal behavior. Fortunately, this group of offenders accounts for the small proportion of delinquent offenders (less than 10% of all delinquents). The other group, called **adolescent-limited offenders**, don't begin offending until their teen years, and they typically do not have the early childhood antisocial and behavioral problems seen in life-course-persistent offenders. As Moffitt and Caspi comment, "Their delinquent activity emerges alongside puberty, when otherwise healthy youngsters experience dysphoria during the relatively roleless years between their biological maturation and their access to mature privileges and responsibility, a period we call the maturity gap" (p. 356). Moffitt and Caspi consider delinquent behavior to be normative for this group, as a way of establishing autonomy from parents and to gain acceptance from peers. Indeed, adolescent-limited offenders are heavily influenced by peers when engaging in delinquent behavior. Adolescent-limited offending is by far the most common type of offending but although smaller in number, the life-course-persistent offenders are more persistent and pathological.

The importance of Moffitt's category of early offending is illustrated in the work of Loeber and Farrington (2001), who provide some interesting statistics on crime rates of child delinquency, which they define as offending at ages 7 to 12 years. They note that in 1997, 250,000 child delinquents were arrested in the United States, with boys outnumbering girls at a 4:1 ratio. Their crimes are often minor ones, but Loeber and Farrington reported that child delinquents were involved in about 2% (about 600) of the murders committed by all juveniles during an 18-year period. They are also involved in other serious crimes: 1 in 3 juvenile arrests for arson, 1 in 5 arrests for sex offenses and vandalism, and 1 in 8 for burglary and forcible rape. They also found that the rates of violent crimes by child delinquents increased by 45% between 1988 and 1997, and weapons violations increased by 76%. Based on extensive longitudinal studies, Loeber and Farrington found that "about one-third to two-thirds of child delinquents are at risk for escalating to serious delinquency" (p. xxiii). Extrapolating from Moffitt's theory, they are also at risk for persistent criminal behavior into adulthood.

It is important to keep in mind that the delinquent behaviors of the adolescent-limited and life-course-persistent offenders may not be substantively different. Both groups can be involved in the same range of criminal activity, including violent offenses. What is different is that the delinquent behavior of life-course offenders is predicted by early onset developmental and behavioral problems.

Moffitt's research was initially conducted on male samples, but she has since extended her studies to females. She finds that her model does predict antisocial behavior of both sexes, but at a much smaller ratio due to the fact that life-course-persistent criminal behavior is extremely rare for females. While the ratio of life-course-persistent criminality is about 10:1 for males identified with early onset conduct problems, the ratio is 100:1 for females. Thus, most female delinquent behavior best fits the adolescence-limited type.

Psychosocial Maturity

Another line of theory development has focused on psychosocial maturity. Scott, Reppucci, and Woolard (1995) proposed a framework for understanding adolescent judgment and decision making, arguing that legal policy should take into account that adolescents make decisions quite differently than do adults, due to differences in peer influences, risk taking, and temporal perspectives. Cauffman and Steinberg (2000) expanded on this theory by defining the concept of **psychosocial maturity**. They define this term as "the complexity and sophistication of the process of individual decision-making as it is affected by a range of cognitive, emotional, and social factors" (p. 743). They delineate three development capacities that affect decision making:

1. *Responsibility*. This involves the adolescent's capacity to make autonomous choices, independent of external influences, including

adults but particularly peers. As adolescents mature, they become less responsive to peer influences but also more independent from parental influences. Responsibility also involves the development of a coherent sense of identity.

2. *Temperance.* Risk taking is higher among adolescents. Adolescents are higher on sensation seeking and impulsivity, and are more susceptible to mood changes due to hormonal changes. Temperance involves the ability to control impulses and exercise self-restraint. Steinberg argues that the increased risk taking of adolescents is due to heightened sensation seeking that increases with puberty which is not held in check by the development of regulatory competence as this occurs later in adolescence. He adds that this risk-taking behavior is unlikely to be changed by educational interventions and suggests instead that interventions focus on reducing harm associated with risk-taking behavior.

3. *Perspective.* This involves the adolescent's ability to see both short- and long-term consequences (time perspective), the ability to understand how one's actions might affect others (perspective taking), and the ability to weigh costs and benefits of a decision. Borum and Grisso (2007) note that "before adulthood, greater weight is given to acquiring potential gains than to avoiding potential losses, and to short-term rather than long-term (future) consequences" (p. 559).

Cauffman and Steinberg (2000) examined these three dimensions in a sample of over 1,000 individuals ranging in age from 12 to 48. They found that individuals did differ significantly on the three domains of psychosocial maturity as a function of age. These results provide support for the conclusion that psychosocial maturity does develop over the period of adolescence. By age 19, the level of maturity was the same as the adult sample. In general, the average adolescent is less psychosocially mature than the average adult, and younger adolescents are less mature than older adolescents. But age alone does not account for differences in decision-making abilities, because there was considerable variation in judgment within each age group. Cauffman and Steinberg note that, "psychosocially mature 13-year-olds demonstrate less antisocial decision-making than psychosocially immature adults" (p. 757). This is important to keep in mind, as the research describes average differences between adults and youth, but there is considerable variation within and between age groups. Thus, some 13-year-olds may be more mature and are better decision makers than some 17-year-olds, even though, on average, 17-year-olds are more mature than 13-year-olds.

The Developing Brain

One of the reasons that adolescents may have lower capacities in key decision-making areas is that adolescent brains have not reached adult maturity, particularly in the frontal lobes, which control executive functions of the brain related to decision making. This area of the brain is typically not fully developed until the early twenties (Giedd et al., 1999). As adolescents mature, they typically become better problem solvers, are less influenced by peers, less impulsive, and more sophisticated in the way they think and make decisions. The research on brain development was cited in the APA brief in the *Roper v. Simmons* (2005) case (see a detailed discussion of this case in Chapter 11 of this text), although the U.S. Supreme Court did not explicitly cite this research in its decision that the death penalty for juveniles was unconstitutional. The question remains about how useful this research is when determining the culpability of adolescents. Aronson (2007) comments that while some researchers support its use in the legal system, "others are uncomfortable with introducing scientific evidence into the legal system before it is understood exactly how specific brain traits relate to the real-life decision making and behavior of teens in high-stress situations" (p. 134).

ASSESSMENT OF YOUTH IN THE JUVENILE JUSTICE SYSTEM

The rights reforms brought on by *Kent* and *In re Gault* established an increased need for forensic assessments of youth with respect to a number of issues (Grisso, 2003). These include capacity to understand arrest rights, competency to stand trial, waiver to adult court, danger or risk to the community, and sentencing or dispositional assessments.

Capacity to Understand Arrest Rights

The *Kent* and *Gault* decisions establish the rights of youth in a variety of legal contexts. This includes rights at arrest, which prior to *Kent* and *Gault* were nonexistent for youth. Owen-Kostelnik, Reppucci, and Meyer (2006) note that "the characterization of young people has shifted between *paternalistic logic* models, which portray youths as children in need of protection and thus deprive them of certain rights when being questioned, and *liberationist logic* models, which depict youths as autonomous individuals entitled to the same rights as adults when being questioned" (pp. 287–288). Thus, as discussed in Chapter 6, the arrest rights established in the case of *Miranda v. Arizona* (1966) apply equally to youth, and forensic psychologists have increasingly been involved in assessing the capacity of youth to understand their rights at arrest (Viljoen & Roesch, 2007). For more details on these assessments, see Chapter 6.

Competency to Stand Trial

The issue of **competency to stand trial** was discussed in detail in Chapter 2. It is important to note that many juvenile courts have become more punishment oriented, and there is an increased possibility that youth may be transferred to adult courts. For these reasons, competency issues have come to the forefront in juvenile court.

There has been considerable discussion about whether the *Dusky* criteria that define adult competence to stand trial (see Chapter 2) can be readily used as a foundation for a finding of incompetence in juvenile populations. Certainly, the functional component of competence that has been established for adults (e.g., understanding of charges and possible consequences of trial, understanding and appreciation of the role of participants in the legal process—defense attorney prosecutor, judge—and decision-making ability in the context of decisions such as pleading guilty or deciding to testify) would also apply to juveniles. However, as Grisso (2003) comments, the causal component is less clear for juveniles. For adults, psychosis, particularly in the form of delusional symptoms, or mental retardation are the primary reasons for a finding of incompetence when a defendant's functional abilities are impaired (Zapf & Roesch, 2005). Although many juveniles have mental health problems, most do not show signs of severe mental illness, as research has shown that fewer than 20% of incompetent adolescents have psychotic disorders (McGaha, Otto, McClaren, & Petrila, 2001). For juveniles, issues related to age, cognitive development, and maturity are more salient (Scott et al., 1995; Viljoen & Roesch, 2005). Factors such as attention deficits and hyperactivity, impaired verbal abilities, and low intelligence may also impair an adolescent's ability to stand trial (Viljoen & Roesch, 2005). However, states have typically not recognized immaturity as a basis for a finding of incompetence (Grisso, 2003).

Although many forensic assessment instruments have been developed for assessing competency in adults (see Chapter 2), this has not been the case for youth. Only one instrument, the *Juvenile Competency Assessment Interview* (JACI) has been designed specifically for youth competency assessments (Grisso, 2005). The JACI is a structured interview that can be used by forensic psychologists to obtain information about the relevant legal capacities and developmental issues in assessing juveniles' adjudicative competence. The *Fitness Interview Test-Revised* (FIT-R; see Chapter 2 for a review), although developed for adult assessments, has also been used with juveniles. Viljoen, Vincent, and Roesch (2006) provided support for its reliability and validity with adolescents, and also noted that scores of young adolescents, particularly those with low IQ scores, showed greater impairment than older adolescents and adults (Viljoen & Roesch, 2005). Nevertheless, it is likely that most incompetent youth are restored to competence within a relatively brief restoration period (McGaha et al., 2001).

If a youth is found to be incompetent to proceed with trial, juvenile restoration services are usually provided in the community, unless there is evidence that an inpatient setting is needed (Redding & Frost, 2001). Restoration may be difficult to achieve, though, especially for youth who have been found incompetent due to developmental deficits. For example, Viljoen, Odgers, Grisso, and Tillbrook (2007) found that teaching did not affect developmental differences in youths' and adults' legal understanding.

Waiver (Transfer) to Adult Court

This central issue in *Kent v. United States* (1966) was whether a youth can be transferred (waived) to adult court. This transfer can occur in one of three ways (Salekin, 2002). *Judicial waiver* allows a judge to transfer a youth to adult court following a hearing in which it is determined that a youth satisfies the criteria established in *Kent v. United States*. As summarized in Box 8.2, these criteria focus on both the youth (e.g., treatment amenability, sophistication and maturity, prior record, seriousness of current charge or charges) as well as the degree of risk the youth would pose to the community once released. *Automatic waiver* is used in over half of the states. In these states, waiver is automatic if a youth is charged with certain offenses, such as murder or other serious violence. Some states limit this to adolescents age 16 or 17, while other states don't provide any age restriction. In fact, young offenders as young as age 8 can face adult penalties for serious offences. Nevada is one of just a few states that don't specify any age limit for exclusion of certain serious offenses (see also Delaware, Mississippi, Nevada, Ohio, and Pennsylvania). In Nevada, anyone regardless of age who is charged with murder or attempted murder is tried in adult court. Those age 14 and older who are charged with other crimes could also be raised to adult court. A third option, which is available in nearly one-third of the states, is *prosecutor direct file*, in which prosecutors can decide whether to try the youth in adult or juvenile court.

The transfer of juveniles to adult court has increased since the *Kent* decision. A recent estimate shows that about 2,000 youth are incarcerated in adult prisons (Ryan & Ziedenberg, 2007). This may in part be due to the support of a majority of citizens for increased sanctions on young offenders, and may be driven by both a fear of violent crime as well as a goal of holding youth more accountable for their offenses. The increase in transfers is attributed to a justice philosophy that holds that some youth are too violent to be managed in the juvenile justice system, that some youth cannot be rehabilitated, and that a more punishment-oriented approach with longer potential sentences would provide better protection for the public. The extent of public support is reflected in a national opinion survey in which Mears (2001) found widespread community support for adult sanctions. Mears found that 87% supported transfer for youth charged with violent offenses. He also found that 64% supported waiver for youth charged with property crimes. Thus, support for increased sanctions of youth may not be limited to those charged with violent crimes.

Psychologists may be asked to evaluate juveniles who are being considered for transfer to adult court. The evaluations would typically focus on three factors: risk (dangerousness) to the community, maturity and sophistication, and amenability to treatment. Psychologists might use standard risk instruments such as the SAVRY (see review of this evaluation later in this chapter), personality testing such as the MMPI-A, tests of intellectual functioning, and measures of treatment responsivity. Salekin (2004) has developed a measure of all three of these factors. The *Risk-Sophistication-Treatment-Inventory* (RSTI) is a semistructured interview and rating scale that is scored based on an interview with the youth; collateral sources such as school, police, detention; and previous treatment records. Interviews with parents and guardians can also provide important information.

Impact of Waiver

The assumptions underlying the use of waivers have not been supported by research. Lotke and Schiraldi (1996) compared youth homicide rates of states with high transfer rates with states with low transfer rates. The results show that transferring youth does not impact homicide rates. "Connecticut has the highest transfer rate in the nation, and it has the same youth homicide rate as Colorado, whose transfer rate is nearly zero. Michigan and Massachusetts have nearly the same transfer rates, but their youth homicide rates are among the highest and lowest, respectively" (p. 7). These studies suggest that the increased transfer rate has not resulted in greater protection of the public, at least in terms of lower rates of homicide.

Another assumption is that an increase in transfer will result in lower recidivism rates. In fact, the opposite appears to be the reality. Bishop and her colleagues (1996) compared the recidivism of youths transferred to adult court with youths retained in the juvenile justice system in Florida.

One limitation of the research on this issue is that the youths in the two systems were not comparable in terms of seriousness of the transfer offense, number of charges, prior record, severity of prior offenses, and sociodemographic factors such as age, gender, and race. Bishop and colleagues overcame this methodological limitation by matching the youth on these variables so that the two samples were in fact comparable on the most relevant dimensions. They examined recidivism rates, defined as *rearrest*, and also looked at the severity of charges at rearrest and the time to failure among those rearrested. Their results are counter to the expectation that raising youth to the adult system will reduce recidivism. They found that the recidivism rates were actually higher in the transfer group: 30% were rearrested during a follow-up period of up to four years compared to 19% of the nontransfer matches. This difference held up even when the researchers controlled for days at risk (since the transfer youth were detained longer, they had fewer days at risk for rearrest). The transfer group averaged 1.9 offenses per year of exposure, compared to 1.7 for the nontransfer group. The transfer group was also more likely to be charged with a felony, and reoffended at a faster rate than the nontransfer group.

Transfer and Race

Minority youth appear to be more likely to be transferred to adult court, even when type and severity of offense is controlled. In a study in Los Angeles, Males and Macallair (2000) found that the rate of violent arrests of minority youth was substantially higher than for white youth. Of course, since more minority youth are arrested, one would expect to see a higher number of such youth who are transferred. Nevertheless, the proportion of youth transferred to adult court should be equivalent across racial groups. This was not the case. While 37% of white youth were transferred, the rate for nonwhite youth was 82%. Thus, minority youth charged with violent offenses were more than twice as likely to be transferred when compared to white youth charged with violent crimes. This disparity is also evident in the type of sentence received, with minority youth more likely to be incarcerated. Ryan & Ziedenberg (2007) noted that while African American, Latino, and other nonwhite youth represent a minority of the youth population in states, they represent up to 70% of youth tried as adults.

Impact of Incarceration in Prisons Rather Than Juvenile Institutions

Prisons, with a primary focus on punishment, do not typically have comparable rehabilitative programs targeted at adolescents' needs. Furthermore, prisons are more violent environments, and juveniles appear to be at increased risk for victimization. According to a report on youth violence by the U.S. Surgeon General, "young people placed in adult correctional institutions, compared to those placed in institutions designed for youths, are eight times as likely to commit suicide, five times as likely to be sexually assaulted, twice as likely to be beaten by staff, and 50 percent as likely to be attacked with a weapon" (U.S. Department of Health and Human Services, 2001). More recent reports confirm that youth remain at high risk for victimization (see Ryan & Ziedenberg, 2007).

In summary, the research suggests that raising youth to adult court and incarceration in prisons rather than juvenile facilities appears to have effects that run counter to the expectations that this would serve as a deterrent, that recidivism would be lower, and the public would be better protected. In fact, the research shows that recidivism of transferred youth is higher than comparable youths not transferred, and there has not been a reduction in homicide rates. Further, minorities are overrepresented in transfer cases. Finally, once sentenced in adult court, youth are at greater risk of victimization in prison.

Risk Assessment

Research findings support the conclusion that no single cause accounts for all delinquency and no single pathway leads to a life of crime (Loeber & Farrington, 1998). Thus, no single intervention is appropriate for all young offenders, and the risk research can help us identify factors that might guide intervention strategies as well as identify those youth who are at the highest risk for reoffending.

Identification of risk factors is important for two reasons. One, it provides information about the likelihood of future criminal behavior, although it is always important to remember that longer term predictions can be made with less certainty, especially for youth. Two, it identifies areas in which appropriate interventions might be targeted that would serve to reduce this likelihood of recidivism. **Risk assessment** should always focus on both of these uses of risk information, since it is essential that risk be both identified and managed. A risk assessment provides an opportunity to identify interventions that could change the expected outcomes.

Risk for violence can be assessed in terms of present and future risk. The difficulties of risk prediction have been well documented (Borum, 1996; Monahan & Steadman, 1994). While the accuracy rate has improved in the past decade, there continues to be a high false positive rate (incorrectly predicting an individual will be violent). For youth in particular, short-term predictions are generally more accurate than long-term ones, since as the time frame of the prediction increases, accuracy decreases. This is particularly true for the assessment of the future risk of adolescents, because most delinquent youth do not continue to engage in criminal acts as adults.

This is the case even for youth who have committed violent acts, as most studies show that less than 30% of these youth are arrested for violent acts as adults. For example, a report from the Washington State Institute for Public Policy presented follow-up data on violent juvenile offenders. They found that, through age 25, only 20% of these violent young offenders were subsequently sentenced for a violent felony as an adult. Thus, the majority of violent youth do not represent a substantial long-term risk of violence (Elliott, Huizinga, & Morse, 1986). The reasons for this are complex, but from a developmental perspective, it is likely due to the fact that adolescents, compared to adults, are more likely to respond impulsively, to be influenced by peers, take greater risks, and think less about long-term consequences of their behavior (Arnett, 1992).

The National Academy of Sciences released the report of the Panel on Juvenile Crime: Prevention, Treatment, and Control (McCord, Widom, & Crowell, 2001). This report addressed a range of issues related to juvenile crime, one of which focused on risk assessement. With respect to risk prediction, the Panel commented, "Public policy on juvenile crime, particularly the trend toward more punitive sanctions, appears to have been influenced in part by predictions of future crime rates—predictions that have proven notoriously inaccurate" (p. ES-6). The Panel recommended that, "Because of the inaccuracies inherent in long-range predictions of behavior, public policy should not be based on the assumption that any specific forecast will be true. The periods over which crime forecasts are made should be as short as possible and the forecasts should be reviewed frequently" (p. ES-6).

Risk Instruments

Several youth risk instruments are available that are useful for assessing risk and identifying areas in which intervention might serve to reduce future risk of criminal behavior (see Corrado, Roesch, Hart, & Gierowski, 2002, for a review). Augimeri, Koegl, Webster, and Levene (2001) developed the *Early Assessment Risk List for Boys* (EARL-20B), which measures several areas of risk for boys under 12, including *family* (stressors, parenting style), *child* (ADHD, peer socialization), and *responsivity to interventions* for both child and family. They have also developed a version for assessing risk for girls under 12 (Levene et al., 2001).

Table 8.1 shows the items from perhaps the most comprehensive structured professional judgment instrument. Borum, Bartel, and Forth (2002) developed the *Structured Assessment of Violence Risk in Youth* (SAVRY). The SAVRY is a 30-item structured guide for evaluating risk for violence in adolescents age 12 to 18. The items are based on factors identified in research as being related to risk for future violence (see Loeber & Farrington, 1998). The categories included are: historical, social/contextual, and clinical risk factors, as well as protective factors. Each risk item is given a rating of low, medium, or high risk based on scoring criteria contained in the manual. The protective factors are

Table 8.1   Structured Assessment of Violence Risk in Youth (SAVRY)

Historical Risk Factors

1. History of violence
2. History of nonviolent offending
3. Early initiation of violence
4. Past supervision/intervention failures
5. History of self-harm or suicide attempts
6. Exposure to violence in the home
7. Childhood history of maltreatment
8. Parental/caregiver criminality
9. Early caregiver disruption
10. Poor school achievement

Social/Contextual Risk Factors

11. Peer delinquency
12. Peer rejection
13. Stress and poor coping
14. Poor parental management
15. Lack of personal/social support
16. Community disorganization

Individual/Clinical Risk Factors

17. Negative attitudes
18. Risk taking/impulsivity
19. Substance use difficulties
20. Anger management problems
21. Low empathy/remorse
22. Attention deficit/hyperactivity difficulties
23. Poor compliance
24. Low interest/commitment to school

Protective Factors

P1. Prosocial involvement
P2. Strong social support
P3. Strong attachment and bonds
P4. Positive attitude toward intervention and authority
P5. Strong commitment to school
P6. Resilient personality traits

Source: Borum, Bartel, & Forth, 2002.

rated as either present or absent. All items are rated on the basis of interview information, prior record information, and when appropriate, psychological test data and interviews with family members. Research has provided promising initial results showing significant correlations of the SAVRY and various violence outcome indicators (Borum & Verhaagen, 2006). Perhaps most important, the protective factors have been negatively associated with violent outcomes, indicating that factors such as prosocial involvement, strong attachments and social support, and resilient personality traits can indeed serve a protective function.

Gender Differences in Risk Factors

Much of the research on risk factors for juvenile offenders has focused on male samples. Research on female adolescent offenders has shown that the rate of violent offending is increasing, although the level of violence is much less severe when compared to male offenders (Moretti, Odgers, & Jackson, 2004). Further, while there is some overlap in risk factors, there are many factors that are more prevalent in adolescent female offenders. For example, Cauffman, Feldman, Waterman, and Steiner (1998) found that 65% of girls in custody in California had symptoms of posttraumatic stress disorder (PTSD) compared to 11% in general female adolescent population. This is likely due to higher rates of sexual or physical victimization and other forms of family violence. Studies of incarcerated girls have shown rates as high as 50% of girls with a history of sexual victimization, whereas boys were rarely sexually victimized. Depression and suicide rates were also found to be higher among girls. Moffitt and colleagues (2001) found that 21-year-old women diagnosed with conduct disorders in childhood or adolescence were significantly more likely to have mental health symptoms (anxiety, depression, psychosis, mania, and suicidality), have more medical problems, require social assistance, be victimized by their partners, and perpetrate physical abuse against them in return. It is important to recognize that much of the research on risk and interventions is based on male samples. There is less research on girls and aggression, but we do know that the level of violence as well as the type of risk factors differ substantially, as boys significantly outnumber girls in the prevalence, frequency, and severity of their violent behavior (Odgers, Schmidt, & Reppucci, 2004). These gender differences suggest that risk assessments normed on male populations may not be suited for use with females (Moretti et al., 2004).

Mental Health and Co-occurring Disorders

One risk factor that merits particular attention is the presence of mental health problems. The rate of mental disorders is higher among youth in the juvenile system than for peers in the general population. Suicide threats and actual suicide attempts by young offenders are not uncommon, and many of these youth have experienced physical and sexual abuse, as well as parental neglect (Smith & Thornberry, 1995). These experiences have a marked effect on the mental health and self-esteem of victims, and they are clear risk factors as they are correlated with delinquent behavior.

A study by Teplin and colleagues (2002) of 1,829 youth in detention in Cook County, Illinois, showed that two-thirds of the male youth and three-quarters of the female youth had one or more psychiatric disorders; about half of the sample had indications of substance abuse; about 20% had a major depression; and approximately 16% of male offenders and 21% of female offenders were considered to have attention-deficit/hyperactivity disorder (ADHD). While psychotic disorders were rare, about 21% of male offenders and 31% of female offenders had an anxiety disorder. Other research has shown that conduct disorder is quite high, in some studies up to 90%, so the presence of conduct disorder is not particularly useful as an assessment focus or a guide for intervention.

Many youth experience more than one type of disorder, which is known as **co-morbidity**. Co-morbidity may be common among young offenders, especially mental health problems such as depression and anxiety co-occurring with other problems such as substance abuse or ADHD (Lexcen & Redding, 2002). In a study of 419 adolescents aged 12–18 years, Sterling and Weisner (2005) found that treating substance abuse alone is often not effective due to the high percentage of co-occurring disorders. Over half of the sample had at least one psychiatric diagnosis in addition to a substance use disorder. They also found that those youth who received treatment for both substance abuse and mental health problems were more likely to refrain from both alcohol and drugs compared to youth who received substance abuse treatment only.

Given the prevalence of mental health problems in adolescent offender groups, it is important that juvenile facilities assess all incoming youth to identify appropriate interventions. This is not yet a widespread practice, but that is slowly changing with the introduction of screening instruments. One such instrument is the Massachusetts Youth Screening Instrument (MAYSI-2) developed by Grisso and Barnum (2003). The MAYSI-2 is a 52-item screening instrument that can be administered by nonprofessionals in about 15 minutes and was designed to identify signs of mental/emotional disturbance or stress. The youth are asked to describe their behavior over the past few months by responding *yes* or *no* to statements about their behavior (e.g., Have you had a lot of problems concentrating or paying attention? Have you felt lonely too much of the time?). There are seven subscales: Alcohol/Drug Use, Angry-Irritable, Depressed-Anxious, Somatic Complaints, Suicide Ideation, Thought Disturbance, and Traumatic Experience. Scores allow a determination of whether the youth is above either of two critical scores: *caution* or *warning*. *Caution* indicates possible clinical significance of the scale score. Grisso (2004) found that 66% of boys and 79% of girls had at least one scale score in this range; 45% of boys and 57% of girls had at least two scales above this range. *Warning* indicates that the youth has scored exceptionally high on a scale, for example, in the top 10% compared to other juvenile youth (27% of boys and 40% of girls had at least one scale score in this range; 11% and 18% at least two scales above this range).

Dispositional Assessments

Grisso (2003, p. 319) identified four questions that should be addressed in forensic evaluations of youth who have been convicted of an offense:

1. What are the youth's important characteristics (e.g., personality, family factors, mental or intellectual problems, delinquency history)?
2. What needs to change (e.g., what factors that have contributed to delinquency will need to be modified to reduce the likelihood of recidivism)?
3. What modes of intervention could be applied toward the rehabilitation objective?
4. What is the likelihood of change, given the relevant interventions?

A report to the court that addresses these questions will be useful for determining the most appropriate sentence, including rehabilitation programs that will help the youth address areas in need of change.

Interventions

There is considerable evidence that intervention, especially early intervention, can reduce delinquency, including serious and violent offending. Lipsey (1995) conducted a **meta-analysis** (a statistical analysis of a large number of empirical studies) of about 400 studies on treatment of juvenile delinquency and found that treatment was effective in reducing general delinquent recidivism by an average of approximately 10%. This may not seem like a substantial difference, but the impact is important in terms of reduced incarceration costs, victim costs, and the positive benefits of contributions by youth who do not recidivate.

Research on risk assessment has identified risk factors that can be used as a foundation for interventions designed to reduce or manage that risk. For example, research has shown that the children of young, single mothers are at higher risk for delinquency (Yoshikawa, 1994). Programs such as the Nurse-Family Partnership (NFP), a home visitation program in which nurses work with low-income, first-time parents and their children, can have both immediate and long-term effects. The goal of NFP is to enhance parenting skills, improve health prevention activities, and improve economic self-sufficiency. In a follow-up conducted 15 years after going through one such program, 15-year-old children of low-income, unmarried mothers who were visited by nurses had fewer arrests, convictions, lower measures of alcohol and cigarette usage, and fewer sexual partners than the children from similar families who did not receive home visits (Olds et al., 1999).

Programs such as the NFP clearly demonstrate that early interventions can have long-term positive benefits. Risk research has also shown that youth with early indications of problems in school, such as bullying, attention problems, and interpersonal difficulties, are more likely to be involved in later delinquency (Loeber & Farrington, 1998). School-based interventions can be effective in addressing these problem behaviors and perhaps lower the incidence of later problems, including delinquent behavior (see the discussion of the bullying program developed by Olweus later in this section).

Conceptually, we can think of interventions along two dimensions: the *timing* of the intervention and the *target* of the intervention (Roesch, 1995). Both the timing and target dimensions of interventions have been found to be important concepts in the development of interventions for young offenders. *Timing* of interventions is usually considered in the context of prevention activities. While each prevention activity includes a target population generally or specifically, it is important to note the dimension of activities exist on a continuum of prevention concepts: primary, secondary, and tertiary prevention.

Primary prevention interventions take place before a problem is developed and are directed at a general population rather than specific individuals. An example of a primary prevention activity is a media campaign warning of the risks of alcohol use for expectant mothers. It is now well established that use of alcohol or drugs during pregnancy can result in Fetal Alcohol Spectrum Disorders (FASD), which in turn is related to the onset of behavioral and mental health problems, and according to some research, individuals with this disorder are at higher risk for juvenile and adult criminality. Streissguth and Kanter (1997) followed 400 individuals with FASD into adulthood and found that 60% had been suspended, expelled, or dropped out of school; 60% had been charged or convicted of a crime; 50% had been confined—either as an inpatient for mental health or substance abuse treatment or incarcerated for committing a crime; 50% exhibited inappropriate sexual behavior; and 30% had alcohol and/or drug problems. A program to address peer victimization in elementary schools by providing curriculum for teachers and students and teaching skills to cope with aggressive behavior is another type of primary prevention (Leadbetter, Dhami, Hoglund, & Dickinson, 2004). Programs such as Project Head Start (Zigler & Styfco, 2004) for high-risk pre-school children promote school readiness by enhancing social and cognitive development, and thus may prevent later school adjustment problems. An example of a largely primary intervention program designed to prevent violent behavior can be found in the creative programs designed by Olweus (2003) in Norway. His program targeted the problem of bullying behavior in elementary schools. Using a multilevel approach, he focused on changes in the school, the classroom, and individuals that would create an atmosphere less conducive to such behavior. The interventions were successful in reducing bullying behavior and also seemed to have a broader effect on antisocial behavior.

Secondary prevention programs are directed at specific groups, but the intervention takes place before significant problems have developed. Youth who show the early risk signs discussed previously in this chapter might be targeted for special programs. An example is the Montreal Preventive Treatment Program, a two-year program aimed at 7- to 9-year-old boys who were identified as having high levels of disruptive behavior in kindergarten. The program focuses on school-based social skills and parent training (Tremblay, Masse, Pagani, & Vitaro, 1996). Follow-up studies showed improvements in school performance and lower levels of delinquent behavior for treated boys compared to a group of untreated boys. Another example is a diversion program, in which first-time, less serious offenders are diverted out of the juvenile justice system (Davidson, Redner, Blakely, Mitchell, & Emshoff, 1987).

Tertiary prevention is the third type of prevention. It takes place long after problems have developed. Tertiary prevention programs are usually quite costly as they often involve institutional care and intensive case management. Furthermore, they usually take place after serious criminal behavior, including violence, has already taken place. Obviously, the focus is to reduce risk of future criminal behavior but the opportunity is lost to prevent any criminal behavior at all. This is why earlier intervention programs can potentially have a greater impact, but there remains a high need to provide treatment for youth who are further along the delinquent path. Most of these programs are in detention facilities but one example of a tertiary program that provides an alternative to detention is Multidimensional Treatment Foster Care, in which trained foster families provide treatment and intensive supervision at home, school, and in the community (Chamberlin, 2003). Notably, follow-up studies show that treated youth compared to a control group had lower arrest rates, less drug use, and better school attendance.

The other conceptual dimension is the *target* of the intervention. We can focus interventions on individuals who are at risk or who have already offended (e.g., psychotherapy with an identified youth in conflict with the law), but we can also focus on families, schools, peers, and communities as important components of effective intervention. A good example of a multitarget approach is Multisystemic Therapy (MST), which targets all the groups as essential parts of an overall intervention program (Henggeler, Cunningham, Pickrel, Schoenwald, & Brondino, 1996). MST provides intensive individual, family, and community support, with an average of 60 hours of direct services. Henggeler and colleagues report significant positive effects on behavior problems, family relations, and self-reported offences. In a 59-week, after referral follow-up, the treated group had less than half as many arrests as controls, had 73 fewer days incarcerated, and had reduced peer aggression. Over two years later, youth who underwent MST were half as likely to be rearrested. While this initial study provided promising results, a subsequent study in Canada found that treated and nontreated youth were not different on any of the outcome measures, suggesting that there was no treatment effect (Cunningham, 2002).

Cost Benefits of Interventions

Table 8.2 shows that there are substantial long-term cost benefits of prevention programs. Aos, Phipps, Barnoski, and Lieb (2001) calculated the

Table 8.2   Cost/Benefit Analysis of the Economic Impact of Interventions

Program	Average Size of the Crime Reduction Effect*	Net Direct Cost Per Participant	Net Benefits Per Participant (i.e., Benefits Minus Costs)[†]
Mentoring (e.g., Big Brothers, Big Sisters)	−0.04	$1,054	$225–$4,524
Intensive Probation (versus regular caseloads)	−0.05	$2,234	$176–$6,812
Early Childhood Education (e.g., Perry Preschool)	−0.10	$8,936	−$4,754–$6,972
Seattle Social Development Project	−0.13	$4,355	−$456–$14,169
Functional Family Therapy	−0.25	$2,161	$14,149–$59,067
Nurse–Family Partnership	−0.29	$7,733	−$2,067–$15,918
Multisystemic Therapy	−0.31	$4,743	$31,661–$131,918

*Negative effect size means lower crime.
[†]Lower end of range includes taxpayer benefits only; upper end of range includes taxpayer and crime victim benefits.
Source: Aos et al., 2001.

benefit of a range of prevention programs in a 30-year follow-up. They estimated the impact that reduced recidivism would have, in terms of benefits resulting from reduced costs of incarceration, increased employment, and lower welfare costs. Programs specifically for juvenile offenders (e.g., Multisystemic Therapy, Functional Family Therapy) had the largest and most consistent economic returns. Programs targeting younger children and youth not already involved in the criminal justice system (e.g., early childhood education programs) had smaller but still positive benefits.

SUMMARY

This chapter provides an overview of the juvenile justice system, from its early history to the present day. Our approach toward children and adolescents has undergone many changes. Some of these changes have been positive, such as increased protection of individual rights, but some have been negative, particularly in terms of less focus on rehabilitation and more emphasis on punishment. Developmental theories were reviewed, suggesting that adolescents, particularly younger ones, are less capable of making decisions compared to adults. We also reviewed approaches to assessing youth, in terms of their capacity to waive arrest rights, competency to stand trial, and waiver to adult court. Finally, interventions with youth were reviewed, revealing that rehabilitation can be effective in reducing recidivism for high-risk youth.

SUGGESTED READINGS AND WEBSITES

Cauffman, E., & Steinberg, L. (2000). (Im)Maturity of judgment in adolescence: Why adolescents may be less culpable than adults. *Behavioral Sciences & the Law, 18*, 741–760.

Loeber, R., & Farrington, D. P. (Eds.). (2001). *Child delinquents: Development, intervention, and service needs.* Thousand Oaks, CA: Sage.

Moretti, M. M., Odgers, C. L., & Jackson, M. A. (Eds.). (2004). *Girls and aggression: Contributing factors and intervention principles.* New York: Kluwer Academic/Plenum.

National Criminal Justice Reference Service. http://www.ncjrs.gov/App/Topics/Topic.aspx?TopicID=122.

Office of Juvenile Justice and Delinquency Prevention. http://ojjdp.ncjrs.org/.

Scott, E. S., Reppucci, N. D., & Woolard, J. L. (1995). Evaluating adolescent decision-making in legal contexts. *Law and Human Behavior, 19*, 221–244.

KEY TERMS

- *Adolescent-limited offenders*
- *Co-morbidity*
- *Competency to stand trial*
- *Life-course-persistent offenders*
- *Meta-analysis*
- *Parens patriae*
- *Primary prevention*
- *Psychosocial maturity*
- *Risk assessment*
- *Secondary prevention*
- *Status offenses*
- *Tertiary prevention*
- *Transfer (waiver) to adult court*

References

Aos, S., Phipps, P., Barnoski, R., & Lieb, R. (2001). *The comparative costs and benefits of programs to reduce crime*. Olympia, WA: Washington State Institute for Public Policy.

Arnett, J. (1992). Reckless behavior in adolescence: A developmental perspective. *Developmental Review, 12*, 339–373.

Aronson, J. D. (2007). Brain imaging, culpability, and the juvenile death penalty. *Psychology, Public Policy, and Law, 13*, 115–142.

Augimeri, L. K., Koegl, C. J., Webster, C. D., & Levene, K. S. (2001). *Early assessment risk list for boys, EARL-20B* (Version 2). Toronto, ON: Earlscourt Child and Family Centre.

Bishop, D. M., Frazier, C. E., Lanza-Kaduce, L., & Winner, L. (1996). The transfer of juveniles to criminal court: Does it make a difference? *Crime & Delinquency, 42*, 171–191.

Borum, R. (1996). Improving the clinical practice of violence risk assessment: Technology, guidelines and training. *American Psychologist, 51*, 945–956.

Borum, R., Bartel, P., & Forth, A. E. (2002). *Structured Assessment of Violence Risk in Youth: Professional manual*. Lutz, FL: Psychological Assessment Resources.

Borum, R., & Grisso, T. (2007). Developmental considerations for forensic assessments in delinquency cases. In A. L. Goldstein (Ed.), *Forensic psychology: Emerging topics and expanding roles* (pp. 553–570). New York: Wiley.

Borum, R., & Verhaagen, D. (2006). *A practical guide to assessing and managing violence risk in juveniles*. New York: Guilford.

Cauffman, E., Feldman, S., Waterman, J., & Steiner, H. (1998). Posttraumatic stress disorder among female juvenile offenders. *Journal of the American Academy of Child and Adolescent Psychiatry, 37*, 1209–1216.

Cauffman, E., & Steinberg, L. (2000). (Im)Maturity of judgment in adolescence: Why adolescents may be less culpable than adults. *Behavioral Sciences & the Law, 18*, 741–760.

Chamberlin, P. (2003). *Treating chronic juvenile offenders: Advances made through the Oregon Multidimensional Treatment Foster Care model*. Washington, DC: American Psychological Association.

Corrado, R. R., Roesch, R., Hart, S. D., & Gierowski, J. K. (2002). *Multi-problem violent youth: A foundation for comparative research on needs, interventions, and outcomes*. NATO Science Series. Amsterdam: IOS.

Cunningham, A. (2002). *Lessons learned from a randomized study of multisystemic therapy in Canada*. London: Centre for Children and Families in the Justice System.

Davidson, W. S., Redner, R., Blakely, C., Mitchell, C., & Emshoff, J. (1987). Diversion of juvenile offenders: An experimental comparison. *Journal of Consulting and Clinical Psychology, 55*, 68–75.

Elliott, D., Huizinga, D., & Morse, B. (1986). Self-reported violent offending: A descriptive analysis of juvenile violent offenders and their offending careers. *Journal of Interpersonal Violence, 1*, 472–514.

Fox, S. J. (1996). The early history of the court. *The Juvenile Court, 6*, 29–39.

Giedd, J., Blumenthal, J., Jeffries, N., Castellanos, F., Liu, H., Ijdenbos, A., Paus, T., Evans, A., & Rapoport, J. (1999). Brain development during childhood and adolescence: A longitudinal MRI study. *Nature Neuroscience, 2*, 861–863.

Grisso, T. (2003). *Evaluating competencies: Forensic assessments and instruments*. New York: Kluwer Academic/Plenum.

Grisso, T. (2004). *Double jeopardy: Adolescent offenders with mental disorders*. Chicago: University of Chicago Press.

Grisso, T. (2005). *Evaluating juveniles' adjudicative competence: A guide for clinical practice*. Sarasota, FL: Professional Resource Press.

Grisso, T., & Barnum, R. (2003). *Massachusetts Youth Screening Instrument-2*. Sarasota, FL: Professional Resource Press.

Henggeler, S. W., Cunningham, P. B., Pickrel, S. G., Schoenwald, S. K., & Brondino, M. J. (1996). Multisystemic therapy: An effective alternative to incarcerating serious juvenile offenders. *Journal of Adolescence, 19*, 47–61.

In re Gault, 387 U.S. 1 (1967).

Juvenile Court Act, Illinois Laws, 131, 131-37 (1899).

Kent v. United States, 383 U.S. 541 (1966).

Leadbetter, B. J., Dhami, M. K., Hoglund, W. L., & Dickinson, E. M. (2004). Prediction and prevention of peer victimization in early elementary school: How does gender matter? In M. M. Moretti, C. L. Odgers, & M. A. Jackson

(Eds.), *Girls and aggression: Contributing factors and intervention princi-ples*. New York: Kluwer Academic/Plenum.

Levene, K. S., Augimeri, L. K., Pepler, D. J., Walsh, M. M., Koegl, C. J., & Webster, C. D. (2001). *Early Risk Assessment List for Girls-Version 1 Consultation Edition*. Toronto: Earlscourt Child and Family Centre.

Lexcen, F., & Redding, R. E. (2002). Mental health needs of juvenile offenders. *Juvenile Correctional Mental Health Report, 3*, 1–16.

Lipsey, M. (1995). What do we learn from 400 research studies on the effec-tiveness of treatment with juvenile delinquents? In J. McGuire (Ed.), *What works? Reducing reoffending* (pp. 63–78). New York: Wiley.

Loeber, R., & Farrington, D. P. (Eds.). (1998). *Serious and violent juvenile offend-ers: Risk factors and successful interventions*. Thousand Oaks, CA: Sage.

Loeber, R., & Farrington, D. P. (Eds.). (2001). *Child delinquents: Development, intervention, and service needs*. Thousand Oaks, CA: Sage.

Lotke, E., & Schiraldi, V. (1996). *An analysis of juvenile homicides: Where they occur and the effectiveness of court interventions*. Alexandria, VA: National Center of Institutions and Alternatives.

Males, M., & Macallair, D. (2000). *The color of justice: An analysis of juvenile adult court transfers in California*. San Francisco: The Center on Juvenile and Criminal Justice.

McCord, J., Widom, C. S., & Crowell, N. A. (2001). *Juvenile crime, juvenile jus-tice*. Washington, DC: National Academy Press.

McGaha, A., Otto, R. K., McClaren, M. D., & Petrila, J. (2001). Juveniles adju-dicated incompetent to proceed: A descriptive study of Florida's competence restoration program. *Journal of the American Academy of Psychiatry and the Law, 29*, 427–437.

Mears, D. (2001). Critical challenges in addressing the mental health needs of juvenile offenders. *Justice Policy Journal, 1*, 41–61.

Miranda v. Arizona, 384 U.S. 436 (1966).

Moffitt, T. E. (1993). Adolescence-limited and life-course-persistent antiso-cial behavior: A developmental taxonomy. *Psychological Review, 100*, 674–701.

Moffitt, T. E. (2003). Life-course-persistent and adolescent-limited antisocial behavior: A 10-year research review and research agenda. In B. B. Lahey, T. E. Moffitt, and A. Caspi (Eds.), *Causes of conduct disorder and juvenile delinquency* (pp. 49–75). New York: Guilford.

Moffitt, T. E., & Caspi, A. (2001). Childhood predictors differentiate life-course-persistent and adolescence-limited antisocial pathways, among males and females. *Development & Psychopathology, 13*, 355–375.

Moffitt, T. E., Caspi, A., Rutter, M., & Silva, P. A. (2001). *Sex differences in anti-social behavior: Conduct disorder, delinquency, and violence in the Dunedin Longitudinal Study*. Cambridge: Cambridge University Press.

Monahan, J., & Steadman, H. J. (1994). *Violence and mental disorder: Developments in risk assessment*. Chicago: University of Chicago Press.

Moretti, M. M., Odgers, C. L., & Jackson, M. A. (Eds.). (2004). *Girls and aggression: Contributing factors and intervention principles.* New York: Kluwer Academic/Plenum.

Odgers, C. L., Schmidt, M. G., & Reppucci, N. D. (2004). Reframing violence risk assessment for female juvenile offenders. In M. M. Moretti, C. L. Odgers, & M. A. Jackson (Eds.), *Girls and aggression: Contributing factors and intervention principles.* New York: Kluwer Academic/Plenum.

Olds, D. L., Henderson, C. R., Kitzman, H. J., Eckenrode, J. J., Cole, R. E., & Tatelbaum, R. C. (1999). Prenatal and infancy home visitation by nurses: Recent findings. *The Future of Children, 9,* 44–65.

Olweus, D. (2003). *Bullying at school.* Oxford: Blackwell.

Owen-Kostelnik, J., Reppucci, N. D., & Meyer, J. R. (2006). Testimony and interrogation of minors: Assumptions about maturity and morality. *American Psychologist, 61,* 286–304.

Redding, R. E., & Frost, L. (2001). Adjudicative competence in the modern juvenile court. *Virginia Journal of Social Policy and the Law, 9,* 353–410.

Roesch, R. (1995). Creating change in the legal system: Contributions from community psychology. *Law and Human Behavior, 19,* 325–343.

Roper v. Simmons, 543 U.S. 541 (2005).

Ryan, L., & Ziedenberg, J. (Eds.). (2007). *The consequences aren't minor: The impact of trying youth as adults and strategies for reform.* Washington, DC: Campaign for Youth Justice.

Salekin, R. T. (2002). Clinical evaluation of youth considered for transfer to adult criminal court: Refining practice and directions for science. *Journal of Forensic Psychology Practice, 2,* 55–72.

Salekin, R. T. (2004). *Risk-Sophistication-Treatment-Inventory.* Lutz, FL: Psychological Assessment Resources.

Scott, E. S., Reppucci, N. D., & Woolard, J. L. (1995). Evaluating adolescent decision-making in legal contexts. *Law and Human Behavior, 19,* 221–244.

Smith, C., & Thornberry, T. (1995). The relationship between childhood maltreatment and adolescent involvement in delinquency. *Criminology, 33,* 451–477.

Sterling, S., & Weisner, C. (2005). Chemical dependency and psychiatric services for adolescents in private managed care: Implications for outcomes. *Alcoholism: Clinical and Experimental Research, 25,* 801–809.

Streissguth, A. P., & Kanter J. (Eds.). (1997). *The challenge of fetal alcohol syndrome: overcoming secondary disabilities.* Seattle: University of Washington Press.

Synder, H. (2003). *Juvenile arrests.* Washington, DC: Office of Juvenile Justice and Delinquency Programs.

Teplin, L. A., Abram, K. M., McClelland, G., M., Dulcan, M. K., & Mericle, A. A. (2002). Psychiatric disorders in youth in juvenile detention. *Archives of General Psychiatry, 59,* 1133–1143.

Tremblay, R. E., Masse, L., Pagani, L., & Vitaro, F. (1996). From childhood physical aggression to adolescent maladjustment: The Montreal Prevention Experiment. In R. D. Peters & R. J. McMahon (Eds.), *Preventing childhood disorders, substance abuse, and delinquency.* Thousand Oaks: Sage.

U.S. Department of Health and Human Services. (2001). *Youth violence: A report of the Surgeon General.* Rockville, MD: U.S. Department of Health and Human Services.

Viljoen, J. L., Odgers, C. L., Grisso, T., & Tillbrook, C. E. (2007). Teaching adolescents and adults about legal proceedings: A comparison of pre- and post-teaching scores on the MacCAT-CA. *Law and Human Behavior, 31,* 419–432.

Viljoen, J. L., & Roesch, R. (2005). Competency to waive interrogation rights and adjudicative competence in adolescent defendants: Cognitive development, attorney contact, and psychological symptoms. *Law and Human Behavior, 29,* 723–742.

Viljoen, J. L., & Roesch, R. (2007). Assessing adolescents' adjudicative competence. In R. Jackson (Ed.), *Learning forensic assessment* (pp. 291–312). New York: Taylor & Francis.

Viljoen, J. L., Vincent, G. M., & Roesch, R. (2006). Assessing child and adolescent defendants' adjudicative competency: Interrater reliability and factor structure of the Fitness Interview Test. *Criminal Justice and Behavior, 33,* 467–487.

Yoshikawa, H. (1994). Prevention as cumulative protection: Effects of early family support and education on chronic delinquency and its risk. *Psychological Bulletin, 115,* 28–54.

Zapf, P. A., & Roesch, R. (2005). Competency to stand trial: A guide for evaluators. In I. B. Weiner & A. K. Hess (Eds.), *Handbook of forensic psychology* (3rd ed., pp. 305–331). New York: Wiley.

Zigler, E., & Styfco, S. J. (Eds.). (2004). *The Head Start debates.* Baltimore, MD: Brookes.

Chapter 9

POLICE PSYCHOLOGY

CHAPTER OBJECTIVES

In this chapter, you will become familiar with:
- The diverse nature of law enforcement agencies operating in the United States
- The practice of police psychology and how it has changed over time
- The four major domains of practice in police psychology
- Some of the specific proficiencies of police psychologists

Police psychology is the application of psychological theory and research to law enforcement or, more specifically, "the delivery of psychological services to and on behalf of law enforcement agencies, their executives, and employees" (Aumiller et al., 2007, p. 65). As we will see, the field of law enforcement is broad. It certainly includes the local agencies, typically city or county police and sheriff departments, with which we are most familiar. But it is much broader, and includes various public safety, corrections, and national security agencies at all levels of government. We begin this chapter with overviews of law enforcement and the history of police psychology in the United States. Next, we discuss in greater detail four core domains of police psychology: assessment, intervention, operational support, and organizational consulting. Specific topics in the field of correctional psychology, including the assessment and management of offenders, are covered in Chapter 9.

Modern societies give law enforcement agencies the responsibility to uphold their laws and protect their citizens, and give them special powers to do so. But how do we make sure that law enforcement agencies hire the best possible officers, give them the best possible education and training, and support them to do the best job possible? And what can law enforcement agencies do to minimize the chances that a tragedy such as the shooting of Jean-Charles de Menezes does not happen again? These are the kinds of questions that interest police psychologists.

CASE STUDY

London, England. It is July 22, 2005, two weeks after suicide bombings on the transit system killed 52 people, and just one day after another suicide bombing attempt failed. Officers of the London Metropolitan Police are watching the apartment building where a suspected terrorist is being kept under surveillance. Police believe the suspect was part of the network responsible for the bombings and may be planning more attacks. Jean-Charles de Menezes, a 27-year-old electrician from Brazil who has been in the country for three years, has the misfortune to live in the same building as the suspect. When de Menezes leaves his apartment that morning carrying a knapsack, he is mistakenly identified as the suspected terrorist. Officers become concerned when he boards a bus, and an armed response unit is placed on alert. They continue to follow de Menezes, even after they realize he is not the original surveillance target. The officers become concerned when de Menezes leaves the bus and, still carrying a knapsack, enters the Stockwell tube station. Fearful de Menezes may be somehow connected with the suspected terrorist and that his knapsack may contain a bomb, several officers follow him onto a waiting subway train. As de Menezes takes a seat, members of the armed response unit rush into the subway car with their weapons raised. When de Menezes stands up, officers of the armed response unit fear he may be trying to set off a bomb and shoot him seven times in the head and once in the shoulder; he dies immediately. In the aftermath of the shooting, the police apologized to de Menezes's family for his death and acknowledged they made mistakes, but also emphasized they were under tremendous pressure at the time to thwart more terrorist attacks. A jury subsequently found the London Metropolitan Police guilty of violating several health and safety laws.

Jean-Charles de Menezes

Source: http://en.wikipedia.org/wiki/File:Menezes.jpg.

POLICING IN THE UNITED STATES

Police or **law enforcement agencies** are bureaucracies created by governing bodies to maintain public order and safety by ensuring compliance with laws, rules, and regulations (Skolnick, 2001). The term *governing* *bodies* is somewhat vague, because it covers a wide range of organizations. Many are governmental organizations, such as elected federal, state, county, or city governments and their executives. Others are intergovernmental or even nongovernmental organizations. The powers of any given law enforcement agency are limited by the jurisdiction or powers of its governing body, as well as by jurisdictional laws and policies. Some of the limits are geographical in nature, due to the fact that a governing body has jurisdiction only within specified areas. Other limits are authoritative, due to the fact that the powers of a governing body are restricted to certain activities or domains.

A few concrete examples will help illustrate the diversity of law enforcement agencies. Most people in the United States live in an area under the jurisdiction of local or regional law enforcement agencies, such as a city police department or a county sheriff department. These agencies are often responsible for enforcing the criminal laws of a state, as well as the other quasicriminal or administrative laws passed by a state, county, or city government. But depending on where people live and what they have been doing (or are suspected of doing), they may also fall under the jurisdiction of other agencies. For example, someone who travels overseas or communicates with people in other countries for certain criminal purposes, such as trafficking drugs or distributing child pornography, may fall under the jurisdiction of international police—the International Criminal Police Organization, known as ICPO or Interpol. Someone who commits a crime or motor vehicle offense while on a major highway may be under the jurisdiction of state police. Someone who commits currency crimes, crosses state lines to commit a crime, or commits crimes using telecommunications or on an Indian reservation may be under the jurisdiction of federal police, such as the Federal Bureau of Investigation (FBI) or the U.S. Secret Service. Someone who violates laws on a military base or on the territorial waters of the United States may be under the jurisdiction of military police or the Coast Guard. Someone who has been charged with or convicted of a criminal offense may be under the jurisdiction of city, county, state, or federal agencies, such as the U.S. Marshals Service, the Federal Bureau of Prisons, a state probation or parole office, or a county sheriff. Even some universities, hospitals, and museums have their own law enforcement agencies (e.g., the Hospital Police Officers of the California Department of Mental Health, the Smithsonian Institution Office of Protection Services).

The early history of law enforcement in the United States can be traced back to colonial days, with the appointment of night watchmen in Boston and county sheriffs in Maryland as far back as the 1630s, as well as to the establishment of several federal law enforcement agencies—such as the

Postal Inspector, Customs Service, Revenue Cutter Service (now the Coast Guard), and Marshals Service—in the 1770s and 1780s. But modern U.S. law enforcement probably can be dated to the early 1800s, with the evolution of metropolitan police departments in large cities such as Boston and New York (White & Escobar, 2008). The original motivation for establishing these metropolitan police was to deal with social disorder, such as the ethnic and racial riots plaguing the United States; it was only in the 1900s that policing began to focus more on crime and law enforcement than on social disorder (Skolnick, 2001). Yet, social disorder continued to have an important influence on the nature of law enforcement throughout the century. For example, in the 1920s and 1930s, Prohibition caused many problems for law enforcement, including a subsequent rise in corruption among local governments and their police departments; and in the 1960s (and again in the 1990s), there was a resurgence in racial and ethnic tensions in many large cities.

An important development began, starting in the 1960s and 1970s and becoming mainstream by the 1980s and 1990s, when there was a move away from reactive, incident-oriented policing—in which law enforcement responded to reported or detected crimes—and a move toward community- and problem-oriented policing. These new approaches emphasized the need for law enforcement agencies to work more closely with members of the public, to mobilize and cooperate with other community agencies, and to help prevent crime whenever possible by taking steps to address its root causes (Moore, 1992; White & Escobar, 2008). Perhaps unsurprisingly, also starting in the 1960s and 1970s, the demographics of law enforcement started to undergo major changes, with increasing representation of women and ethnic and racial minorities among sworn officers (Sklansky, 2006; Skolnick, 2008).

The number and size of law enforcement agencies has increased dramatically over time, along with the number of laws governing the behavior of the citizens of the United States. It is impossible to determine exactly how many law enforcement agencies and law enforcement officers there are in the United States today. According to the Bureau of Justice Statistics, there were about 18,000 law enforcement agencies in the United States in 2004, employing more than 800,000 full-time law enforcement officers (see Table 9.1). These numbers are low-bound estimates, because they include only sworn officers—those authorized to make arrests and carry firearms— and exclude officers working for military law enforcement agencies.

Most police psychologists function in the role of nonsworn or civilian support staff, working in a variety of roles. (Only a handful of psychologists are sworn police officers.) There are also a number of psychologists who are not employed directly by law enforcement agencies, but instead operate as external consultants or contractors. These police psychologists have backgrounds in many different subfields of psychology and do many

Table 9.1   Number of Law Enforcement Agencies and Full-Time Officers in the United States in 2004

Type of Agency	Number of Agencies	Number of Officers
Federal	N/A	104,884
State and Local	17,876	731,903
State police	49	58,190
Local police	12,766	446,974
Sheriff	3,067	175,018
Other	1,994	51,721
Total	N/A	836,787

N/A = Not available. *Federal* includes nonmilitary federal officers authorized to carry firearms and make arrests. *Local police* includes consolidated police/sheriffs. *Other* includes constable, marshal, and special jurisdiction agencies.
Source: Bureau of Justice Statistics (http://www.ojp.usdoj.gov/bjs/lawenf.htm).

different kinds of work, but regardless of the particulars of their employment, the essence of their work is to improve the effectiveness, productivity, and well-being of law enforcement officers.

The History of Police Psychology

It is impossible to date precisely the birth of police psychology as a specialization within the broader field of forensic psychology. Although psychologists had consulted on law enforcement topics on an informal or occasional basis for decades, an eminent police psychologist and the first manager of Psychological Services for the Royal Canadian Mounted Police, Dr. Robert Loo, put its emergence as a formal specialization sometime in the late 1960s (Loo, 1986). For example, in 1966, the first full-time police psychologist in Germany was hired; in 1968, Martin Reiser (sometimes referred to the as "father of police psychology" in the United States) was hired by the Los Angeles Police Department as the first full-time police psychologist; and in 1971, the Society of Police and Criminal Psychology was established and began to hold annual meetings that included papers on topics related to police psychology (Allen, 2008; Bartol, 1996).

It is much easier to date the coming-of-age of police psychology: the mid-1980s. Several important events occurred around that time. For example, the section on Police and Public Safety in Division 18 (Psychology in Public Service) of the American Psychological Association was founded in 1983. Also, there was increasing recognition of the importance of police psychology within law enforcement agencies. The FBI hosted an influential National Symposium on Police Psychological Services in 1984 (Bartol, 1996), and the International Chiefs of Police formed a standing committee on Police Psychology in 1985 (Ostrov, 1986).

Another important event was the release of a special issue on "Psychology in Law Enforcement" published in the journal *Behavioral Sciences & the Law* in 1986. In the introduction, the editors of the special issue referred to police psychology as "one of the most exciting 'new areas' . . . in the field" (Cavanaugh & Rogers, 1986, p. 351). An article included in the special issue reviewed the history of police psychology in the United States (Ostrov, 1986). Ostrov lamented that as late as 1967, national reviews of law enforcement practice indicated that the only real involvement of psychology was with respect to screening of police applicants—and even that role was greatly restricted in scope—and there were probably only a half dozen or so law enforcement agencies that employed police psychologists on a full-time basis (Bartol, 1996). But the use of psychologists in screening applicants expanded greatly in the ensuing years, and psychologists also took on new roles. Ostrov was encouraged that by the 1980s, psychologists were being used in many other roles in law enforcement, including fitness for duty evaluations of and interventions for law enforcement officers, and support of police operations such as hostage negotiation, antiterrorism, undercover work, and criminal profiling (see also Bartol, 1996).

Police psychology is now fully established as a specialization. Aumiller and colleagues (2007) provided a thorough description of the work of police psychologists in their summary of the final report of the Joint Committee on Police Psychology Competencies established by the International Association of Chiefs of Police, the Police Psychological Services Section of the Society for Police & Criminal Psychology, and Police & Public Safety Section of Division 18 of the American Psychological Association. The Joint Committee identified more than 50 specific distinct proficiencies, or areas of practice, within police psychology, comprising four general domains of proficiency. The **assessment domain** comprises activities associated with the development, implementation, and evaluation of procedures for evaluating individuals, primarily law enforcement applicants, officers, and administrators. The assessment procedures include such things as self-report questionnaires, interviews, performance tests, and case history reviews; they are used to make decisions about such things as hiring, placement, and promotion. The **intervention domain** comprises activities associated with provision of clinical services to law enforcement personnel. These clinical services are designed to promote and improve the health and well-being of officers. The **operational domain** comprises activities associated with supporting and enhancing the work of law enforcement officers, including investigation and incident management. Finally, the **consulting domain** comprises activities associated with supporting and enhancing the administration of law enforcement agencies. Table 9.2 presents some examples of distinct proficiencies within each of these four domains.

Table 9.2   Core Domains and Specific Proficiencies of Police Psychology

| Core Domain | Specific Proficiencies | |
	Example	Description
Assessment Domain	Job analysis	Identification of the relevant knowledge, skills, and abilities (KSAOs) required for various positions within a law enforcement agency
	Pre-employment (pre- and postoffer) psychological evaluations of job candidates	Evaluation of applicants to ensure that they have the minimum KSAOs required in the positions for which they are applying
	Psychological fitness-for-duty evaluations of incumbents	Evaluation of officers already on the job to determine whether they are able to safely and effectively carry out essential job duties
Intervention Domain	Employee assistance counseling	Interventions provided by agencies to officers experiencing personal, psychological, or behavioral problems that may adversely affect their job performance
	Critical incident counseling	Interventions provided by agencies to offices impacted by traumatic events occurring at work
	Wellness programs	Interventions provided by agencies to prevent or reduce the negative impact of stress on health by promoting physical and mental well-being
Operational Domain	Criminal profiling	Identification of personality, behavioral, and demographic factors characteristic of the perpetrators of particular crimes or criminal patterns to assist investigation
	Threat assessment	Evaluation and management of people who may pose a risk of harm to the assets or mission of an agency
	Operations-related education and training	Development of officers' KSAOs to support and enhance their performance of essential job duties
Consulting Domain	Organizational development	Development, implementation, and evaluation of initiatives designed to improve organizational performance
	Executive consultation	Assistance provided to agency executives to support and enhance their job performance
	Development of performance appraisal systems	Design and implementation of policies, processes, and instruments for measurement and feedback of individual job performance

Source: Aumiller et al., 2007, Table 9.3.

THE PRACTICE OF POLICE PSYCHOLOGY: SOME EXAMPLES

We have space in this chapter to discuss only a few aspects of the practice of police psychology. We focus on job analysis and applicant screening from the assessment domain and, from the operational domain, operations-related education and training with respect to use of force. Chapters 5 and 6 present more information regarding other distinct proficiencies from the operational domain, such as operations-related education, training, and research with respect to eyewitness testimony, interviewing, and interrogation.

Job Analysis

What specific knowledge, skills, abilities, and other personal characteristics —sometimes referred to as **KSAOs** (Christal & Weissmuller, 1988)—are required to perform well as a law enforcement officer? The answer to this question is critically important to law enforcement agencies, so they can try to hire the best applicants as officers, make sure these applicants receive the best training possible, and place them in or promote them to the most suitable positions. But the answer depends in part on the agency for which officers will work, as well as the positions they will hold within that agency. For example, an officer responsible for enforcing vehicle safety and maintenance on highways must have a different set of KSAOs than another who is responsible for enforcing wildlife regulations, investigating suspicious fires, or border patrol. To make matters more complicated, the specific responsibilities of agencies and positions change over time. Every major law enforcement agency in the United States now requires officers who know how to investigate computer-related crimes, including distribution of child pornography, commercial fraud, and terrorism.

   Job analysis is the process of identifying the relevant knowledge, skills, and abilities required for various positions within a law enforcement agency (Christal & Weissmuller, 1988). Police psychologists help to identify, describe, and quantify the performance components of a position in terms of such things as nature, frequency, and criticality (Aumiller et al., 2007). This may be done in many different ways. One is to survey officers or their supervisors and ask them to identify important KSAOs. Another is to ask these same people to describe prototypical "successful" or "ideal" officers, and see which KSAOs characterize the prototypes. Also, experts can follow officers on the job to observe the actual tasks they engage in on a daily basis, and then analyze the KSAOs required for successful completion of those tasks.

   An excellent example of job analysis was the one conducted by Kaczmarek and Packer (1996). They set out to identify the critical KSAOs for "general duties" police officers in Australia. In the first phase of their research, they surveyed 913 general duties police officers and their supervisors, asking them to rate 87 specific job activities in terms of how important they perceived them, how frequently they performed them, and how difficult they were to learn. (The job activities had been identified through previous research with other general duties police officers.) Ratings of importance were correlated positively with ratings of frequency, $r = .37$, but negatively with ratings of difficulty, $r = -.15$. A set of 31 job activities were identified as being of core importance, regardless of the experience, rank, gender, or geographic location of the survey respondents (see Table 9.3). Respondents were also asked to identify the characteristics they considered necessary to perform what they believed were the five most important job activities. In the second phase, the researchers consulted a group of experts, comprising 17 police psychologists and 50 psychology graduate students, to identify the psychological characteristics required for successful completion of the core activities. In total, 42 psychological characteristics were identified by at least one-third of the sample (see Table 9.4). The characteristics identified by the experts were, in general terms, similar to those identified by police officers.

Although different law enforcement positions (e.g., administrator, supervisor, undercover officer, emergency response officer) obviously require different KSAOs, there may be a core set that applies to all law enforcement officers (Sanders, 2003) and is very similar to that identified by Kaczmarek and Packer (1996). In general, then, law enforcement requires cognitive characteristics such as reading, writing, and memory abilities that facilitate the understanding of and adherence to laws, policies, and regulations; physical characteristics such as health and fitness that facilitate performance of challenging tasks (e.g., rescue, shift work, self-defense, use of weapons); interpersonal characteristics such as good communication skills, sensitivity, and a sense of humor that facilitate positive interaction with fellow officers and with members of the public; psychological characteristics such as motivation, resilience, and flexibility that facilitate problem- and emotion-focused coping with job-related tasks and stresses; and moral characteristics such as honesty, sound judgment, integrity, and reliability that facilitate sound decisions, some of which involve matters of life and death (e.g., use of deadly force).

Applicant Screening

Identifying the core and specific KSAOs for law enforcement makes it much easier to develop sound procedures for identifying the job applicants who are best suited for a career in a given agency. **Applicant screening**,

Table 9.3   Importance, Frequency, and Difficulty Ratings for Core Job Activities Identified by General Duties Police Officers and Supervisors in Australia

Activities	Importance	Frequency	Difficulty
1. Use firearms	1	4	3
2. Maintain a safe working environment	1	1	3
3. Investigate incidents/offenses	2	1	3
4. Respond to reported crime, inquiries, or requests for assistance	2	1	3
5. Prioritize tasks	2	1	3
6. Adapt communication strategies to meet the needs of individuals	2	1	3
7. Utilize problem-solving techniques	2	1	3
8. Record information using notes, plans, photos, etc.	2	1	3
9. Establish good relationships with the community	2	1	3
10. Participate in teamwork or encourage team morale	2	1	3
11. Manage personal stress	2	1	3
12. Carry out tasks/allocated tasks	2	1	3
13. Respond to jobs via radio calls	2	1	4
14. Adhere to/apply the code of ethics/conduct	2	1	4
15. Provide customer service	2	1	4
16. Establish local knowledge of a specific patrol area	2	1	4
17. Use/maintain operational equipment	2	1	4
18. Utilize police databases	2	1	4
19. Keep up-to-date with current affairs	2	1	4
20. Undertake mobile patrols as a preventative measure	2	1	4
21. Use police communications equipment	2	1	4
22. Maintain communication with other members and sections	2	1	4
23. Maintain notebook/diary/mobile duty returns	2	1	4
24. Act in accordance with OH&S regulations and guidelines	2	1	4
25. Complete departmental forms/reports	2	1	4
26. Use safe driving procedures	2	1	4
27. Use keyboard skills	3	1	3
28. Provide information to the community	3	1	4
29. Prevent/detect traffic offenses	3	1	4
30. Adhere to guidelines relating to uniform	3	1	5
31. Deal with aggressive people	2	2	2

Source: Kaczmarek & Packer, 1996. Ratings were made on a 5-point scale (1 = *High*, 5 = *Low*).

Table 9.4   Psychological Characteristics Identified by Experts as Essential for Performing Core Activities of General Duties Police Officers

Manual dexterity	Finger dexterity	Speed and accuracy
Agreeableness	Mechanical ability	Clerical ability
Writing ability	Responsibility	Conformity
Motor skills	Spatial relations	Reading comprehension
Self-control	Cooperativeness	Flexibility
Sociability	Interpersonal relations skills	Listening comprehension
Communication skills	Judgment	Objectivity
Conscientiousness	Observation skills	Memory
Decision-making skills	Assertiveness	Empathy
Sensitivity	Integrity	Conflict-resolution skills
Tolerance	Deductive reasoning	Inductive reasoning
Abstract reasoning	Perception	Trustworthiness
Self-esteem	Moral judgment	Internal locus of control
Orderliness	Vocabulary	Spelling

Source: Kaczmarek & Packer, 1996.

also known as *police selection*, is the process of evaluating applicants— either before or after an initial offer of employment is made—to ensure that they have the minimum KSAOs required for their jobs. Police psychologists help to develop and evaluate applicant screening procedures, as well as conduct actual evaluations through the administration of various assessment procedures. Guidelines to assist applicant screening have been developed by the Police Psychological Services Section of the International Association of Chiefs of Police. The applicant screening procedures used by some agencies also are guided by statutory requirements or national accreditation standards.

In most circumstances, applicant screening conducted prior to an offer of employment is not conducted directly by police psychologists; rather, police psychologists assist in the development and evaluation of screening procedures, and may also supervise the administration and interpretation of assessment procedures. Screening at this stage focuses on general cognitive or intellectual abilities, basic or normal personality functions, and physical fitness. Psychological assessment procedures used at this stage may include intelligence tests to assess cognitive abilities and self-report questionnaires to assess personality functions. In addition to any psychological assessment procedures, applicants typically undergo background checks, medical exams, personal interviews, situational tests (a sort of structured role-play exercise), and physical ability tests. Once the pool of applicants has been narrowed and initial offers of employment have been made, a second screening process then focuses on assessment of mental health, substance use, and morals or values. This is the stage at which direct involvement of police psychologists is required. Psychological assessment procedures used at this stage may include clinical interviews to assess mental health. In addition, candidates may undergo further interviews and situational tests, drug testing, and even polygraph tests (Cochrane, Tett, & Vandecreek, 2003; Gallo, 2008).

Applicant screening sounds like a good idea, but does it work? Research on the effectiveness of applicant screening procedures has yielded three general findings:

1. Many individual assessment procedures predict some aspects of job success, although their predictive power is limited. For example, Weiss, Zehner, Davis, Rostow, and DeCoster-Martin (2005) examined the predictive validity of the Personality Assessment Inventory (PAI; Morey, 1996, 2007), a self-report test of personality and psychopathology, with respect to subsequent performance problems in a sample of 800 police officer candidates in the United States. The specific performance problems they examined were related to insubordination, citizen complaints, and neglect of duty. Looking at specific scales of the PAI that measures antisocial behavior, attitudes, and personality, they found small but statistically significant correlations with performance problems. Similar findings have been reported for other personality tests, as well as for interviews, cognitive ability and personality tests, and situational tests (Detrick, Chibnall, & Luebbert, 2004; De Meijer, Born, Terlouw, & Van der Molen, 2008; Pynes & Bernardin, 1992; Sellbom, Fischler, & Ben-Porath, 2007; Scogin, Schumacher, Gardner, & Chaplin, 1995).

2. Various assessment procedures have small to moderate correlations with each other, suggesting they may all tap aspects of job suitability but with only limited overlap or redundancy. This is illustrated by the findings of a recent study by Dayan, Fox, and Kasten (2008). They studied a cohort of 423 police officer candidates in Israel, all of whom had passed initial physical, medical, and background screening. The candidates then completed additional screening, including an interview, cognitive ability testing, and situational tests at an assessment center. Candidates were interviewed individually by a trained police officer. The interview was structured in nature, focusing on the candidate's current attitudes and behavioral history, and lasted about 30 minutes. The interviewer then made a number of discrete ratings of the candidate, as well as a summary rating of suitability, on a 7-point scale. The cognitive ability testing included three standardized intelligence tests, and scores on each test were averaged to create an overall ability score. At the assessment center, candidates were divided into groups of 13 to 15 and completed two days of activities, including individual and group tasks. Individual tasks included situational tests in which they role-played police officers completing various assignments, such as seizing property, searching and arresting suspects, and issuing traffic tickets. Group tasks included moving a log over a wall under strict conditions, developing a strategy

for recruiting new police officers, and designing security features for a new police station. Two assessors made independent ratings for each candidates in several specific areas, as well as a summary rating of suitability on a 7-point scale; as well, candidates were asked to nominate three peers in their group who had outstanding qualities. The interview, cognitive ability testing, and assessment center ratings were all reliable. The cognitive ability testing had small to moderate correlations with interview and assessment center ratings, $r = .18$ to .44, and the correlations between the cognitive ability testing and assessment center ratings were also moderate, $r = .34$ to .37. All three sets of ratings were significantly correlated with the final acceptance decisions made by a senior police psychologist, with each containing unique (i.e., nonredundant) information.

3. Well-constructed screening procedures—batteries that combine standardized assessment procedures, each of which taps different KSAOs—improve prediction of job performance. A good example is a recent study by Lough and Ryan (2006). They compared the job performance of two groups of police officer candidates. One group underwent a standard or low-intensity applicant screening after the initial offer of employment and the other underwent an intensive screening program, based on a model developed in the United States. The researchers used nine indicators to judge the subsequent occupational performance of both groups, including such things as the number of public and internal complaints; motor vehicle accidents; compensation claims for stress and other reasons; and days off work due to sickness, stress, and other reasons. At the end of the first year on the job, the group that underwent intensive screening performed better than the other group on eight of the nine indicators. At the end of the second year, the performance advantage of the intensively screened group was somewhat small, although their performance was still better on six of nine indicators. Aggregated across two years, there were statistically significant ($p < .05$) differences between the two groups on four indicators, with the intensively screened group having fewer motor vehicle accidents, sick days, nonstress compensation claims, and nonstress days off. The intensively screened group did not perform significantly worse than the other group on any of the nine indicators.

Despite the apparent success of intensive applicant screening procedures, there are still reasons to be cautious regarding their implementation. First, the predictive validity of assessment procedures is limited. To be fair, individual assessment procedures were not designed to be used in isolation, and each may be useful for screening in or out applicants with different kinds of strengths or weaknesses. But even intensive screening procedures typically have predictive validity that is moderate at best. This may be the result of weaknesses in the scientific research, such as problems measuring overall job performance in a reliable and valid manner, and difficulties controlling for organizational characteristics, which may have as much influence on job performance as do an officer's personal characteristics (Sanders, 2003).

Second, intensive screening procedures are difficult and expensive to implement. For example, assessment centers require careful planning and administration, trained staff, considerable space and equipment, and lots of time with applicants; it is difficult to estimate their cost–benefit ratio relative to more traditional assessment procedures, such as tests of cognitive ability and personality (Hale, 2005; McLaurin, 2005). Finally, it is important to consider issues of fairness and acceptability. For example, Carless (2006) found that screening procedures perceived as focusing too much on the past (e.g., background checks) or on general psychological characteristics (e.g., tests of cognitive ability and personality) were viewed by applicants as less fair or relevant than those perceived as focusing on the present (e.g., interviews) or actual performance in job-related situations (e.g., physical ability tests, situational tests, assessment centers).

Criminal Profiling

It can be difficult for law enforcement agencies to investigate complaints of criminal offenses and gather sufficient evidence to lay charges or support convictions; it is even more difficult when the identities of the perpetrators of those offenses are unknown. **Criminal profiling** is an investigative support method that attempts to identify the personality, behavioral, and demographic characteristics of unknown criminal perpetrators based on an analysis of offense-related behaviors either in the case at hand or in similar cases. The purpose of a criminal profile is to help identify, apprehend, or interview suspects.

It is probably more accurate to refer to criminal profiling as a set of methods or approaches, rather than as a specific method. Regardless of the specific method employed, the underlying general principle is the same: Inferences regarding what happened during an offense are used to draw inferences about the identity of the perpetrator. Some methods add an intermediate step, with behavior being used to draw inferences about the likely goals and motivations of the perpetrator, which in turn are used to make inferences about identity. Put simply, investigators work backward in time from the "What?" of a crime to understand the "Why?" and, ultimately, the "Who?" (Pinizzotto & Finkel, 1990).

Criminal profiling clearly involves a lot of inference, which really is just a technical term for educated guesswork. The inferential process is most likely to yield accurate, useful information when three conditions are met.

- First, the quantity and quality of offense-related information—physical evidence, witness reports, and so forth—must be sufficient to permit a reliable behavioral reconstruction. This means criminal profiling should only occur after an offense has been thoroughly investigated using standard operating procedures, and may be particularly useful in cases that involve a series of offenses rather than a single offense.

- Second, the offense-related behavior must be sufficiently unusual to permit a detailed and specific motivational reconstruction. This means criminal profiling is unlikely to be helpful in cases involving, say, ordinary property crimes, as the motivations underlying them are rather commonplace and straightforward. Instead, criminal profiling is most often used to investigate offenses such as homicide, kidnapping, hostage taking, sexual assault, arson, bombing, and some offenses that involve threats, stalking, or extortion—and, once again, especially when there is a series of such offenses. (It may also be used to investigate more commonplace offenses that involve unusual offense-related behavior.)

- Third, there must be enough known about "typical" perpetrators that the criminal profiler can link certain offense-related behaviors and motivations with specific personal characteristics. The knowledge of typical perpetrators may come from the personal experience of the criminal profiler, or it may come from scientific research on known groups of offenders or databases of past offenses.

The notion that offense-related behavior can be used to infer identity isn't a new one. It is likely that since the first law enforcement agencies were established, good investigators all relied on this notion at times. Attesting to this view are famous cases, such as the profile of the serial murderer, Jack the Ripper, by London police surgeon Dr. Thomas Bond in the 1890s, or the profile of George Metesky, the Mad Bomber of New York, by psychiatrist James Brussel in the 1950s (Petherick, 2005). What is new about criminal profiling, however, is the attempt to make the process a more rigorous one. This has been done in two major ways. First, criminal profilers made the process more systematic by specifying the way a profile should be constructed, according to their preferred approach. Systematization is crucial to enhancing the replicability or reliability of an approach. Second, criminal profilers have attempted to ground their approaches in scientific theory and research. Reliance on a sound evidence base is crucial to enhancing the accuracy or validity of an approach.

As noted previously, there are several different methods of or approaches to criminal profiling. These methods are often contrasted in terms of where they rely on deductive versus inductive analytic techniques (Alison, West, & Goodwill, 2004). **Deductive analytic techniques** are case-focused or idiographic in nature: They attempt to infer characteristics of a perpetrator from review of the evidence surrounding a particular offense or series of offenses, without explicit consideration of or reference to more general knowledge about other perpetrators or other offenses. The inferences are based on the reasoning, experience, insight, and intuition of the criminal profiler. The inferential process puts a heavy emphasis on the mediating role of motivations. It is assumed that a perpetrator's offense-related behavior reflects specific motivations, which in turn will be associated with specific personal characteristics of the perpetrator. An important strength of deductive analytic techniques is their focus on the uniqueness and dynamic nature of offense-related behavior and motivations, and so they are most likely to be useful when an offense or offense series includes rare or unusual behavior, or when a perpetrator's behavior or motivation appears to be changing over time. **Inductive analytic techniques**, in contrast, are comparative or statistical (also referred to as *nomothetic*) in nature: They infer a perpetrator's characteristics from knowledge of general patterns of criminal behavior, as reflected in scientific theory and research. The inferences are based on the apparent similarity of the offense-related behavior in the case at hand to the behavior of known groups of perpetrators. The inferences do not require any speculation concerning mediating factors such as motivations. An important strength of inductive analytic techniques is their focus on established patterns of criminal behavior, so they are most likely to be useful when an offense or offense series includes common or typical and stable behaviors. All approaches to criminal profiling recognize the importance of both deductive and inductive analytic techniques; the differences between the approaches lie in terms of which analytic techniques are used earliest or most often in the profiling process. Regardless of the type of analytic techniques used, police psychologists may play a role either as criminal profilers or, more commonly, members of a team of criminal profilers; they also may conduct research on offenders to assist inductive analytic approaches.

The first systematic approach to profiling was **Criminal Investigative Analysis**, which was developed by the FBI's Behavioral Science Unit in the 1970s and 1980s. Many people made important contributions to this approach, including FBI officers such as Patrick Mullany, Howard Teten, Robert Ressler, John Douglas, and Roy Hazelwood, as well as consulting mental health professionals such as Park Dietz. The hallmark of the FBI's approach is a strong reliance on offense motivational typologies to infer offender characteristics, based on the assumption that similar behavior with similar motivation reflects similar personal characteristics (Dietz, 1985; O'Toole, 1999). To assist this process, the FBI devoted considerable effort to the development of motivational typologies based on qualitative analyses of cases or case series, initially for sexual homicide (Burgess, Douglas, Hartman, McCormack, & Ressler, 1986) and later for a range of violent offenses (Douglas, Burgess, Burgess, & Ressler, 1992). As it is currently used, Criminal Investigative Analysis begins by using information about offenses—and, in particular, information about crime scenes—to classify the offense according to a motivational typology (O'Toole, 1999). This is followed by a full reconstruction of the circumstances surrounding the offense, including the perpetrator's personality, mood, and mental health; the role of fantasy and planning; victim selection; and interactions with the victim before, during, and after the offense, including the method and manner of any physical or sexual assault and any evidence of travel. Next, investigators look for evidence of "signatures," idiosyncratic aspects of offense-related behavior that may be specific to the offender. The final step is to generate a profile that speculates about the personal characteristics of the perpetrator, such as gender, race, family background, education and employment, intimate and general social relationships, medical and mental health problems, criminal history, and residence. Note that the process begins with a straightforward inductive analytic technique—namely, classification using a motivational typology—followed by extensive deductive analysis.

Critical of the FBI's heavy reliance on deductive analytic techniques, Canter developed the **Investigative Psychology** approach to criminal profiling in the 1990s. His goal was to make criminal profiling less of an art—the success of which depends directly on the talents of profilers—and more of a science. He started with the basic assumption that criminal behavior can be understood much like any other form of human behavior, all of which is essentially lawful or rule-governed. The Investigative Psychology approach has two hallmarks. The first is the incorporation of various psychological theories to guide the analysis of offense behavior and personal characteristics of offenders. The second is the central role of statistically derived offender typologies. Both of these features are inductive analytic techniques that use information about other offenders to make inferences about the perpetrators in the case at hand.

Behavioral Evidence Analysis (Turvey, 2008) is a strongly deductive approach, developed in reaction to the reliance on typologies, psychological theory, and statistical analysis that characterize Criminal Investigative Analysis and Investigative Psychology. In Behavioral Evidence Analysis, profilers make rational inferences about the personal characteristics of perpetrators based directly on the facts of the case at hand; there is no reference to "other offenders" as a means of justifying conclusions.

The final approach we discuss here is **geographic profiling**, which uses criminological theory, quantitative analysis of geospatial data, and typologies of offender mobility to determine the personal characteristics of perpetrators. A particular focus of geographic profiling is identifying the likely residence or travel routes of perpetrators. Rossmo (1995, 1998) apparently was the first to use principles derived from environmental criminology to develop a quantitative means of doing this. He and others have since developed specialized software to implement sophisticated mathematical models, called *criminal geographic targeting algorithms*, that use data about the location of criminal activity (in the form of addresses or coordinates) to yield information relevant to the search for suspects. The nature of the output varies, but it may be geo-profile (an ordinary two-dimensional street map that contains search instructions) or a jeopardy surface (a two-dimensional map that also includes a third dimension, reflecting probability density information about the suspect's location). This is obviously a highly inductive technique. But geographical profiling that uses mobility typologies to infer other personal characteristics such as age, gender, psychopathology, criminal history, and so forth may also incorporate deductive techniques (Beauregard, Proulx, & Rossmo, 2005).

Criminal profiling is a fascinating activity that has attracted the attention and interest of the general public. But there are several good reasons to be cautious about the usefulness of criminal profiling.

- First, it is used in very rare and specific circumstances. A suspect's identity usually is known to police; the problem they face is gathering the evidence that will support arrest, charge, or conviction of the suspect. (Consider the fact that the more than 80% of physical and sexual assaults in the United States are committed by close acquaintances, including family members or intimate partners.) Even when the suspect's identity is unknown, police have a wide range of investigative procedures they use before they turn to criminal profiling. In essence, criminal profiling is an investigative tool of last resort.

- A second reason to be cautious about criminal profiling is that it carries some risks. An inaccurate profile may mislead investigators, leading them down irrelevant avenues, ignoring or foreclosing potentially useful lines of inquiry. Profiling may also lead investigators to alter their strategies to focus on a particular suspect in ways that may be viewed as harassment or entrapment.

- Third, a range of methods are used by people with diverse backgrounds. It is difficult to ensure that criminal profilers are adequately trained and using accepted methods. The establishment of professional organizations (e.g., the International Association of Investigative Psychology) and credentialing processes (e.g., International Criminal Investigative Analysis Fellowship) are important in this regard.

- Fourth, and most important, the reliability (consistency) and validity (accuracy) of criminal profiling are not well established. Research in this area is hampered by the fact that many profiles contain claims that are vague, of little investigatory relevance, or difficult to either verify or falsify (e.g., Almond, Alison, & Porter, 2007; Dowden, Bennell, & Bloomfield, 2007). For example, some studies have attempted to evaluate the effectiveness of criminal profiling by comparing the judgments of experts to those of untrained professionals, including law enforcement officers, psychologists, university students, and even self-identified psychics; others have evaluated the accuracy of geographical profiles generated by sophisticated software to those generated by people given a few simple rules. Systematic reviews of the literature have reached dramatically different conclusions: Some argue there is no evidence that criminal profiling is anything but "smoke and mirrors" (Bennell, Taylor, & Snook, 2007; Snook, Cullen, Bennell, Taylor, & Gendreau, 2008; Snook, Eastwood, Gendreau, Goggin, & Cullen, 2007), whereas others argue there is at least limited support for its reliability and validity (Kocsis, Middledorp, & Karpin, 2008; Rossmo & Filer, 2005).

Operations-Related Education and Training: Use of Force

Operations-related education and training is intended to help improve the success of law enforcement agencies and officers in the specific jobs or missions they undertake. One focus of education and training is improving police decision making. Law enforcement officers have broad powers regarding such things as search or seizure of property; detention, arrest, or charge of people suspected of violating the law; and the use of force—up to and including deadly force—to enforce the law or protect the safety of citizens. Exercised properly, these powers are essential for successful performance of their duties; exercised improperly, they can result in the loss of citizen's faith in and respect for the justice system. Although the use of police powers is limited by law and guided by agency policy, individual officers must use their discretion to interpret the application of law and policy in specific situations. For this reason, decision making by law enforcement officers has been a focus of considerable research, education, and training in police psychology, examining topics such as how police make decisions about traffic stops, arrest in cases of suspected domestic violence, or handling of people suffering from mental illness.

One of the most important topics in police decision making concerns the use of force. This is obviously a high-stakes decision: Improper exercise of discretion can result in psychological trauma, physical injury, or death of innocent people. (See Box 9.1 for an example of controversy regarding police use of force.) But the context of these decisions is also unusual, as they often must be made under conditions of extreme stress. Imagine, for example, you are a uniformed member of a large metropolitan police force, armed with many of the weapons given to typical general duties officers. While on patrol one night, you receive a radio call reporting a domestic disturbance at a nearby residence. You and your partner respond and are first on scene. When you arrive, the front door of the residence is open and you can hear people screaming and shouting, including both adults and children, but you cannot see anyone. You assume they must be in the back of house, probably in the kitchen. You pound on the open door and announce your presence, but no one responds. A few seconds later, you hear the sounds of a scuffle and a woman screams, "Oh! He's killing me, he's killing me!" Your partner immediately gets on his radio to call for back-up. What do you do? Consider the following options; think about why you would or would not choose each one.

a. Wait with your partner for back-up to arrive before entering the residence.
b. Pound on the door and announce your presence again, but louder this time.
c. Enter the residence, with no weapon in hand.
d. Enter the residence, with your nightstick (flashlight, pepper spray, etc.) in hand.
e. Enter the residence, with your conducted electricity weapon (Taser) in hand.
f. Enter the residence, with your firearm (handgun or shotgun) in hand.

The difficult thing about this scenario is that no matter how you respond, someone—the woman who is being assaulted, the man who is assaulting her, their children, you, your partner—could end up dead. If you respond with insufficient force, you may be unable to protect the safety of the victim or bystanders; if you use too much, you may provoke an escalation of violence, and even end up using your weapon. Even if you respond in a way that seems entirely reasonable, someone could end up dead, prompting you (and a lot of other people) to second-guess your original decision.

There is a large body of theory and research on decision making in the fields of cognitive and social psychology that has been of great assistance to police psychologists. But much of this theory and research is not directly relevant to the use of force by police. More relevant is research directly on police, which has examined the impact of personal characteristics such as age, gender, education, job-related experience, and race on use of force (e.g., McElvain & Kposowa, 2008). Even better is research directly relevant to education and training. Police psychologists increasingly are relying on an

Box 9.1 A Controversy Concerning Police Use of Force

Robert Dziekanski, a 40-year-old Polish man, was traveling to Canada to visit his mother, a recent immigrant. He arrived at the Vancouver International Airport on October 14, 2007 at about four o'clock in the afternoon and cleared the immigration checks required for international visitors, but apparently had difficulty retrieving his luggage and did not clear Customs for more than eight hours. During this time, he became increasingly agitated, a situation that was exacerbated by his limited ability to communicate in English. When he cleared Customs, his behavior attracted the attention of border patrol officers: He walked aimlessly, talked loudly to himself, and picked up furniture and moved it around. He was sweating profusely and did not respond to attempts to communicate with him. Border patrol officers secured and cleared the area where Mr. Dziekanski was located, then summoned the Royal Canadian Mounted Police (RCMP), the federal police who have jurisdiction at the airport. Four RCMP officers attended the scene about 10 minutes later. The subsequent interaction was captured on video by a private citizen at the airport. The RCMP approached Mr. Dziekanski at a safe distance and attempted to calm him down by talking to him, but he was again unresponsive. His behavior was still agitated, and at one point picked up a computer monitor and threw it on the floor. The RCMP officers drew their conducted electricity weapons, also known as Tasers, and approached Mr. Dziekanski directly. About 25 seconds later, one of the officers discharged a weapon, and Mr. Dziekanski stumbled and fell to the floor, screaming and convulsing. A few seconds later, another loud crack was heard, apparently the result of a second Taser being fired. The officers then attempted to restrain Mr. Dziekanski, who was still screaming and convulsing on the floor, by kneeling on him and handcuffing him. In the videotape, one of the officers can be heard to say, "Hit him again, hit him again," and there may have been as many as two additional Taser discharges. Only 90 seconds after the first Taser shot was fired at Mr. Dziekanski, he fell silent and stopped moving. The RCMP immediately called for emergency assistance and administered first aid, but Mr. Dziekanski died of heart failure. This tragic incident caused public outrage in Canada and resulted in a number of investigations and reviews, including internal reviews by the RCMP of its own whether the officers involved complied with the agency's policies regarding use of force and the policy itself.

Robert Dziekanski lies on the floor of the Vancouver International Airport after being Tasered by Royal Canadian Mounted Police officers, as one officer looks on.
(Paul Pritchard)

approach originally developed in military psychology sometimes referred to as **operational psychology**, the goal of which is to use basic psychology to "generate empirical knowledge on individual and contextual factors influencing human behavior in dynamic settings that produce a hazard to life, health, or basic values" (Johnsen & Eid, 2006, S1; see also Staal & Stephenson, 2006).

From an operational psychology perspective, police decisions regarding use of force have some important characteristics. First, and most obvious, these decisions involve use of skills under very difficult conditions, including physical and social environments that are complex and dynamic; incomplete and uncertain information about those environments; and extreme emotional arousal, including fear. Second, the decisions always involve moral reasoning, which requires decision makers to understand, accept, and consider institutional values as they are reflected in law and policy. Third, use-of-force decisions often involve the need to work closely with one or more team members. So, these are the problems faced by law enforcement officers; how have police psychologists tried to improve education and training regarding use-of-force decisions?

A major contribution of police psychology has been to support the movement toward simulation-based training, in which law enforcement officers are given the opportunity to practice decision making and use of force under controlled circumstances that closely resemble situations they are likely to encounter in the course of their employment. Training in real-world context sounds ideal, but it has some important limitations (Bennell, Jones, & Corey, 2007). Perhaps the biggest is that trainees may encounter few relevant situations in the field, and so have limited opportunity to practice skills or observe others practice their skills. Real-world training also exposes trainees to potentially dangerous situations before they have acquired a good skill set for managing those situations. And training in highly controlled situations, like a classroom or a traditional firing range, may actually be counterproductive, as trainees may be forced to acquire skills that later they will need to unlearn in the real world. For example, learning how to fire a handgun accurately at a stationary bull's-eye target under ideal lighting while calm and wearing earplugs does not necessarily help, and may even hinder, accurate shooting while chasing a human target at night with a police cruiser's lights flashing and sirens blaring. In contrast, simulation-based training allows repeated exposure to challenging and changing situations, and gives instructors the ability to work with trainees to improve their performance.

A common method for training police officers in use of force is the use of computer-based simulators (Bennell, Jones, & Corey, 2007). A typical simulator involves projection of various job-relevant scenarios via high-quality, life-size video with accompanying audio. Trainees are required to engage in interactive role play during the scenarios, armed with various weapons that emit infrared light when deployed. The presentation of scenarios is controlled by computer, so the conditions or progress of the scenario can be changed by instructors or automatically changed in response to the trainee's deployment of weapons. This means a trainee's actions can result in immediate feedback during the simulation. The entire simulation may be taped so it can be reviewed with the trainee, or a report may be generated to gauge performance (e.g., number of times or accuracy with which a weapon was used). Instructors can present trainees with the same scenarios, modify the outcome of the scenario, or change the scenario altogether.

Bennell, Jones, and Corey (2007) discussed how **cognitive load theory** can be used to understand and improve use-of-force training for police. Three concepts are crucial in cognitive load theory. **Intrinsic cognitive load** reflects the inherent complexity of the information trainees are learning. **Extraneous cognitive load**, on the other hand, is due to the unnecessary demands placed on the mental information processing resources of trainees due to the learning materials and instructional methods used by instructors. Finally, **germane cognitive load** reflects the direct efforts of instructors to help trainees develop relevant schemas, cognitive structures or "mental maps" they can use to organize the new information they acquire into meaningful concepts.

According to theory, there is little instructors can do to reduce intrinsic cognitive load; to put it simply, the relevant task "is what it is." Instead, instructors should try to use training techniques that reduce extraneous cognitive load but increase germane cognitive load. To decrease extraneous cognitive load, instructors can present problems to trainees in different formats, such as partially completed or completed examples. (Partially completed examples present a problem with only a few steps missing or unsolved; completed examples provide a problem with the full solution.) These formats allow trainees to observe correct problem-solving techniques from the outset, instead of wasting their information-processing resources learning how to make mistakes before they learn correct performance. Alternatively, instructors can make sure that learning methods allow trainees to focus their attention and minimize redundancy. To increase germane cognitive load, instructors can use a diverse set of examples or exercises that helps trainees generalize their learning across situations, or have them talk aloud while engaging in tasks so they can concretize and process the information they are acquiring.

An excellent example of the application of operational psychology principles to police psychology is a study conducted by Saus et al.

(2006). They discussed the concept of **situational awareness**, a cognitive process that involves understanding the immediate physical environment. Situational awareness requires that a person perceives the environment accurately, uses those perceptions to develop an appreciation of what is happening right now, and can use that appreciation to make projections about what might happen in the immediate future. Just as the ability to visualize the field of play helps professional athletes to improve their performance in team sports, the ability to visualize the environment during a critical incident—the features of the surrounding terrain, where people are, what they are doing, what might be coming next—is crucial to good decision making in use-of-force scenarios. Improving situational awareness is one potential way to improve use-of-force decisions; it can be viewed as a way to increase germane cognitive load, according to cognitive load theory. One technique that is used to improve situational awareness is the *freeze technique*, which involves stopping a simulated training exercise at various points in time and posing questions to trainees that will help them to develop microskills related to perception, appreciation, and projection.

Saus and colleagues (2006) evaluated the effectiveness of standard firearms training that involved the use of the freeze technique. In Norway, they studied 40 police recruits—20 males and 20 females. They were randomly assigned to the standard or experimental training conditions. The standard condition involved classroom instruction in the use of firearms, practice on a target range under increasing levels of difficulty, and discussion of the upcoming computerized simulation test. The experimental training condition received scenario-based instruction, which involved sessions in the computerized simulator using the freeze technique and discussion of situational awareness. The length of training was the same for both groups. After completion of training, all subjects completed the same scenario test in the computerized simulator, one that required them to use their firearms for successful outcome. To evaluate success, the researchers stopped the simulator at specific points and asked questions to determine each subject's level of situational awareness, recorded the total shots taken and number of hits, and recorded heart rate during the exercise. Recruits in the experimental training condition had significantly higher levels of situational awareness according to both self-report and ratings made by instructors; they also fired significantly more shots, as well as significantly more accurate shots. Finally, recruits in the experimental training condition demonstrated less heart rate variability, which the authors interpreted as indicating the expenditure of less cognitive effort during the simulation exercise.

SUMMARY

Although some of the basic job requirements for law enforcement officers have remained unchanged for more than a hundred years, policing increasingly requires a set of knowledge, skills, abilities, and other personal characteristics that is both more diverse and more specialized. Psychologists have helped law enforcement agencies cope with the challenges of modern policing in a variety of ways. Some of the work done by police psychologists involves more traditional activities, such as assessment, counseling, and evaluation; but some of the work is novel, involving the application of general psychological theory and research to the specific problems faced by officers in the field.

SUGGESTED READINGS

Kaczmarek, A., & Packer, J. (1996). *Defining the role of the general duties constable: A job analysis* (Report Series No. 124.1). Payneham, Austalia: National Police Research Unit. (Available through the website of the Australian Centre for Policing Research, http://www.acpr.gov.au.)

Kocsis, R. N. (Ed.). (2008). *Criminal profiling: International theory, research, and practice.* Totowa, NJ: Humana Press.

KEY TERMS

- *Applicant screening*
- *Assessment domain*
- *Behavioral Evidence Analysis*
- *Cognitive load theory*
- *Consulting domain*
- *Criminal Investigative Analysis*
- *Criminal profiling*
- *Deductive analytic techniques*
- *Extraneous cognitive load*
- *Geographic profiling*
- *Germane cognitive load*
- *Inductive analytic techniques*
- *Intervention domain*
- *Intrinsic cognitive load*
- *Investigative Psychology*

- *Job analysis*
- *KSAOs*
- *Law enforcement agencies*
- *Operational domain*
- *Operational psychology*
- *Operations-related education and training*
- *Police*
- *Police psychology*
- *Situational awareness*

References

Alison, L., West, A., & Goodwill, A. (2004). The academic and the practitioner: Pragmatists' views of offender profiling. *Psychology, Public Policy, and Law, 10*, 71–101.

Allen, S. W. (2008). Police psychologists. In B. L. Cutler (Ed.), *Encyclopedia of psychology and law* (pp. 575–580). Thousand Oaks, CA: Sage.

Almond, L., Alison, L., & Porter, L. (2007). An evaluation and comparison of claims made in behavioural investigative advice reports compiled by the National Policing Improvements Agency in the United Kingdom. *Journal of Investigative Psychology and Offender Profiling, 4*, 71–83.

Aumiller, G. S., Corey, D., Allen, S., Brewster, J., Cuttler, M., Gupton, H., & Honig, A. (2007). Defining the field of police psychology: Core domains & proficiencies. *Journal of Police and Criminal Psychology, 22*, 65–76.

Bartol, C. R. (1996). Police psychology: Then, now, and beyond. *Criminal Justice and Behavior, 23*, 70–89.

Beauregard, E., Proulx, J., & Rossmo, D. K. (2005). Spatial patterns of sex offenders: Theoretical, empirical, and practical issues. *Aggression and Violent Behavior, 10*, 579–603.

Bennell, C., Jones, N. J., & Corey, S. (2007). Does use-of-force simulation training in Canadian police agencies incorporate principles of effective training? *Psychology, Public Policy, and Law, 13*, 35–58.

Bennell, C., Taylor, P. J., & Snook, B. (2007). Clinical versus actuarial geographic profiling strategies: A review of the research. *Police Practice and Research, 8*, 335–345.

Burgess, A., Douglas, J., Hartman, C., McCormack, A., & Ressler, R. K. (1986). Sexual homicide: A motivational model. *Journal of Interpersonal Violence, 1*, 251–272.

Carless, S. A. (2006). Applicant reactions to multiple selection procedures for the police force. *Applied Psychology, 55*, 145–167.

Cavanaugh, J. L., & Rogers, R. R. (1986). Psychology in law enforcement. *Criminal Justice and Behavior, 4*, 351–352.

Christal, R. E., & Weissmuller, J. J. (1988). Job-task inventory analysis. In S. Gael (Ed.), *The job analysis handbook for business, industry, and government, Vol. 2* (pp. 1036–1050). New York: Wiley.

Cochrane, R. E., Tett, R. P., & Vandecreek, L. (2003). Psychological testing and the selection of police officers: A national survey. *Criminal Justice and Behavior, 30*, 511–537.

Dayan, K., Fox, S. J., & Kasten R. (2008). The preliminary employment interview as a predictor of assessment center outcomes. *International Journal of Selection and Assessment, 16*, 102–111.

De Meijer, L., Born, M., Terlouw, G., & Van der Molen, H. T. (2008). Criterion-related validity of Dutch police-selection measures and differences between ethnic groups. *International Journal of Selection and Assessment, 16*, 321–332.

Detrick, P., Chibnall, J. T., & Luebbert, M. C. (2004). The Revised NEO Personality Inventory as predictor of police academy performance. *Criminal Justice and Behavior, 31*, 676–694.

Dietz, P. E. (1985). Sex offender profiling by the FBI: A preliminary conceptual model. In M. H. Ben-Aron, S. J. Hucker, & C. D. Webster (Eds.), *Clinical criminology: The assessment and treatment of criminal behavior* (pp. 207–219). Toronto: Clarke Institute of Psychiatry and M & M Graphics.

Douglas, J. E., Burgess, A. W., Burgess, A. G., & Ressler, R. K. (1992). *Crime classification manual: A standard system for investigating and classifying violent crime.* New York: Simon and Schuster.

Dowden, C., Bennell, C., & Bloomfield, S. (2007). Advances in offender profiling: A systematic review of the profiling literature published over the past three decades. *Journal of Police and Criminal Psychology, 22*, 44–56.

Gallo, F. J. (2008). Police psychology. In B. Cutler (Ed.), *Encyclopedia of psychology and law* (pp. 580–584). Thousand Oaks, CA: Sage.

Hale, C. (2005). Pros and cons of assessment centers. *Law and Order, 53*(4), 18, 20–21.

Johnsen, B. H., & Eid, J. (2006). Operational psychology: Training and development issues. *Military Psychology, 18*, S1–S2.

Kaczmarek, A., & Packer, J. (1996). *Defining the role of the general duties constable: A job analysis* (Report Series No. 124.1). Payneham, Australia: National Police Research Unit.

Kocsis, R. N., Middledorp, J., & Karpin, A. (2008). Taking stock of accuracy in criminal profiling: The theoretical quandary for investigative psychology. *Journal of Forensic Psychology Practice, 8*, 244–261.

Loo, R. (1986). Police psychology: The emergence of a new field. *Police Chief, 53*(2), 26–30.

Lough, J., & Ryan, M. (2006). Psychological profiling of Australian police officers: A longitudinal examination of post-selection performance. *International Journal of Police Science and Management, 8*, 143–152.

McElvain, J. P., & Kposowa, A. J. (2008). Police officer characteristics and the likelihood of using deadly force. *Criminal Justice and Behavior, 35*, 505–521.

McLaurin, M. (2005). How to run an assessment center. *Police: The Law Enforcement Magazine, 29*(3), 18, 20, 22, 24–26.

Moore, M. H. (1992). Problem solving and community policing. In M. Tonry & N. Morris (Eds.), *Modern policing* (pp. 99–158). Chicago: University of Chicago Press.

Morey, L. C. (1996). *An interpretive guide to the Personality Assessment Inventory (PAI)*. Odessa, FL: Psychological Assessment Resources.

Morey, L. (2007). *The Personality Assessment Inventory professional manual* (2nd ed.). Odessa, FL: Psychological Assessment Resources.

Ostrov, E. (1986). Police/law enforcement and psychology. *Criminal Justice and Behavior, 4*, 353–370.

O'Toole, M. E. (1999). Criminal profiling: The FBI uses criminal investigative analysis to solve crimes. *Corrections Today, 61*(11), 44–46.

Petherick, W. (Ed.). (2005). *Serial crime: Theoretical and practical issues in behavioral profiling*. Burlington, MA: Academic Press.

Pinizzotto, A. J., & Finkel, N. J. (1990). Criminal personality profiling: An outcome and process study. *Law and Human Behavior, 14*, 215–233.

Pynes, J. E., & Bernardin, H. J. (1992). Entry-level police selection: The assessment center is an alternative. *Journal of Criminal Justice, 20*, 41–52.

Rossmo, D. K. (1995). Place, space, and police investigations: Hunting serial violent criminals. In J. E. Eck & D. Weisburd (Eds.), *Crime and place* (pp. 217–235). Onsey, NY: Criminal Justice Press.

Rossmo, D. K. (1998). Target patterns of serial murderers: A methodological model. In R. M. Holmes & S. T. Holmes (Eds.), *Contemporary perspectives on serial murder* (pp. 199–217). Thousand Oaks, CA: Sage.

Rossmo, D. K., & Filer, S. (2005). Analysis versus guesswork: The case for professional geographic profiling. *Blue Line, 17*(7), 24–25.

Sanders, B. A. (2003). Maybe there's no such thing as a "good cop": Organizational challenges in selecting quality officers. *Policing: An International Journal of Police Strategies and Management, 26*, 313–328.

Saus, E. R., Johnsen, B. H., Eid, J., Riisem, P. K., Andersen, R., & Thayer, J. F. (2006). The effect of brief Situational Awareness Training in a police shooting simulator: An experimental study. *Military Psychology, 18*, S3–S21.

Scogin, F., Schumacher, J., Gardner, J., & Chaplin, W. (1995). Predictive validity of psychological testing in law enforcement settings. *Professional Psychology: Research and Practice, 26*, 68–71.

Sellbom, M., Fischler, G. L., & Ben-Porath, Y. S. (2007). Identifying MMPI-2 Predictors of police officer integrity and misconduct. *Criminal Justice and Behavior, 34*, 985–1004.

Sklansky, D. A. (2006). Not your father's police department: Making sense of the new demographics of law enforcement. *Journal of Criminal Law and Criminology, 96*, 1209–1243.

Skolnick, J. H. (2001). Policing. In N. J. Smelser & P. B. Baltes (Eds.), *International encyclopedia of the social & behavioral sciences* (pp. 11535–11541). New York: Elsevier.

Skolnick, J. H. (2008). Enduring issues of police culture and demographics. *Policing and Society, 18*, 35–45.

Snook, R., Cullen, R. M., Bennell, C., Taylor, P. J., & Gendreau, P. (2008). The criminal profiling illusion: What's behind the smoke and mirrors? *Criminal Justice and Behavior, 35*, 1257–1276.

Snook, B., Eastwood, J., Gendreau, P., Goggin, C., & Cullen, R. M. (2007). Taking stock of criminal profiling: A narrative review and meta-analysis. *Criminal Justice and Behavior, 34*, 437–453.

Staal, M. A., & Stephenson, J. A. (2006). Operational psychology: An emerging subdiscipline. *Military Psychology, 18*, 269–282.

Turvey, B. (2008). *Criminal profiling: An introduction to Behavioral Evidence Analysis* (3rd ed.). San Diego: Elsevier.

Weiss, W. U., Zehner, S. N., Davis, R. D., Rostow, C., & DeCoster-Martin, E. (2005). Problematic police performance and the Personality Assessment Inventory. *Journal of Police and Criminal Psychology, 20*, 16–21.

White, M. D., & Escobar, G. (2008). Making good cops in the twenty-first century: Emerging issues for the effective recruitment, selection and training of police in the United States and abroad. *International Review of Law, Computers & Technology, 22*, 119–134.

Chapter 10

CORRECTIONAL PSYCHOLOGY

CHAPTER OBJECTIVES

In this chapter, you will become familiar with:

- The structure of the correctional system in the United States
- The practice of correctional psychology and how it has changed over time
- The importance of risk assessment and risk management in correctional psychology
- The major approaches to risk assessment and risk management, as well as some specific examples of risk assessment instruments and correctional treatment programs

Correctional psychology is the application of psychological theory and research to the correctional system (Clements et al., 2007; Magaletta, Patry, Dietz, & Ax, 2007). We begin this chapter with overviews of the structure of the correctional system and the history of correctional psychology in the United States. Next, we discuss in greater detail two of the most important topics in correctional psychology: offender assessment and management. The selection, training, and support of correctional staff are covered in Chapter 9.

CASE STUDY

Suppose you are a judge trying to determine the proper sentence for the following case: white male, divorced, about 36 years old. Will plead no contest to drug-related offenses after being found intoxicated in violation of the conditions of probation. History of polysubstance abuse, including cocaine and heroin, since the age of about 8 years old. A penchant for self-destructive behavior—in the offender's own words, "It's like I have a loaded gun in my mouth and my finger's on the trigger, and I like the taste of the gunmetal."[1] Substance abuse has caused serious family and employment problems, including divorce and inability to get steady work. Numerous arrests for drug-related offenses including driving, carrying a handgun, and housebreaking while intoxicated. Multiple incarcerations, with sentences ranging up to three years. Repeated failure on community supervision, including probation and parole violations, some stemming from refusal to provide or failure of court-ordered drug tests. Repeated attempts at substance use treatment, including community-based programs and more than a year spent in a correctional treatment facility, invariably followed by relapse.

As a judge, what kind of a sentence are you leaning toward? You could sentence the offender to lengthy probation and yet more treatment in an attempt to rehabilitate him and help him become a productive member of society, although this has been tried repeatedly and over many years without apparent success. Alternatively, you could sentence the offender to a lengthy prison term in an attempt to deter him ("scare him straight"); at least this would protect the general public from his reckless and irresponsible behavior.

This was the situation faced by a California judge in 2001, hearing charges against the actor, Robert Downey, Jr. The judge, influenced in part by state law regarding sentencing of nonviolent drug offenders and recognizing Downey's long struggle to get control over his addictions, came down in favor of rehabilitation.

Mug Shot of Robert Downey Jr., as Photographed by the California Department of Correction in April 2001
Retrieved May 1, 2008 from http://news.bbc.co.uk/2/hi/americas/413283.stm.
Source: The Smoking Gun Date: April, 2001 Author: Uncredited.

---

[1]From "Addicted Downey Jnr jailed." *BBC News,* 8/6/1999.

The story of Robert Downey, Jr., reminds us that many offenders in the criminal justice system have serious problems and the corrections system provides an opportunity to make positive changes. The challenge is to identify which offenders are in need of help, what kind of help they need, and whether this help can be delivered in a way that also protects public safety.

So far, Robert Downey, Jr., has made the best of the opportunity given him by the sentencing judge. Downey achieved full sobriety in 2003 and has maintained it since then with the assistance of 12-step programs, meditation, and yoga. He established a positive relationship with his son. He met a woman and established a stable intimate relationship, marrying her in 2005. His career blossomed: Although he always received critical acclaim for his acting, he has been working more steadily and on important productions. For example, he received a Golden Globe award and an Academy Award nomination for his supporting role in the 2008 film, *Tropic Thunder*.

CORRECTIONAL PSYCHOLOGY IN THE UNITED STATES

Part of the larger criminal justice system, the **corrections system** is responsible for supervising people who have been arrested for, charged with, or convicted of criminal offenses. When most laypeople think of the corrections system, they think about prisons. But depriving people of their liberty by institutionalizing them is considered a major infringement of civil rights, and it is permitted only in limited circumstances. Only a small percentage of people in the criminal justice system, perhaps 20% or so, are institutionalized; the rest are supervised in the community.

Several types of institutions are used in the criminal justice system. *Jails* are most often used for pretrial detention (i.e., to hold people who have been arrested until they must go to court) and to house people convicted of relatively short sentences (typically, up to 6 or 12 months). Most jails are closed, maximum security facilities—movement in or out of the facility is very restricted, and the perimeter is demarked with high walls or fences and razor wire. The population of jail detainees includes people whose lives are in a state of major disruption or confusion: some are acutely distressed about being separated from their loved ones or losing their jobs due to arrest; others are intoxicated or in withdrawal, or suffering symptoms of mental disorder; yet others are fearful of the possibility that they may be sentenced to many years in prison. But because the typical stay in jail is quite short in duration—a few weeks or a few months, on average—the opportunities to offer programs or services are limited.

Prisons and **penitentiaries** are used to house people who receive custodial sentences. The length of the sentences may range from weeks or months to many years, or even life, reflecting the diversity of offenders and crimes for which they have been convicted. To deal with this diversity, there are typically several types of prisons in a jurisdiction's correctional system. Some institutions are very low security, perhaps including open or unsecured institutions such as work camps. These low-security institutions permit the semblance of a normal life for offenders and facilitate rehabilitation and readjustment to the community. Medium- and high-security institutions, in contrast, focus on keeping offenders separated from the community, but also may offer a variety of treatment and rehabilitation programs.

Most offenders—perhaps 80% or more—are supervised in the community. There are three major forms of community supervision: bail, probation, and parole. **Bail** is also known as *pretrial release.* It is used for people who have been arrested for or charged with criminal offenses and released into the community to await trial, and for people who have been convicted but are awaiting sentencing. The term of bail is often open-ended, and may last for many months. People may be granted bail based solely on their promise to attend court as directed, or they may be asked to guarantee attendance at court by putting up a bond or surety. In either case, people may have conditions placed on them that will (temporarily) restrict their rights and freedoms. The most common conditions include such things as reporting to a police, bail, or probation officer on a regular basis; not leaving the jurisdiction without permission; and not having contact with people who are alleged victims or witnesses to the offenses for which the person has been arrested. Violation of the conditions of bail is a criminal offense that may result in immediate pretrial detention and new charges.

Probation (and the related concept of *conditional sentence*) is a punishment following conviction for a criminal offense, typically considered more serious than community service or fines but less serious than imprisonment. People also may be sentenced to probation, either instead of a term of imprisonment or following (consecutive to) a term of imprisonment. The term of probation generally is fixed, lasting from six months to several years. Probation may include conditions similar to those used for people on bail, but often the conditions are more strict and may include such things as not using alcohol or other intoxicating substances or not associating with people who are known criminal offenders. Violation of the conditions of probation is a criminal offense that may result in imprisonment (i.e., serving the rest of the term of probation in custody) or new charges.

Parole is a conditional release from imprisonment intended to facilitate an offender's return and readjustment to the community. It is typically granted when the offender has served a substantial portion of a term of imprisonment with good behavior and is released from custody early as a reward. The term of parole varies greatly, from weeks to many years, depending on the length of the original sentence given to the offender. Parole is very similar to probation in terms of the conditions imposed on people. Suspected violation of the conditions of parole may result in a temporary return to custody, and if proved they may result in the offender serving the rest of the original sentence in custody.

The History of Correctional Psychology

Although health care and social service professionals have worked in the correctional system for more than a hundred years, the birth of correctional psychology probably can be dated to around World War II (Bartol & Freeman, 2005; Brodsky, 2007; Daly, 2000; Megargee, 2003). Raymond Corsini (1945), working as a correctional psychologist at that time, estimated that there were about 200,000 adults imprisoned in the United States (which then had a population of about 149 million) and about 100 psychologists delivering services to them. Many of these psychologists came together in 1953 to found the organization now known as the American Association for Correctional and Forensic Psychology (AACFP). According to the organization's first official publication, the *Journal of Correctional Psychology*, it had 92 members in 1956.

The decade of the 1970s was a time of special growth in correctional psychology (Bartol & Freeman, 2005; Brodsky, 2007). Membership in what is now the AACFP expanded to over 300 people. Its official journal was revamped and renamed *Criminal Justice and Behavior*. The organization developed the *Standards for Psychology Services in Adult Jails and Prisons*, which were published in the journal (Levinson, 1980). A new generation of "practitioner-scholars"—correctional psychologists who delivered services in prison but also conducted research—emerged from within its ranks.

The AACFP now has more than 400 members. But it is not the only professional organization that serves correctional psychologists. Many correctional psychologists belong to organizations such as the American Psychological Association's Division 18 (Psychologists in Public Service) and Division 41 (the American Psychology-Law Society), in addition to or instead of the AACFP. *Criminal Justice and Behavior* is regarded internationally as one of the most important and prestigious journals in the field of forensic psychology.

Several factors may be responsible for the growth of correctional psychology (Bartol & Freeman, 2005; Brodsky, 2007). One is a tremendous increase in the prison population in the United States. Recall the statistics Corsini cited in his 1945 article, summarized above, and then compare them to contemporary statistics from the Bureau of Justice Statistics: Right now, more than 2.25 million people are in penitentiaries, prisons, or jails, and another 5 million are on probation or parole on any given day. Put another way, almost 1% of the entire population of the United States is incarcerated in a correctional facility and almost 2% is under community supervision. And these numbers have grown steadily, at the rate of about 2% and 3% per year, over the past decade.

Another factor is that the correctional system has paid more attention to offender rehabilitation over the past 50 years. There has always been a tension in the philosophy underlying the correctional system between the ethics of *control* versus *care*. The **ethic of control** serves the goals of protection of public safety, retribution, and individual and general deterrence. It emphasizes the need to ensure that offenders are detained or supervised in a safe and just manner. In contrast, the **ethic of care** serves rehabilitative goals. It emphasizes the need to provide offenders with the services needed to help them become law-abiding and productive members of society. Correctional psychology has tried to balance these ethics by developing effective offender assessment and treatment services. The services offered usually address common and most important risk factors for crime, such as impulsivity, antisocial attitudes, educational and vocational problems, substance abuse, anger, disturbed family relationships, and mental disorder. The primary goal of these programs, and the primary outcome used to evaluate their effectiveness, is reduction in recidivism rates. If a program results in fewer offenders committing new crimes, this benefits everyone; it is thus consistent with both control and care. Implementing good correctional treatment programs is costly, but even a small reduction in recidivism rates may result in huge economic (not to mention humanitarian!) benefits.

OFFENDER RISK ASSESSMENT AND MANAGEMENT

The process of identifying risk and protective factors for crime is referred to as **offender risk assessment**. Similarly, the process of preventing crime by influencing risk and protective factors is sometimes referred to as **offender risk management**. Offender risk assessment and management are integral to contemporary criminal justice responses to crime.

A **risk** is a hazard that is incompletely understood; its occurrence can be forecast only with uncertainty. The hazard we are concerned with in this chapter is crime, and crime clearly is a complex phenomenon. Criminal acts can vary greatly with respect to such things as nature, motivation, severity of consequences, and so forth. Accordingly, risk is multifaceted and cannot be conceptualized or quantified simply, for example, in terms of the probability that someone will engage in crime. Instead, one must also consider the nature, seriousness, frequency or duration, and imminence of any future criminal conduct. Also, risk is inherently dynamic and contextual. For example, the risk posed by offenders depends on where they reside, what kinds of services they receive, their motivation to establish a prosocial adjustment, whether they experience adverse life events, and so forth.

In essence, then, risk is not a characteristic of the physical world that can be evaluated objectively, but a subjective perception—something that exists not in fact, but in the eye of the beholder. These perceptions regarding the nature and degree or quantum of risk in a given case, as well as the selection of risk management strategies and tactics, are based in turn on judgments regarding the collective influence of myriad individual things or elements, referred to as **risk factors.** But what exactly is a risk factor? It is relatively easy to demonstrate using a wide range of research designs that a thing is, on average, correlated with crime. But things that are correlated with crime may be causes, features, concomitants, or even consequences of crime. A risk factor is a correlate that also precedes the occurrence of the hazard and, therefore, may play a causal role. Demonstrating that something is a risk factor requires longitudinal research or well-substantiated theory. Risk factors may be further subdivided into three types.

1. **Fixed risk markers** do not change status over time.
2. **Variable risk markers** change status over time, but these changes do not influence the outcome.
3. **Causal risk factors** change status over time, and these changes influence the outcome.

Differentiating among these three types of risk factors also requires longitudinal designs, and ideally experimental or quasiexperimental longitudinal designs.

Considerable attention has been devoted to the identification of important risk factors for crime. One family of theories that has proven quite useful for this purpose may be referred to as **decision theories**. They posit that crime is a voluntary, purposeful human behavior; or, put differently, that people engage in crime because they made a decision to do so. The decision is, in essence, a cost–benefit analysis in which the offender perceived a situation in which engaging in crime was one potential course of action; evaluated the potential benefits of crime and viewed it as a means of successfully achieving one or more desired goals; evaluated the potential costs of crime and found them acceptable; and then implemented plans to engage in crime. According to these theories, risk factors are things that influence offenders' decisions about crime—how and why they make decisions to engage in crime. One decision theory that is popular in correctional psychology is sometimes referred to as the Psychology of Criminal Conduct (PCC) or the General Personality and Cognitive Social Learning (GPCSL) perspective (Andrews & Bonta, 2006). It focuses most heavily on offender's personality, attitudes, and experiences.

Assessment is the process of gathering information for use in decision making. The specific assessment procedures used are determined by what is being assessed and the nature of the decisions to be made. In the case of offender risk assessment, we must assess what offenders have done in the past, how they are functioning currently, and what they might do in the future. The decisions to be made are strategic in nature, including what should be done to cope with or manage the risks posed by an offender.

In sum, offender risk assessment can be defined as the process of evaluating offenders to: (1) characterize the risk that they will commit crime in the future; and (2) develop interventions to manage or reduce that risk (Andrews, Bonta, & Wormith, 2006; Hart, 2001). The task is to understand how and why an offender chose to commit crime in the past, and then to determine what could be done to discourage the person from choosing to commit crime again in the future. The specific procedures used to gather relevant information typically include: interviews with and observations of the person being evaluated; direct psychological or medical testing of the person; careful review of available documentary records; and interviews with collateral informants such as family members, friends, employers, and service providers.

The ultimate goal of offender risk assessment is crime prevention, or the minimization of the likelihood of and negative consequences stemming from any future violence. But offender assessment should achieve a number of goals in addition to the protection of public safety (Hart, 2001). A "good" offender risk assessment procedure should also yield reliable (i.e., consistent or replicable) results. That is, correctional psychologists should reach similar findings when evaluating the same offender at about the same time. It is highly unlikely that unreliable decisions can be of any practical use. Furthermore, a good offender risk assessment procedure should be prescriptive; it should identify, evaluate, and prioritize the mental health, social service, and criminal justice interventions that could be used to manage an offender's risk. Finally, a good offender risk assessment procedure should be open or transparent. Put another way, correctional professionals are accountable for the decisions they make, and it is therefore important for them to make explicit, as much as is possible, the basis for their opinions. A transparent offender assessment procedure allows offenders and the public a chance to scrutinize professional opinions. The transparency should protect correctional professionals when an offender commits crime despite the fact that a good risk assessment was conducted, as it can be demonstrated easily that standard or proper procedures were followed. Transparency should also protect offenders and the public by making it obvious when an improper offender risk assessment is conducted.

It is impossible for any single offender risk assessment procedure to achieve all these goals with maximum efficiency. Similarly, it is impossible for the various parties interested in offender risk assessment (correctional psychologists, prison administrators, offenders, lawyers, judges, victims, parole board members, etc.) to reach a consensus regarding which procedure is best for all purposes and in all contexts. Instead, correctional professionals should choose the best procedure or set of procedures for a particular assessment of a particular offender.

Approaches to Offender Risk Assessment

Correctional psychologists use two basic approaches to reach opinions about offender risk: professional judgment and actuarial decision making. These terms refer to how information is weighted and combined to reach a final decision, regardless of the information that is considered and how it was collected. The hallmark of professional judgment procedures is that the evaluator exercises some degree of discretion in the decision-making process, although it is also generally the case that evaluators have wide discretion concerning how assessment information is gathered and which information is considered. It comes as no surprise that unstructured clinical judgment is also described as "informal, subjective, [and] impressionistic." In contrast, the hallmark of the actuarial approach is that, based on the information available to them, evaluators make an ultimate decision according to fixed and explicit rules. It is also generally the case that actuarial decisions are based on specific assessment data, selected because they have been demonstrated empirically to be associated with violence and coded in a predetermined manner. The actuarial approach also has been described as "mechanical" and "algorithmic."

Professional Judgment Procedures

The professional judgment approach comprises at least three different procedures. The first is **unstructured professional judgment**. This is decision making in the complete absence of structure, a process that could be characterized as "intuitive" or "experiential." Historically, it is the most commonly used procedure for assessing offender risk and, therefore, is very familiar to correctional psychologists as well as to courts and tribunals. It has the advantage of being highly adaptable and efficient; it is possible to use intuition in any context, with minimal cost in terms of time and other resources. It is also person centered, focusing on the unique aspects of the case at hand, and thus can be of great assistance in planning interventions to manage offender risk. The major problem is that there is little empirical evidence that intuitive decisions are consistent across professionals or, indeed, that they are helpful in preventing crime. As well, intuitive decisions are unimpeachable; it is difficult even for the people who make them to explain how they were made. This means that the credibility of the decision often rests on charismatic authority—that is, the credibility of the person who made the decision. Finally, intuitive decisions tend to be broad or general in scope, so that they become dispositional statements about the offender ("Offender X is a very dangerous person") rather than a series of speculative statements about what the offender might do in the future assuming various release conditions.

The second professional judgment procedure is sometimes referred to as **anamnestic risk assessment**. (*Anamnesis* is a medical term that refers to the construction of a patient's history through his or her accounts or recollections.) This procedure imposes a limited degree of structure on the assessment as the evaluator must, at a minimum, identify the personal and situational factors that resulted in crime in the past. The assumption here is that a series of events and circumstances, a kind of behavioral chain, led up to the offender's antisocial behavior. The professional's task therefore is to understand the links in this chain and suggest ways in which the chain could be broken. However, there is no empirical evidence supporting the consistency or usefulness of anamnestic risk assessments. Anamnestic risk assessment also seems to assume that history will repeat itself—that offenders are static over time, so the only thing they are at risk to do in the future is what they have done in the past. Nothing could be farther from the truth, of course; there are many different "criminal careers." Some offenders will escalate in terms of the frequency or severity of crime over time, some change the types of crime they commit, and some will de-escalate or even desist altogether.

The third procedure is known as **structured professional judgment**. Here, decision making is assisted by guidelines that have been developed to reflect the state of the discipline with respect to scientific knowledge and professional practice. Such guidelines—sometimes referred to as *clinical guidelines*, *consensus guidelines*, or *clinical practice parameters*—are quite common in medicine, although used less frequently in psychiatric and psychological assessment. The guidelines attempt to define the risk being considered; discuss necessary qualifications for conducting an assessment; recommend what information should be considered as part of the evaluation and how it should be gathered; and identify a set of core risk factors that, according to the scientific and professional literature, should be considered as part of any reasonably comprehensive assessment. Structured professional guidelines help to improve the consistency and usefulness of decisions, and certainly improve the transparency of decision making. They may, however, require considerable time or resources to develop and implement. Also, some evaluators dislike this middle ground or compromise approach, either because it lacks the freedom of intuitive decision making or because it lacks the objectivity of actuarial procedures.

Actuarial Procedures

There are at least two types of **actuarial decision making**. The first is the actuarial use of psychological tests. Classically, psychological tests are structured samples of behavior designed to measure a personal disposition; that is, an attempt to quantify an individual's standing on some trait dimension. Research indicates that some dispositions—such as psychopathy, major mental illness, and impulsivity—are associated with offender risk in a meaningful way. On the basis of research results, one can identify cutoff scores on the test that maximize some aspect of predictive accuracy. This procedure has several strengths, most importantly its transparency and the demonstrated consistency and utility of decisions made using tests. One major problem is that the use of psychological tests requires considerable discretion: Correctional psychologists must decide which tests are appropriate in a given case, and judgment also may be required in test scoring and interpretation. Another problem is that reliance on a single test does not constitute a comprehensive evaluation and will provide only limited information for use in developing management strategies and tactics. More generally, the actuarial use of psychological tests focuses professional efforts on passive crime *prediction* rather than crime *prevention*.

The second type of procedure is the use of actuarial risk assessment instruments. In contrast to psychological tests, actuarial instruments are designed not to measure anything but solely to predict the future. Typically, they are constructed with great precision, optimized to predict a specific outcome in a specific population over a specific period of time. The items in the scale are selected either rationally (on the basis of theory or experience) or empirically (on the basis of their association with the outcome in test construction research). The items are weighted and combined according to some algorithm to yield a decision. In offender risk assessment, the "decision" generally is the estimated likelihood of future crime (e.g., arrest, charge, or conviction for a new offense) over some period of time. Like psychological tests, actuarial instruments have the advantage of transparency and direct empirical support; they also suffer many of the same weaknesses including the need for discretion in selecting a test, interpreting findings, and the limitations of the test findings for use in planning interventions. There are additional problems with actuarial instruments that estimate the absolute likelihood or probability of recidivism. One is that they require tremendous time and effort to construct and validate. In cases when the time frame of the prediction is long, true cross-validation may require decades. Also, when constructing actuarial tests there is an unavoidable trade-off between the precision of estimated recidivism rates and their generalizability: The more precisely one estimates the recidivism rate of a particular group or sample, the less likely it is that the estimate will accurately describe the recidivism rate of other groups or samples (and vice versa). The same statistical procedures that optimize predictive accuracy in one setting will decrease that test's accuracy in others. Finally, it is easy to accord too much weight to information concerning the estimated likelihood of recidivism provided by actuarial tests. Most actuarial tests of offender risk yield very precise likelihood estimates, proportions with two or three decimal places, but they do not provide the information necessary to understand the error inherent in these estimates. When one considers the fact that many of these estimates were derived from relatively small construction samples and have not been validated in independent samples, it is clear that the actuarial test results are only pseudoprecise. It is important for any professional who uses actuarial tests to understand and explain to others the limitations of absolute likelihood estimates of recidivism.

Example: The Level of Service-Case Management Inventory

The Level of Service-Case Management Inventory (LS-CMI) was developed by a group of correctional psychologists working in Canada that included Don Andrews, James Bonta, and Steve Wormith (Andrews, Bonta, & Wormith, 2004). It is a set of structured professional judgment (SPJ) guidelines that assist the assessment and management of risk for general criminality. It is intended for use by a variety of correctional professionals, including correctional psychologists. The original version of the test, the *Level of Supervision Inventory* (LSI), was published in 1982, and later renamed the *Level of Service Inventory*. A revised version, the LSI-R, was published in 1995. Most recently, it was revised yet again and renamed the *Level of Service-Case Management Inventory*, or LS-CMI, in 2004.

The LS-CMI is intended for use with male and female offenders, aged 16 and older, in institutions or the community. It comprises 11 sections that require evaluators to make a series of ratings based on a semistructured interview with the offender and a review of relevant records, then document various opinions, recommendations, and decisions (see Table 10.1 for an

Table 10.1   Overview of the Level of Service-Case Management Inventory (LS-CMI)

Section	Activity
1. General Risk/Need Factors	Assess factors from the "Big 8" domains that are reliably associated with risk for criminality
2. Specific Risk/Need Factors	Assess factors that are possibly associated with risk for criminality, including some related to personal adjustment and criminal history
3. Prison Experience—Institutional Factors	Assess factors associated with institutional adjustment problems, including history of incarceration and barriers to release
4. Other Client Issues	Assess other factors relevant to case management, including problems related to psychological and physical health, finances, accommodation, and victimization
5. Special Responsivity Considerations	Assess factors that should be considered when determining how best to deliver correctional services, such as supervision and treatment
6. Risk-Need Summary and Override	Summarize risk-need scores and rationale for any override of classification based on scores
7. Risk-Need Profile	Graphically summarize of risk-need scores
8. Program/Placement Decision	Summarize decisions made about case management, including classification and treatment
9. Case Management Plan	Prioritize primary (criminogenic) needs, other needs, and responsivity factors
10. Progress Record	Log activities and events that reflect changes in risk, including response to correctional programming
11. Discharge Summary	Summarize case information that should be reviewed if the offender returns to custody or community supervision

Source: Andrews, Bonta, & Wormith (2004).

overview). Section 1 contains 43 items that are summed to yield an actuarial (i.e., formulaic or algorithmic) risk/need score. This section is the core of the LS-CMI; it was in the original LSI, and the other sections were added to it over time. The items in Section 1 tap eight domains of psychosocial functioning: Criminal History, Education/Employment, Leisure/Recreation, Family/Marital, Companions, Alcohol/Drug Problems, Pro-Criminal Attitude/Orientation, and Antisocial Pattern. They were selected rationally, according to PCC and GPSCL theoretical frameworks. Sections 2 through 5 contain items that reflect other specific risk, need, and responsivity factors. These items are considered less important than those in Section 1, according to theory and research, but are still potentially relevant to risk. In Sections

6 and 7, evaluators reach final opinions concerning the risks posed by the offender. First, they use cutoff scores to interpret actuarial risk/need scores. Next, they use their professional judgment to adjust or override the actuarial risk/need scores, when they think it necessary or appropriate (e.g., when a case presents with unusual circumstances). Finally, in Sections 8 through 11, evaluators recommend, implement, evaluate, and document case management strategies based on the findings of Sections 1 through 7. This is done rationally or logically, rather than using an algorithm or formula.

Even from this brief description, it is clear that the LS-CMI is not a simple, quantitative test. It specifies the type of information evaluators should gather, and contains tools that evaluators can use for this purpose (e.g., a semistructured interview guide). It forces evaluators to consider a standard list of risk, need, and responsivity factors identified from theory and research, but it also encourages evaluators to consider factors not included in the list. Evaluators calculate actuarial risk scores, which can be interpreted with respect to various norms and cutoffs, but they are encouraged to override the mechanical interpretations when appropriate. Evaluators are encouraged to think systematically about case management, based on the test findings. It is the reliance on discretion or judgment that makes the LS-CMI a form of SPJ—also known as empirically guided judgment or anchored clinical judgment—rather than a form of actuarial decision making.

The LSI and its progeny, although originally developed in Canada for use with male offenders in community settings, are now used routinely by various correctional systems around the world. It is no exaggeration to say that the LS-CMI is the "gold standard" for offender assessment. It is used with the entire range of offenders, including those in custody, adult females, juvenile delinquents, mentally disordered offenders (MDOs), violent offenders, and so on. Its ability to predict future criminal behavior has been confirmed by a number of empirical evaluations. For example, according to recent meta-analyses, the average correlation between total scores on the LSI, LSI-R, or Section 1 of the LS-CMI and general recidivism among offenders on community supervision is about $r = .25$; the average correlation with institutional infractions is about $r = .15$. There is also some research indicating that the LS-CMI is sensitive to changes in risk over time—that is, it can be used to measure whether an offender's risk is increasing or decreasing over time.

Other Risk Assessment Instruments and Related Tests

Despite its successes, there are at least three important limitations of the LS-CMI as a risk assessment measure. First, it uses a simplistic definition of *risk*: the probability that an offender will be officially sanctioned for antisocial or criminal behavior over a given period of time. The LS-CMI can't be used to forecast an offender's risk for specific types of crime (e.g., sexual violence, intimate partner violence), or the severity of any future crime (e.g., no physical harm versus serious or life-threatening violence), or the risk during other time periods (e.g., the next 2 to 4 weeks, the next 15 years).

Second, because of its definition of risk, the LS-CMI ignores important risk factors for specific forms of antisocial behavior, such as drug crimes, child abuse and exploitation, intimate partner violence, sexual violence, stalking, gang violence, or political terrorism. In particular, it pays relatively little attention to mental disorder as a risk factor for violence. For example, paraphilic disorders such as pedophilia or sexual sadism are an important risk factor for sexual violence in some cases; delusional disorders such as erotomania may be important risk factors for stalking; and personality disorders such as psychopathy may be associated with a wide range of violence. Serious mental disorder is certainly not rare in offender populations, but mental disorder does not play a role in PCC/GPSCL and is therefore accorded little weight in the LS-CMI.

Third, the structure of the LS-CMI still reflects its origins. It seems best suited for assessing adult males under community supervision in urban centers in the United States or Canada. It is perhaps less appropriate for use with the most serious offenders (e.g., those incarcerated in maximum security institutions), female offenders, or offenders from ethnocultural minority backgrounds who are often overrepresented in correctional systems (especially indigenous peoples, such as Aborigines in Australia; First Nations, Inuit, and Métis in Canada; Maori in New Zealand; and American Indians in the United States).

In light of these limitations, it should come as no surprise that several other risk assessment instruments are often used in addition to or instead of the LS-CMI (see Table 10.2). Some of these tests are intended to assess specific risks. For example, correctional psychologists who work with sexual offenders may use tests such as the STATIC-99 (Hanson & Thornton, 1999), an actuarial test developed to estimate offender's risk for specific forms of sexual violence, or special-to-purpose SPJ guidelines such as the Sexual Violence Risk-20 (SVR-20; Boer, Hart, Kropp, & Webster, 1997) or the Risk for Sexual Violence Protocol (RSVP; Hart et al., 2003). Others are intended for specific settings. For example, correctional psychologists who work with offenders newly admitted to jail may use management-focused SPJ guidelines such as the Jail Screening Assessment Tool (JSAT; Nicholls, Roesch, Olley, Ogloff, & Hemphill, 2005). Still others are intended for offenders with specific types of problems. For example, the Historical, Clinical, Risk Management-20 (HCR-20; Webster, Douglas, Eaves, & Hart, 1997) may be used by correctional psychologists who work with offenders to assess offender risk, especially with offenders who may be suffering from mental health problems.

Table 10.2   Examples of Specialized Risk Assessment Instruments

Instrument	Format	Purpose	Target Population
VRAG	Actuarial	Assessment of risk for violence	Adult males with a history of violence and mental health problems
HCR-20	SPJ	Comprehensive assessment and management of risk for institutional and community violence	Adult males and females in correctional or mental health settings
SAVRY	SPJ	Comprehensive assessment and management of risk for institutional and community violence	Adolescent males and females in correctional or mental health settings
STATIC-99	Actuarial	Brief assessment of risk for sexual violence	Adult males with a history of sexual offenses
JSOAP	Actuarial	Brief assessment of risk for sexual violence	Adolescent males with a history of sexual offenses
SVR-20	SPJ	Comprehensive assessment and management of risk for sexual violence	Adult males and females
ERRASOR	SPJ	Comprehensive assessment and management of risk for sexual violence	Adolescent males
ODARA	Actuarial	Assessment of risk for intimate partner violence	Adult males with a recent history of intimate partner violence
DA	Actuarial	Assessment and management of risk for life-threatening intimate partner violence	Adult males with a recent history of intimate partner violence
SARA	SPJ	Comprehensive assessment and management of risk for intimate partner violence	Adult males and females
JSAT	SPJ	Comprehensive assessment and management of short-term risk for institutional adjustment problems	Adult males and females admitted to correctional settings
START	SPJ	Comprehensive assessment and management of short-term risk for institutional adjustment problems	Adult males and females admitted to mental health settings

Note: More information about these instruments can be found in Otto & Douglas, 2009.

Specialized actuarial risk assessment instruments tend to be relatively brief tests that closely resemble Section 1 of the LS-CMI, except that the content reflects more specific risk factors. A good example is the STATIC-99. It comprises 10 items, several of which reflect prior sexual offenses (see Table 10.3). Evaluators rate each item based on a review of official records. Item ratings are summed to yield a total score. Cutoffs are used to categorize offenders into several groups. Norms are used to estimate, for offenders in each group, the probability of charge or conviction for future sexual offenses over periods of 5 or 15 years. Although the test is relatively

Table 10.3   Risk Factors in the STATIC-99

Item	Content	Coding
1. Young	Under age 25?	0 = No 1 = Yes
2. Single	Ever lived with lover for at least two years?	0 = Yes 1 = No
3. Index Nonsexual Violence	Any convictions?	0 = No 1 = Yes
4. Prior Nonsexual Violence	Any prior convictions?	0 = No 1 = Yes
5. Prior Sex Offenses	Number of prior charges or convictions?	0 = 0 charges/0 convictions 1 = 1–2 charges/1 conviction 2 = 3–5 charges/2–3 convictions 3 = 6+ charges/4+ convictions
6. Prior Sentencing Dates	Number of prior sentences?	0 = 3 or fewer 1 = 4 or more
7. Noncontact Sex Offenses	Any convictions?	0 = No 1 = Yes
8. Unrelated Victims	Any unrelated victims?	0 = No 1 = Yes
9. Stranger Victims	Any stranger victims?	0 = No 1 = Yes
10. Male Victims	Any male victims?	0 = No 1 = Yes
Total	Sum of item scores	0–1 = Low 2–3 = Moderate-Low 4–5 = Moderate-High 6+ = High

Source: Accessed July 24, 2009 at http://www.static99.org.

simple, it now has a lengthy manual that contains detailed administration instructions (Harris, Phenix, Hanson, & Thornton, 2003). The STATIC-99 is not intended as a stand-alone test, because it focuses on a small number of historical factors; the test authors recommend consideration of dynamic factors to ensure a comprehensive assessment, and have developed additional instruments for this purpose.

In contrast, specialized SPJ guidelines tend to be longer, more comprehensive, and management focused. In this respect, they resemble the full LS-CMI. A good example here is the RSVP. Its administration process comprises six steps. In Step 1, evaluators gather relevant information. In Step 2, they consider the presence of 22 standard risk factors (see Table 10.4), as well as any other case-specific risk factors. In Step

Table 10.4   Risk Factors in the Risk for Sexual Violence Protocol (RSVP)

Domain	Risk Factor
Sexual Violence History	1. Chronicity of sexual violence
	2. Diversity of sexual violence
	3. Escalation of sexual violence
	4. Physical coercion in sexual violence
	5. Psychological coercion in sexual violence
Psychological Adjustment	6. Extreme minimization or denial of sexual violence
	7. Attitudes that support or condone sexual violence
	8. Problems with self-awareness
	9. Problems with stress or coping
	10. Problems resulting from child abuse
Mental Disorder	11. Sexual deviance
	12. Psychopathic personality disorder
	13. Major mental illness
	14. Problems with substance use
	15. Violent or suicidal ideation
Social Adjustment	16. Problems with intimate relationships
	17. Problems with nonintimate relationships
	18. Problems with employment
	19. Nonsexual criminality
Manageability	20. Problems with planning
	21. Problems with treatment
	22. Problems with supervision

3, they consider the relevance of each factor with respect to risk for sexual violence. In Step 4, they consider risk scenarios—that is, speculate about the possible nature, severity, imminence, frequency, and likelihood of any future sexual violence. In Step 5, they develop risk management strategies based on relevant risk factors and risk scenarios. Finally, in Step 6, they make a number of conclusory opinions. The manual is relatively long (although only about half the length of the STATIC-99 manual, in terms of word count).

Specialized risk assessment instruments such as those in Table 10.2 are used frequently in correctional systems. Research indicates they are about as successful for their specialized purpose (e.g., assessing risk for intimate partner violence) as the LS-CMI is for assessing and managing risk for general criminality. They also provide more detailed information that may be useful for making risk management decisions.

Correctional psychologists also have developed tests that are used to assess specific risk factors or aspects of risk. One example is the Hare Psychopathy Checklist-Revised (PCL-R; Hare, 1991, 2003). The PCL-R was developed to assess symptoms of psychopathic personality disorder, which subsequent research indicated is a robust risk factor for several forms of serious and violent crime. The PCL-R is used in many correctional systems around the world as part of comprehensive offender risk assessments, and it is also used as part of other actuarial and SPJ risk assessment instruments such as the Violence Risk Appraisal Guide (VRAG; Quinsey, Harris, Rice, & Cormier, 1998, 2006), the HCR-20 (Webster et al., 1997), and the SVR-20 (Boer, Hart, Kropp, & Webster, 1997). Other tests have been designed to tap an offender's self-reports related to several aspects of risk. Although research indicates that these tests are predictive of future criminality, their primary utility is as one part of a more comprehensive risk assessment.

Strategies for Offender Risk Management

Risk management activities can be divided into four basic categories: monitoring, treatment, supervision, and victim safety planning.

Monitoring, or repeated assessment, is always a part of good risk management. The goal of monitoring is to evaluate changes in risk over time so that risk management strategies and tactics can be revised as appropriate. Monitoring, unlike supervision, focuses on surveillance rather than control or restriction of liberties; it is therefore minimally intrusive. Monitoring tactics may include contacts with the offender, as well as with potential victims and other relevant people (e.g., therapists, correctional officers, family members, coworkers) in the form of face-to-face or telephonic meetings. Where appropriate, they may also include field visits (e.g., at home or work), electronic surveillance, polygraphic interviews, drug testing (urine, blood, or hair analysis), and inspection of mail or telecommunications (telephone records, fax logs, e-mail, etc.).

Treatment involves the provision of (re-)habilitative services. The goal of treatment is to improve an offender's psychosocial adjustment. Treatments may include training programs designed to improve interpersonal, anger management, and vocational skills; psychoeducational programs designed to change attitudes toward crime; individual or group psychotherapy; chemical dependency programs; and psychoactive medications, such as antipsychotics or mood stabilizers.

Supervision involves the restriction of the offender's rights or freedoms. The goal of supervision is to make it (more) difficult for the offender to engage in further violence. An extreme form of supervision is incapacitation, that is, involuntary institutionalization of the offender in a correctional or health care facility. Incapacitation clearly is an effective means of reducing the offender's access to potential victims. It is, however, by no means perfectly effective: The offender may escape from the institution or even commit crimes while institutionalized. Incapacitation also has other disadvantages: It is expensive; it restricts accessibility to treatment services; and it may promote the development of antisocial attitudes by increasing contact with antisocial peers and by creating a sense of powerlessness or frustration. Community supervision is much more common than institutionalization. Typically, it involves allowing the offender to reside in the community with restrictions on activity, movement, association, and communication. Restrictions on activity may include requirements to attend vocational or educational programs, not to use alcohol or drugs, and so on. Restrictions on movement may include house arrest, travel bans, "no go" orders (i.e., orders not to visit specific geographic areas), and travel only with identified chaperones. Restrictions on association may include orders not to socialize or communicate with specific people or groups of people who may encourage antisocial acts or with past or potential victims.

Victim safety planning involves improving the security resources of potential victims, a process sometimes referred to as *target hardening*. The goal is to ensure that, if crime recurs—despite all monitoring, treatment, and supervision efforts—any negative impact on the victims' psychological and physical well-being is minimized. Victim safety planning is most relevant in situations that involve "targeted violence."

An Integrated Approach to Offender Management: The Risk-Need-Responsivity (RNR) Model

Over the past 20 years, what has come to be known as the Risk-Need-Responsivity (RNR) model has emerged as the dominant approach to offender treatment in correctional psychology. It was developed by the same people responsible for the LS-CMI, together with colleagues such as Paul Gendreau, Robert Hoge, and Robert Ross (e.g., Andrews, Bonta, & Hoge, 1990; Gendreau & Ross, 1979).

The RNR model comprises three core principles, derived from research on correctional treatment and interpreted within the broader framework of PCC/GPCSL theory. According to the **risk principle**, the level of services delivered to offenders should be commensurate with the risks they pose to reoffend. This means offenders at high risk for recidivism should receive more intensive assessment and management, relative to offenders at moderate or low risk. According to the **need principle**, offender assessment and management should focus on criminogenic (crime-causing) needs. This means services for offenders should target causal risk factors for antisocial behavior that have been validated by empirical research. According to the **responsivity principle**, services should be delivered that maximize their effectiveness. This means two things. First, in general terms, the focus of management programs should be on skills acquisition and enhancement through prosocial modeling, the appropriate use of reinforcement and disapproval, and problem solving, because research suggests this is the most efficient and effective way to change people's behavior. Second, more specifically, it means that the management programs delivered to offenders should match their individual learning styles, motivations, abilities, and strengths.

Development of the RNR model was motivated by the rather unhappy state of the research literature on the effectiveness of correctional treatment that existed in the 1970s. At that time, there was no good evidence that correctional treatment reduced recidivism rates in offenders, or even that it made offenders feel much better. Systematic reviews of the research literature concluded that correctional treatment was largely ineffective— or, in the words of Robert Martinson, that "nothing works" with respect to offender treatment (Martinson, 1974).

Andrews, Bonta, and colleagues rejected the Martinson verdict. They argued that the correctional treatments reviewed by Martinson should not be lumped together, due to their heterogeneity. They conducted their own reviews and found treatment programs that reported positive findings tended to have some important similarities (Bonta & Andrews, 2007; Wormith et al., 2007). For example, effective programs:

- targeted high-risk rather than low-risk offenders;
- focused on concrete goals such as changing criminal behavior rather than improving self-esteem;
- relied on structured or skills-focused interventions rather than unstructured or psychotherapeutic interventions; and
- were often delivered to groups rather than individuals.

Based on these findings, they formalized the RNR principles. Their conclusion is that the effectiveness of a correctional treatment depends directly on its consistency with RNR principles. For example, in a recent study (Bonta & Andrews, 2007), residential and community-based offender treatment programs were reviewed and scored according to the number of RNR core principles to which they adhered (0 = no adherence, 3 = complete adherence). The effectiveness of each treatment program was

indexed using *r* as an effect size measure. The mean effectiveness
was calculated for each adherence score. Institutional and community
programs with adherence scores of 3 (i.e., adherence to all RNR core
principles) had effect sizes of .17 and .35; this corresponds to reduction
in recidivism rates of roughly 17 and 35 percentage points, respectively,
for treated versus untreated offenders. In contrast, the effect size for
adherence scores of 0 (adherence to no RNR core principles) were actually negative: −.10 for institutional programs and −.02 for community
programs. Treatment programs that ignored RNR principles were either
ineffective or may have actually increased recidivism rates by up to 10%.
(See Figure 10.1.)

The RNR approach has had some positive impacts on correctional psychology. First, and perhaps most important, it replaced the nihilistic dogma
that "Nothing works!" with a more constructive question, "What works?"
This promoted the development of systematic, evidence-based offender
treatment programs. Second, it highlighted the need for routine evaluation of treatment programs, which led to a great increase in high-quality
empirical research. Third, in combination with the underlying PCC or
GPSCL theoretical framework, it helped correctional psychologists
practice in a rational and reasonable manner, and especially balance the
conflicting ethics of control and care. It is an excellent conceptual tool
for guiding the development and delivery of psychological services in
corrections.

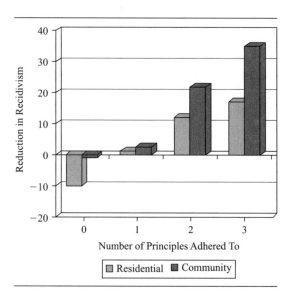

**Figure 10.1   Reduction in Recidivism Rates as a Function of Adherence to Risk-Need-Responsivity
(RNR) Principles in Residential and Community Correctional Treatment Programs**

But the approach also has its limitations. Tony Ward and colleagues (Ward, 2002; Ward & Brown, 2004; Whitehead, Ward, & Collie, 2007) have pointed out that although the RNR approach has good research support, most of it has come from research focusing on male offenders with a history of general criminality and without serious mental health problems. There is relatively little research examining the utility of RNR with respect to more specific offender populations, including females, offenders suffering from major mental illnesses, and serious violent offenders. With respect to theory, Ward and colleagues argued that the RNR approach focuses too much on reducing recidivism—encouraging offenders *not* to commit crime, but without giving them enough help to develop prosocial alternatives to crime. This limits the potential impact of correctional programs by failing to maximize treatment engagement or motivation. In essence, this latter argument is that RNR values the ethic of control more than the ethic of care.

As an alternative, Ward and colleagues developed the Good Lives (GL) model. GL focuses on promoting the important personal goals of offenders, while at the same time reducing and managing their risk for future crime. The basic idea is by helping people fulfill their basic human needs and desires—what the GL model calls "primary goods"—treatment naturally discourages or minimizes involvement in crime. According to GL, primary goods are "activities, experiences, or situations that are sought for their own sake and that benefit individuals and increase their sense of fulfillment and happiness" (Whitehead et al., 2007, p. 580), including such things as relatedness, autonomy, knowledge, mastery, play, and physical health. Problems arise when the strategies can't obtain primary goods. Such problems typically take four forms: neglect of important primary goods; use of ineffective strategies to secure goods; conflict of strategies to secure goods; and inability to implement strategies for securing goods.

RNR and GL are similar in many respects, as proponents of both approaches acknowledge. In theory, GL may be seen as an expansion of RNR to include some factors deemed *noncriminogenic needs* by the latter but *primary human goods* by the former. In practice, the major differences between them are that, compared to RNR, GL treatment: (1) deals more explicitly with the goals and values of offenders; and, (2) includes a focus on the process by which offenders attempt to construct meaning in their lives.

Example: Reasoning and Rehabilitation-Revised Program

The Reasoning and Rehabilitation-Revised Program, formerly known as Cognitive Skills Training Program, was developed concurrent with RNR principles (see Andrews & Bonta, 2006). Its goal is to prevent general criminality. It was the first offender treatment program to be implemented nationally in Canada, and subsequently has been implemented in correctional systems in the United States as well as countries such as Australia, Germany, New Zealand, Norway, Sweden, and the United Kingdom.

The program is a cognitive-behavioral treatment designed to train offenders in skills that address a wide range of problems commonly associated with criminal behavior, such as poor planning and decision-making skills, deficits in empathy and perspective taking, attitudes and beliefs that condone criminal behavior, association with peers who lead a criminal lifestyle, and so on. It was developed for use with adult male offenders who are at moderate to high risk for general criminality. It is delivered in small-group format (usually 8 to 10 participants) in classroom settings, either in institutions or in the community. The assessment and treatment procedures are highly structured, set out in detailed manuals. The standard curriculum comprises about four individual sessions in which the evaluator assesses the offender using motivational interviewing techniques, followed by 35 to 40 treatment sessions of two to three hours duration delivered over 8 to 12 weeks. The overall goal of treatment is to teach offenders to think before they act by providing them with more effective skills to anticipate problems and plan their reactions, solve problems, and consider other people's points of view. Specific topics covered in treatment include interpersonal problem solving, self-control and self-management, assertiveness and social interaction, social perspective taking, critical reasoning, and values reasoning. Treatment delivery is designed to maximize the motivation and participation of offenders.

Research has shown that offenders who participate in the Reasoning and Rehabilitation-Revised Program improve on measures of skill development. For example, a recent evaluation in Sweden examined the effectiveness of treated offenders compared to matched controls over a period of five years. Of offenders who started treatment, 77% completed successfully. According to various questionnaires completed at the end of treatment, treated offenders exhibited significant improvements with respect to such things as impulsivity and prosocial attitudes. A follow-up of offenders subsequently released indicated that offenders who completed treatment had a 48% reconviction rate, compared to 60% for untreated offenders and 73% for dropouts.

Findings such as these give reason for optimism, but it is important to note some important limitations of the Reasoning and Rehabilitation-Revised Program. First, the dropout rate is too high: About 1 of 4 offenders *do not* complete treatment. More must be done to build and maintain offender motivation. Second, the reconviction rate is too high, even among offenders who complete treatment: About 1 in 2 reoffend within 2 to 5 years. Third, evaluations rely too heavily on quasiexperimental designs, rather than randomized trials. Fourth, the program is targeted at general criminality, rather than specific forms of offending. Its effectiveness with, say, intimate partner violence or sexual offenders is unknown. Finally, the active process (i.e., mechanism of change) underlying treatment is not clear. According to theory, it works by changing the thinking styles of offenders—increasing prosocial attitudes, decreasing impulsivity, and so forth. But there is not good research support for this assumption; indeed, some evaluations have found that offenders who report greater attitude change have higher reconviction rates than those who report less attitude change.

Other Offender Treatment Programs

To address risk for general criminality, some correctional systems also offer programs to enhance life skills in such areas as employment, education, anger management, parenting, and leisure activities. To address more specific forms of criminality, some offer programs for sexual violence, family violence, or other violence. To address mental health problems related to risk for general or violent criminality, some offer programs for offenders with substance use problems, acute mental illness, intellectual deficits, or personality disorder. Many of these programs are modeled closely after the Reasoning and Rehabilitation-Revised Program in terms of format and structure.

Evaluations of these treatment programs have yielded generally positive findings, insofar as they are often associated with short-term improvements in attitudes, adjustment, and skills, and sometimes with long-term reductions in recidivism rates. But these evaluations also have found evidence of the same problems that have plagued the Reasoning and Rehabilitation-Revised Program: high attrition (dropout) rates, typically in the range of 30% to 60%; high recidivism rates, even among offenders who successfully complete treatment; lack of high-quality evaluations, in the form of randomized controlled trials; and lack of research on mechanisms of change. For example, systematic reviews of the effectiveness of sex offender treatment programs include scores of studies, but only a few of these are randomized controlled trials. Although there is evidence that successful treatment on average reduces the rate of sex offense recidivism by about one-quarter to one-third, the results of randomized controlled trials indicated the reduction in recidivism associated with treatment was very small or even nonexistent. The same pattern of findings is evident in evaluations of intimate partner violence treatment programs.

SUMMARY

The corrections system in the United States is highly complex in nature, responsible for managing offenders in both institutions and the community. The corrections system has grown dramatically over the past 50 years and increasingly has taken responsibility for not just supervising but also rehabilitating offenders. Correctional psychology has grown and evolved along with the system is services. Correctional psychologists have made important contributions to the development, implementation, and evaluation of a wide range of theory-grounded and evidence-based offender risk assessment procedures and offender risk management programs. Their work is critical to improving the lives of offenders while protecting and enhancing public safety.

SUGGESTED READINGS

Andrews, D. A., & Bonta, J. (2006). *The psychology of criminal conduct* (4th ed.). Cincinnati, OH: Anderson.

Clements, C. B., Althouse, R., Ax, R. K., Magaletta, P. R., Fagan, T. J., & Wormith, J. S. (2007). Systemic issues and correctional outcomes: Expanding the scope of correctional psychology. *Criminal Justice and Behavior, 34,* 919–932.

Wormith, J. S., Althouse, R., Simpson, M., Reitzel, L. R., Fagan, T. J., & Morgan, R. D. (2007). The rehabilitation and reintegration of offenders: The current landscape and some future directions for correctional psychology. *Criminal Justice and Behavior, 34,* 879–892.

KEY TERMS

- *Actuarial decision making*
- *Anamnestic risk assessment*
- *Assessment*
- *Bail*
- *Causal risk factors*
- *Correctional psychology*
- *Corrections system*
- *Decision theories*
- *Ethic of care*
- *Ethic of control*
- *Fixed risk markers*

- *Monitoring*
- *Need principle*
- *Offender risk assessment*
- *Offender risk management*
- *Parole*
- *Penitentiaries*
- *Prisons*
- *Probation*
- *Responsivity principle*
- *Risk*
- *Risk factors*
- *Risk principle*
- *Structured professional judgment*
- *Supervision*
- *Treatment*
- *Unstructured professional judgment*
- *Variable risk markers*
- *Victim safety planning*

References

Andrews, D. A., & Bonta, J. (2006). *The psychology of criminal conduct* (4th ed.). Cincinnati, OH: Anderson.

Andrews, D. A., Bonta, J., & Hoge, R. D. (1990). Classification for effective rehabilitation: Rediscovering psychology. *Criminal Justice and Behavior, 17*, 19–52.

Andrews, D. A., Bonta, J., & Wormith, S. J. (2004). *Level of Service-Case Management Inventory (LS-CMI)*. Toronto: Multi-Health Systems Inc.

Andrews, D. A., Bonta, J., & Wormith, S. J. (2006). The recent past and near future of risk and/or need assessment. *Crime & Delinquency, 52*, 7–27.

Bartol, C. R., & Freeman, N. J. (2005). History of the American Association for Correctional Psychology. *Criminal Justice and Behavior, 32*, 123–142.

Boer, D. P., Hart, S. D., Kropp, P. R., & Webster, C. D. (1997). *Manual for the Sexual Violence Risk-20: Professional guidelines for assessing risk of sexual violence*. Vancouver, British Columbia: British Columbia Institute Against Family Violence, and co-published with the Mental Health, Law, & Policy Institute, Simon Fraser University.

Bonta, J., & Andrews, D. A. (2007). *Risk-need-responsivity model for offender assessment and rehabilitation*, Report 2007–06. Ottawa: Public Safety Canada.

Brodsky, S. L. (2007). Correctional psychology and the American Association of Correctional Psychology: A revisionist history. *Criminal Justice and Behavior, 34*, 862–869.

Clements, C. B., Althouse, R., Ax, R. K., Magaletta, P. R., Fagan, T. J., & Wormith, J. S. (2007). Systemic issues and correctional outcomes: Expanding the scope of correctional psychology. *Criminal Justice and Behavior, 34*, 919–932.

Corsini, R. (1945). Functions of the prison psychologist. *Journal of Consulting Psychology, 9*, 101–104.

Daly, W. C. (2000). A half century of prison psychology: 1950–2000. *Education, 120*, 469–476.

Gendreau, P., & Ross, B. (1979). Effective correctional treatment: Bibliotherapy for cynics. *Crime & Delinquency, 25*, 463–489.

Hanson, R. K., & Thornton, D. (1999). *STATIC-99: Improving actuarial risk assessments for sex offenders*. Ottawa: Ministry of the Solicitor General of Canada.

Hare, R. D. (1991). *Manual for the Hare Psychopathy Checklist-Revised (PCL-R)*. Toronto: Multi-Health Systems Inc.

Hare, R. D. (2003). *Manual for the Hare Psychopathy Checklist-Revised (PCL-R)* (2nd ed.). Toronto: Multi-Health Systems Inc.

Harris, A. J., Phenix, A., Hanson, R. K., & Thornton, D. (2003). *STATIC-99 coding rules revised—2003*. Ottawa: Public Safety and Emergency Preparedness Canada.

Hart, S. D. (2001). Assessing and managing violence risk. In K. S. Douglas, C. D. Webster, S. D. Hart, D. Eaves, & J. R. P. Ogloff (Eds.), *HCR-20 violence risk management companion guide* (pp. 13–25). Burnaby, British Columbia: Mental Health, Law, and Policy Institute, Simon Fraser University.

Hart, S. D., Kropp, P. R., Laws, D. R., Klaver, J., Logan, C., & Watt, K. A. (2003). *The Risk for Sexual Violence Protocol (RSVP): Structured professional guidelines for assessing risk of sexual violence*. Burnaby, British Columbia: Mental Health, Law, and Policy Institute, Simon Fraser University.

Levinson, R. B. (1980). Standards for psychology services in adult jails and prisons. *Criminal Justice and Behavior, 7*, 81–127.

Magaletta, P. R., Patry, M. W., Dietz, E. F., & Ax, R. K. (2007). What is correctional about clinical practice in corrections? *Criminal Justice and Behavior, 34*, 7–21.

Martinson, R. (1974). What works? Questions and answers about prison reform. *The Public Interest, 35*, 22–54.

Megargee, E. I. (2003). Psychological assessment in correctional settings. In J. R. Graham & J. A. Naglieri (Eds.), *Handbook of psychology, Vol. 10: Assessment psychology* (pp. 365–388). New York: John Wiley & Sons.

Nicholls, T., Roesch, R., Olley, M., Ogloff, J. R. P., & Hemphill, J. F. (2005). *Jail Screening Assessment Tool (JSAT): Guidelines for mental health screening in jails*. Burnaby, Canada: Mental Health, Law, and Policy Institute, Simon Fraser University.

Otto, R. K. & Douglas, K. S. (2009). *The handbook of violence risk assessment.* New York: Routledge.

Quinsey, V. L., Harris, G. T., Rice, M. E., & Cormier, C. A. (1998). *Violent offenders: Appraising and managing risk.* Washington, DC: American Psychological Association.

Quinsey, V. L., Harris, G. T., Rice, M. E., & Cormier, C. A. (2006). *Violent offenders: Appraising and managing risk* (2nd ed.). Washington, DC: American Psychological Association.

Ward, T. (2002). Good lives and the rehabilitation of offenders: Promises and problems. *Aggression and Violent Behavior, 7*, 513–528.

Ward, T., & Brown, M. (2004). The Good Lives model and conceptual issues in offender rehabilitation. *Psychology, Crime & Law, 10*, 243–257.

Webster, C. D., Douglas, K. S., Eaves, D., & Hart, S. D. (1997). *HCR-20: Assessing risk for violence, version 2.* Burnaby, British Columbia: Mental Health, Law, and Policy Institute, Simon Fraser University.

Whitehead, P. R., Ward, T., & Collie, R, M. (2007). Applying the Good Lives model of rehabilitation to a high-risk violent offender. *International Journal of Offender Therapy and Comparative Criminology, 51*, 578–598.

Wormith, J. S., Althouse, R., Simpson, M., Reitzel, L. R., Fagan, T. J., & Morgan, R. D. (2007). The rehabilitation and reintegration of offenders: The current landscape and some future directions for correctional psychology. *Criminal Justice and Behavior, 34*, 879–892.

Chapter 11

PSYCHOLOGY, LAW, AND PUBLIC POLICY

CHAPTER OBJECTIVES

In this chapter, you will become familiar with:

- The roles that **expert witnesses** play in civil and criminal cases
- Federal and state guidelines for evaluating the admissibility of expert testimony
- The use of **amicus curiae** briefs

Expert witnesses are often called upon in court to provide evidence in a range of criminal and civil cases. Expert evidence is often a critical component of a criminal or civil trial. Indeed, the use of experts can have an impact on the outcome of a case. Kovera, Russano, and McAuliff (2002) summarize research that shows that the introduction of expert testimony does influence jury decisions. Expert testimony introduced by the prosecution tends to increase conviction rates, while defense experts tend to decrease the likelihood of conviction. Schuller and Hastings (1996), in a mock jury study, found that expert testimony about battered woman syndrome, compared to a no expert control group, was associated with more lenient verdicts and more favorable evaluations of the defendant's claim of self-defense.

The need for expert testimony is based on the belief that experts have specialized knowledge that is beyond the ordinary knowledge and understanding of a judge and/or jury. Indeed, research suggests that jurors not only lack certain critical information, but may also hold incorrect beliefs, assumptions, or expectations. In an ideal world, experts would present evidence that is based on reliable and valid science. As we see in this chapter, the real world of the courtroom may fall short of this ideal. For this reason, the courts have established a number of rules for determining whether scientific evidence should be admitted. Before reviewing these rules, we will discuss more general issues related to the roles that experts might play in court.

ROLES OF EXPERT WITNESSES

Experts can be asked to testify in court in several different ways. One is to provide testimony resulting from an evaluation of a criminal defendant or a plaintiff in a civil case. For example, a forensic psychologist might testify about the results of an evaluation of a defendant's competency to stand trial or a plaintiff's psychological functioning in a civil suit involving damages resulting from a traumatic event. A second type of testimony involves an expert in an educative role providing information about psychological research. For example, an expert might testify about the research on the reliability and validity of eyewitness testimony or the effect that media coverage prior to trial might have on jury decisions.

Saks (1990) discussed the dilemmas and pitfalls faced by expert witnesses, and he identified three possible roles that expert witnesses can adopt:

1. *Mere Conduit/Educator.* "My first duty is to share the most faithful picture of my field's knowledge with those who have been assigned the responsibility to make the decisions. To do this may be to be a mere technocrat, rather than a complete human being concerned with the moral implications of what I say and with the greater good of society. The central difficulty of this role is whether it is all right for me to contribute hard-won knowledge to causes I would just as soon see lose" (p. 295).

2. *Philosopher-Ruler/Advocate.* "There is a greater good at stake in this case, and that is (fill in the blank: desegregating schools, seeing to it that this child goes to the right home, keeping people from being executed, seeing to it that people are executed, etc.). I must advocate for those outcomes, and that obviously means giving testimony that involves clever editing, selecting, shading, exaggerating, or glossing over" (p. 296). Chesler, Sanders, and Kalmuss (1989) comment that experts may rationalize adopting this role because of the adversarial nature of the courtroom: "I understood the partisan nature of the courtroom and I realized that I would be on the stand arguing for a position without also presenting evidence that might be contrary to my . . . side. But you see, that didn't bother me, because I knew that the other side was also doing that" (p. 1271).

3. *Hired Gun.* "This role is much like the one immediately preceding, but the hired gun works in the service of someone else's values rather than advancing his or her own. This role sees the job this way: I must do what I can to help the people who hired me. This style of expert witnessing raises the question of whether it is all right to mislead in a cause in which one does not believe" (p. 296).

Saks adds a fourth category, but concluded that as a practical matter, this type does not exist in practice. This role is considered to be the ideal circumstance for an expert witness:

> Everything is in harmony, no dilemmas, you can have your cake and eat it too. The data are so helpful to a cause you believe in that you can be entirely forthcoming about them. This fourth cell is a triviality precisely because it presents no choices. An expert who would testify only under the harmonious conditions of this cell raises a different ethical problem, for which lawyers have a more ready answer than we do. As a practical matter, however, this cell does not exist. No matter how good the data are, they never are good enough for an advocate's purposes. Pressures may develop to stretch or to overstate, or to make more clear and unambiguous data that are never altogether clear and unambiguous. (p. 297)

The dilemma for experts is that working in an adversarial legal system places unique demands and expectations on experts. Saks (1990) summarizes the difficulties faced by expert witnesses:

> The black-letter rules of law are clear enough in their prescription for the behavior of experts who are witnesses at trial: They are to be witnesses and not advocates. And yet the process by which experts are selected, retained, and prepared for trial inevitably socializes them into feeling as if they are members of the adversary team. The law says be a witness, but the process by which experts become witnesses sends them the opposite message. Typically, the message that they owe their first loyalty to the fact finders and not to the party that hired them is delivered only as they take the witness stand. Yet missing that fundamental point is unlikely to have immediate consequences for the individual expert. (p. 309)

The Role of Psychologists as Experts in Court

Although psychologists have testified in court for over 100 years (see discussion in Chapter 1), their testimony was largely restricted to the interpretation of psychological tests (Smith, 1976). Testifying about issues such as the insanity defense was generally not permitted, in large part because the courts viewed this as falling within the domain of the medical profession, notably psychiatrists. *People v. Hawthorne* (1940) is illustrative of the court's view. In *Hawthorne*, a psychologist's testimony was restricted to observations from an evaluation of the defendant, but the psychologist could not offer an opinion on the defendant's mental state at the time of the offense. The court noted that insanity was a *disease*, and physicians, not psychologists, were qualified to make diagnoses about diseases. However, this ruling was appealed, and the appeals court overturned the decision of the lower court.

In the *Hawthorne* decision, Judge Butzel wrote, "I do not think it can be said that his [the psychologist's] ability to detect insanity is inferior to that of a medical man whose experience along such lines is not so intensive" (p. 208), and added that "There is no magic in particular titles or degrees, and in our age of intense scientific specialization we might deny ourselves the use of the best knowledge available by a rule that would immutably fix the educational qualifications to a particular degree" (p. 209).

This decision was not viewed positively by the American Psychiatric Association, which would argue over the next 20 years that psychologists were not competent to offer diagnostic opinions, and further, that the proper role of psychologists was to serve in the role of an assistant or helpmate to the psychiatrist, as the latter had the ultimate authority for patients. In 1954, the American Psychiatric Association passed a Resolution that emphasized that mental disorders are, like physical ailments, *illnesses*, which must be diagnosed and treated by physicians. The resolution commented that

> Other professional groups such as psychologists, teachers, ministers, lawyers, social workers, and vocational counselors, of course, use psychological understanding in carrying out their professional functions. Members of these professional groups are not thereby practicing medicine. The application of psychological methods to the treatment of illness is a medical function. Any physician may utilize the skills of others in his professional work, but he remains responsible, legally and morally, for the diagnosis and for the treatment of his patient. The medical profession fully endorses the appropriate utilization of the skills of psychologists, social workers, and other professional personnel in contributing roles in settings directly supervised by physicians. It further recognizes that these professions are entirely independent and autonomous when medical questions are not involved; but, when members of these professions contribute to the diagnosis and treatment of illness, their professional contributions must be coordinated under medical responsibility. (obtained from http://www.psych.org/edu/other_res/lib_archives/archives/195702.pdf)

In a resolution passed in 1964, the American Psychiatric Association discussed the principles underlying the relationship between psychiatrists and psychologists. The resolution again emphasized the point made clear that the physician had the primary and ultimate authority in defining patient care:

> To place the most critical aspect of the problem under specific discussion in its proper perspective, namely the professional need for cooperatively

defining and respecting the areas of activity and responsibility for scientists who participate in the care of the patient, it must be fully realized that physicians have the ultimate responsibility for patient care, and that they, and they alone, are trained to assume this responsibility. In the public interest, other scientists, when contributing to this patient care, must recognize and respect this ultimate responsibility. (obtained from http://www.psych.org/edu/other_res/lib_archives/archives/196401.pdf)

It is of particular interest that this 1964 resolution was passed after the case of *Jenkins v. the United States* was decided in 1962. This case established the independent role of psychologists as experts in matters related to diagnosis of mental disease. In *Jenkins*, the defendant was charged with assault and breaking into a house. At the trial, the defense called three psychologists and two psychiatrists to testify about the defendant's sanity. All three psychologists testified that the defendant met the criteria for a diagnosis of schizophrenia, and two of the three psychologists testified that the crimes were a product of the defendant's mental illness. The trial judge instructed the jury to disregard the psychologists' testimony, stating that psychologists are not qualified to diagnose mental disease.

The case was appealed and the American Psychological Association prepared an *amicus curiae* brief (see discussion later in this chapter), which asserted that psychology was a well-established discipline grounded in the science of human behavior, and that clinical psychologists were, by training, competent to offer opinions on mental status and causal relationships of mental status and criminal behavior. The American Psychiatric Association filed its own brief, which made a point similar to its resolution in 1964, that psychiatrists are the only profession competent to provide expert medical opinions about mental disease.

The U.S. Court of Appeals held that the trial court, by excluding psychological testimony, had erred. It directed that a psychologist's lack of medical training could not, in and of itself, be used to justify an automatic disqualification of psychological testimony. Instead, it asserted that such decisions must be made by looking at the knowledge and experience of a particular witness, and the probative value of his or her opinion.

The groundbreaking case of *Jenkins* opened the courtroom doors to psychologists, and in many ways set the stage for the rapid development of the field of forensic psychology that has taken place since the 1960s. It is important to remember, however, that *Jenkins* did not allow the automatic qualification of psychologists as experts who could offer opinions about diagnosis. Rather, the *Jenkins* decision clearly specified a case-by-case approach, in which an expert's qualification would be evaluated in the context of the specific issues before a particular court. Nevertheless, it is now generally accepted that psychologists can qualify as experts on matters related to issues such as competence to stand trial and criminal responsibility, as a survey by Farkas, DeLeon, and Newman (1997) found that all but three U.S. states allow psychologists to testify on these matters.

Admissibility of Expert Testimony

Psychologists (and other experts) must meet certain legal criteria in order to be qualified as an expert and be allowed to testify in court. These criteria have been established through several court decisions and federal guidelines. These criteria will be reviewed in the following sections.

The Frye Test

The earliest standard for the admissibility of expert testimony was established in 1923 in the case of *Frye v. United States*. In this case, the defense asked to introduce evidence from an expert who would testify about the results of a physiological deception test, the results of which, the defense claimed, would support the defendant's innocence. The expert in this case was prepared to testify that the research supported the use of polygraph results to detect deception. The prosecution objected and the court did not allow the expert's testimony. The appeal was considered by the Court of Appeals of the District of Columbia. The appeals court, in considering whether this evidence should have been admitted, established what has become known as the Frye Rule:

> Just when a scientific principle or discovery crosses the line between the experimental and demonstrable stages is difficult to define. Somewhere in this twilight zone the evidential force of the principle must be recognized, and while courts will go a long way in admitting expert testimony deduced from a well-recognized scientific principle or discovery, the thing from which the deduction is made must be sufficiently established to have gained general acceptance in the particular field in which it belongs.

This is also known as the **general acceptance** test. In the *Frye* case, the appeals court held that the trial court did not err in denying this testimony, concluding that "We think the systolic blood pressure deception test has not yet gained such standing and scientific recognition among physiological and psychological authorities as would justify the courts in admitting expert testimony deduced from the discovery, development, and experiments thus far made." The **Frye test** is considered a conservative test of admissibility, and critics have suggested that it excludes evidence that is novel yet still reliable and valid (Melton, Petrila, Poythress, & Slobogin, 2007). The Frye test has been replaced in most states by the test established in the **Daubert** decision, which is discussed later in this section.

Federal Rules of Evidence

These rules govern the introduction of evidence in civil and criminal proceedings in federal courts, although many state statutes are modeled on these rules. There are two rules that focus on the admissibility of expert testimony.

Rule 702 Testimony by experts. If scientific, technical, or other specialized knowledge will assist the trier of fact to understand the evidence or to determine a fact in issue, a witness qualified as an expert by knowledge, skill, experience, training, or education, may testify thereto in the form of an opinion or otherwise, if (1) the testimony is sufficiently based upon reliable facts or data, (2) the testimony is the product of reliable principles and methods, and (3) the witness has applied the principles and methods reliably to the facts of the case.

*Rule 703 Bases of **Opinion Testimony** by Experts*. The facts or data in the particular case upon which an expert bases an opinion or inference may be those perceived by or made known to the expert at or before the hearing. If the facts or data are of a type reasonably relied upon by experts in the particular field in forming opinions or inferences upon the subject, they need not be admissible in evidence in order for the opinion or inference to be admitted. Facts or data that are otherwise inadmissible shall not be disclosed to the jury by the proponent of the opinion or inference unless the court determines that their probative value in assisting the jury to evaluate the expert's opinion substantially outweighs their prejudicial impact.

Daubert v. Merrell Dow Pharmaceuticals *(1993)*

In this case, Jason Daubert and Eric Schuller, who were minor children born with serious birth defects, and their parents sued Merrell Dow Pharmaceuticals in California state court, alleging that the birth defects had been caused by the mothers' ingestion of a prescription antinausea drug marketed by the drug company. In trial, Merrell Dow introduced the testimony of an expert who presented a literature review concluding that maternal use of the drug during the first trimester of pregnancy was not a risk factor for human birth defects. The plaintiffs countered with eight experts who testified about research showing that the drug could cause birth defects. The District Court granted Merrell Dow's motion for summary judgment, ruling that the testimony of the plaintiff's experts did not meet the general acceptance test.

First, the Supreme Court ruled that the **Federal Rules of Evidence**, and not *Frye*, is the standard for admitting expert scientific testimony in a federal trial, and further, that *Frye*'s general acceptance test was superseded by the Rules' adoption.

Next, the Supreme Court established four criteria to assist judges in evaluating the admissibility of scientific evidence in court. In effect, *Daubert* established the role of the trial court judge as a gatekeeper to ensure that expert evidence is admitted only if it is scientifically valid. The four criteria judges should apply in making this determination are:

1. Whether the theory or technique can be (and has been) tested empirically. Citing psychologists such as Karl Popper, the Court discussed the importance of falsifiability through experimental testing.
2. Whether the theory or technique has been subjected to peer review and publication. The Court noted that publication is not necessarily a requirement for admissibility, as some propositions may be too new or of limited interest to be published. Nonetheless, the Court emphasized that "submission to the scrutiny of the scientific community is a component of 'good science,' in part because it increases the likelihood that substantive flaws in methodology will be detected. . . . The fact of publication (or lack thereof) in a peer reviewed journal thus will be a relevant, though not dispositive, consideration in assessing the scientific validity of a particular technique or methodology on which an opinion is premised."
3. Whether the particular scientific technique has a known or potential rate of error, and the existence and maintenance of standards controlling the technique's operation.
4. Consideration of general acceptance within a relevant scientific community. The Court noted that widespread acceptance can be an important factor in ruling particular evidence admissible, but a known technique that has only minimal support within the community may properly be viewed with skepticism.

The Court of Appeals affirmed the district court judge's decision. The Supreme Court, noting that the District Court and the Court of Appeals focused almost exclusively on "general acceptance" as gauged by publication and the decisions of other courts, vacated (i.e., set aside or annul an order or judgment which the Court finds was improper) the judgment of the Court of Appeals and remanded the case back to trial court for further proceedings consistent with its opinion.

The *Daubert* decision also addressed concerns expressed by the parties involved in the case and by the briefs submitted to the Court that abandoning the general acceptance test as the sole test for admissibility would result "in a 'free for all' in which befuddled juries are confounded by absurd and irrational pseudoscientific assertions." The Court commented that "In this regard respondent seems to us to be overly pessimistic about the capabilities of the jury, and of the adversary system generally. Vigorous cross-examination, presentation of contrary evidence, and careful instruction on the burden of proof are the traditional and appropriate means of attacking shaky but admissible evidence."

Daubert is legally binding in federal courts but states may choose whether to adopt this standard. Indeed, some states have adopted *Daubert*, other states retain the Frye standard, and still others have adopted their own standards of admissibility. The differences in state standards allow a natural comparison of whether the type of standard makes a difference. In other words, are there differences in admission of expert testimony under the two primary standards? Cheng and Yoon (2005) conducted a study of state courts to answer this question. They found that a state's adoption of *Frye* or *Daubert* did not make a difference in practice. They concluded that:

> The results of this study are consistent with the theory that the power of the Supreme Court's *Daubert* decision was not so much in its formal doctrinal test, but rather in its ability to create greater awareness of the problems of junk science. This suggests that courts apply some generalized level of scrutiny when considering the reliability of scientific evidence, regardless of the governing standard. (p. 503)

It would follow from Cheng and Yoon's conclusion about judges' heightened awareness of the problems of junk science that it should translate to an increased scrutiny of experts. Dixon and Gill (2002) provide empirical support for this, as they found that post-*Daubert*, there was an increase in both the proportion of challenged evidence in which reliability was discussed and the proportion of expert evidence found unreliable. Dixon and Gill concluded that "It appears that once judges started acting as more vigilant gatekeepers, they became more careful in examining relevance, qualifications, and other considerations for admitting evidence, in addition to reliability" (p. 298).

Despite the fact that there might be some confusion about the application of the *Daubert* criteria, it seems that judges are scrutinizing experts more carefully. Krafka, Dunn, Johnson, Cecil, and Miletich (2002) conducted two surveys of federal judges, one two years before the *Daubert* decision and one in 1998. They reported that one-third of the judges in 1998 said they admitted expert evidence less often than they did before *Daubert*. This was supported by their decisions, as judges in 1998 permitted 59% of cases to proceed to trial without limitation on the evidence, compared to a 75% rate in the earlier survey.

General Electric Co. v. Joiner *(1997)*

This case established the trial judge's role in determining admissibility of expert testimony. In this case, the U.S. Supreme Court held that a court of appeals could not overturn a trial court's decision about admissibility unless it determined that it abused its discretion in applying *Daubert*. When *Kumho* was decided two years later, this case became part of what is known as the *Daubert trilogy*.

Kumho Tire Company v. Carmichael *(1999)*

The *Daubert* decision left open the question that many mental health professionals asked, which was whether the *Daubert* criteria was limited to scientific testimony or would apply to all expert testimony? *Kumho Tire* was a civil product liability case against a tire manufacturer. A tire blowout was alleged to have caused an accident resulting in injuries to several individuals and one death. An expert testified that the blowout was the result of a defect in the tire's design. The trial court ruled that the expert's methodology, involving observational and technical information about tire design and wear, did not satisfy *Daubert's* reliability criteria, so it was not admissible. The U.S. Supreme Court reviewed the case and its decision emphasized the flexibility of the *Daubert* criteria, and also held that *Daubert* could not logically be applied to all types of expert testimony. Specifically, the Court ruled that a trial judge can use any other factors he or she deemed appropriate when evaluating the admissibility of an expert who might base conclusions from observations based on extensive and specialized experience. *Kumho Tire* established the trial judge's role as a gatekeeper and applied it to all expert testimony, including testimony that might be considered nonscientific. Thus, *Kumho Tire* clearly provides a basis for the admissibility of expert testimony based on clinical observations and evaluations.

Opinion Testimony

Previously, we discussed two of the Federal Rules of Evidence dealing with the admissibility of expert evidence. A third rule focuses specifically on the issue of whether an expert can offer an opinion on the ultimate issue before the courts (e.g., the defendant is incompetent to stand trial).

Rule 704 Opinion on Ultimate Issue. This rule deals with whether an expert can provide an opinion about the ultimate issue before the court. There are two parts to this rule:

a. Except as provided in subdivision (b), testimony in the form of an opinion or inference otherwise admissible is not objectionable because it embraces an ultimate issue to be decided by the trier of fact.
b. No expert witness testifying with respect to the mental state or condition of a defendant in a criminal case may state an opinion or inference as to whether the defendant did or did not have the mental state or condition constituting an element of the crime charged or of a defense thereto. Such ultimate issues are matters for the trier of fact alone.

The issue of whether experts should give an opinion about an ultimate legal issue (e.g., whether the defendant is competent or incompetent) has long been debated among mental health professionals and legal scholars (Bazelon, 1974; Melton et al., 2007; Morse, 1978; Slobogin, 1989). Rule 704(a) allows experts to give opinions about an ultimate issue before the court, such as whether a defendant is competent to stand trial. However, Rule 704(b) provides an exception, that an expert cannot provide an opinion about mental state with respect to the issue of criminal responsibility (e.g., an insanity defense). Melton et al. (2007) take the position that this evidentiary prohibition should apply to all types of cases. Those who believe that forensic evaluators should not offer an opinion on the ultimate legal issue argue that evaluators can offer scientific and clinical opinions but that legal decisions (which encompass moral and social considerations) are beyond their area of expertise. To offer an opinion on the ultimate legal issue of a defendant's competency would be to intrude on the role of the legal fact finder. Grisso (2003) noted that the question of *"how much of a deficit in abilities is enough to justify the restriction of individual liberties?"* requires a social and moral judgment, as it cannot be answered without applying personal values (p. 15).

On the other hand, those who believe that forensic evaluators should offer an opinion on the ultimate legal issue argue that the fact finder should be able to consider all available information, including ultimate opinions of forensic evaluators, and weigh the evidence accordingly when arriving at a final determination on the issue. No requirement that the fact finder accept the evaluator's opinion on the ultimate issue exists. In addition, stating an opinion on the ultimate issue might assist the fact finder in following the evaluator's testimony since the direction of the testimony is made obvious.

Despite guidelines prohibiting some forms of ultimate opinion testimony, the courts often encourage such testimony (Redding, Floyd, & Hawk, 2001). Forensic professionals themselves do not agree about whether ultimate opinions should be provided to the court. Approximately 25% of the forensic experts surveyed by Borum and Grisso (1996) indicated that ultimate opinions were to be avoided, whereas the other 75% were either neutral on the issue or believed it was important to offer such opinions. Robbins, Waters, and Herbert (1997) found that about 90% of the competency evaluation reports they examined offered ultimate opinions and Skeem, Golding, Cohn, and Berge (1998) noted that ultimate opinions were offered in about 75% of the reports they examined.

Judges as Gatekeepers

How effective are judges as gatekeepers? Justice Rehnquist, in his dissent in *Daubert*, commented on his skepticism about the ability of judges to apply the criteria specified in *Daubert*. He commented that:

> I defer to no one in my confidence in federal judges; but I am at a loss to know what is meant when it is said that the scientific status of a theory depends on its "falsifiability," and I suspect some of them will be, too. I do not doubt that Rule 702 confides to the judge some gatekeeping responsibility in deciding questions of the admissibility of proffered expert testimony. But I do not think it imposes on them either the obligation or the authority to become amateur scientists in order to perform that role. (p. 600)

The results of several studies by Margaret Kovera and her colleagues provide support for Justice Rehnquist's reservations, as her research suggests that judges may not recognize flawed research when they confront it and they may indeed admit invalid research into evidence. Kovera and McAuliff (2000) presented a description of expert testimony in a hostile work environment sexual harassment case to Florida judges. They manipulated the description of a research study that would be part of the expert's testimony. Judges received descriptions containing one of three methodological flaws and also manipulated whether the study had been subject to peer review. They found that the judges' ratings of the quality of the research did not differ as a function of the manipulations of methodological quality. Kovera et al. (2002) summarized their research showing similar results for attorneys and jurors, as neither group demonstrated an ability to recognize research flaws.

Surveys have also been conducted that provide confirmation that judges may find it difficult to apply the *Daubert* criteria. Gatowski et al. (2001) obtained a national survey of 400 state court judges to obtain information about their understanding of the *Daubert* guidelines and how they would apply them when evaluating the admissibility of scientific evidence. Nearly all the surveyed judges expressed support for the gatekeeping role established by *Daubert*, and they also reported that they found the *Daubert* criteria useful guidelines for determining the admissibility of expert testimony. Despite their acceptance of *Daubert*, the survey also found that judges had difficulty defining the four *Daubert* criteria, especially falsifiability and error rate. Gatowski and colleagues concluded that their survey points to the need for judicial education about how to evaluate research:

> What judges need to know is not how to design the best scientific study, but how to evaluate imperfect ones. Judges do not need to be trained to become scientists, they need to be trained to be critical consumers of the science that comes before them. Judges need to know what critical questions to ask, they need to know what methodological and statistical issues scientific experts, and other purveyors of science, should address and comment on when proffering science for use in the court. Judges need to know what to listen and look for when expert evidence is presented and what they should be asking about when the information is not forthcoming. (p. 455)

On the Witness Stand

An expert witness may be asked to provide a court with information that may assist in the court's understanding of a particular issue. An expert might be asked to summarize the psychological research on a particular topic, such as eyewitness testimony. A forensic expert may be asked to testify about the findings of an evaluation of an issue before the court, such as a defendant's competency to stand trial. Due to the adversarial nature of the judicial system, expert testimony can be a stressful experience (see Loftus, 1986, and Loftus & Ketchum, 1991, for a discussion of the experiences of an expert witness).

Prior to testimony, an expert must be qualified as a witness. The court will apply either the *Daubert* or *Frye* criteria, depending on which is applicable in a given jurisdiction. Once qualified, the expert will present his or her findings in the direct examination by the defense or prosecution (depending on which side asked the expert to provide services), and that is followed by the cross-examination which is led by the opposing side. The primary purpose of a cross-examination is to challenge the findings or opinions of the expert. A number of books are available to help experts and attorneys prepare for and cope with cross-examination (e.g., Brodsky, 1991; Ceci & Hembrooke, 1998; Stern, 1997; Tsushima & Anderson, 1996; Ziskin & Faust, 1997). These resources provide excellent information on the role of the expert witness and include descriptions of possible rebuttal tactics to cross-examination questions, including numerous references and examples of how the expert can respond.

INFLUENCING THE LEGAL SYSTEM

Psychological research might influence court decisions or legal policy in a number of ways. First, psychological research can have an indirect influence. It is indirect because researchers do not take an active role in directly communicating their research results to the judiciary. Rather, research is published in journal articles, books, or even popular periodicals, and judges may cite them as secondary sources for their opinions. Ellsworth and Getman (1987) argue that perhaps the greatest impact may occur when research is so widely disseminated and accepted in the community at large that judges consider them to be truisms. However, since judges or legislators rarely read social science journals, this method of influencing the legal system may not have a substantial impact. Second, psychologists can communicate research results to the legal system directly by providing expert testimony. Psychologists who have specialized knowledge about a particular issue before the courts may be asked to provide expert testimony. They may, for example, summarize research on the reliability and validity of eyewitness testimony, or the effects of sexual harassment on workers. Third, psychologists can participate in the preparation of what are referred to as *amicus curiae* briefs. These briefs summarize research on a given issue before the courts.

Amicus Curiae Briefs

Amicus curiae briefs are also known as "friends of the court" briefs. A *brief* is a written document that is presented to a court, prepared by a group or organization that is not a party to the litigation. Briefs typically summarize the body of research that might address a particular issue before the court. Briefs have been submitted by diverse interest and professional groups (see Box 11.1). The American Psychological Association, through its Committee on Legal Issues (COLI) has prepared numerous briefs to court cases involving a diverse range of topics, including the juvenile death penalty; competence to be executed; school desegregation; same-sex marriages; gay, lesbian, and bisexual parenting; battered woman's syndrome; abortion; child witnesses; and affirmative action (see the APA web site link at the end of this chapter for a list of all briefs). Since 1962, when the APA submitted its first brief in the *Jenkins* case discussed earlier in this chapter, APA has submitted over 160 briefs, with over half submitted to the Supreme Court.

Bersoff and Ogden (1991) identified five functions of briefs:

1. Briefs can supply information not readily available to the parties in the case.

Box 11.1 Example of an American Psychological Association Brief

Comfort v. Lynn School Committee; Bollen v. Lynn School Committee (U.S. Court of Appeals for the First Circuit)

This case involves a school voluntary desegregation plan in Lynn, Massachusetts, that uses race as a factor in assigning children to K–12 schools in the event that they do not want to attend their local neighborhood school and request a transfer. APA's brief presents social, psychological, and developmental research as a backdrop for the court's consideration of the Plan. Central to the discussion is the "Intergroup Contact Hypothesis," including recent meta-analytic research linking intergroup contact under appropriate conditions with decreased levels of intergroup prejudice. The brief also educates the court concerning some of the processes involved in prejudice and discriminatory behavior, including negative stereotypes, in-group bias, aversive racism, intergroup anxiety, and implicit stereotypes. The relationship between cross-race friendships and reduced prejudice and negative stereotypes in children, and the importance of intergroup contact for the development of children's social and moral reasoning are also included to assist the court's thinking. Finally, the brief discusses the ineffectiveness of several alternatives to the Plan advanced by the appellants related to their argument that integrated classrooms were not necessary.

Source: http://www.apa.org/psyclaw/issues.html.

---

2. Briefs can develop and enlarge arguments that a party, because of limits in the amount of space it is allotted in its own brief, is forced to make in summary form.
3. Briefs can present arguments that a party would like to make but cannot make itself because it lacks the resources, data, or credibility to do so.
4. Briefs can present arguments that a party prefers not to make.
5. Briefs can inform the court of the broader policy interests involved in a case, or of broader implications of its holding.

Roesch, Golding, Hans, and Reppucci (1991) suggested that briefs may be analyzed along a continuum. At one end is a *science translation* brief, which is intended to be an objective summary of a body of research. At the other end is an *advocacy* brief, which takes a clear position on some legal or public policy issue. Some briefs may attempt to be neutral in their portrayal of a body of literature, but many are more adversarial in nature. Indeed, some have argued that adversarial briefs represent the predominant method (see Tremper, 1987, for a review), a perception that may lead judges to regard briefs as suspect. Our view is that all briefs must evaluate and interpret research, so the distinction between science translation and advocacy briefs may often be blurred. Although it is a laudable goal to strive to represent a body of research objectively, even a science translation brief will reflect the knowledge, perspectives, and values of the brief writers.

Suedfeld and Tetlock (1992) summarized the arguments against advocacy briefs: "These include the danger of degrading the level of psychological discourse, the infringement of the ethics of scientific/professional roles, and possible negative repercussions for psychology itself if its practitioners get too embroiled in policy debates" (p. 4).

Melton and Saks (1990) discussed the difficulties in deciding how much interpretation versus summary a brief should contain:

> Either alternative can end up misleading a reader, especially a law reader, which is what the judges are when they read these kinds of briefs. The solution, we think, is in approaching the writing with an honest desire to share with the courts a faithful picture of the available psychological knowledge, and to interpret the research only to the extent that doing so will clarify its meaning. (p. 5)

Suedfield and Tetlock (1992) also suggested a more cautious approach. They commented that "We are comfortable with psychology taking on the role of compiling and disseminating information . . . we are much less comfortable with the idea that the discipline should act as a policy advocate" (p. 10). In contrast, Roesch et al. (1991) have suggested that it may be possible to balance the roles of science and advocacy. They wrote:

> It is possible to be scientific without being neutral, to be objective yet form an opinion about the implications of the research. If the data warrant a particular conclusion, then it may be reasonable for brief writers to advocate for a legal decision that would reflect the knowledge gained from the research. (p. 12)

Elizabeth Loftus, a psychologist who has testified in numerous cases involving issues such as eyewitness testimony and recovered memory (Loftus, 1986), has commented on the advocacy versus impartial role of experts in the context of courtroom testimony. She questioned, "Should a psychologist in a court of law act as an advocate for the defense or an impartial educator? My answer to that question is *both*. If I believe a defendant is innocent, if I believe in his innocence with all my heart and soul, then I probably can't help but become an advocate of sorts" (p. 238).

An Example of a Brief

To illustrate the use of briefs, we will highlight the brief submitted by the American Psychological Association in an adolescent death penalty case. In *Roper v. Simmons* (2005), the U.S. Supreme Court considered whether

---

**Box 11.2 Summary of APA Brief in
Roper v. Simmons**

Adolescents, as a group, think and behave differently from adults in ways that undermine the court's constitutional rationale for capital punishment in cases of adolescent offenders.

Adolescence is a period in which character is forming and often involves heightened risk taking and even criminal conduct, which are moderated or eliminated by the individual in adulthood.

Adolescent decision makers on average are less future oriented and less likely to consider properly the consequences of their actions.

Neuropsychological research demonstrates that the adolescent brain has not reached adult maturity.

Given that 16- and 17-year-olds as a group are less mature developmentally than adults, imposing capital punishment on such adolescents does not serve the judicially recognized purposes of the sanction.

The unsettled nature of adolescent personality confounds attempts to make sufficiently reliable determinations about the character and future behavior of adolescent defendants to support execution.

The lapse of time between a crime and sentencing tends to complicate assessment of the adolescent capital defendant.

Unconscious racism may falsely attribute greater culpability to African American adolescent offenders.

---

it was permissible, under the U.S. Constitution, to execute a juvenile offender (older than 15 but younger than 18) when a capital crime was committed. Christopher Simmons was 17 years old when he murdered a woman during an attempt to burglarize her home. Due to his age, he was automatically raised to adult court in the state of Missouri. Simmons confessed to the crime and was sentenced to death.

The APA brief reviewed the developmental research that shows that adolescents have considerably less capacity than adults in terms of judgment and decision making (see Box 11.2). A number of key findings from psychological research were highlighted. Adolescence is marked by an increase in risk taking (Arnett, 1992), including engaging in criminal behavior. As Moffitt (1993) notes, this involvement in criminal activity, particularly when initiated in adolescence rather than childhood, typically does not persist into adulthood, and may reflect the fact that adolescents are immature and more heavily influenced by peers (Haynie, 2002). Adolescents are also less future oriented, and are less likely to weigh the consequences of their decisions (Cauffman & Steinberg, 2000). In other words, they often act impulsively. One compelling explanation for these differences between adolescents and adults is that cognitive capacities of adolescents are simply underdeveloped. Recent research on brain development shows that adolescent brains have not reached adult maturity, particularly in the frontal lobes, which control executive functions of the brain related to decision making (Giedd et al., 1999). This area of the brain is typically not fully developed until the person is in his or her early twenties. Research suggests that younger children and adolescents are simply less likely to think strategically about their decisions (Peterson-Badali & Abramovitch, 1993). As adolescents mature, they typically become better problem solvers, are less influenced by peers, less impulsive, and more sophisticated in the way they think.

The Supreme Court considered this brief as well as briefs from other groups and oral testimony. The Court held, in a 5–4 decision, that those under 18 cannot be executed. The key issues cited by the Court were:

- Adolescents are overrepresented statistically in virtually every category of reckless behavior.
- Almost every state prohibits those under 18 years of age from voting, serving on juries, or marrying without parental consent—in recognition of comparative immaturity and irresponsibility of juveniles.
- Juveniles are also more vulnerable or susceptible to negative influences and outside pressures, including peer pressure.
- Youth as a mitigating factor: the signature qualities of youth are transient. As they mature, recklessness may subside. Likelihood that a teenage offender has made cost–benefit analysis that attaches any weight to the possibility of execution is virtually nonexistent.

The *Simmons* case appears to have been highly influenced by the psychological research that was presented in the APA brief. But not all Supreme Court Justices agreed about how the psychological research could or should be applied to individual cases. In his dissent, Justice Scalia wrote that:

> Even putting aside questions of methodology, the studies cited by the Court offer scant support for a categorical prohibition of the death penalty for murderers under 18. At most, these studies conclude that, *on average*, or *in most cases*, persons under 18 are unable to take moral responsibility for their actions. Not one of the cited studies opines that all individuals under 18 are unable to appreciate the nature of their crimes.

Justice Scalia's dissent highlights the problems in applying psychological research to legal cases. Psychological research is primarily based on group differences, and we are well aware of the considerable variation within groups. Research shows, for example, that on average, adolescents are less capable decision makers than adults. But the law deals only with the individual case, so judges want to know only about the individual case before them. In this sense, Justice Scalia is quite correct—we cannot generalize the research cited in the APA brief to an individual such as Christopher Simmons.

Another criticism of *amicus curiae* briefs is that organizations submitting briefs have not been consistent in their interpretation and application of research results. For example, the American Psychological Association submitted briefs in *Thornburgh v. American College of Gynecologists and Obstetricians* (1986) and *Hartigan v. Zbaraz* (1986). Both cases involved the rights of adolescents to consent to an abortion. As summarized by Gardner, Scherer, and Tester (1989), the briefs concluded that cognitive developmental theory implies that most adolescents are competent to make abortion decisions, and that research shows that most adolescents are capable of making sound decisions about health care, including decisions about abortions.

The briefs were criticized for their claim that "there are authoritative grounds for the positive assertion that adolescents and adults have equivalent decision-making competence" (Gardner et al., 1989, p. 897). Contrast this with the APA brief in the *Simmons* case, which concluded that adolescents do not have the same decision-making capacity as adults (see Box 11.2). To be sure, there was considerable research in the years between the abortion and death penalty briefs, so this may have led to different conclusions about adolescent decision making. To the extent that this is true, it points to another reason that courts have been reluctant to rely on social science research in its decisions. If results and implications of research change over time, courts may view social science research as too unstable to apply to legal decisions.

SUMMARY

The focus of this chapter was on the role that expert witnesses may play in civil and criminal cases. The standards for admitting expert testimony were reviewed. One controversial issue centers around whether experts should be allowed to provide an opinion about the ultimate issue before a court. The use of *amicus curiae* briefs was also discussed. Briefs provide an alternative to court testimony as a way of introducing psychological research that may be relevant to a legal issue before a court. The brief in the juvenile death penalty case of *Roper v. Simmons* was presented to illustrate how psychological research can be conveyed to the court.

SUGGESTED READINGS AND WEBSITES

American Psychological Association, list of briefs. http://www.apa.org/psyclaw/issues.html.

Bazelon, D. L. (1974). Psychiatrists and the adversary process. *Scientific American, 230*, 18–23.

Faust, D., & Ziskin, J. (1988). The expert witness is psychology and psychiatry. *Science, 241*, 31–35.

Loftus, E. F. (1986). Ten years in the life of an expert witness. *Law and Human Behavior, 10,* 241–263.

Roesch, R., Golding, S. L., Hans, V. P., & Reppucci, N. D. (1991). Social science and the courts: The role of *amicus curiae* briefs. *Law and Human Behavior, 15,* 1–11.

KEY TERMS

- *Amicus curiae brief*
- *Daubert*
- *Expert witness*
- *Federal Rules of Evidence*
- *Frye test*
- *General acceptance*
- *Opinion testimony*

References

Arnett, J. (1992). Reckless behavior in adolescence: A developmental perspective. *Developmental Review, 12,* 339–373.

Bazelon, D. L. (1974). Psychiatrists and the adversary process. *Scientific American, 230,* 18–23.

Bersoff, D. N., & Ogden, D. W. (1991). APA *amicus curiae* briefs: Furthering lesbian and gay male civil rights. *American Psychologist, 46,* 950–956.

Borum, R., & Grisso, T. (1996). Establishing standards for criminal forensic reports: An empirical analysis. *Bulletin of the American Academy of Psychiatry and the Law, 24,* 297–317.

Brodsky, S. L. (1991). *Testifying in court: Guidelines and maxims for the expert witness.* Washington, DC: American Psychological Association.

Cauffman, E., & Steinberg, L. (2000). (Im)maturity of judgment in adolescence: Why adolescents may be less culpable than adults. *Behavioral Sciences and the Law, 18,* 741–760.

Ceci, S. J. & Hembrooke, H. (1998). *What can (and should) be said in court?: Expert witnesses in child abuse cases.* Washington, DC: American Psychological Association.

Cheng, E. K., & Yoon, A. H. (2005). Does Frye or Daubert matter? A study of scientific admissibility standards. *Virginia Law Review, 91,* 471–513.

Chesler, M. A., Sanders, J., & Kalmuss, D. S. (1989). *Social science in court: Mobilizing experts in the school desegregation cases*. Madison: University of Wisconsin Press.

Daubert v. Merrell Dow Pharmaceuticals, Inc., 509 U.S. 579 (1993).

Dixon, L., & Gill, B. (2002). Changes in the standards for admitting expert evidence in federal civil cases since the Daubert decision. *Psychology, Public Policy, and Law, 8*, 251–308.

Ellsworth, P. C., & Getman, J. G. (1987). Social science in legal decision making. In L. Lipson & S. Wheeler (Eds.), *Law and the social sciences* (pp. 581–636). New York: Russell Sage.

Farkas, G. M., DeLeon, P. H., & Newman, R. (1997). Sanity examiner certification: An evolving national agenda. *Professional Psychology: Research and Practice, 28*, 73–76.

Frye v. United States, 293 F. 1013 (D.C. Cir. 1923).

Gardner, W., Scherer, D., & Tester, M. (1989). Asserting scientific authority: Cognitive development and adolescent legal rights. *American Psychologist, 44*, 895–902.

Gatowski, S. I., Dobbin, S. A., Richardson, J. T., Ginsburg, G. P., Merlino, M. L., & Dahir, V. (2001). Asking the gatekeepers: A national survey of judges on judging expert evidence in a post-*Daubert* world. *Law and Human Behavior, 25*, 433–458.

General Electric Co. v. Joiner, 522 U.S. 136 (1997).

Giedd, J., Blumenthal, J., Jeffries, N., Castellanos, F., Liu, H., Ijdenbos, A., Paus, T., Evans, A., & Rapoport, J. (1999). Brain development during childhood and adolescence: A longitudinal MRI study. *Nature Neuroscience, 2*, 861–863.

Grisso, T. (2003). *Evaluating competencies: Forensic assessments and instruments*. New York: Kluwer Academic/Plenum Press.

Hartigan v. Zbaraz, cert. granted, 55 U.S.L.W. 3247 (U.S. Oct. 14, 1986).

Haynie, D. L. (2002). Friendship networks and delinquency: The relative nature of peer delinquency. *Journal of Quantitative Criminology, 18*, 99–123.

Jenkins v. United States, 307 F.2d 637 (D.C. Cir. 1962).

Kovera, M. B., & McAuliff, B. D. (2000). The effects of peer review and evidence quality on judge evaluations of psychological science: Are judges effective gatekeepers? *Journal of Applied Psychology, 85*, 574–586.

Kovera, M. B., Russano, M. B., & McAuliff, B. D. (2002). Assessment of the commonsense psychology underlying Daubert: Legal decision makers' abilities to evaluate expert evidence in hostile work environment cases. *Psychology, Public Policy, and Law, 8*, 180–200.

Krafka C. L., Dunn, M. A., Johnson, M. T., Cecil, J. S., & Miletich, D. (2002). A survey of judges' and attorneys' experiences, in federal civil trials. *Psychology, Public Policy, and Law, 8*, 309–332.

Kumho Tire Company v. Carmichael, 526 U.S. 137 (1999).

Loftus, E. F. (1986). Ten years in the life of an expert witness. *Law and Human Behavior, 10*, 241–263.

Loftus, E. F., & Ketchum, K. (1991). *Witness for the defense: The accused, the eyewitness and the expert who puts memory on trial.* New York: St. Martin's Press.

Melton, G. B., Petrila, J., Poythress, N. G., & Slobogin, C. (2007). *Psychological evaluations for the courts: A handbook for mental health professionals and lawyers* (3rd ed.). New York: Guilford.

Melton, G. B., & Saks, M. J. (1990). AP-LS's pro bono amicus brief project. *American Psychology-Law Society News, 10*, 5.

Moffitt, T. E. (1993). Adolescence-limited and life-course-persistent antisocial behavior: A developmental taxonomy. *Psychological Review, 100*, 674–701.

Morse, S. J. (1978). Law and mental health professionals: The limits of expertise. *Professional Psychology, 9*, 389–399.

People v. Hawthorne, 291 N.W. 205 (Mich. 1940).

Peterson-Badali, M., & Abramovitch, R. (1993). Grade related changes in young people's reasoning about plea decisions. *Law and Human Behavior, 17*, 537–552.

Redding, R. E., Floyd, M. Y., & Hawk, G. L. (2001). What judges and lawyers think about the testimony of mental health experts: A survey of the courts and bar. *Behavioral Sciences & the Law, 19*, 583–594.

Robbins, E., Waters, J., & Herbert, P. (1997). Competency to stand trial evaluations: A study of actual practice in two states. *Journal of the American Academy of Psychiatry and Law, 25*, 469–483.

Roesch, R., Golding, S. L., Hans, V. P., & Reppucci, N. D. (1991). Social science and the courts: The role of *amicus curiae* briefs. *Law and Human Behavior, 15*, 1–11.

Roper v. Simmons, 543 U.S. 541 (2005).

Saks, M. J. (1990). Expert witnesses, nonexpert witnesses, and nonwitness experts. *Law and Human Behavior, 14*, 291–313.

Schuller, R. A., & Hastings, P. A. (1996). Trials of battered women who kill: The impact of alternative forms of expert testimony. *Law and Human Behavior, 2*, 167–188.

Skeem, J. L., Golding, S. L., Cohn, N., & Berge, G. (1998). Logic and reliability of evaluations of competence to stand trial. *Law and Human Behavior, 22*, 519–547.

Slobogin, C. (1989). The "ultimate issue" issue. *Behavioral Sciences and the Law, 7*, 259–266.

Smith, J. T. (1976). The forensic psychologist as an expert witness in the District of Columbia. *Journal of Psychiatry and Law, 4*, 277–285.

Stern, P. (1997). *Preparing and presenting expert testimony in child abuse litigation: A Guide for expert witnesses and attorneys.* Thousand Oaks, CA: Sage.

Suedfeld, P., & Tetlock, P. E. (1992). *Psychology and social policy.* New York: Hemisphere.

Thornburgh v. American College of Gynecologists and Obstetricians, 106 S. Ct. 2169 (1986).

Tremper, C. R. (1987). The high road to the bench: Presenting research findings in Appellate briefs. In G. B. Melton (Ed.), *Reforming the law: Impact of child development research* (pp. 199–231). New York: Guilford.

Tsushima, W. T., & Anderson, R. M. (1996). *Mastering expert testimony: A courtroom handbook for mental health professionals*. Mahwah, NJ: Erlbaum.

Ziskin, J., & Faust, D. (1997). *Coping with psychiatric and psychological testimony* (5th ed.). Los Angeles, CA: Law and Psychology Press.

Chapter 12

ETHICS AND PROFESSIONAL ISSUES

CHAPTER OBJECTIVES

In this chapter, you will become familiar with:

- The roles and responsibilities of the forensic psychologist
- Issues of licensure and certification for psychologists
- The core ethical principles for psychologists
- Procedures for resolving ethical issues
- The general principles and ethical standards of the American Psychological Association's Ethics Code
- Common ethical issues that arise in each of the roles of a forensic psychologist

---

Just as there are multiple definitions for forensic psychology (as discussed in Chapter 1), the term **forensic psychologist** may mean different things to different people. There are many and varied roles that a forensic psychologist may play and in this chapter we examine some of those roles in more detail. In addition, we discuss the forensic psychologist's professional responsibilities as well as some relevant ethical issues that are often faced.

ROLES AND RESPONSIBILITIES OF THE FORENSIC PSYCHOLOGIST

Forensic psychologists may take on many roles. Examination of the Student Section/Careers portion of the website for the American Psychology-Law Society (AP-LS; Division 41 of the American Psychological Association, www.ap-ls.org) indicates that there is no one particular path to becoming a forensic psychologist and that forensic psychologists may be employed in a wide variety of settings. In addition, the roles and responsibilities of the forensic psychologist are many and varied. In general, a forensic psychologist will take on one primary role but may engage in additional roles depending on his or her interests and training. The various roles that may be played by a forensic psychologist include, but are not limited to: trial consultant, expert witness, evaluator, treatment provider, researcher, academic, and correctional psychologist. Of course, it is possible (in fact, common) for an individual to take on more than one of these roles or to take on additional roles not mentioned here.

The Trial Consultant

A trial consultant (or jury consultant) is someone who works with legal professionals, mainly attorneys, to assist in various aspects of case preparation including jury selection, development of case strategy, and witness preparation. Many trial consultants rely on their research training to develop and execute research that will assist attorneys in preparing a case. Research and data collection strategies might include community surveys, focus groups, jury simulations, shadow juries, and mock trials. Trial consultants (or jury consultants) may be involved in both civil and criminal cases and may assist at any (or all) stage(s) of the proceedings—in preparation for trial, during trial, or after trial. There is no one avenue to becoming a trial consultant; however, trial consultants usually have advanced degrees in one of the behavioral sciences, such as psychology or criminology. There are many trial consulting firms across the United States that employ individuals in this role; however, it is also possible to maintain a private practice as a trial consultant without working for a trial consulting firm.

The Expert Witness

An expert witness is someone who testifies in court about specialized knowledge that he or she possesses. Forensic psychologists are often called upon to testify regarding matters of mental health (in the case of a clinical forensic psychologist) or general theory and research in psychology and law. Generally, clinical forensic psychologists are involved as expert witnesses after having evaluated a defendant and thus are called to testify regarding that defendant's mental state and how it relates to the legal issue at hand (such as insanity, competency, dangerousness, civil commitment, etc.). It is possible, however, for forensic psychologists to serve as general expert witnesses where, instead of testifying regarding specialized knowledge about a particular defendant/complainant, they may be called to testify regarding broader psychological principles in which they have specialized knowledge or expertise. This role is usually performed in conjunction with another role, such as that of researcher, academic, or evaluator and thus is not generally the only (or even the primary) role in which a forensic psychologist engages. Forensic psychologists in the expert witness role may participate in both criminal and civil proceedings and are usually trained either in general psychology or in a particular psychological specialty such as clinical psychology.

The Evaluator

Many forensic psychologists take the role of evaluators. In general, this refers to the evaluation of criminal defendants or parties to civil litigation with respect to mental health issues that relate to the legal issue at hand; however, this may also refer to the evaluation of service delivery or treatment programs. In the criminal realm, forensic psychologists may be called upon to evaluate defendants with respect to their competency to stand trial, their mental state at the time of the offense (insanity), their risk for future dangerousness, or other such issues. In the civil realm, forensic psychologists may be called upon to evaluate an individual's psychological state after having been injured or in an accident or may evaluate families involved in custody and access disputes. The evaluator role usually goes hand in hand with the expert witness role as many evaluators are called into court to testify about the opinions they formed during their evaluations. Forensic psychologists who take on the role of an evaluator are employed in a wide variety of settings, including forensic hospitals, state psychiatric hospitals, community mental health centers, and private practice. Forensic psychologists who evaluate defendants or parties to civil litigation usually have been trained as clinical psychologists and have some specialization in forensic psychology and are usually required to be licensed as psychologists.

The Treatment Provider

Treatment providers offer psychological treatment to individuals requiring or desiring these services. Forensic psychologists who take on the role of the treatment provider work in a wide variety of settings, similar to those who take on the evaluator role, including forensic hospitals, state psychiatric hospitals, community mental health centers, and private practices. In addition, similar to the evaluator, treatment providers may work with individuals (or groups) involved in both criminal and civil proceedings. In the criminal realm, treatment providers may be called upon to offer psychological interventions to individuals who have been deemed by the courts as incompetent to stand trial (and thus require treatment for the restoration of competency), insane at the time of the crime (and thus require treatment for their mental illness), or at a high risk to commit a violent offense (and thus require treatment to minimize the likelihood of acting violently in the future), as well as a number of other criminal law-related issues. Within the civil realm, forensic psychologists may be called upon to provide treatment to families who are going through divorce proceedings or to individuals who sustained psychological injuries as a result of some trauma that they endured or a host of other civil law-related issues. The roles of treatment provider and evaluator may both be performed by the same forensic psychologist, although ethical guidelines (discussed later in this chapter) attempt to limit the chances that both of these roles will be fulfilled with the same client or patient.

The Researcher

Forensic psychologists who take on the role of researcher design and implement research on various issues relevant to forensic psychology or psychology and the law, both criminal and civil. In addition, these professionals may conduct research on mental health law and policy or program evaluation. These professionals may be employed in a number of settings including universities and colleges, but also at research institutes, government or private agencies, and psychiatric hospitals or other mental health agencies.

The Academic

Forensic psychologists who take on the role of the academic are involved in teaching, research, and a host of other education-related activities such as training and supervision of students. Psychologists who take on this role can be trained either generally in psychology or in one of the specialties such as clinical psychology. In addition, these professionals usually have an advanced degree in psychology, typically a PhD. It is often the case that academics will also take on one or more of the aforementioned roles in addition to the role of academic. In general, academics are employed by institutions of higher learning—colleges or universities.

The Correctional Psychologist

A correctional psychologist is a forensic psychologist who works in a correctional setting with inmates and offenders. These psychologists often engage in direct service delivery—both evaluation and treatment—of individuals who have been incarcerated or who are out on probation or parole. Thus, in addition to the roles of evaluator and treatment provider, correctional psychologists may also take on the role of researcher or expert witness.

PROFESSIONAL ISSUES

Licensure and Certification

Every state has developed statutory provisions for the practice of psychology and in every state an individual must be licensed as a psychologist in order to practice psychology independently (without supervision). In most every state, a doctoral-level degree is required to become licensed as a psychologist; however, some states have provisions for becoming licensed as a psychological technician (or some other similar title) with a master's degree. Although not licensed as a *psychologist* and therefore unable to practice psychology independently, being licensed as a psychological technician allows for the practice of many aspects of psychology under the supervision of a doctoral-level licensed psychologist. Depending on the state, licensed psychological technicians may be able to conduct assessments and provide treatment as long as they are supervised by a licensed psychologist.

An individual need not be licensed to participate in many of the roles described earlier. It is necessary to be licensed to engage in the role of evaluator, treatment provider, or expert witness (unless the testimony is to be general and not specifically in regard to an individual that the psychologist has evaluated or treated); however, it is possible to engage in the role of trial consultant, researcher, academic, correctional psychologist, and expert witness (for general testimony about psychological theory and research) without being licensed to practice as a psychologist or psychological technician. As a general statement, it is necessary to be licensed as a psychologist whenever one engages in the practice of psychology with an individual or a group of people. The one exception to this is when one engages in the practice of psychology within a correctional setting. In this case, it is possible to practice psychology without a license and it is the correctional institution that retains responsibility for its psychological personnel.

Psychology is a self-regulating profession, thus decisions regarding competence to practice psychology and the conduct expected of psychologists are made by members of the profession as well as members of the public who sit on a self-regulating board. The primary purpose of the self-regulating board is the protection of the public. Each state has a regulatory board that controls the profession of psychology. Practitioners apply to this regulatory board to become licensed (which usually requires that the individual have completed a series of specific courses in psychology, have completed a certain number of hours of supervised clinical contact, and have passed a national licensing exam) and this board is responsible for implementing and administering the relevant Act or statutes pertaining to the practice of psychology. In each state, the regulatory board is usually responsible for: protecting the public from incompetent or unethical psychologists; determining the requirements for becoming licensed as a psychologist; periodic review of licensed psychologists' competence to practice psychology; developing and enforcing codes of ethical and professional conduct to be followed by licensed psychologists; educating and informing the public about the regulation of psychology; and developing and enforcing complaint and disciplinary procedures brought against psychologists.

Resolving Ethical Issues

When a client, patient, member of the public, or another psychologist has a complaint about the professional behavior of a psychologist, there are a couple courses of action that may be taken. The first action to be considered is to bring the complaint to the attention of the offending psychologist. This informal mechanism may not be appropriate for every complaint but, for those in which it is appropriate, it represents an efficient way of resolving the issue. For example, this may be an appropriate course of action when a psychologist has taken on a multiple role relationship with a client; simply bringing this to the attention of the psychologist may be enough to remediate the concern. If an informal means of resolving the issue is ineffective or inappropriate, the complainant may file a complaint with the licensing board of the state in which the psychologist practices. In addition, if the offending psychologist is a member of the American Psychological Association (APA) a complaint may also be registered with the APA, which has an ethics office to hear and deal with complaints about a psychologist's behavior. The state licensing boards and the APA have formal mechanisms for resolving complaints about a psychologist's behavior. This can be a stressful and time-consuming process, but it is generally considered to be a fair means of adjudicating complaints.

ETHICAL AND LEGAL ISSUES

As discussed in the previous section, psychology is a self-regulating profession that uses ethical principles and standards as one means of regulation. Although there is no set number of ethical principles and numerous authors and commentators have used various terms to describe these principles, Koocher and Keith-Spiegel (1998) have compiled a list of nine core ethical principles relevant to the profession of psychology that appear to capture the essence of the values to which the profession of psychology subscribes (see Table 12.1).

The American Psychological Association's Ethics Code

While numerous ethics codes pertaining to the conduct of psychological services exist, the most relevant code, and therefore the one on

Table 12.1   Core Ethical Principles for Psychologists

1. *Doing no harm (nonmaleficence).* Through commission or omission, psychologists strive to benefit those with whom they work, at the same time taking care to ensure that the potential for damage is eliminated or minimized to the greatest extent possible.
2. *Respecting autonomy.* The rights of individuals to decide how to live their lives as long as their actions do not interfere with the welfare of others is accepted by psychologists as an ultimate goal for clients, students, research participants, and others with whom psychologists work.
3. *Benefiting others.* All decisions that psychologists make should have the potential for a positive effect on others. Often, this principle must be balanced against doing no harm, respect for autonomy, available resources, and utility.
4. *Being just.* Actions should be fair and equitable. Others should be treated as psychologists would want to be treated under similar circumstances.
5. *Being faithful.* Issues of fidelity, loyalty, trustfulness, trust, promise keeping, and respect for those with whom psychologists work converge to form the delicate standards necessary in fiduciary relationships. When psychologists are straightforward, sincere, candid, and without intent to mislead or deceive anyone, ethical action is more likely.
6. *According dignity.* Psychologists view others as worthy of respect. This enhances the probability that decisions will be ethical.
7. *Treating others with care and compassion.* Psychologists should be considerate and kind to those with whom they work, yet maintain professional boundaries.
8. *Pursuit of excellence.* Maintaining competence, doing one's best, and taking pride in one's work are important in ensuring high-quality professional services, as well as providing hedges against unprofessional and unethical actions.
9. *Accepting accountability.* Psychologists who act with a consideration of possible consequences, who accept responsibility for actions and inactions, and who avoid shifting blame or making excuses are acting with integrity. Putting principles over expediency is sometimes the longer and more arduous route, but in the long run it is the one that ensures self-respect.

Source: Koocher & Keith-Spiegel (1998, p. 4–5).

which we will focus this discussion, is the American Psychological Association's Ethical Principles of Psychologists and Code of Conduct (also called the Ethics Code). The most recent version of the Ethics Code was published in 2002 and represents a revision and update of the 1992 Ethics Code.

The APA first developed and published a code of ethics for psychologists in 1953 and, since that time, has continually worked to revise and update this code. The current APA Ethics Code consists of two parts: general principles and ethical standards.

General Principles

The general principles section of the Code contains five principles, which represent aspirational goals meant to guide psychologists to the highest ideals of psychology. These five general principles are not enforceable rules (it is the Ethical Standards section of the Code that sets out enforceable rules), but rather, are principles to be considered by psychologists when attempting to determine an ethical course of action. (Note that the nine core principles outlined earlier by Koocher and

Keith-Spiegel are represented in these five principles.) The five general principles are as follows:

1. *Beneficence and Nonmaleficence.* "Psychologists strive to benefit those with whom they work and take care to do no harm. In their professional actions, psychologists seek to safeguard the welfare and rights of those with whom they interact professionally and other affected persons, and the welfare of animal subjects of research" (APA Ethics Code, p. 1062).

2. *Fidelity and Responsibility.* "Psychologists establish relationships of trust with those with whom they work. They are aware of their professional and scientific responsibilities to society and to the specific communities in which they work" (p. 1062).

3. *Integrity.* "Psychologists seek to promote accuracy, honesty, and truthfulness in the science, teaching, and practice of psychology" (p. 1062).

4. *Justice.* "Psychologists recognize that fairness and justice entitle all persons to access to and benefit from the contributions of psychology and to equal quality in the processes, procedures, and services being conducted by psychologists" (p. 1062).

5. *Respect for People's Rights and Dignity.* "Psychologists respect the dignity and worth of all people, and the rights of individuals to privacy, confidentiality, and self-determination" (p. 1063).

Ethical Standards

The ethical standards section of the Ethics Code consists of enforceable ethical standards that fall into the following 10 different content areas: resolving ethical issues, competence, human relations, privacy and confidentiality, advertising and other public statements, record keeping and fees, education and training, research and publication, assessment, and therapy.

Within each of these 10 content areas are standards that serve to provide more detailed information regarding ethical courses of action and guidelines for behavior. The underlying basis of each of these ethical standards is a concern for the welfare of those individuals with whom psychologists interact on a professional basis.

Discussion of the ethical standards within each of these 10 content areas is beyond the scope of this chapter but Table 12.2 provides a sample of some of the guidelines within each of these areas.

Forensic psychologists, like psychologists who do not interact with the legal system, are bound by these ethical guidelines; however, there

Table 12.2 Sample of Ethical Standards within each of Ten Content Areas

Content Area	Sample of Ethical Standards
Resolving Ethical Issues	**1.04 Informal Resolution of Ethical Violations** When psychologists believe that there may have been an ethical violation by another psychologist, they attempt to resolve the issue by bringing it to the attention of that individual, if an informal resolution appears appropriate and the intervention does not violate any confidentiality rights that may be involved.
Competence	**2.01 Boundaries of Competence** Psychologists provide services, teach, and conduct research with populations and in areas only within the boundaries of their competence, based on their education, training, supervised experience, consultation, study, or professional experience.
Human Relations	**3.05 Multiple Relationships** A multiple relationship occurs when a psychologist is in a professional role with a person and (1) at the same time is in another role with the same person, (2) at the same time is in a relationship with a person closely associated with or related to the person with whom the psychologist has a professional relationship, or (3) promises to enter into another relationship in the future with the person or a person closely associated with or related to the person. A psychologist refrains from entering into a multiple relationship if the multiple relationship could reasonably be expected to impair the psychologist's objectivity, competence, or effectiveness in performing his or her functions as a psychologist, or otherwise risks exploitation or harm to the person with whom the professional relationship exists. Multiple relationships that would not reasonably be expected to cause impairment or risk exploitation or harm are not unethical.
Privacy and Confidentiality	**4.01 Maintaining Confidentiality** Psychologists have a primary obligation and take reasonable precautions to protect confidential information obtained through or stored in any medium, recognizing that the extent and limits of confidentiality may be regulated by law or established by institutional rules or professional or scientific relationship.
	4.04 Minimizing Intrusions on Privacy Psychologists include in written and oral reports and consultations, only information germane to the purpose for which the communication is made.
Advertising and Other Public Statements	**5.01 Avoidance of False or Deceptive Statements** Psychologists do not knowingly make public statements that are false, deceptive, or fraudulent concerning their research, practice, or other work activities or those of persons or organizations with which they are affiliated.

(continued)

Table 12.2   *(Continued)*

Content Area	Sample of Ethical Standards
Record Keeping and Fees	**6.04 Fees and Financial Arrangements** As early as is feasible in a professional or scientific relationship, psychologists and recipients of psychological services reach an agreement specifying compensation and billing arrangements.
Education and Training	**7.03 Accuracy in Teaching** Psychologists take reasonable steps to ensure that course syllabi are accurate regarding the subject matter to be covered, bases for evaluating progress, and the nature of course experiences. This standard does not preclude an instructor from modifying the course content or requirements when the instructor considers it pedagogically necessary or desirable, so long as students are made aware of these modifications in a manner that enables when to fulfill course requirements.
Research and Publication	**8.07 Deception in Research** Psychologists do not conduct a study involving deception unless they have determined that the use of deceptive techniques is justified by the study's significant prospective scientific, educational, or applied value and that effective nondeceptive alternative procedures are not feasible. Psychologists do not deceive prospective participants about research that is reasonably expected to cause physical pain or severe emotional distress.
Assessment	**9.06 Interpreting Assessment Results** When interpreting assessment results, including automated interpretations, psychologists take into account the purpose of the assessment as well as the various test factors, test-taking abilities, and other characteristics of the person being assessed, such as situational, personal, linguistic, and cultural differences, that might affect psychologists' judgments or reduce the accuracy of their interpretations. They indicate any significant limitations of their interpretations.
Therapy	**10.01 Informed Consent to Therapy** When obtaining informed consent to therapy as required in Standard 3.10, Informed Consent, psychologists inform clients/patients as early as is feasible in the therapeutic relationship about the nature and anticipated course of therapy, fees, involvement of third parties, and limits of confidentiality and provide sufficient opportunity for the client/patient to ask questions and receive answers.

Source: APA Ethical Principles of Psychologists and Code of Conduct (2002).

also exist Specialty Guidelines for Forensic Psychologists (Committee on Ethical Guidelines for Forensic Psychologists, 1991), which focus on issues specific to working in conjunction with the legal system.

The Specialty Guidelines for Forensic Psychology

The Specialty Guidelines for Forensic Psychology were first published in 1991 and are currently undergoing an update and revision (most recent draft available at www.ap-ls.org). These guidelines represent joint endorsement by the American Psychology-Law Society (AP-LS; Division 41 of the American Psychological Association) and the American Academy of Forensic Psychology but are not an official statement of the American Psychological Association. That is, these Specialty Guidelines are not enforceable by the APA but they were developed to provide further guidance than that offered by the APA's Ethical Code for those professionals who engage in the practice of psychology within the forensic arena.

The Guidelines provide guidance and information to be considered in attempting to determine the most ethical course of action in 12 different areas, including: responsibilities; competence; diligence; relationships; fees; notification, assent, consent, and informed consent; conflicts in practice; privacy, confidentiality, and privilege; methods and procedures; assessment; documentation; and professional and other public communications.

There are a number of ethical issues that psychologists and forensic psychologists deal with on a regular basis. Some of the most common issues include taking on multiple roles and confidentiality, privacy, and privilege.

Ethical Issues in the Various Roles of the Forensic Psychologist

Many of the ethical issues that psychologists deal with cut across the various roles that they take on. For example, when psychologists interact with students, they may take on the role of researcher, academic, or supervisor. When they interact with clients, they may be involved as a treatment provider or evaluator. Each role carries with it ethical issues and we will discuss the most common role conflicts next.

Among other ethical issues, such as taking on multiple roles with the patient or client, psychologists acting in the roles of evaluators and treatment providers must often think about issues related to informed consent, confidentiality, and whether they are practicing within the bounds of their competence. When the evaluator or treatment provider is working within the forensic context, he or she must also grapple with the issue of who is the client. In many situations, the client or patient is the person being evaluated or receiving treatment services; however, in the forensic context, it is the attorney or the court who is the client, rather than the person being evaluated or treated. Recall also that working within the forensic context means that there is often no confidentiality for the person being evaluated or treated. In addition, there is an assumption that the evaluator or treatment provider will be objective and neutral—not favoring one side over the other and thus not concealing information that may be favorable to one party to the proceedings but not the other (for example, not concealing how the offender's previous violent history may increase his or her risk for future violence, even when being retained by the defense to present mitigating testimony at a sentencing hearing). The same issue regarding being objective and neutral is of concern to psychologists taking on the role of the expert witness. In the expert witness role, psychologists are expected to maintain their objectivity and to provide information that will assist the court in making a legal decision; thus, it would be unethical for expert witnesses to agree to be paid on a contingency basis (the expert would get paid for his/her services only if the desired outcome is reached in a case).

When psychologists take on the role of a researcher, they need to adhere to ethical guidelines regarding the design and implementation of research. Issues of concern in this role include the honest reporting of data, obtaining informed consent from research participants, being honest about the risk of harm that may occur as a result of research participation (for example, some research designs may require that the participants are initially deceived, which may cause them to feel duped and perhaps mistrustful), ensuring that research participation is voluntary and not coerced, and ensuring that participants are able to withdraw from participation without any undue consequences. In addition, when the research involves treatment for a psychological problem or condition, the psychologist-researcher must also consider the right of everyone to treatment when designing the research. The role of researcher is often inherent in the role of academic but a few additional ethical issues arise in this role including being aware of multiple roles with students, respecting the power differential between the academic and the student, and ensuring that proper credit is given to students and other individuals involved in academic work and publication.

In the role of trial consultant, psychologists must be sure to practice within the bounds of their competence, guard against guaranteeing the outcome of a case, ensure that research is performed on sample sizes large enough to demonstrate any desired effects, honestly report research results or data, and be careful not to taint witnesses during preparation.

Finally, psychologists working within the correctional system also deal with numerous ethical issues on a daily basis, such as confidentiality, informed consent, competence, and who is the client (the person being treated or evaluated or the correctional institution for whom the psychologist works). In addition, correctional psychologists are often put in the awkward position of performing multiple roles on a daily basis—consider the psychologist who works with inmates on a daily basis but who is also expected to be able to discipline an inmate or even turn a firearm on an inmate in a time of institutional crisis (psychologists working in the federal correctional system receive firearms training and are expected to take arms during institutional upheaval).

These are just some of the ethical issues that arise for psychologists in each of the various roles they may assume. Of course, this list is neither comprehensive nor exhaustive. We now turn to a discussion of two of the most common ethical issues for psychologists in almost any role: multiple roles and confidentiality.

Multiple Roles

Although psychologists may take on many different professional roles, it is important that a psychologist use caution when taking on multiple professional roles with the same client/student/patient. For example, although a psychologist may be a researcher, a clinical supervisor, and a treatment provider, it would be important that the psychologist not engage in each of these roles with the same student. Thus, a student may act as a research assistant as well as a clinical supervisee for the psychologist but should not also receive treatment for his or her own psychological issues from the same psychologist. The responsibility for ensuring that the student not engage with the psychologist in too many roles rests on the psychologist, not on the student. Psychologists must maintain an awareness of the power differential that occurs in certain situations and use caution so as not to exert undue power over the actions of others with whom they interact. See Box 12.1 for a case study of multiple roles.

Of course, nothing is ever as simple as it seems. What would happen if Dr. Smart were the only forensic psychologist in the small town where the McDonalds live and thus referring the McDonalds to another psychologist is not an option? The Ethics Code warns against psychologists engaging in multiple roles but sometimes this is impossible to avoid. The main purpose of the Ethics Code is to protect the public and to ensure that psychologists carefully consider the various ways in which their behavior may affect others. Of course, that is not to say that there are easy resolutions for every situation. What is important, however, is that psychologists use the Ethics Code to guide their actions and to assist them in thinking through all the possible issues involved in a particular situation.

Confidentiality and Privilege

One of the main issues that psychologists deal with on a daily basis is that of *confidentiality*. That is, psychologists are ethically bound to keep information about their clients confidential. But what happens when the client

========   **Box 12.1 Case Study: Multiple Roles**   ========

Situation: Dr. Smart, a forensic psychologist, has been seeing Mrs. McDonald in therapy for almost a year at the request of the court. Mrs. McDonald pled guilty to shoplifting and, as a condition of receiving probation, agreed to attend counseling sessions with Dr. Smart for one year. Over the last year, Dr. Smart and Mrs. McDonald have worked on Mrs. McDonald's various personal issues and the increasing tension in Mrs. McDonald's marriage. Mrs. McDonald has recently made the decision to divorce her husband and things have escalated to the point where she and her husband are no longer speaking to each other. In addition, he has decided to sue Mrs. McDonald for full custody of their 6-year-old daughter. The Judge who is to hear Mr. McDonald's petition in family court has requested a custody evaluation of the family to assist in his determination regarding the best interests of Mr. and Mrs. McDonald's daughter. Mrs. McDonald has asked Dr. Smart to conduct this custody evaluation since she will have completed her required one-year of counseling with Dr. Smart and thus Dr. Smart will no longer be her therapist. Mrs. McDonald believes that Dr. Smart will be an objective evaluator and will make the process somewhat easier since Dr. Smart already has a good understanding of Mrs. McDonald's background and functioning. Should Dr. Smart participate in this evaluation?

Issues: Dr. Smart is being asked to perform a custody evaluation, which would entail an assessment of all relevant parties—Mr. McDonald, Mrs. MacDonald, and their 6-year-old daughter—in order to make a recommendation to the Court regarding which parent should receive custody. Although Mrs. McDonald has completed her counseling with Dr. Smart, and is thus no longer a patient of Dr. Smart, this is a somewhat tricky situation. Dr. Smart is being asked to participate as an evaluator in a custody suit; however, Dr. Smart has already engaged with Mrs. McDonald as a treatment provider for a year.

Resolution: In this situation, it would be unwise for Dr. Smart to engage in the role of evaluator since she has already engaged with Mrs. McDonald as a treatment provider. The concern is that it may be difficult for Dr. Smart to remain objective and neutral in the custody evaluation. This may work in either of two ways— Dr. Smart may be swayed in favor of Mrs. McDonald since she has come to know her and is familiar with the struggles in the McDonald's marriage; or Dr. Smart may be swayed in favor of Mr. McDonald since she has knowledge of Mrs. McDonald's troubles with the law and is familiar with the struggles in the McDonald's marriage. The best course of action may be for Dr. Smart to refer the McDonald's to a colleague for the custody evaluation.

tells the psychologist something that may end up harming someone else? Or, what happens when the psychologist believes that the client is going to hurt him- or herself or even someone else? These are not easy issues to deal with by any means. Fortunately, one way of attempting to guard against these situations is for psychologists to tell their clients up front what information might require them to break the client's confidentiality. Psychologists are legally bound to report certain types of information—such as learning about known or suspected child abuse (or, in some states, elder abuse). It is important that the client know ahead of time the limits on confidentiality.

What about the specific case of the forensic psychologist? Is a forensic psychologist who is retained by the courts to evaluate a defendant's mental state required to keep this information confidential? The short answer is no. In the case of the forensic psychologist, the purpose of the evaluation is to assist the courts in making a decision about a particular legal issue (e.g., competency to stand trial, or mental state at the time of the offense) and, thus, the psychologist is unable to maintain confidentiality of the information obtained from the defendant. It is, however, important that the defendant understand that there is no confidentiality in this situation. In addition, simply because confidentiality does not apply in the forensic context, does not mean that the forensic psychologist is free to divulge the details of the case to other people not involved in the case. The forensic psychologist must still respect the defendant's right to privacy and must still act ethically by divulging information about the defendant to only those relevant parties—usually the judge, the defense, and the prosecution.

Confusion often exists regarding *confidentiality* and *privilege*. **Confidentiality** is an ethical principle prohibiting psychologists from divulging information about their clients to third parties except under certain circumstances that have been agreed to by both parties. **Privilege**, on the other hand, is a legal protection belonging to the client that ensures protection of communications from disclosure in legal proceedings. Every state recognizes attorney-client, physician-patient, husband-wife, and priest-penitent privilege; however, some, but not all, states also recognize a psychotherapist-patient privilege. In those states where a psychotherapist-patient privilege exists, communications between psychotherapist and patient are protected from disclosure in legal proceedings, unless the patient waives that privilege. (Read the sample case study on confidentiality in Box 12.2.)

Again, however, nothing is as simple as it seems. What if the crimes were violent and people were getting hurt? What if Mr. Schneider were to identify a specific target of his crimes? What if Mr. Schneider were a forensic examinee sent to Dr. Blake by the courts for an evaluation and he divulged this information to Dr. Blake?

In the case of violent crimes wherein innocent people are getting hurt, Dr. Blake's course of action might depend on whether the potential victims of future crimes committed by Mr. Schneider were identifiable. If they were clearly identifiable and could be harmed, Dr. Blake might need to consider breaking Mr. Schneider's confidence and warning either the intended victim, or the authorities, or both. If the potential victims were not clearly

---

Box 12.2 Case Study: Confidentiality

Situation: Dr. Blake is a clinical psychologist whose private practice mainly involves treating adults who are suffering from depression. He has recently begun to conduct some forensic evaluations for the courts, but this comprises only about 10% of his practice. Dr. Blake has been seeing Mr. Schneider, a general therapy client, for his depression for the last three months. Before beginning therapy with Mr. Schneider, Dr. Blake informed him about the limits of confidentiality—that Dr. Blake would keep everything Mr. Schneider told him confidential unless Mr. Schneider divulged information to Dr. Blake regarding known or suspected child or elder abuse or an intention to hurt himself or someone else. During the last therapy session, Mr. Schneider told Dr. Blake that he had been involved in a series of crimes over the last six months. As Mr. Schneider elaborated on his behaviors, it became clear to Dr. Blake that these were highly publicized crimes that the city police were actively attempting to solve. What should Dr. Blake do in this situation? Can Dr. Blake inform the police of the information he learned from Mr. Schneider?

Issues: Dr. Blake has entered into an agreement with Mr. Schneider wherein he promised confidentiality within certain limits. Mr. Schneider has divulged information to Dr. Blake that implicates himself in a number of well-known crimes that the city police are actively attempting to solve; in fact, the police have posted a reward for the arrest and conviction of the person or persons involved in these crimes. The crimes have nothing to do with child or elder abuse and Mr. Schneider has not voiced an intention to hurt himself or anyone else; although there is a possibility that someone could get hurt if the crimes were to continue to happen.

Resolution: Dr. Blake clearly laid out the limits on confidentiality with Mr. Schneider before commencing treatment. The information provided does not suggest that there are any child/elder abuse concerns nor does it suggest that Mr. Schneider intends to hurt himself or someone else. In this situation, the most appropriate course of action for Dr. Blake is to maintain Mr. Schneider's confidence and not divulge the details of his crimes to the authorities or anyone else. Of course, this does not prohibit Dr. Blake from making this a focus of treatment or from attempting to convince Mr. Schneider to turn himself in to the police.

---

identifiable, Dr. Blake would most likely need to maintain Mr. Schneider's confidence. If, however, Mr. Schneider was a forensic examinee and divulged this information to Dr. Blake during the course of an evaluation for the courts, Dr. Blake could then include this information in the report to court. Recall that in forensic evaluations, confidentiality does not apply and the authority requesting the evaluation has a right to any of the information obtained from the examinee.

With issues of confidentiality, as well as with any other ethical issue, there are rarely easy answers—the situation is rarely black or white. The ethical guidelines to which psychologists must adhere provide useful information to assist psychologists think through these dilemmas; however, the decisions that psychologists make about these dilemmas are often the product of lengthy discussion with colleagues and painstaking weighing of options. In this respect, the ethical guidelines are invaluable, both to psychologists as well as to the people and groups with whom psychologists work.

SUMMARY

One of the most intriguing things about becoming a psychologist is the ability to participate in many different roles and activities. While we have only touched on some of the various roles that psychologists play in this chapter, one thing is clear: psychologists perform a wide variety of activities and participate in a large variation of professional roles, sometimes on a daily basis.

The fact that psychology is a self-regulating profession means that it is up to psychologists to ensure that their own behavior, as well as the behavior of their colleagues, is ethical and will not lead to harm for those people with whom psychologists interact. Psychologists are guided by a number of core ethical principles including: doing no harm, respecting autonomy, benefiting others, being just, being faithful, according dignity, treating others with care and compassion, pursuing excellence, and accepting accountability.

Professional licensing boards in each state are responsible for regulating the practice of psychology and for protecting the public through the adjudication of any complaints against a practicing psychologist. In addition, the American Psychological Association has an ethics committee that is responsible for hearing complaints against any of its members. For the most part, psychologists are careful and conscientious about their interactions and often painstakingly engage in consultation and deliberation with colleagues regarding ethical issues that they may face.

SUGGESTED READINGS

American Psychological Association. (2002). Ethical principles of psychologists and code of conduct. *American Psychologist, 57*, 1060–1073.

Bersoff, D. N. (2003). *Ethical conflicts in psychology* (3rd ed.). Washington, DC: American Psychological Association.

Committee on Ethical Guidelines for Forensic Psychologists. (1991). Specialty guidelines for forensic psychologists. *Law and Human Behavior, 15*, 655–665.

Koocher, G. P., & Keith-Spiegel, P. (1998). *Ethics in psychology: Professional standards and cases* (2nd ed.). New York: Oxford.

KEY TERMS

- *Confidentiality*
- *Forensic psychologist*
- *Privilege*

References

American Psychological Association. (2002). Ethical principles of psychologists and code of conduct. *American Psychologist, 57*, 1060–1073.

Committee on Ethical Guidelines for Forensic Psychologists. (1991). Specialty guidelines for forensic psychologists. *Law and Human Behavior, 15*, 655–665.

Koocher, G. P., & Keith-Spiegel, P. (1998). *Ethics in psychology: Professional standards and cases* (2nd ed.). New York: Oxford.

Author Index

Subject Index

FASD (Fetal Alcohol Spectrum Disorders), 229
FBI, *see* Federal Bureau of Investigation
Federal Bureau of Investigation (FBI), 2, 242, 255, 256
Federal Bureau of Prisons, 242
Federal Court system, 14–15
Federal Rules of Evidence, 305, 306, 308–309
Federline, Kevin, 60, 61
Fees, ethical standards about, 332
Feldman, S., 226
Female offenders, 214, 216, 291
Ferguson, Colin, 32
Fetal Alcohol Spectrum Disorders (FASD), 229
Fidelity, in APA Ethics Code, 330
Field experiments, of juries, 183
Fifth Amendment, 17, 32
Financial arrangements: ethical standards for, 332
Finkelhor, D., 84
Finkelmann, D., 4
First Amendment, 189
Fitness for duty, 64
Fitness Interview Test (FIT), 36
Fitness Interview Test-Revised (FIT-R), 35, 219–220
Fixed risk markers, 275
Flesch-Kincaid reading level analysis, 151
Florida, recidivism of juveniles in, 221–222
Force, police use of, 258–260
Forcible medication, 38
Ford, Tony, 120–121
Forensic (term), 4
Forensic psychologists, 323–339
    clinical vs. nonclinical, 3
    determinations of legal issues by, 29
    ethical guidelines for, 328–333
    ethical issues of, 328, 333–339
    licensure and certification of, 327–328
    professional associations for, 12
    roles and responsibilities of, 10–12, 323–326
    training of, 22–26
Forensic psychology, 1–12, 18–26
    community-oriented approach to, vii
    criminal profiling in, 1–2
    defined, vii, 2–5
    differences between law and, 18–26
    and Haney's taxonomy, 21–22
    history of, 5–9
    as influence on law, 312–317
    practice vs. research in, 4
    and roles of psychologists, 10–12
    training in, 22–26
Forensic treatment, *see* Treatment
Forensis, 4
Forgetting, rate of, 125, 140

Fortas, Abe, 209, 210
Forth, A., 224
Fourteenth Amendment, 9
Fourth Amendment, 17
Fox, S. J., 208, 251
Freeze technique, 263
French, S., 110–111
Frequency of violence, risk assessment for, 48
Freud, Sigmund, 6
FRI (Function of Rights in Interrogation), 153
Friends of the court briefs, 312. *See also Amicus curiae* briefs
Frye test (Rule), 304–306
Frye v. United States, 304
The Fugitive (television series), 189
Fulero, S. M., 5
Function of Rights in Interrogation (FRI), 153
Fundamental attribution error, 148

G
Gangs, 214
Gardner, W., 317
Gatowski, S. I., 311
Gault, Gerald Francis, 211
Gault case, 151
GCCT (Georgia Court Competency Test), 36
GCS (Gudjonsson Compliance Scale), 165–166
Geier, J. L., 162
Gemot, 181
Gender differences, 123, 226
Gendreau, P., 110–111, 288
General acceptance, 306
General acceptance test, 304
General Electric Co. v. Joiner, 308
General jurisdiction, 15, 16
General Personality and Cognitive Social Learning (GPSCL) perspective, 276, 291
Geographic profiling, 257
Georgia Court Competency Test (GCCT), 36
Germane cognitive load, 262
Getman, J. G., 312
Gibbons, Barbara, 163
Gill, B., 307
GL (Good Lives) model, 291
GMBI (Guilty But Mentally Ill) provisions, 41
Godinez v. Moran, 32
Golding, S. L., 310, 312
Goldstein, A. M., 3, 4
Goldstein, C. J., 158
Goldstein, N. E. S., 162, 163
Good Lives (GL) model, 291
Goodman, G. S., 133–134
Goodman, S., 166
Governing bodies, police as, 241
Governments, 65, 86–87